The Dialogue in Hell between Machiavelli and Montesquieu

APPLICATIONS OF POLITICAL THEORY

Series Editors: Harvey Mansfield, Harvard University, and Daniel J. Mahoney, Assumption College

This series encourages analysis of the applications of political theory to various domains of thought and action. Such analysis will include works on political thought and literature, statesmanship, American political thought, and contemporary political theory. The editors also anticipate and welcome examinations of the place of religion in public life and commentary on classic works of political philosophy.

The Dialogue in Hell between Machiavelli and Montesquieu

Humanitarian Despotism and the Conditions of Modern Tyranny

Maurice Joly

Translated, edited, and
with commentary by
John S. Waggoner

LEXINGTON BOOKS
Lanham • Boulder • New York • Toronto • Oxford

LEXINGTON BOOKS

Published in the United States of America
by Lexington Books
4501 Forbes Boulevard, Suite 2003, Lanham, Maryland 20706

PO Box 317
Oxford
OX2 9RU, UK

Copyright © 2002 by Lexington Books
First paperback edition 2003

British Library Cataloguing in Publication Information Available

Library of Congress Cataloging-in-Publication Data

Joly, Maurice, 1831–1878.
  [Dialogue aux enfers entre Machiavel et Montesquieu. English]
  The dialogue in hell between Machiavelli and Montesquieu : humanitarian despotism
and the conditions of modern tyranny / Maurice Joly ; edited and translated by John S.
Waggoner.
     p. cm. — (Applications of political theory)
  Includes bibliographical references and index.
  ISBN 0-7391-0337-7 (cloth : alk. paper) — ISBN 0-7391-0699-6 (pbk. : alk. paper)
  1. France—Politics and government—1852–1870. 2. Political ethics. I Waggoner,
John S., 1947– II. Title. III. Series.

JC229 .J5713 2002
320.944'09'034—dc21

                                                        2001038969

Printed in the United States of America

♾™ The paper used in this publication meets the minimum requirements of American
National Standard for Information Sciences—Permanence of Paper for Printed Library
Materials, ANSI/NISO Z39.48–1992.

Contents

Preface

Maurice Joly is the author of the *Dialogue in Hell*, the major source of the world's most infamous forgery, *The Protocols of the Elders of Zion*. The present consideration of Joly follows precedent by first mentioning this association and briefly discussing the *Protocols*. The fact remains that it is principally through the *Protocols* and not as an author in his own right that the name Maurice Joly ever became known to later generations.

The *Protocols* was concocted at the turn of the century, about two decades after Joly's death. This anti-Semitic tract had a formative influence on many of the principal founders of the Nazi regime in Germany. In the face of evidence proving the *Protocols'* fraudulence, Hitler himself still tried to vindicate the essential "truth" of its teaching about the Jews. He also put the *Protocols* to frequent use as propaganda and intended to indoctrinate future leaders of his Reich by having it read in his "Youth Schools."

The *Protocols* purported to tell the real purpose behind the Congress of the Zionist Movement, which met in Basel, Switzerland, (1897) and was called by Theodor Herzl to explore the possibilities for founding a Jewish homeland. The "secret protocols" of that Congress were presented as evidence of a political project of a wholly different character from that framed largely in response to the aspirations of a beleaguered and persecuted people. The *Protocols* would have the Basel meeting understood as only the latest convocation of Jews who, dispersed to key centers of influence around the world, secretly met to coordinate their activities in pursuit of their common goal of universal domination. Nazi propaganda used them as stunning "proof" of the existence of a Jewish world conspiracy, then supposedly on the verge of bringing to fruition an age-old dream of universal rule.

The *Protocols*, remarkably enough, has been connected with many of the more prominent political figures of the twentieth century as well as some of its most cataclysmic events. Scholars have surmised that the *Protocols* was fabricated in Russia to influence the direction of policy under Czar Nicholas II. Its revelations were meant to serve a dual purpose of impressing the gullible Nicholas and mobilizing mass support for a counterrevolutionary move against the agents of liberalism and change. Key figures in the government of Nicholas were said to be the tools of the *Protocols* conspiracy to undermine the Czar and Holy Russia.

The Czar was impressed by the *Protocols* and apparently kept it close at hand. The Bolsheviks even found a copy in his family's immediate possession at the time of its bloody assassination. The role it played in several of the more infamous pogroms of the era give evidence of its capacity to incite the Russian masses. After the 1917 Revolution, White Russian émigrés evidently brought copies of the *Protocols* to Germany. There it found wider publication and quickly appeared in translation in most of the literate countries of the world.

The influence of the *Protocols* did not end with the fall of the Third Reich. It has found a new lease on life among the enemies of Israel in the Middle East. An updated version, tailored to the politics of that region, is today making new converts to its teaching. It is also back in vogue in Russia among the many far-right groups that have mushroomed in the troubled times of post-Communism. Brisk sales of the *Protocols* have been reported in other areas of the world. It was linked to neo-Nazi movements that plagued Argentina when the anarchy of the 1970s momentarily opened the door to power for Fascist groups that eerily patterned themselves on the doctrines and tactics of Hitler. More recently, the *Protocols* has found its way to Muslim countries in Asia and have reportedly even appeared in Japan. Mahatin bin Mohammad of Malaysia appeals to a mindset, not too distant from the *Protocols*, when he purports to see the economic crisis in Southeast Asia at the end of the century as a product of global capitalism led by Jewish financiers. Such events remind us of the continued virulence of political anti-Semitism and its capacity to break out anew long after the end of the Nazi era and far from the borders of Israel.

It is important to emphasize that Joly himself is not an anti-Semite.[1] Moreover, the *Dialogue* shows him to be an intransigent enemy of the kind of tyrannical politics which, ironically, the *Protocols* served in a later century. The present study endeavors to restore the integrity of Joly's intentions in writing the *Dialogue* and to fairly assess his still timely contribution to the understanding of modern politics. It is the first attempt at a full commentary on the *Dialogue in Hell*. Repressed in Joly's own time, it largely remains in an unwarranted obscurity today because of its unfortunate association with the infamous forgery that continues to overshadow it.

Notes

1. According to Hans Speier, "The Truth in Hell: Maurice Joly on Modern Despotism," *Polity* 10 (1977): 32, "genocidal anti-Semitism" is "the only trait of modern totalitarianism that Joly did not foresee." Yet, "ironically enough," it was "precisely that which his book—perverted by forgers—helped so much to promote."

Acknowledgments

Early television had a show, *Ted Mack's Original Amateur Hour*, and Ted himself acted as impresario for all the talent that graced this deservedly acclaimed and widely watched telecast. There appeared a nervous little girl from Hoboken who shed her nervousness as she passed deeper into raucous song—*Lady of Spain*—hands simultaneously pumping and gliding along the keys of her accordion, as body rocked on tapping feet. She concluded to much applause and Ted asked the girl her name and if she would like to thank anyone. On cue, she set into her "thank-yous." It began with her parents and continued in machine gun fashion. The television audience could hear "and Aunt Bertha and Uncle Sam." It was all gathering speed, as she was about to descend into cousins, teachers, schoolmates, then friends, neighbors, and domestic pets. But Ted intervened and our little lady of Spain faded from the screen. He was obliged to cut away to pitch for an American elixir that promised the elderly faithful, nodding before magnified television screens, "to feel stronger...fast!"

I remember very well when I worked in the State Legislature of Massachusetts and a conversation I had with an old "pol," who was unsurpassed in his knowledge of how "the Game" was played "up there on Beacon Hill." He told me: "Never get into any long list of 'thank-yous.' The ones you thank don't give a (expletive deleted) and the ones you don't remember to thank get ticked off."

The wisdom of the "pol" is probably unassailable and I risk being classed among the "re-tahds," which, in case you don't know, was State House for persons of very meager intelligence. But I stand with the kid from Hoboken. The heart too has to have its say and I'm willing to risk ridicule and take some time doing it.

I would first like to thank Prof. David Lowenthal. I remember the day the secretary, with uncharacteristic formality, summoned me to "The Chairman's Office." I had many a "summons" in numerous other such offices through the years.

For example, I had never quite made "The Dean's List" as an undergraduate but my name periodically found a place on a certain Dean's list. It was this the Dean himself waved at me while peering over spectacles. And if my name appeared again on it, he would be forced to take the "appropriate action" that he threatened the last time. The same anecdote could be recounted about my whole sophomore year in high school. I was being watched. Another town, another sheriff. And if I didn't mend my ways, I was being told again, I'd have to pack up and get out of Dodge. To escape such ignominy and avoid taking precipitate leave from friends, I vowed to the Dean right there and then to attend all my classes. And I'm sure I did, for a while.

You can understand how I was momentarily disoriented by the novelty of what Professor Lowenthal was asking. I was, I marveled, being invited to stay on at a school. I joined the Ph.D. program at Boston College. Little did David know, but that day ranks as one of the happier days of my life. I subsequently learned my Montesquieu from him, but even more, he introduced me to Shakespeare and made him a lifetime companion. Can anyone think of a more precious gift?

Professor Lowenthal's invitation allowed me to study with the likes of Chrstopher Bruell, Robert Faulkner, Father Ernest Fortin, David Manwaring, and Robert Scigliano, among others. Only someone fortunate enough truly to have had a real teacher can appreciate the gratitude I feel. We at Boston College had many. From them I learned many sublime things but I also learned to think manfully about certain harsher necessities. We were a Political Science Department, after all.

I later even taught at Boston College. Bob Faulkner imaginatively designed courses for me that I could plausibly teach. He knew I was facing the job market and my thin résumé needed some strategic padding.

Unlike many of my more gifted friends and acquaintances, I was not compelled to philosophic studies by keen intellect. I was rather drawn to certain men and women already engaged in them. It was a longish process that tentatively started at Cornell, but was interrupted when all hell broke loose. It also began with great skepticism. I was drawn to them by something inchoate in me which I was not even remotely aware of at the time.

And as I subsequently knew these people better and heard them talk, I wanted to be like them. So, on any measure of existential "authenticity," I merit a bad failing grade and wouldn't even try to talk my way around it. They proved to be very wise, appropriately "tough," and like Bob Faulkner, incredibly kind. As with one's parents, I came to call them all by their first names. I am to this day, and in advanced years, still self-conscious in doing so. It somehow affronts the respect I feel for them.

I would also like to thank the people I lived with in the course of my studies. This includes Abe Shulsky, still the smartest individual I have ever met. It also includes Wayne Ambler, Michael Kieselbach, Roger Karz and the late Jim Leake. What a disparate set of *hombres*. I look back to them all with affection and gratitude for having shared in their special lives.

Wayne is my oldest friend with whom I'm still fortunate to have regular contact. We literally grew up together, intellectually and otherwise. I invited him to my small apartment when I first came to Boston College. It was for a long weekend, mainly to hear Chris Bruell's seminar on Plato's *Laws*. He immediately enrolled and stayed roughly eight years, both at B.C. and my apartment. We sat in on just about every course Chris subsequently offered. Chris's mind is the most powerful I've ever encountered. Time flew in his seminars. For a brief, exhilarating moment I would be conscious of thinking at higher levels. It is difficult to describe the power and charm of such a mind, set off by an understated manner and quiet humor.

I often wondered what the administration thought about him. A hapless teacher, no doubt. This was because there were typically only two or three graduate students, brave souls, officially registered in his courses. Yet, his classrooms were always full. I remember on more than one occasion hunting for chairs to accommodate the auditors—anyone within driving distance of his classroom, who, like me, my roommates, and friends, sought the privilege of spending a couple of hours with Xenophon and Plato.

Wayne's misfortune is to have installed his family in Italy a trifle late. He missed the "great Alfonso," who ruled Naples toward the middle of the fifteenth century. *Il Magnifico* commissioned the celebrated Poggio for an unheard of sum (five hundred pieces of gold, to be exact) to translate Xenophon's *Cyropaedia*. But that was then and now is now. At any rate, I'm sure that Poggio's translation cannot hold a candle to Wayne's.

I would also like to mention and thank Richard Crosby. As with Wayne, the friendship goes back to undergraduate days and has been recently renewed. As an older student back then, he benevolently tried to shape my education. He introduced me to good scotch, great books, and good music. And one part of his lessons, it has to be said, took immediate and fast hold. He also introduced me to Joly and we worked on a translation together for a short time.

While I am at it, I would like to thank Stuart Appelbaum, my best friend and roommate from undergraduate years. To no other person have I ever so unburdened my heart. Though it was an adolescent one, it is, despite encroaching old age and much water under the bridge, still the same one. He would probably be curious to know.

I had come to think that friendship, like love, were mainly affairs for the young. I found an exception in Terence Marshall. Some of my fondest memories of France involve him and his wife, Annie, sitting around a table in Paris or Arcachon about to tuck into French foods, wine, and cheeses. From the very first, Terry was solicitous of my welfare. I had to find appropriate employment. He had me to talk about Joly at the University of Paris and arranged for other speaking engagements on other topics at other universities. If we shook the tree hard enough, an employment "plum" might fall my way. He put me into contact with delightful and very able people.

He is a kind of older brother to me. and had to show me how to survive in France. He has an inflated impression of my talents and I am flattered by this and the kindness he shows me. Who wouldn't be? For me, he is the model of a scholar. But he shows that good humor, in both senses of the term, are compatible with his serious occupations.

We often would gather late Friday afternoons at his apartment to grouse about American politics, French politics, and Franco-American relations. We are very good at these things and there was always much to talk about. We also did justice to the bottle of "unblended" that sat before us. I have had some nibbles through the years regarding publications of my book. But it is thanks to Terry and his connections that it will see the light of day.

I do not have an Aunt Bertha or an Uncle Sam. But I do have an Uncle Jim and an Aunt Margot and would also like to thank them for their interest in me and my education. My debt to my parents is beyond words.

It is an honor to be involved in any project, as I am at Lexington Books, under the aegis of the likes of Daniel Mahoney and Harvey Mansfield. The latter is the world's greatest interpreter of Machiavelli and the teacher of thinkers I most admire. Of him it can be said: "he is among those who have *truly* read and understood Machiavelli." The former is becoming one of our most important political thinkers. I share this opinion with the French thinker I most admire, by the way.

I would also like to thank Gilbert Hamamjian at the French Cultural Center in Cairo. Let me explain. It fell to Gilbert to help me prepare my manuscript for what in publishing jargon is called "camera ready" condition. He stands on soil where his great countryman Champollion stood, and, like him, shows incredible patience and genius in deciphering exotic texts.

Computers bought in Cairo have Arabic as the operating mode. A few clicks, he showed me, would bring it into conformity with more familiar tongues. Once, near the end of my long labors, the manuscript suddenly seized. All was instantly transformed into a potpourri of English, French, and Arabic. Accents, *aigus et graves*, appeared everywhere. Snake like configurations were being emitted at a terrifying rate and were marching across the pages from right to left. *Mayday! Mayday!* I stabbed the escape key repeatedly with my index finger, as he once counseled me to do. This seemed to make things worse. The squiggles were carrying the day. Mind and pulse raced. For some strange reason I thought of Samuel P. Huntington as the Western languages succumbed. Was this what they talked about when they talked about a deadly *virus*? And yet I had not opened any electronic mail, which beckoned "I love you" from Manila, or anywhere else, I assure you. (Sickos.) I was face to face with something all my Egyptian acquaintances (including the auto mechanic of the twenty-three-year-old Chrysler I drive) were very loath to admit even existed. Yes, I had a *mushkila*, big time. In case you don't know, *mushkila* is Arabic for "problem."

With phone tucked under chin, I composed myself and made a call to Gilbert. "It is normal," he blandly assured me. It was not "normal." "Obviously, all is *foutu*," I shouted, as if it was his fault. I was sure the manuscript was right then hurtling through cyberspace to that irretrievable bin out there in virtual reality that had inhaled my résumé, and other documents of greater and lesser importance. Efforts to correct the *mushkila* over the phone came to naught. I watched him descend from his cab and I could read the thoughts settling in his mind, as he made his way into the apartment. "The woman is *normale* but *ce mec* is really bizarre. How is it that these people are the last *hyper*power? It is strange, no?" But he saluted me, as always, in a friendly manner. He made house calls on more than one occasion, and I greeted him like I used to greet the French doctor in the night. First time authors would all be lucky to have a Gilbert.

I would also like to thank the many foundations for their generous support through my long labors. But, unfortunately, I can't. And this brings me to the main reason I am writing these acknowledgments.

There is a simply horrible piece of "folk wisdom" I have heard recounted on more than one occasion here. I can be forgiven retelling it since my openness to all foreign cultures is by now obvious. After all, I worked in the Boston State House for more than five years. It advises that when you go home at night, men, beat your wives! Because even if you don't know why, it is reasoned, they certainly do. My wife has suffered from everything except beatings. In a twist on the above, I would like now to thank her for all the things I know about, and the millions of others she does for us, of which I'm not aware.

I've come to realize that the few good things I've done in life were done because of her. If I flatter myself that this book is among them, it is because it is largely hers. I started it because of her, work was sustained on it because of her, and it was brought to completion because of her.

At cocktail or dinner parties, an *innocente* would sometimes intone, "What are you writing about?" I would launch into my subject. Ready to pass into a higher gear, I would suddenly be brought to a stall by a swift kick to the shin under the table. It was Sylviane's foot and it acted in deference to host and hostess. She was also intervening once again to save me from myself. She had seen guests' eyes glaze over, jaws slacken, and spoons discreetly being put back to rest on the table. I still think that Joly is important, as is obvious. But by her acts, I've come to look at my book in more realistic terms. It has been a painful lesson that has been delivered forcefully on several occasions. She always steps in when my enthusiasms or moroseness take a dangerous and ridiculous turn.

I never wanted to be misunderstood about such a thing, so I've never breathed this to any other human soul. But, you see, I too have a *daimonion*. I dedicate my book to it. And I hope that this once she figures out that I'm not kidding her.

Introduction

Biographical information on Joly is sketchy at best.[1] There are numerous inconsistencies even concerning the years of his birth and death. A recent writer on the *Dialogue* takes this as indicative of the cavalier way in which posterity has treated Maurice Joly.[2] He was in fact born in Lons-le-Saunier, France in 1821. He died in 1878. His father was French and served for a time as Councillor General of the Jura and his mother was Italian. Joly was not of Jewish descent as was later asserted by Nazi apologists who, after the revelations of the *Protocols* forgery, still sought a Jewish connection to his work.

Joly's moralism, which was later to degenerate into misanthropy, was evident at an early age. He was known for his sharp tongue and biting wit that had for its target many of his closest associates. As an adolescent, he was a habitual truant, having run away from his boarding school no less than five times. He was described as fitting the classic mold of a rebel.

To support himself in higher studies, he had to work for seven years in a tedious bureaucratic post. He then found employment as a tutor at the Ecole Supérieure du Commerce. He successfully completed a course of study in law and was admitted to the Paris bar in 1859. He was then hired as a secretary to Jules Grevy. A former member of the Constituent Assembly of 1848, Grevy was out of office and practicing law while also involving himself in various republican political causes. Joly was soon to have a falling out with the man who was later to be President of the General Assembly.

Joly's first book was written shortly thereafter and was entitled *le Barreau de Paris*, a series of sketches portraying then-prominent lawyers and jurists. It was described as caustic and totally lacking in any indulgence for human foibles. His second work, *César*, vigorously attacked Napoleon III and anticipates the modern Caesar as he appears in the *Dialogue*. While he was a prolific writer, his articles were seen as "philosophic and severe." They did not suit the literary tastes of his times and were not often accepted by Parisian journals.

The *Dialogue in Hell* was published in Brussels in 1864. Joly's efforts to have copies of it smuggled into France were compromised by police infiltrators. Arrest followed quickly. Society did not welcome him after his release from prison. Defenders of the Empire denounced him while republicans saw him as someone to avoid—more a troublemaker than a martyr to their cause. He fell into a sullen solitude that he used for research into his *l'Art du Parvenir*, which pilloried his contemporaries for the acts that brought the profit and esteem he perhaps secretly craved for himself.

He became editor of a new journal, *le Palais*, a position that ended after a confrontation with his principal collaborator in the enterprise. After the fall of the Empire in 1870, he sought a government position from Grevy. He failed in this and joined the radical resistance under Louis Auguste Blanqui and Louis Charles Delacruze, after vehemently having denounced the terms of armistice with Germany. In November, he was arrested again but was freed a few months later by the Council of War. During his detention, he wrote an autobiographical sketch that, among other things, is noteworthy for its reference to the circumstances surrounding the writing of the *Dialogue*. Though he states that he was a revolutionary during the Resistance, he is emphatic in affirming that his motives were patriotic and denying he had any communist sympathies.[3]

For a while, the new Republic seemed more congenial to Joly. In 1872, he was offered a position with the journal *la Liberté*. In 1878, during the political crisis that saw the Chamber dissolved, Joly publicly attacked Grevy who was a candidate for the presidency against General MacMahon. He had posters plastered all over Paris that said of his former associate that "he had done all the evil one man can do to another without killing him." He was attacked in return. He brought suit against certain journals charging defamation. Representing his own cause in court, he also used the occasion to assail his political enemies, then important figures in the Republic. He died the same year, by suicide. Near the revolver he used to kill himself was found the manuscript of his novel, *les Affamés*, published two years earlier.

Beyond scant biographical details, what we can know of this unhappy individual largely depends on a proper interpretation of the *Dialogue in Hell*, his most complex and far-reaching statement on contemporary politics. In his short introductory statement, Joly professes to be giving voice to the public's "conscience" and to be describing abiding truths about politics. It is his lasting achievement to have uncovered in the analysis of his own times the vulnerabilities of modern politics to a new form of tyranny. His work remains one of the earliest and richest investigations of the essential conditions of modern despotism, the threat of which he sensed in the historic project of Napoleon III.

The *Dialogue in Hell* rightfully can be viewed as Joly's consummate achievement. The conversation in hell between the celebrated Montesquieu and the infamous Machiavelli draws upon his considerable literary skills and his deep study of political theory. Literary tastes, which he offended in his earlier works, are pleasantly engaged while he elaborates a political teaching to modern men framed in philosophic seriousness and, indeed, world-historic significance.

The court that sentenced Joly for authorship of the *Dialogue* condemned his work for its implied criticism of the policies of the Emperor Napoleon III. Its general thesis had succeeded in showing how "the dreadful despotism taught by

Machiavelli in *The Prince*" could, "by artifice and evil ways," impose itself on modern society. But this concealed a more specific charge against the French government, which was portrayed as having "through shameful means, hypocritical ways, and perfidious contrivances, led the public astray, degraded the character of the nation and corrupted its morals." Machiavelli's "dreadful despotism" was current reality and a theoretical conversation between two philosophers was an exposé of the reigning sovereign of the Second Empire.[4]

Napoleon's police immediately confiscated what were probably thought to be all extant copies of the *Dialogue*. But the text, surprisingly enough, later somehow found its way to Istanbul. It was there, in 1921, that a correspondent of the London *Times* made the connection with the *Protocols* when he stumbled upon Joly's work. That prestigious newspaper had previously published the *Protocols* and was involved in a polemic about its authenticity.

The rediscovery of the *Dialogue in Hell* in conjunction with the *Protocols* has seriously affected posterity's treatment of Joly, who has come to be known more as a historic curiosity than as an author and political thinker. His name may surface from time to time in talks of literary forgeries, as it notably did in the 1980s during discussions of the Hitler's supposed diaries, and most recently with regard to the authenticity of the *Tiananmin Papers*. For the most part, however, he has been consigned to a footnote in intellectual history. Such summary treatment inevitably contributes to misconceptions about Joly while it unfairly associates him with some of history's most unsavory anti-Semites.

Given the momentous legacy of the *Protocols*, it is not surprising that a "great amount of critical intelligence" has been spent in unraveling the riddle of such a hoax. Humane concerns have combined with the devotion to the truth to expose a lie with such murderous consequences. This has resulted in a "truly staggering" amount of books and studies on the *Protocols*.[5] Such scholarly endeavors inevitably placed first-rate thinkers into contact with Joly's *Dialogue*. Though their overriding concern was with the *Protocols* in an attempt to piece together all the relevant material and events in its sordid history, such scholars have given Joly large (if passing) tribute as a student of contemporary despotism and an author of considerable talent. Their comments have long pointed the way to a more serious treatment of Joly but the fact remains that Joly's *Dialogue* has never been read as it should nor extensively commented upon.

Konrad Heiden, one of the earliest biographers of Hitler and, arguably, still the best, writes that Maurice Joly

> has seen the secret disease of his epoch and that is something that men do not like. Today we read Joly with quite different eyes. Today the evils are no longer secret. To us, living in the present day, some of the sentences of this forgotten work seem like a lightning flash bathing the present in dazzling light.

According to Heiden, Joly's great achievement was to take the thought of Machiavelli and apply its teaching to modern conditions. Joly combines "timeless Machiavellian wisdom, and understanding of domination, with a knowledge of the modern mass and its state of mind."[6]

Heiden does not stand alone among scholars who, drawn to Joly from their study of the *Protocols*, have come to appreciate the author of the *Dialogue*. Norman Cohn, whose investigation of the *Protocols* inspired the title for his most celebrated study—*Warrant for Genocide*—refers to the *Dialogue* as "an admirable work, incisive, ruthlessly logical, beautifully constructed." He sees Joly not only as a "brilliant stylist," but as having a "fine intuition for the forces which, gathering strength after his death, were to produce the cataclysms of the present century."[7]

Herman Bernstein in his *History of a Lie* went so far as to translate the complete text of the *Dialogue in Hell* as well as other documents used to concoct the *Protocols*.[8] Despite accessibility to English-speaking readers through Bernstein's effort, and the inviting comments of thinkers such as Heiden and Cohn, scholarship continued to deal only sparingly with Joly and the *Dialogue*. Indeed, as the Nazi era receded and the political influence of the discredited *Protocols* temporarily began to wane, Joly and his *Dialogue* seemed to retreat once again into obscurity.

More recently, however, there is evidence that Joly is coming into his own as an author and thinker. The *Dialogue in Hell* was published in France in 1968 as an integral text. It is there, appropriately enough, that interest in Joly tentatively blossomed, no doubt due in part to the prestige that Raymond Aron, who directed its publication, had lent it. *France Culture* broadcast a radio presentation of the *Dialogue*, along with excerpts from other of Joly's works, in 1983. The program was taken from a staging of the *Dialogue in Hell* at the Theatre de Petit Odeon in 1982 with members of the prestigious Académie Française playing the roles of Machiavelli and Montesquieu. It has since been restaged in Paris. Coincidental to such interest is, of course, the incredible revival of the political influence of the *Protocols*. For different reasons, then, attention is again turning to Joly. This opens the way for the present study and a more thorough investigation of his thought and dramatic art.

Joly's "lightning flash" of illumination impressed Jean-François Revel, who wrote the introduction to the 1968 French edition of the *Dialogue*. With the Fifth Republic in mind, this eminent member of the Académie Française sees something prophetic in Joly's description of the modern media and the use to which it could be put in shaping public opinion. Revel implies that students today will continue to find relevance in Joly's teaching and marvel at the multiple examples of his "startlingly prophetic powers."[9]

Hans Speier, an even more recent commentator on the *Dialogue*, speaks of the "bitter freshness" of the *Dialogue*. He remarked that Joly's powers of prediction "can be traced to the paradox that, strictly speaking, Joly's foresight was insight." Speier distinguishes Joly's insight from the statistical extrapolations of the "futurology" studies that are current academic fad.

> Instead, it was derived from certain firmly held views of human nature in combination with very close analytical observations of the political scene. Sensitized by his liberal predilections to the hazards of liberty in the industrialized society of nineteenth century France, he described Bonapartism as though it was a prototype of twentieth century despotism.[10]

According to Speier, Joly's fairest and most appreciative critic, no author of distinction has been treated more capriciously than Maurice Joly. Speier's short essay—"The Truth in Hell" (1977)—intends to redeem the *Dialogue* from obscurity in order to open the way to a fuller assessment of Joly's contribution to our understanding of modern despotism. The journal *Commentaire* reprinted a translation of his article in France in 1991.

The present study follows on the enterprise begun by Speier but, beyond him, endeavors to show what in fact is the deepest source of what inspires "Machiavelli's Politics in the Nineteenth Century," the subtitle of Joly's work. This will lead to fresh insights into the mind of Napoleon III while it opens readers to a body of nineteenth century political thought that Joly saw as inspiring the policies of the Second Empire. The threat to liberal freedoms and the path to a radically new form of despotism can be found in Napoleon's implementation of Saint-Simonian doctrine. An examination of the influence of Saint-Simonianism on the *Dialogue in Hell* will provide a key to the full understanding of Joly's work.

Chapters 1 through 6 are devoted to a close analysis of Joly's text. Two chapters devoted to Saint-Simonian thought and its connection to the *Dialogue* follow them. Chapter 10 is an essay that uses Joly's analysis as an entry into the historical controversy surrounding Napoleon III. There it will be argued that the ambiguities of the Second Empire can be traced to the complex ideological goals of Napoleon that Saint-Simonianism inspired. Chapter 9 treats the *Dialogue*'s drama, an element that goes relatively unexamined by those who have written about Joly. The staging of the *Dialogue in Hell* in France indicates that the literary talent of Joly has come to be appreciated. However, Joly himself makes clear in his short introductory statement that he intends his book to be read and studied as containing political lessons of great importance.

Like the staging of Platonic *Dialogues*, the staging of Joly's *Dialogue* perhaps risks diverting students from sustained reflection to matters of literary aesthetics—secondary considerations of all too questionable value. Speier criticizes those readers of the *Dialogue* who concentrate on such matters, thinking that therein lies the truly worthy element of what is viewed as an "artistic achievement."[11] They are as guilty of misreading Joly as those who, despite his introductory warning, dismiss the *Dialogue in Hell* as a mere "lampoon" or political satire. The author of the *Dialogue* surely would have been shocked by the perversion of his thought and the use to which it was put in the *Protocols*. He probably would have been as much surprised by its appearance later in this century in dramatic form, "sanitized' of the political concerns that prompted him to write in the first place.

The last chapter of the work takes a more detailed look at the *Protocols* and the *Dialogue*'s connection to it. A short Appendix has been added on Thomas Babington Macaulay, a nineteenth-thinker who was very influential on Machiavellian scholarship, someone to whom Joly too may have been indebted.

Readers of Joly today will find his voice still amazingly pertinent. The post-Communist world we live in has been marked, to say the least, by controversy over liberalism and its global relevancy. To a large extent, the preeminent dispute in the *Dialogue in Hell* is once again our own. Joly raises the whole issue of historical "endism" well before Francis Fukuyama, drawing on the thought of Kojeve and Hegel, made it popularly topical in our day.[12] Our most explicit domestic preoccupation is arguably the culture war between "secularists" and "traditionalists" and there are strong echoes of this in the *Dialogue*. Until recently, it was a bitter dispute over the merits, even the morality, of deficit financing. And this, too, figures prominently in its pages. There are even references to the amorous adventures of the ruler, which, if conducted honorably, redound to his advantage, short, of course, but also long term. In brief, I have tried (unsuccessfully) to eschew repeated references to our situation and conditions today. Otherwise I would never have finished and the readers Joly wanted to reach are not in need of this anyway.[13]

Readers of the *Dialogue* will work through timeless issues of politics, guided by Machiavelli and Montesquieu.[14] Substantial effort has been made in this book to reintroduce a perhaps forgotten body of political doctrine, Saint-Simonianism, to establish its relevancy to the drama and substance of the *Dialogue* as well as to the politics of Napoleon III. Joly's text is noteworthy in drawing parallels between the Caesars and the Bonapartes to describe the most ambitious of political projects. As a study of modern tyranny, his work is perhaps unsurpassed. Readers will undoubtedly be prompted at certain points of Machiavelli's and Montesquieu's debate to think of thinkers within Joly's intellectual universe: Rousseau, Constant, DeBonald, De Maistre, Guizot, J. S. Mill, de Tocqueville, Marx, Smith, Jefferson, the *Federalist*; and to think of others that post-date Joly's world: Galbraith, C. W. Mills, Keynes, Huxley, Orwell, Aron, Nietzsche, among others. The better-informed reader surely will be drawn to think of additional thinkers and historic personages, I'm sure.

*****

A final word about the subtitle, which has been added to the paperback edition. Joly wrote at a time of complacency and optimism. This is personified in the thinking of the Montesquieu of the *Dialogue*. The most significant book of the last decade espoused a position not too distant from Joly's presentation of the great French thinker. It brought "tidings of great joy"—that the ideological conflicts of the twentieth century, humanity's most sanguinary, had issued into the undisputed triumph of liberal politics and marketplace economics. The historic path had been cleared. International trade would multiply the interconnectedness of peoples and underpin the planet's prosperity. Liberal polities, which safeguard the rights and dignity of the individual, would help guarantee the planet's peace. As one influenced by this thesis would have it, "the zones of peace" would spread and absorb "the zones of conflict."

Things have changed since then. Confident optimism is no longer ours. There is a populist backlash ("anti"-globalisation) against liberal economics and trade. There is an elitist attack on liberal politics in the name of supranational institutions. These would place vital spheres of the life of citizens beyond salutary checks and democratic control, the hallmark of the liberal polity. And there are new despotic (indeed, totalitarian) threats from "the zones of conflict."

For Joly, despotism was an eternal possibility and liberal politics is never a "settled" one. He has delineated the "conditions of modern tyranny," the new forms in which despotism would appear. He has elaborated one such species of the new genus of despotism—a most sedulous one and, for that, difficult to recognize. I have called it "humanitarian despotism." It is the regime of the French Emperor, Napoleon III.

In all too obvious ways, we are today menaced by movements that violently reject liberal freedoms. And we are also menaced by antagonistic forces that all too often claim a "humanitarian" label, it should be pointed out.

Scholars sympathetic to the author of the *Dialogue in Hell* think they praise him best by underscoring his remarkable powers of prediction. This praise is misplaced. We are not dealing with another Nostradamus here. As Hans Speier has sensed, his powers of prediction are based on "insight." He has demonstrated the "eternal" possibility of despotism by showing it springing up in soil that seemed least congenial to its propagation. (Who would have thought that Nazism would spring up in the home of Kant, Goethe, and Schiller?) In the present context, this is another way of saying that liberal freedoms are "always" vulnerable. And the threats "ever-present." Joly has made good his claims for his book. His little "dialogue" between the two giants of modern philosophy has uncovered "abiding truths" about our political condition. (We would expect as much from the likes of a Machiavelli and a Montesquieu and their dramatic confrontation). This is why Joly's work remains "fresh" and this is why his warning is always "timely." He forces us to think about "the conditions of freedom." And this would also be a good subtitle to Joly's work. It's the most important "lesson" he bequeaths us.[15]

Notes

1. Most biographical detail of any substance comes from Henri Rollin, *l'Apocalypse de notre temps* (Paris: Gallimard, 1939). Information on the life of Joly in the "Avant Propos" of the best known French edition of the *Dialogue* is taken from this source. See Maurice Joly, *Dialogue aux Enfers entre Machiavel et Montesquieu*, published in the collection "Liberte de l'esprit" dirigée par Raymond Aron (Paris: Calmann-Levy, 1968), vii-xii. Biographical material for this introduction is taken mainly from there.

2. In "The Truth in Hell," 31, Hans Speier notes these discrepancies in some of the more prominent works on Joly:

> The article on Joly in *Grande Encyclopedie*, Hans Leisegang, *Gesprache in der Unterwelt*, and Hans Barth, "Maurice Joly," state that Maurice Joly lived from 1821 to 1878. Herman Bernstein gives the dates 1831-1878. Norman Cohn, *Warrant for Genocide*, has 1829-1879. Finally, Henri Rollin in his "Avant Propos" to Maurice Joly, *Dialogue aux Enfers entre Machiavel et Montesquieu*, states that Joly was born in 1829 and died 17 July 1877.

To underscore the heedless way in which posterity has treated Joly, consider that the only English translation until now, that of Bernstein, inexplicably mistranslates even the title of the *Dialogue*.

3. Excerpts from the "autobiography" can be found in Herman Bernstein, *The Truth About* The Protocols of Zion (New York: Covici-Freide, 1935), 16-17.

4. See Bernstein for excerpts of the court decision as reported by *Le Droit*, a Paris newspaper, on April 26, 1865.

5. Walter Laqueur, *Russia and Germany* (Boston: Little, Brown, 1965), 97. Laqueur also lists "the more substantial investigations" in solving the riddle of what he calls "the greatest politico-literary hoax in modern history." See note 43, 339.

6. Konrad Heiden, *Der Feuhrer*, tr. Ralph Manheim (Boston: Houghton-Miflin, 1944), 6. We are beholden to Pierre-Andre Taguieff and the monumental efforts he made to collect all important documents relevant to the *Protocols*. Within his work is a collection of scholarly efforts to bring to light once again its entire sordid legacy. See his two volume work, *Les Protocols Des Sages de Sion* (Paris: Berg International, 1992). The first volume is by Taguieff and is an introduction to the study of the fabrication of the *Protocols* and the uses to which it was put in this century. The second volume is an impressive collection of studies and documents under his editorial direction. I refer those who might have further interest in the *Protocols* to these works, a kind of "one stop shopping" for interested scholars. Taguieff does in a much better way what Herman Bernstein earlier tried to do. He works with much more material. One of the reasons for this is the astonishing influence the nefarious document has again exerted, subsequent to Bernstein's time. See note 8 in this regard.

7. Norman Cohn, *Warrant for Genocide* (London: Eyre & Spottiswoode, 1967), 73.

8. The English translation of Godsche's "Jewish Cemetary in Prague," the *Protocols* itself, as well as the *Dialogue* can be found in Bernstein, *The Truth About* The Protocols. Bernstein was the first to trace Godsche's tale to the forgery. More will be said of this connection in chapter 11. Perhaps one of the reasons Joly's text has failed to draw commentary from English readers is the terribly flawed quality of Bernstein's translation. This was the motive for including a new translation as part of this work.

9. See Jean Francois Revel's Preface to the *Dialogue aux Enfers*, xvii-xix.

10. Speier, "The Truth in Hell," 32.

11. This is the view of Hans Liesegang, who considers the *Dialogue* a literary "masterpiece" and compares the author to Dostoyevsky. See Speier, "The Truth in Hell," 31.

12. See Francis Fukuyama, "The End of History?" *The National Interest*, 16 (summer 1989). His book (1992) drops the question mark but adds "And the Last Man." The idea of an "end" to history comes from Hegel. The idea of "the Last Man" comes from Nietzsche. One might be tempted to think, by his dropping the question mark, that he grew more optimistic about the prospects for liberalism in the interval between the article and the book. And by adding "the Last Man," that he became more reflective of its ultimate conclusions. In the interval, and shortly thereafter, four generations of Soviet Communist rule were openly repudiated and the party deposed. The USSR ceased to exist. Power passed from Gorbachev to Yeltsin as President of the Russian Federation. A vigorous reformer and Westernizer was now in the saddle and he was soon to prove himself strong enough to quell any attempt at counterrevolution. News from Asia was still astonishingly encouraging. Things have changed since, to say the least. Internal struggle and external conflict appear everywhere and the upshot of such things cannot really be foreseen with confidence. This certain looks like "history" as we all know it and the thesis that it is benignly coming to an end seems more and more implausible. Such is the fate of any thesis that is tied to unpredictable events. The "phenomena can be saved" if we posit, like the Communists of old, that history's cunning is beyond the ken of naive simpletons. Long term, indeed, now, it seems, over the *very* long term, things will prove the thesis right. But "in the long term, we are all dead." So, it seems, Fukuyama's thesis will never be proved right by us, or wrong. Joly, we will see, has something to tell us about these things.

13. About two decades ago, in the United States, there was an advertisement about a ragù sauce, if I remember correctly. Not all the power of the woman's movement has been able to purge such things from American popular culture. A man's voice (the husband) asked: "Are there tomatoes in it? (A stupid question.) Is there beef in it? Is there oregano—and basil in it?" A woman's voice (the wife) would refrain in dulcet tones, ever smugger and more reassuring (or was it really controlled exasperation?) to the repeated queries: "It's *in theeeere.*" With respect to Joly, I would not go as far as this woman would, but almost. I don't want to grate too much.

14. Raymond Aron, one of the last century's greatest thinkers and political analysts, explained why "for over four centuries the quarrel over Machiavellianism has not ceased being of contemporary interest." It is "because at bottom this quarrel is eternal." Aron had planned a multi-volume work on Machiavelli that was to be his magnum opus. He

abandoned the work after the war. This quote is taken from a generally favorable review of the work of the Christian, Jacques Maritain, in his quarrel with the Florentine. The reservations Aron expressed give us a sketch of the lines of critique he himself probably would have developed in his abandoned work. It is no wonder that Joly and his Machiavellian teaching saw the light of day in France under the aegis of Aron. He figured prominently in my thoughts as I delved deeper in the *Dialogue*, as you will see. I also contend that the thought of Montesquieu has particular relevance to today's political dilemmas. Pierre Manent is the finest of Raymond Aron's progeny. He also thinks Montesquieu particularly relevant to us as "decidedly the modern philosopher most capable of losing us as well as saving us." See Aron's essay entitled "French Thought in Exile: Jacques Maritain and the Quarrel over Machiavellianism," in *In Defense of Political Reason. Essays by Raymond Aron,* Daniel J. Mahoney, ed. (Lanham, Md: Roman & Littlefield), 53. Manent's quote can be found in his profound study of modern consciousness in *La Cité de l'homme* (Paris: Fayard, 1994), 109.

15. This book, about freedom and character was finished shortly before the events of September 11, 2001. I would have said certain things with a different nuance (and more strongly) if I had written it after. But, for many reasons, I decided to change nothing and let things stand as they were written. (Subsequently, only a subtitle was added to the paperback version of the book and this little addendum, which explains why I added it.)

I wrote that America had never suffered a tragedy, at least at the hands of others. I still think this the case. September 11 was a personal tragedy for all the victims of that day, American and non-American. We all shared in that deeply. Indeed, it shook our very soul. The nation's real tragedy would be, by gross blunder or weakness of will, to succumb to the forces that were unleashed that day. Writing now, six months after the "events," this does not seem to be the case.

Abraham Lincoln led us through our only real tragedy. He set high standards for us, in peace, for sure, but in war, also. He waged it vigorously because freedom and other dear principles were at stake. But he also waged it with malice towards none.

The better angels of our nation were in display on that horrible September day. They struck a mystic chord in all of us. I, for one, never thought that they had abandoned our spirit. It's just that they seemed to have sat silent for so long. Looking to the future, we hope, fondly, and pray, fervently, that they continue to play upon us.

TRANSLATION

DIALOGUE IN HELL

BETWEEN

MACHIAVELLI[*]

AND MONTESQUIEU

OR

THE POLITICS OF MACHIAVELLI

IN THE 19TH CENTURY

by a Contemporary

Soon we should see a frightening calm during which everyone will
unite against the power which had violated the laws.

When Sulla wanted to give Rome freedom, she was no longer able to
receive it.

(Montesquieu, *The Spirit of the Laws*)

Drussels

Published by A. Mertens and Son

Rue de L'escalier, 22

1864

---

[*] The emphasis on Machiavelli is as it appeared in original publication.

A Short Introductory Statement

This book delineates certain attributes applicable to all governments. However, it aims at something more precise: the quintessential features of a political system whose practices have not varied a single day since the fatal and, alas, already too distant date of its *enthronement*.

The appropriate response to this situation is not to write lampoons or pamphlets. The sensibilities of modern peoples are too *civilized* to accept harsh truths about contemporary politics. The enduring success of certain others tracts is mystifying and cause enough to corrupt integrity itself. But the public conscience still lives, and heaven will some day take an active role in settling scores with those that trifle with it.

Certain facts and principles are better judged when seen outside the framework they customarily appear to us. The change of perspective can sometimes be very troubling!

Here, everything is presented as fiction. It would be superfluous to give the key to it in advance. If this book has significance, if it conceals a teaching, the reader must understand it himself and not have it explained to him. Moreover, reading this will not be without its lively pleasures. Still, one must proceed slowly through it as befits writings that are not about frivolous matters.

No one should ask whose hand wrote these pages. In a certain sense, a work like this is anonymous. It answers a call to conscience. Everyone hears this call. The ideas take form. The author withdraws to the background because he merely records a thought that is generally held. He is merely a more or less obscure instrument of the partisans who seek the good.

Geneva, October 15, 1864

First Part

First Dialogue

Machiavelli: At the edge of this shore, I was told I would meet the shade of the great Montesquieu. Is this it in front of me?

Montesquieu: The name "great" belongs to no one here, O Machiavelli. But I am the one you seek.

Machiavelli: Among the illustrious persons whose spirits populate this gloomy stopping place, there is no one I wished to meet more than Montesquieu. Forced into these unknown regions by the migration of souls, I thank fortune for finally placing me in the presence of the author of *The Spirit of the Laws*.

Montesquieu: The former Secretary of State of the Florentine Republic has not yet forgotten the language of courts. But what can those who have crossed to these dismal shores have to exchange but anguish and regrets?

Machiavelli: Is this the philosopher, the statesman, who speaks like this? What does death matter to those who have lived by thought, since thought is immortal? For myself, I do not know a more tolerable situation than that which is ours here until Judgment Day. We are delivered from the cares and worries of material existence, live in the domain of pure reason, and are able to converse with the great men whose names have resounded throughout the universe. We may follow from afar the revolutions of states, the fall and transformation of empires. It is open to us to meditate upon their new constitutions, upon the changes brought about in the morals and the ideas of the peoples of Europe, upon the progress of civilization in politics, arts, industry, as well as the sphere of philosophical ideas. What a spectacle to contemplate! What astonishing marvels—if the shades that have descended here are to be believed! Death is for us like a remote refuge where we can assimilate the final lessons of history and the vindication of human rights. Even the void of death is not able to break all the ties that keep us attached to earthly existence, for posterity still demonstrates its dependence on men like you who have wrought great changes in the human spirit. At this moment your political principles reign over almost half of Europe. Who should be freer from fear in undertaking this somber passage which leads to hell or heaven than someone like you who can appear before Eternal Justice with such pure claims to glory?

Montesquieu: You ought to speak for yourself, Machiavelli. You're being too modest for one who has left behind immense renown as the author of *The Prince*.

Machiavelli: I think I catch the drift of your irony. Would the great French publicist judge me like the crowd, which knows me only as a name and through blind prejudice? I know that book has given me a disastrous reputation. It has made me responsible for all sorts of tyrannies. It has earned me the enmity of peoples as the hated personification of despotism. It has poisoned my last days and the reprobation of posterity seems to have followed me even here. But what have I done? For fifteen years I served my country, which was a republic. I conspired for its independence and defended it staunchly against Louis XII, the Spanish, Julius II, and Borgia himself, who, but for me, would have snuffed it out. I protected it against bloody intrigues that riddled it everywhere, combating them with diplomacy when another would have used the sword. I treated, negotiated, made or broke ties in accordance with the interests of the republic which found itself crushed between great powers and which war tossed about like a skiff. And it was not an oppressive or autocratic government but popular institutions that we supported in Florence. Was I one of those who was seen changing with fortune?

The Medici's executioners knew where to find me after the fall of Soderini. I advanced with the rise of liberty and fell with it. I was proscribed and no prince deigned to glance on me. I died impoverished and forgotten. That was my life, and those the crimes that earned me the ingratitude of my country and the hatred of posterity. Perhaps heaven will be more just toward me.

Montesquieu: I know all that, Machiavelli. That's why I could never understand how the Florentine patriot, the servant of a republic, became the founder of that sinister school which includes all the crowned heads as disciples and is put to use to justify tyrannies' most heinous crimes.

Machiavelli: And what if I told you that that book was only the product of a diplomat's imagination, that it was not intended for print, that the notorious uses to which it has been put are alien to its author?—That it was conceived under the influence of ideas which were then common to all Italian principalities avid to aggrandize themselves at each other's expense and directed by a cunning politics in which the most perfidious was reputed to be the most skillful....

Montesquieu: Are these your real thoughts on the matter? Since you are speaking so candidly, I can assure you that this is what I always thought. Indeed, I share such convictions with those few that know your life and have attentively read your works. Yes, yes Machiavelli, your avowals in this regard do you honor. So, you did not say what you really thought, or you only spoke under the sway of personal feelings which for a moment clouded your exalted mind.

Machiavelli: There you are mistaken, Montesquieu, as are those who have judged this matter like you. My only crime was to speak the truth to peoples and to kings—not the moral truth, but the political truth, not the truth as it ought to be, but as it is and always will be. I am not the founder of the doctrine whose paternity is attributed to me. It is grounded in the human heart. *Machiavellianism preceded Machiavelli*.

Moses, Sesostris, Solomon, Lysander, Phillip and Alexander of Macedon, Agathocles, Romulus, Tarquin, Julius Caesar, Augustus, and even Nero, Charlemagne, Theodoric, Clovis, Hugh Capet, Louis XI, Gonzalo of Cordova, Cesare Borgia—these are the progenitors of my doctrine. I am skipping some even better examples, and of course will not speak of those who came after me. The list would be too long and *The Prince* would teach them nothing but what they already knew by wielding power. Who in your time has rendered me more brilliant homage than Frederick II? To gain popular favor, he took pen in hand to refute me. While in politics, he rigorously applied my doctrines.

What inexplicable quirk of the human mind would hold what I have written in this book against me? Logic dictates that the scientist should be reproached for investigating the physical causes of bodies that fall and harm us, the doctor for describing diseases, the chemist for cataloguing poisons, the moralist for portraying vice, and the historian for writing history.

Montesquieu: Oh, Machiavelli. Would that Socrates was here to untangle the sophistry couched in your remarks. Although I am not by nature endowed with strong debating skills, it is still not very difficult for me to rebut you. You compare to poison and disease the ills engendered by the spirit of domination, cunning, and violence. But your writings teach the ways to communicate diseases to states. You teach how to distill these poisons. When the scientist, the doctor, or moralist investigates evil, it is not to teach its propagation, but to cure it. As soon as you let out that you do not hold to despotism on principle and that you yourself consider it an evil, it seems to me that by this alone you condemn it and that we agree at least on this point.

Machiavelli: We do not, Montesquieu, for you have not understood my thought in its entirety. I have opened myself to attack by using an analogy that can only too easily be turned against me. Socratic irony itself could not disconcert me. It is sophists who are most skillful in wielding the underhanded weapon of *dialectics* in such a way. You are not of this school, nor am I. Therefore let's put aside semantics and facile analogies so that we don't lose sight of certain ideas. Here is the essence of my system, and I doubt that you will shake it, because it is composed only of moral and political facts deduced from one eternal truth: the evil instinct in man is more powerful than the good. Man is more attracted by evil than by good and fear and force have more sway over him than reason. I won't bother to demonstrate these truths. In your country, only the hare-brained coterie of Baron d'Holbach, of which J. J. Rousseau was the high priest and Diderot the apostle, attempted to controvert these truths. All men seek to dominate and no one would not be a tyrant if he could. All, or nearly all, are ready to sacrifice another's rights to their own interests.

By what means can these ravenous beasts we call men be restrained? At the origins of societies, it is brutal and unrestrained force; later, it is the law, that is to say, still force, but institutionalized. You have fully investigated the origins of history. Everywhere force precedes right.

Political liberty is only a secondary idea. The need to live is what dominates states as it does individuals.

In certain regions of Europe, there are people incapable of moderation in the exercise of liberty. Prolonged liberty is transformed into license. Civil or social war follows. The state perishes. This happens either when the state fractures and is dismembered as a result of its convulsions, or when its divisions make it the prey of foreigners. In such situations, people prefer despotism to anarchy. Are they wrong?

Once established, states have two kinds of enemies: internal and external. What arms do states use in making war against foreigners? Will two enemy generals inform each other of their battle plans so that each will be better able to defend himself? Will they forbid attacks by night, traps, ambushes, and battles in which the numbers of troops are unequal? Obviously not. Don't you agree? Such combatants would be a laughing stock. But you don't want to use all the traps, artifices, and stratagems that are indispensable to war against internal enemies and factions? Doubtless, this case calls for less rigor but basically the rules are the same. Can pure reason lead violent masses that are motivated by emotions, passions, and prejudices?

Let the direction of affairs be placed in the hands of an autocrat, an oligarch, or the people themselves. No war, no negotiation, no internal reform would succeed without the help of those stratagems that you seem to condemn but which you yourself would have had to use if the king of France had charged you with the least important affairs of state.

What childish condemnation has dogged *The Prince*! Has politics anything to do with morality? Have you ever seen a single state conduct itself according to the principles that govern private morality? But then every war would be a crime, even when it had fair cause. Given that conquest has no other motive than glory, it would always be a heinous offense. Every treaty in which one power tipped the balance in its favor would be a base fraud. Any usurpation of sovereign power would deserve death. Nothing would be legitimate except what was based on justice! But what I have just related I also maintain even in the face of contemporary history. All sovereign powers find their origin in force or, what is the same thing, in the negation of justice. Does that mean that I proscribe justice? No. But I regard it as having an extremely limited application, both in the relations among nations and in the relations between rulers and ruled.

Moreover, don't you see that this word—"justice"—is infinitely vague? Where do its claims begin? Where do they end? Where should it apply? Where not? I will give some examples. Consider the following state. Its public institutions are poorly organized. It's in the throes of a turbulent democracy. Its laws are powerless before factions. Disorder reigns everywhere—everything precipitates its ruin.

A bold man springs up from the ranks of the aristocrats or from the midst of the people. He demolishes all constitutional power, takes over lawful authority, reforms all institutions, and gives the country twenty years of peace. Had he the right to do what he did?

Pisastatus seizes the citadel in a surprise attack and prepares the way for the century of Pericles. Brutus violates the monarchical constitution of Rome, expels the Tarquins, and with the thrusts of a dagger founds a republic whose grandeur is the most impressive spectacle that the universe has seen. The struggle between patricians and plebeians, so long as it was controlled, made for the vitality of the Republic but it ultimately leads to its dissolution and brings everything to the brink of destruction. Caesar and Augustus appear. They too are violators. But the Roman Empire that succeeded the Republic, thanks to them, lasts as long. It finally falls only after having covered the entire world with its debris. So, was justice on the side of these audacious men? No, according to you. And yet posterity has showered them with glory. In truth, they served their country by saving it. They prolonged its existence through the centuries. You do see that, in states, interest overrules the principle of justice. What emerges from these considerations is *that good can come from evil; that one attains good through evil,* just as someone is cured by poison, or someone's life is saved by the cut of a knife. I have taken societies as they are and have prescribed rules accordingly.

Considered in the abstract, are violence and deceit evil? Yes, but they will have to be used to govern men, as long as men are not angels.

Everything is good or bad according to the use made of it and the advantage derived from it. The ends justify the means. And now, if you ask me why I, a republican, everywhere give preference to absolute government, I will tell you. In my country, I witnessed the inconstancy and cowardice of the people, its predilection for servitude, its incapacity to conceive and respect the conditions of free life. In my view, the people represent a blind force that dissipates sooner or later, unless taken in hand by a single man. I answer that the people, left alone, only know how to destroy themselves. They are incapable of knowing how to administer, judge, and make war. I tell you that the brilliance of Greece shone only during the eclipse of liberty, that without the despotism of the Roman aristocracy, and later, the despotism of the emperors, the brilliant civilization of Europe would never have developed.

Shall I look for examples among modern states? They are so striking and so numerous that I shall cite only the first that come to mind.

The Italian republics shone under what institutions and under which men? Under which sovereigns did Spain, France, and Germany establish their power. The Leo X's, the Julius II's, the Phillip II's, the Barbarossas, the Louis XIV's, the Napoleons are all men of awesome strength, whose hands were placed more often on the hilts of their swords than on the charters of their states.

But I'm surprised to have to speak at such length to convince the illustrious writer who's listening to me now. If I'm not mistaken, aren't a number of these ideas found in *The Spirit of the Laws*? Has this discourse offended that sober and reserved man who has dispassionately meditated upon the problems of politics? The Encyclopedists were no Catos. The author of *The Persian Letters* was not a saint, nor even fervently devout. Our school, which is called immoral, followed the true God more than did philosophers of the eighteenth century.

Montesquieu: I have listened to you attentively. Even your last statement fails to rile me, Machiavelli. Will you be so good as to listen to me and allow me the same liberty to express myself?

Machiavelli: I'll keep quiet and listen in respectful silence to the man they call the *legislator of nations*.

Second Dialogue

Montesquieu: Your doctrines contain nothing new to me, Machiavelli, and if I experience some difficulty in refuting them, it is less because of their frightening implications than because, whether true or false in particular instances, they have no philosophic basis. I understand very well that you are above all a political man, and that facts impress you more than ideas. But you will agree nevertheless that when the question concerns government, it is incumbent on us to lay down certain principles. You leave no place in your politics for morals, religion, or justice. You have on your lips but two words: *force* and *cunning*. A system that can be summed up by saying that force plays a great role in human affairs, and that cunning is a prerequisite for statesmen expresses truisms, you know full well, that need no demonstration. But if you set up violence as a principle and cunning as a maxim of government, and if your calculations take into account none of the laws of human nature, then the code of tyranny you acclaim is no more than the law of the jungle. Animals also are cunning and strong and, in effect, no right is recognized among them other than brute force. But I don't think your reductionist thinking goes that far, for you recognize the existence of good and evil.

It is your principle that good can come from evil, and that it is permitted to do evil when it may result in a good. Thus, you don't say that betraying one's word is good itself, that it is good to put corruption, violence, and murder to use. Rather, you say that a person can be a traitor when it's useful, kill when it's necessary, and take another's goods when it's advantageous. I hasten to add that, in your system, these maxims apply only to princes, and only when it is a question of their interests or those of the state. Consequently, the prince has the right to break his oaths. He may shed torrents of blood to seize and keep power. He may despoil those he has banished, overturn all law, promulgate new ones, then violate these, squander finances, corrupt, repress, punish, and threaten continually.

Machiavelli: But haven't you yourself said that in despotic states fear is necessary, virtue useless, and honor dangerous, that blind obedience is required, and that the prince is lost if he lowers his guard for an instant.[*]

---

[*] *The Spirit of the Laws* IX 3.

Montesquieu: Yes, I did say that. But when I discovered, as you did, the horrible conditions on which tyrannical power depends, it was to excoriate it, not to celebrate it, to incite a horror in my country, which, fortunately for her, has never bent her head under such a yoke. How is it you can't see that the use of force is only an exception in the conduct of orderly societies and that even the most arbitrary powers are forced to search for their sanction in considerations divorced from theories of force? It is not only in the name of interest of state, it is also in the name of duty that all oppressors act. They violate its strictures but they invoke it nevertheless. It follows that state interests are inadequate of themselves to justify the ends and therefore the means that they put to use.

Machiavelli: Here, I must stop you. You do take such interest into account. And that is enough to justify all those political necessities that are not in accord with justice.

Montesquieu: You invoke raison d'état. But look, I won't posit for the basis of societies precisely that which destroys them. In the name of such interests, princes and peoples, in their capacity as citizens, will only commit crimes. State interests, you say! But how do I know whether it is really advantageous for the state to commit this or that iniquity? Don't we both know that the interest of the state most often serves as cover for the interest of the prince and of the corrupt favorites that surround him? I avoid such consequences by positing justice as the basis of the very existence of societies. This is because the notion of justice sets limits that such interest must not pass beyond.

If you were to ask me what is the foundation of justice, I would tell you that it is morality, whose precepts contain nothing doubtful or obscure, because they are written in all religions and are imprinted in luminous characters in the conscience of man. It is from this pure source that all civil, political, economic, and international laws must flow.

Ex eodum jure, sive ex eoded fonte, sive ex eodem principio.

But it is here that the inconsistency of your argument is most flagrant. You are Catholic; you are Christian; we worship the same God. You accept His commandments. You accept morality. You accept justice in human relations. But you trample upon all its rules where the state or prince is concerned. In short, *according to you, politics has nothing at all to do with morality.* You allow the monarch what you forbid the subject. Depending on whether the same actions are done by the weak or the strong, you glorify or condemn them. They are crimes or virtues depending on the rank of the one who performs them. You praise the prince for having done them *and you send the subject to the galleys.* You do not consider the fact that no society based on such maxims could endure. Do you believe that a subject will keep his promises for long when he sees the sovereign betray his? That he will respect the laws when he knows that the lawgiver has violated them, and continues to violate them every day? Do you believe that a subject will hesitate to embark upon the path of violence, corruption, and fraud when he constantly sees walking there those who are charged with leading him? Stop deceiving yourself. Each act of usurpation by the prince in the public domain authorizes a similar infraction where the subject is concerned. Each act of political betrayal engenders the same in society at large. Each act of violence in high places legitimates one in low. Note well what happens to the relations among men in civil society.

And as for the relations between citizens and their rulers, I don't need to tell you that it means the introduction of civil war into the bosom of a society already in a turbulent situation. The silence of the people is only the truce of the vanquished, for which complaint is a crime. Wait until the people awaken. You have devised the theory of force. Rest assured. It will sink into the minds of the people. At the first occasion, they will break their chains on the most trifling of pretexts and take back by force what force has wrested from them.

The maxim of despotism is the Jesuitical saying *Perinde ac Cadaver*—kill or be killed. That's all there is to its law. Today the people are brutalized. Tomorrow—civil war. At least things happen this way in European climes. In the Orient, people doze peacefully in the degradation of slavery.

Thus, princes cannot let themselves do what private morality does not permit. This is my conclusion. It is categorical. You thought that you could confound me by citing examples of many great men who have undertaken bold acts in violation of the laws and given their countries peace and sometimes glory. And from this you draw your great conclusion: *good comes from evil.* I'm not very impressed by it. It hasn't been proved to my satisfaction that these bold men have done more good than evil, nor that society would not have been saved and maintained without them. The measure of safety that they bring does not compensate for the germs of dissolution that they introduce into states. A few years of anarchy are often much less deadly for a kingdom then several years of stultifying despotism.

You admire great men. I admire only great institutions. For people to be happy, I believe that they have less need of men of genius than men of integrity. But, if you wish, I concede that some violent enterprises that you defend could have been advantageous for certain states. These acts might be justified in ancient societies where slavery and the belief in fate prevailed. They reappear in the Middle Ages and even in modern times. But as manners have grown softer, as enlightenment has spread among the diverse peoples of Europe, and above all, as the principles of political science have become better known, justice has been substituted for force in theory and in practice. Undoubtedly, the politics of free societies will always be stormy and many crimes will be committed in liberty's name. But a fatalistic mindset no longer exists. If you could say in your time that despotism was a necessary evil, you could not say so today, because given the present state of manners and political institutions among the principal peoples of Europe, despotism has become impossible.

Machiavelli: Impossible? If you succeed in proving that to me, I'll agree to start turning my thought around to your direction.

Montesquieu: I will prove it, if you are still willing to give me the lead

Machiavelli: I'm quite willing. But be careful. I think that you are undertaking quite a task.

Third Dialogue

Montesquieu: A dense mass of shadows is coming toward this shore. The place where we are now will soon be overrun. Come over to this side, or else we'll soon be separated.

Machiavelli: Your last statement is less tenable than your remarks at the beginning of our conversation. I find that you have overstated the implications of principles found in *The Spirit of the Laws*.

Montesquieu: In that work, I purposely avoided elaborating long theories. If hearsay were not your only access to the work, you would see that the particular developments I mention readily follow from the principles there posited. Moreover, I freely confess that the knowledge I have acquired of recent times has not modified or added anything to my ideas.

Machiavelli: Do you seriously intend to argue that despotism is incompatible with prevailing political conditions in Europe?

Montesquieu: I did not say in every country but, if you wish, I will name the ones where the advance of political science has brought about this grand development.

Machiavelli: Which are these?

Montesquieu: England, France, Belgium, a portion of Italy, Prussia, Switzerland, the German Confederacy, Holland, even Austria, which is to say, as you see, almost all the countries over which the Roman world formerly extended.

Machiavelli: I know a little of what has happened in Europe from 1527 to the present, and I confess I am quite curious to hear you back up your claim.

Montesquieu: Well, listen, and maybe you'll end up being convinced. It is not men but institutions that preserve the reign of liberty and sound morals in states. All the good, indeed all the bad, which redounds to man in society, necessarily depends on the correct or incorrect ordering of institutions. And when I call for the most correct institutions, you understand that, following the fine words of Solon, *I mean the most perfect institutions that peoples are able to support.* That is to say, I don't presuppose impossible conditions and, consequently, I distance myself from those deplorable reformers who claim to found societies on a purely rational basis without taking into account climate, habits, morals, and even prejudices.

Originally, the role of institutions in nation making was narrowly conceived but has since evolved. Antiquity showed us marvelous civilizations and states in which the conditions for free government were admirably understood. The peoples of the Christian era have had more difficulty putting constitutions in harmony with the dynamics of political life, but they have profited from the lessons of antiquity, and with infinitely more complicated civilizations, they have nevertheless arrived at more perfect results.

One of the foremost causes of anarchy and despotism was the theoretical and practical ignorance that had so long existed in the states of Europe regarding the fundamental principles of organizing political power. At a time when sovereignty rested solely in the person of the prince, how could the right of the nation be guaranteed? How could power not be tyrannical when the person who was charged with executing the laws was also the lawmaker? How could the citizens be protected from arbitrary rule, when the legislative and executive powers were from the first mixed together, and when judicial power subsequently came to be united in the same hands?

I know full well that certain ideas of liberty and certain notions of public rights eventually penetrated the consciousness of even the most benighted. Yet they were but feeble obstacles to the unlimited power of absolute monarchy. On the other hand, the fear of popular anarchy and the gentle disposition of certain kings did lead some of them to make moderate use of the excessive powers with which they were invested. But it is no less true that such precarious guarantees existed at the discretion of the monarch who, in principle, possessed the goods, rights, and person of his subjects. In Europe, the separation of powers has solved the problem of free societies, and if anything can alleviate my anxiety in the hours before the Last Judgment, it is the thought that my time on earth had something to do with this great emancipation.

You were born, Machiavelli, at the end of the Middle Ages, and with the renaissance of the arts, you witnessed the dawn of modern times. But let me point out that the society in which you lived was still quite infected with barbarism. Europe was an arena. The ideas of war, domination, and conquest filled the heads of statesmen and princes. I know that force counted for everything and justice very little in those times. Kingdoms were the prey of conquerors. Within states, sovereigns fought lords; the lords crushed cities. In the midst of feudal anarchy that brought all Europe to arms, the people, trampled under foot, had been habituated to regard princes and nobles as preordained divinities, to whom the human race was delivered. You were born into times filled with tumult but also with grandeur. You observed intrepid commanders, men of iron, and audacious geniuses. And this world of disorder in all its complex and colorful variety appeared to you as it would to an artist whose imagination was more affected than his moral sense. In my opinion, this is what explains *The Prince*. A short while ago, your Italian deviousness was put to use to sound me out about what I thought about that work. You were amused. But in attributing *The Prince* to the caprice of a diplomat, you weren't so far from the truth after all. Since your time, however, the world has moved forward. Today people regard themselves as the arbiters of their destinies. The claims of privilege and aristocracy have been destroyed in theory and practice. They have raised in its stead a principle that would be quite novel to you, a descendant of Marquis Hugo—the principle of equality. They see those who govern merely as their representatives. They have fought civil wars to put the principle of equality into practice and it summons an adamant allegiance. They value these laws as their blood, because these laws have in a real sense cost the blood of their ancestors.

A while ago, I spoke to you of wars. I am aware that they are always raging. But one of the primary indications of progress is that conquered states in today's world no longer forfeit their property to the conquerors. Rights and guarantees that you are hardly aware of in international law today regulate the relations among nations as civil law regulates the relations of subjects in each nation.

After having secured their personal rights by civil laws and international obligations by *treaties*, people wanted to put themselves in an ordered relation with their princes and so they secured their political rights by *constitutions*. People were subjected for a long time to arbitrary rule because of the blending of powers. This allowed princes *to make tyrannical laws and to execute them tyrannically*. Now, the three powers of the state—legislative, executive, and judicial— are separated by constitutional demarcations that could not be breached without sounding the alarm to the whole body politic.

By this single reform, itself an immense accomplishment, internal public right was created and the superiority of the principles that constitute it became manifest. The person of the prince ceases to be confounded with the notion of the state. Sovereignty is seen to derive its authority from the very heart of the nation. Power is divided between the prince and other political bodies in a way that preserved their independence. In the presence of such an illustrious statesman, I don't want to go into detail describing what is known in England and France as *the constitutional regime*. Today it is operational in the major European states, not only because it is an expression of the most advanced political science, but above all because it is the only practicable mode of government given the ideas of modern civilization.

Political society is always governed by *laws*. This holds no less in tyrannical regimes than in free societies. Therefore, all the safeguards a citizenry enjoys *depend on the way the laws are made*. If the prince is the sole lawgiver, he will make only tyrannical laws. It would be fortunate if he did not overthrow the state's constitution in a few years but, eventually, we would arrive at absolute rule. If a Senate is the lawgiver, oligarchy is established, a regime odious to the people because it gives to them as many tyrants as there are rulers; if the people are the lawgivers, the tendency is toward anarchy, which is but another route to despotism. If an Assembly elected by the people is the lawgiver, the primary problem is already solved, for this is the very foundation of representative government, which today flourishes in all of southern Europe.

But even an Assembly of the people's representatives, if it alone possessed all legislative power, would not hesitate to abuse its power and expose the state to the greatest dangers. The properly constituted regime, a happy compromise of aristocracy, democracy, and monarchy, simultaneously partakes of these three forms of government through a balance of powers which seems to be the masterpiece of the human mind. The person of the sovereign remains sacred and inviolable. Although he keeps many major prerogatives necessary for the good of the state, his essential role is to be the living embodiment of the laws with *responsibility for their faithful execution*. He is no longer personally accountable for everything. Responsibility is also assumed by the ministers that he brings into his government. The law, which he proposes alone or concurrently with another body of the state, is drawn up by a council composed of men experienced in affairs of state. It is then submitted to an upper chamber which is hereditary or sits for life and which examines the law's provisions to determine whether they contain anything contrary to the constitution. The law is then voted on by a popularly elected legislative body and subsequently interpreted by an independent judicial body. If the law is bad, it is rejected or amended by the legislative body and the upper chamber opposes its adoption if it is contrary to the principles on which the constitution rests.

You understand that the mechanisms of this system can be adapted in a thousand ways according to the temperament of the people to which it is applied. Its great achievement is to reconcile order and liberty, stability and change, and to bring about the participation of all citizens in public life, thereby defusing popular insurrection. Such a country is self-governing. When different majorities are elected to the legislature, new ministers are named to form a new government.

As you see, relations between the prince and subjects rest upon a vast system of guarantees whose unshakable foundations are found in the social order. No administrative act can touch anyone's property. The judiciary protects individual liberty. In criminal cases, the peers of the accused sit in judgment. A Supreme Court oversees all lower courts and is charged with reversing unfortunate decisions. The citizens themselves are armed for the defense of their rights by forming citizen militias that complement the work of the police in the cities. By right of petition, the most humble individual can bring his grievance to the door of the sovereign assemblies that represent the nation. Regional districts are administered by elected government officials. Each year, large provincial assemblies, likewise popularly elected, convene to express the needs and wishes of the surrounding populace.

This is the merest sketch, O Machiavelli, of some of the institutions that flourish today in modern states and notably in my beloved homeland. But as access to information is the essence of free countries, none of these institutions could long survive if they did not function in full view. These institutions were given the breath of life by a power unknown in your century and only born in my time. I refer to the *press*, long proscribed, still decried through ignorance, to which could be applied the felicitous phrase spoken by Adam Smith about credit: *it is a public thoroughfare*. In effect, along this thoroughfare, all the ideas of modern peoples move. In the state, the press performs functions similar to traditional police powers. It voices needs, conveys complaints, denounces abuses and arbitrary acts. It compels the depositories of power to keep within moral bounds, and to do this, it suffices to place them before public opinion.

In societies regulated in such a way, O Machiavelli, how could you advance the ambitions of princes and the designs of tyranny? I am aware of the agonizing convulsions through which these advances triumphed. In France, liberty, steeped in blood during the revolution, returned only with the restoration. Even then, new disturbances were brewing. But all the principles, all the institutions of which I have spoken had already become a part of the mores of France and the peoples who had come under the influence of her civilization. I've finished, Machiavelli. Today, states as well as sovereigns are governed only by the rules of justice. A minister in the present age, inspired by your lessons, would not remain in power a year! The monarch who tried to put into practice the maxims of *The Prince* would bring upon himself the reprobation of his subjects. He would be banished from Europe.

Machiavelli: You think so?

Montesquieu: Please. Excuse my bluntness.

Machiavelli: Certainly.

Montesquieu: May I assume that you have changed your ideas somewhat?

Machiavelli: I intend to demolish, piece by piece, all the fine things you have just said and to demonstrate to you that only my doctrines prevail, even today, despite new ideas, despite new morals, despite your so-called principles of public right, despite all the institutions you have just described. But allow me, first, to ask one question. Your knowledge of contemporary history ends where?

Montesquieu: The information I've collected concerning different European states is current to the end of 1847. My wanderings through these infinite spaces filled with this motley crowd of souls haven't brought me into contact with anyone who could tell me anything about subsequent periods. Since I descended into this dismal dwelling place, I've spent about half a century among ancient peoples, and it has only been for a quarter of a century that I've come across great numbers of modern peoples. Moreover, most of these have been from the most remote corners of the world. I don't even know what year it actually is.

Machiavelli: Here the last are indeed the first, O Montesquieu. The statesman of the Middle Ages, the political man of barbarous times, knows more about the history of modern times than the philosopher of the eighteenth century. It is the year of grace, 1864.

Montesquieu: Please, tell right away, I beg you, O Machiavelli, what has happened in Europe since 1847?

Machiavelli: With your permission, not until I have given myself the pleasure of refuting your core theories.

Montesquieu: As you wish, but rest assured that I have no misgivings in this regard. Centuries are necessary to change the principles and form of government under which people have been accustomed to live. No new political teaching could have any effect in the fifteen years that have just elapsed, and, in any case, even if it were possible, the doctrines of Machiavelli would never be the ones that triumphed.

Machiavelli: That's what you think. Now you listen to me.

Fourth Dialogue

Machiavelli: While listening to your theories on the separation of powers and the benefits the peoples of Europe owe to it, I could not prevent myself, Montesquieu, from marveling at the extent to which the greatest minds could be deluded by such a system.

Impressed by the institutions of England, you thought that the constitutional regime could be made the universal panacea for states. But you did not foresee the irresistible movement of history that tears societies today loose from their old traditions. It will not take two centuries for this form of government that you so admire to be merely a memory in Europe, something antiquated and obsolete, like Aristotle's theory of drama and the rule of the three unities of time, place, and action.

First, let me examine your political mechanism in the abstract. You balance the three powers and you limit each to its sphere. One will make the laws; another will interpret them; a third will execute them. The prince will reign; ministers will govern. A marvelous thing—this constitutional seesaw! You have foreseen everything, regulated everything, but haven't provided for movement. No action would result from such a system. If this system functions precisely as you theorize, it would result in immobility. But in reality, things won't happen this way. At the first opportunity, movement will occur by the release of one of those springs that you have so forcefully compressed. Do you think that the powers will remain for long within the constitutional bounds you have assigned them, and that they will not end up breaking them? Where is the independent Assembly that will not aspire to sovereignty? Where is the court that will not bend to the pressure of public opinion? Above all, where is the prince who will not, in his innermost thoughts, contemplate overthrowing the rival powers that constrain his activities? In reality, you have placed at loggerheads all opposing forces, encouraged usurpation, and given power to all parties involved. You have put the prospect of ruling before all the ambitious and would make the state an arena where factions are unleashed. In a short while there would be disorder everywhere. Longwinded orators would transform deliberative assemblies into debating contests. Audacious journalists and unscrupulous pamphleteers would attack the character of the sovereign every day and discredit the government, ministers, and officials....

Montesquieu: I am well acquainted with these criticisms of free governments. To my mind, they carry no weight. Abuses do not constitute a condemnation of the institutions themselves. I know many states that have lived in peace for a long time under such laws. I pity those that are not able to experience them.

Machiavelli: Hold on! In your theories, you have taken into consideration discreet social groups. But there are huge numbers of people whose poverty chains them to their work in the same way that slavery did in former times. I ask you, what do all your parliamentary conventions have to do with their welfare? After all, this vaunted political development has merely resulted in the triumph of a privileged minority, elevated by chance, as the former nobility was by birth. What does it matter to the proletarian, bent over his work, oppressed by the weight of his fate, that a few orators have the right to speak and a few journalists to write? For the masses, the rights you have created will forever remain unrealized since they are incapable of putting them to use. Theoretically, the law promises the enjoyment of such rights, while circumstances prevent their actual exercise. This merely underscores the bitter irony of their fate. I tell you that some day they will take up their rights and spitefully destroy them in order to give themselves over to despotism.

Montesquieu: What scorn Machiavelli has for humanity and how base he must think modern peoples are! Almighty God, I refuse to believe that You have created men so vile. Whatever Machiavelli may say, he is ignorant of the principles and character of contemporary civilization. Today, both God and society sanction work. And far from being a sign of man's servitude, it is what brings men into social groups and is the means by which their equal rights are asserted.

Political rights are hardly meaningless for people in states where the law recognizes no privileged class and where all careers are open to individual enterprise. Without doubt, inequality in matters of intelligence and fortunes brings about inevitable inequalities among individuals in the enjoyment of their rights. This would hold true in any society. But isn't the recognition of such rights enough to fulfill the promise of the Enlightenment to assure for men their fullest possible emancipation? For those very people destined by birth to the most humble conditions, does the consciousness of their autonomy, and dignity as citizens, mean nothing? But that's only one side of the coin. If the spiritual dignity of peoples is tied to liberty, they are no less strongly attached to liberty by their material interests.

Machiavelli: I was expecting you to bring this up. Your school has posited principles whose ultimate consequences seem to escape you. You believe that they lead to the rule of reason. I am going to show that they bring back the rule of force. As originally conceived, the essence of your political system consists in giving nearly equal influence to each of the various powerful groups composing society, in order to bring an even balance to their social interests. You don't want the aristocratic element to dominate the democratic element. However, the temper of your institutions is to give more power to the aristocracy than to the people and more power to the prince than to the aristocracy, thereby calibrating the powers according to the political capacities of those who are to exercise them.

Montesquieu: That's true.

Machiavelli: You have the different classes of society participating in public affairs according to their aptitude and enlightenment. You put power in the hands of the property-holding classes by giving them the right to vote and they restrain the people through their collective common sense. Freedom of expression empowers popular opinion in such nations. The aristocracy sets the tone by its grand bearing. Through its preeminence, the throne lends majestic brilliance. You tenaciously preserve all traditions, the memory of all great historical events, and the celebration of greatness. On the surface, the society appears monarchical, but at bottom everything is democratic, for in reality there are no barriers between classes and work is the means to all fortunes. Isn't it something like this?

Montesquieu: Yes, Machiavelli. At least you are able to understand thoughts you don't agree with.

Machiavelli: Well, all these things are passé or will disappear like a dream, for you must contend with a new principle that is causing the lightning-like disintegration of all institutions.

Montesquieu: And what is this principle?

Machiavelli: Popular sovereignty. Take it from me. They will find a way to square the circle before the balance of powers will be reconciled with the existence of such a principle in nations where it is accepted. It is absolutely inevitable that the people, one day or another, will take over all power that ultimately resides in them. Will they hold onto it? No. After a few days, they will cast it aside and out of weariness confer it on the first soldier of fortune they come across. You know in your country in 1793 how the French rabble treated the representative monarchy. The people asserted their sovereignty by severing the head of their king. They then squandered all their rights and delivered themselves over to Robespierre, Barras, Bonaparte.

You are a great thinker but you do not appreciate the infinite baseness of the people. I am not describing those of my time but those of yours. They grovel in the face of strength and are without pity in the face of weakness. They are implacable in the face of trifling faults and indulgent toward crimes. They are incapable of tolerating the frustrations of a free society and patient to the point of martyrdom with all the outrages of audacious despotism. They overturn thrones in moments of anger. They hand themselves over to masters in whom they pardon outrages which, for much slighter reason, they would have decapitated twenty constitutional kings.

Try to find justice then, try to find right, stability, order, and respect for complicated forms of your parliamentary machinery, when you're faced with violent, undisciplined, faithless masses whom you've told the following: "You personify justice; you are the masters; you are the arbiters of the state." Oh! I'm quite aware that the prudent, politic Montesquieu, who posited certain principles but was reserved in spelling out all the implications, did not write the doctrine of popular sovereignty into *The Spirit of the Laws*. But, as you said a short while ago, certain things follow implicitly from the principles you set down there. The similarity of your doctrines with those of *The Social Contract* is readily apparent. And the day the French revolutionaries, swearing in *verba magistra*, proclaimed that "a constitution can only be the free compact among equals," monarchic and parliamentary government was sentenced to death in your country. It was useless to try to restore the principles of such government. It was useless for your Louis XVIII, upon returning to France, to try to show that his powers had their source in the declarations of '89, which he pretended were but a royal concession. This pious fraud of the aristocratic monarchy flew in the face of history. It was to disappear in the conflagration of the 1830 revolution, as the government of 1830, in its own right....

Montesquieu: Come on, out with it.

Machiavelli: Let's not jump ahead of ourselves. What we both know of the past allows me to claim that the principle of popular sovereignty destroys all stability and indirectly consecrates the right of revolution. It puts societies in open conflict with all human authorities and even with God. It is the very incarnation of force. It turns the people into a ferocious beast, which goes to sleep when it is surfeited with blood and then is enchained. And here is the inevitable path followed by societies whose conduct is regulated by that principle. Popular sovereignty engenders demagoguery; demagoguery engenders anarchy; anarchy leads to despotism. According to you, despotism is barbarism. Well, don't you see that peoples return to barbarism via civilization?

And what's more, no matter how you look at it, despotism is the only form of government really suited to the social conditions of modern peoples. You said that their material interests attach them to liberty. Surely you jest. In general, what kinds of states require liberty? Those animated by great sentiments and passions, by heroism, by faith, even by honor, as you used to characterize the French monarchy. Stoicism could produce a free people. Christianity, under certain conditions, could do the same. I understand the necessity of liberty for Athenians and Romans, people from nations that thirsted only for military glory, whose every aspiration was satisfied by war, who, moreover, required a most vigorous and enthusiastic patriotism in order to triumph over their enemies.

Public liberties were the natural patrimony of states where manual labor and productive tasks were relegated to slaves and where a man was worthless unless he was a citizen. I also perceive liberty in certain Christian periods, notably in small states, as in Italy or Germany, confederated like the Greek republics. In them, I also find some of the natural causes that make liberty necessary. It was much less problematic when there was an unquestioned principle of authority, when people, working in regimented, tutelary guilds docilely obeyed the beck and call of their pastors. If political emancipation had been attempted then, it would have taken place without danger for it would have been accomplished in conformity with the principles upon which the existence of all societies depend. But your large states depend solely on industry for survival and are populated by the godless and faithless. When popular aspirations are no longer satisfied by war and violent forces turn inward, liberty, and the principles upon which it is founded, can only be a cause of dissolution and ruin. I might add that liberty is no more necessary to the moral needs of individuals than to states.

Bored of ideas and under the shock of revolution, cold and disillusioned societies have emerged, indifferent to politics and religion. They are no longer moved by anything but material possessions and live only in terms of self-interest, worshipping only gold. Their mercantile morals rival those of the Jews whom they have taken for models. Do you really think it is love of liberty itself that leads the lower classes to mount an assault on authority? It is rather hatred for the well-off. Basically, it is to rob them of their riches, the means to pleasures they covet.

The well-off call for law and order, executive energy, and strength. They demand of the state but one thing, its protection against the turmoil that its feeble constitution cannot withstand, the security necessary for the maintenance of their possessions and the conduct of their businesses. What forms of government would you establish in societies where corruption has insinuated itself everywhere, where fortune is acquired only by fraud, where morality can no longer be guaranteed except by repressive laws, and where patriotism itself has been extinguished by an amorphous universal cosmopolitanism?

I don't see any salvation for such societies, veritable colossuses with feet of clay, except by instituting extreme centralization, placing all public power at the disposal of those who govern. What is needed is a hierarchical administration similar to that of the Roman Empire, which regulated with machine-like precision all the movements of the individual. It calls for a vast system of legislation that takes back bit by bit all the liberties that had been imprudently bestowed—in sum, a gigantic despotism that could strike immediately and at any time all who resist and complain. I think the Caesarism of the late Empire answers fairly well to what I would want for the well-being of modern societies. I have been told that such vast apparatuses already exist in more than one country in Europe, and thanks to them, these countries can live in peace, like China, Japan, and India. It's only vulgar prejudice that makes us look down on these oriental civilizations whose institutions one learns to appreciate more every day. The Chinese, for example, are very good businessmen and their lives are very well regulated.

Fifth Dialogue

Montesquieu: I hesitate to respond, Machiavelli, because what you just said is uttered with a kind of fiendish maliciousness that you leave me with the suspicion that your statements are not completely in accord with your real thoughts. Yes, you are capable of devastating rhetorical skills that play with the truth and you are indeed the dark genius whose name is still dreaded by current generations. I also freely grant, however, that too much would be lost if such a powerful mind were to keep its silence. I want to hear you out. And I even want to respond to you, although I now have come to the conclusion that I have little hope of convincing you. You have just painted a truly sinister picture of modern society. I am not able to judge whether it's a good rendering. The least I can say is that it is incomplete. In everything, good is mixed with bad, but you have portrayed only the latter. Furthermore, you have not given me the means to verify the extent to which you are correct. I don't know which people or states you had in mind when you drew this bleak picture of contemporary life.

Machiavelli: All right, let's take as a test case the most civilized nation in Europe, which, I hasten to say, should correspond least to the portrait I have just painted.

Montesquieu: Do you mean France?

Machiavelli: Yes, of course.

Montesquieu: You're right, for it is in France that the sinister doctrines of materialism have penetrated least. France has remained the home of great ideas and great passions, the sources of which you think have dried up. Those great principles of public right that you see as having no role in the government of states emanates from France.

Machiavelli: You might add that it's the field of experiment consecrated to political theories.

Montesquieu: As yet I know of no historical experiment that demonstrates any durable benefits from the establishment of despotism, in France any more than in any other nation. Above all else this brings me to the conclusion that your theories on the inevitability of absolute power are quite inconsistent with the reality of things. Until now, I know of only two European states, Turkey and Russia, completely bereft of liberal institutions, which everywhere else have mitigated the pure monarchical element. And yet if you look closely at the internal changes taking place in the heart of Russia, perhaps you'd find intimations of an approaching transformation. I know you predict that in the more or less distant future, peoples, menaced by inevitable disintegration, will return to despotism as to the ark of their salvation. They will bring into being great absolute monarchies similar to those of Asia. But this is only a prediction. How long will it take?

Machiavelli: No more than a century.

Montesquieu: Aren't you the clairvoyant. A century is still so much time gained. But now let me tell you why your prediction will not be borne out. Modern societies must not be seen through the eyes of the past. Everything has changed— morals, habits, needs. When I come to judging the destiny of modern societies, reasoning from historical analogies is not completely cogent. Above all, one must beware of taking what is contingent for universal laws and of transforming what is particular to certain times and places into general rules. Given that periods of despotism in the past have occurred several times as a result of social upheavals, does it follow that despotism must be taken as the rule for government? I grant it has played a transitional role in history but I am far from concluding from this that it is an appropriate solution for the crises of modern times. Isn't it more reasonable to say that different evils call for different remedies; that different problems call for different solutions; and different social mores call for different political mores? The tendency to perfection and progress is a foreordained social law. Eternal Wisdom, if I may say so, has condemned us to it. It has denied them movement in a contrary direction. Societies are fated to progress.

Machiavelli: Or they die.

Montesquieu: Let's not put too much emphasis on extreme cases. Societies never die in the process of generation. When the constituted order is not suited to them, their institutions can subsequently change, fall into decay, and perish. But the process of generating a new social order takes centuries. In this way, the various peoples of Europe have been successively transformed from a feudal to a monarchic system and from a pure monarchy to a constitutional regime. There is nothing fortuitous in this progressive development, whose inherent direction is so clear. It was the necessary result of a progress in thought being translated into practice.

A society's form of government must be in harmony with its principles, and you run counter to this absolute law when you think that despotism is compatible with modern civilization. As long as people regarded the sovereign as a pure emanation of divine will, they submitted to absolute power without complaint.

As long as the institutions under which they lived were incapable of assuring their welfare, they put up with arbitrary rule. But, from the moment their rights were recognized and solemnly declared, and more responsive institutions, based on free consent, were able to perform all the functions of the social body, princely politics was brought down. Power came to be regarded as subordinate to public purposes. The art of government was changed into administrative science. Today, things in states are organized so that the governing power merely appears as the engine where social power is generated.

Unquestionably, if you take it for granted that these societies are infected by all the corruption and vices that you just mentioned, they will rapidly disintegrate. But don't you see that this really begs the question? Since when does liberty debase souls and degrade character? These are not the lessons of history, which clearly reveal in the clearest terms that the greatest peoples have always been the freest. If morals are debased, as you say, in some part of Europe unknown to me, despotism must have been the cause, and liberty must have been extinguished. Therefore, liberty must be preserved where it exists and reestablished where it no longer exists.

Don't forget. We are basing our discussion on principles. And if yours are different from mine, they must at least be consistent. But you confuse me when you praise liberty in antiquity and condemn it in modern times, rejecting or accepting it depending on the time or place. Even assuming that these distinctions are justified, the principle remains intact, and I am only concerned with principle.

Machiavelli: I see you, like a skilled pilot, avoiding the reefs by keeping to the high seas. Generalizations are very convenient in arguments. But I confess that I am very curious to see how the sober Montesquieu deals with the problem of the principle of popular sovereignty. Up until now, I can't tell whether or not it's part of your system. Do you or do you not accept it?

Montesquieu: I can't answer a question posed in such terms.

Machiavelli: I can appreciate how the specter of popular sovereignty might well disconcert you.

Montesquieu: You're wrong, Machiavelli. But before answering I must remind you of the character of my writings and the function they served. You have tied my name to the iniquities of the French Revolution. This is quite a harsh judgment of a philosopher who proceeded so prudently in his quest for truth. I was born in a century of intellectual ferment, on the eve of a revolution that was to sweep away the ancient forms of monarchical government. I can say that I saw into all the practical consequences that this change of ideas would entail. I could not fail to see that the separation of powers would one day necessarily shift the seat of sovereignty.

This principle—poorly understood, poorly defined, above all, poorly applied—gave rise to terrible misunderstanding and shook French society from top to bottom. The consciousness of these dangers oriented my works. So while important innovators directly attacked the foundations of authority and unknowingly prepared a momentous catastrophe, I single-mindedly applied myself to the study of free governments to discover the fundamental principles upon which they rest. Statesman more than philosopher, jurist more than theologian, practical legislator—if I may be so bold to use such a word—more than theoretician, I think I did more for my country in teaching it to govern itself than calling into question the very principle of authority. Yet, God forbid that I raise myself above those who, like me, have in good faith sought the truth! We all have made mistakes. But each bears the responsibility for his works.

Yes, Machiavelli, there is one thing I do not hesitate to grant. You were right when you said a little while ago that the emancipation of the French people had to take place in accord with the fundamental principles upon which the existence of human societies depend. And from this concession you will see how I am going to judge the principle of popular sovereignty.

For me, I don't accept a meaning of popular sovereignty that would effectively exclude the most enlightened classes in the society from rule. We are talking about a crucial distinction, that between a pure democracy and one that is representative. If sovereignty resides anywhere, it resides in the nation as a whole. Therefore, to begin with, I will call it national sovereignty. But this concept of sovereignty is not absolute. It is only relative. When the unrestrained exercise of man's power is viewed as legitimate, a profoundly subversive idea follows—the unquestioned supremacy of man-made law. This is the materialistic and atheistic doctrine that set the French Revolution upon its bloody course, and, after the delirium of independence, imposed a degrading despotism. It's not quite correct to say that nations are absolute masters of their destinies, for their sovereign master is God Himself, and they can never be beyond His power. If nations were absolutely sovereign, they could do anything—act against eternal justice, even against God. Who dares go so far? But the principle of divine right, as commonly understood, is no less deadly a principle in diminishing the people and delivering them over to obscurantism and arbitrary rule. It leads to a system of castes where the people are turned into a herd of slaves, led, as in India, by the hand of priests and trembling under the rod of the master. How could it be otherwise? If it is God who designates the sovereign as the very representative of the Divine on earth, he has complete power over the human beings under his sway. This power will admit of no restraint except the general rules of fairness, which will always be easy to evade.

The area between these two extreme positions is occupied by furious partisan conflict. Some cry: "no divine authority!" Others: "no human authority!" O Supreme Providence, I refuse to accept either of these alternatives. They both appear to me blasphemous and contrary to Your wisdom. The truth lies between a divine right that does not include man in its considerations and a human right that does not include God, Machiavelli. Nations, like individuals, are free in the hands of God. They possess all rights and all powers provided they are exercised in accord with the rules of eternal justice. Sovereignty is human in the sense that it is men who confer it and that it is men who exercise it. It is divine in the sense that it is God who institutes it and that it can only be exercised according to the precepts He has established.

Sixth Dialogue

Machiavelli: I'd like to determine exactly what follows from what you've just said. To what extent does the hand of God control human affairs? Who determines who is sovereign?

Montesquieu: The people.

Machiavelli: It is written: *Per me regnes regnant.* Which literally means— Through Me kings reign.

Montesquieu: Yours is a translation tailor-made for *The Prince*, O Machiavelli, and in this century was the inspiration of one of your most illustrious partisans. But it doesn't come from Holy Scripture. God established sovereignty. He does not determine sovereigns. His almighty hand stopped at that point because it is there that human free will begins. "Kings reign according to my commandments. They must rule according to my laws." This is the meaning of the Holy Book. If it were otherwise, you'd have to say that Providence invests good and bad princes alike. We would have to bow down before Nero as well as Titus, before Caligula as well as Vespasian. No, God did not will that the most sacrilegious reigns could invoke His sanction and that the vilest tyrannies could claim His ordination. He has left to peoples as he has to kings the responsibility for their actions.

Machiavelli: I strongly doubt the orthodoxy of all this. Be that as it may, isn't it the people, according to you, who confer sovereign authority?

Montesquieu: Be careful, in the event you oppose such an argument, that you do not run up against a truth of pure common sense. What we are talking about is no historical novelty. In ancient times, in the Middle Ages, wherever rule was established other than by invasion or conquest, the free will of the people gave rise to sovereign power, originally by means of election. To cite only one example, in France the leader of the Carolingian line succeeded the descendants of Clovis, and the dynasty of Hugh Capet that of Charlemagne.[*] Of course, heredity eventually took the place of election. Because of their distinguished services and the public's gratitude, various traditions established the right to rule in the

---

[*]*The Spirit of the Laws* XXXI 4.

principal families of Europe. Nothing was more legitimate. But during periods of revolution, we revert to the fundamental principle of popular sovereignty. It is the ultimate appeal whereby authority never fails to gain consecration. This inherent principle has been explicitly recognized only recently in certain constitutions of modern states.

Machiavelli: But if the people choose their masters, can they then overthrow them? If they have the right to establish whatever form of government that suits them, who is to prevent them from changing it at will? A regime of ordered liberty will not be the result of your doctrines, but an era marked by continual revolutions.

Montesquieu: You are confusing the right with an abuse that may or may not result from its exercise. In other words, you are confusing the principle with its application. These are fundamental distinctions that must be understood.

Machiavelli: Don't expect to get off so easily. I am asking you about what logically follows from your principles. Try to avoid the consequences if you wish. But do the people have the right to overthrow their sovereigns or not?

Montesquieu: Yes, in extreme cases and for just cause.

Machiavelli: Who will be the judge of these extreme cases and their justice?

Montesquieu: And who could it be, if not the people themselves? Has it been otherwise since time immemorial? No doubt this is a dangerous prerogative, but it is as salutary as it is necessary. To hold the contrary would command men to respect the most odious governments and force them back under the yoke of a preordained monarchy.

Machiavelli: Your system has only one drawback. It presupposes the infallibility of the people's collective reason. But being men, aren't they prone to passion, error, and injustice?

Montesquieu: If the people are mistaken, they will be punished as men who have sinned against the moral law.

Machiavelli: How so?

Montesquieu: The scourge of discord, anarchy, and despotism itself will be their punishment. There is no other justice on earth while awaiting God's.

Machiavelli: You just mentioned the word despotism. See how we always return to it.

Montesquieu: This comment is not worthy of your great intelligence, Machiavelli. I have considered the most extreme consequences of the principles you oppose, in spite of the fact that taking the extreme case effectively distorts the truth of things. God has granted peoples neither the power nor the will to change so radically those forms of government essential to their existence. In political societies, as with all organic beings, the very nature of things limits the range of the use of freedom. The thrust of your argument must be limited to what is reasonable.

You believe that revolutions will be more frequent because of modern ideas. In fact, they won't be more frequent, and will possibly be much less so. To repeat what you said a little while ago, nations today live through industry. And what seems to you a cause of servitude is instead a factor that leads to order and liberty. I am aware that industrial civilizations are plagued with severe problems, but their benefits must not be denied nor their tendencies distorted. Whatever anyone says, societies that live by means of work, exchange, and credit are essentially Christian, for all such powerful and varied forms of industry are basically applications of several great moral ideas derived from Christianity, the source of all strength and all truth.

Industry plays such a formidable role in the dynamics of modern societies that you can't account for them without considering its influence. Such matters have nothing to do with the way you think. The scientific principles of modern economics are derived from the study of the interconnectedness of modern industrial society which decidedly points away from the concentration of power. The tendency of economics is to see the political apparatus merely as a necessary but very costly mechanism, whose workings must be simplified. It reduces the role of government to such elementary functions that its greatest drawback perhaps is to destroy government's prestige. Industry is the archenemy of revolutions, for without social order, it perishes, and the vital sap that sustains modern peoples is stopped. Industry cannot do without liberty and is itself only a manifestation of liberty. Furthermore, economic liberty necessarily gives rise to political liberty, so that it can be said that the most advanced industrial peoples are also the freest. Forget India and China, whose dismal fate is to live under absolute monarchy. Cast your eyes upon Europe and you will see.

You just mentioned the word *despotism* again. All right, Machiavelli. You are one whose dark genius has completely drunk in all hellish ploys, all occult schemes, all the artifices of law and government that could be used to enchain both the peoples' bodies and minds. You are one who despises men and wishes a terrible oriental domination over them. You are one whose political doctrines are borrowed from the frightful visions of Indian mythology. Please tell me, I beg you, how you could set up despotism among peoples where public right is firmly based on liberty, and where morality and religion also conduce to the same end. How is it possible among Christian nations that are sustained by commerce and industry and in states whose political institutions stand in full view to a free press that casts light into the most obscure recesses of power? Summon all the resources of your powerful imagination. Search. Contrive. And if you solve this problem, I will join you in declaring that the spirit of modernity is vanquished.

Machiavelli: You have dealt me a strong hand. Be careful or I might take you up at your word.

Montesquieu: Do so, I beg you.

Machiavelli: I fully expect to be up to the challenge.

Montesquieu: In a few hours, maybe we'll be separated. You're unfamiliar with this place. Follow me along this winding, dark footpath. For several more hours we can avoid the surging crowd of spirits over there.

Seventh Dialogue

Machiavelli: We can stop here.

Montesquieu: I'm listening.

Machiavelli: First, I must tell you that you are completely mistaken about what my principles imply. You always associate despotism with decadent forms of eastern monarchy, but I don't see things that way. Given new societies, new ways of proceeding are required. To rule today does not require committing atrocities, or decapitating your enemies, confiscating the goods of your subjects, or engaging in widespread torture. No. Death, expropriation, and torture should only play a minor role in the internal politics of modern states.

Montesquieu: That's nice.

Machiavelli: To be sure, I confess that I'm not terribly impressed with your complicated, *clanging machinery of industrial civilizations*. But, rest assured. I do keep up with the times. The strength of those doctrines associated with my name is their adaptability to all times and all situations. Today, Machiavelli has *progeny* who understand the worth of his teachings. Although I am thought to be very old, my eternal youthfulness is always in evidence.

Montesquieu: Are you serious?

Machiavelli: Listen and decide for yourself. Ruling today is less a question of doing men violence than of disarming them, less a question of repressing political passions than of de-politicizing men altogether, less a question of censoring their ideas than of assimilating them and subtly altering them.

Montesquieu: What? I don't understand what you're saying.

Machiavelli: We are talking about the moral dimension of politics and we'll soon see how it can be put to use. The principal secret of governing consists in sapping public spirit to the point where there is a total lack of interest in the ideas and principles that inspire revolutions today. In all times, peoples, like men, are bought off with words. Appearances are almost always enough for them. That's all they ask. Sham institutions can be established that rest on equally empty speech and ideas. *The liberal slogans* that are used by some parties as weapons against the government must be cleverly co-opted. The people must be inundated with these slogans to the point of boredom, even disgust. Today much is made of the power of public opinion. I will show you that it can be made to express whatever one wants if the hidden springs of power are truly understood. But before thinking about controlling opinion, you have to disorient it, to unsettle its convictions by acting in astonishingly contradictory ways, constantly diverting it, mesmerizing it, little by little leading it astray. One of the great secrets of the day is to know how to manipulate popular prejudices and passions so as to create such a confused way of thinking that any common ground of understanding is impossible among people who speak the same language and have the same interests.

Montesquieu: Where are you headed with these thoughts? Their obscurity portends something sinister.

Machiavelli: If the wise Montesquieu intends to let emotions get in the way of politics, perhaps I should stop here. I did not claim to base my position on moral grounds. You challenged me to put a stop to what agitates your societies, constantly wracked by the spirit of anarchy and revolt. Will you let me say how I'd solve the problem? You can indulge your scruples by taking my argument as purely theoretical.

Montesquieu: O.K.

Machiavelli: I acknowledge your request for more clarity. I will make myself clear eventually. But first let me tell you what is essential for the prince if his hopes to consolidate power are to be realized. First of all, he must try to destroy parties and dissolve independent associations, wherever they exist, in order to paralyze individual initiative in all its forms. Civic character would thus be undermined, weakening all resistance to slavery. Absolute power will no longer be an accident of fortune, but will become a need. These political precepts are not entirely new, but, as I was telling you, the techniques must be. Simple police and administrative regulations can attain a great number of these ends. In your societies—so intricate and well ordered—you have put *a monster called the state* in the place of absolute monarchs, a new Briareus whose arms extend everywhere, a colossal, tyrannical organism in whose shadow despotism will always be reborn. So, by invoking the authority of the state, nothing could be so easy as putting into effect the secret project I was talking about a short while ago. And the most powerful means to that end are likely to be precisely those that an able man may gather from this same industrial regime that you find so admirable.

For example, a simple change of a regulation would allow me to bring into existence immense monopolies. The fate of all private fortunes would become completely dependent on these vast reservoirs of public wealth. They could be taken over on the credit of the state the day after my political takeover. You are an economist, Montesquieu. Weigh the value of such a scheme.

As head of the government, all my edicts, all my ordinances would constantly aim at the same goal—the annihilation of independent powers, whether of groups or individuals, to develop the unlimited dominance of the state, making it the most powerful force in protecting, promoting, and remunerating society's activities.

I have another scheme that the industrial order makes opportune. In contemporary times, the aristocracy, as a political force, has disappeared. But the middle class landowners are still an obstacle to governments because they are inherently autonomous. It might be necessary to impoverish them or destroy them completely. In order to do that, all you need to do is increase the taxes on landed property, keep agriculture in a condition of relative inferiority, and aggressively promote commerce and industry. But, above all, speculation must be encouraged to the fullest, for excessive industrial prosperity can itself become a danger by creating too many independent fortunes.

Industrial magnates and manufacturers can be effectively dealt with by heavily stimulating spending for luxuries, increasing the level of wages, and skillfully striking heavy blows at the sources of *production*. I don't need to elaborate on these ideas. You know them well enough and in what circumstances and under what pretexts all this can happen. The public interest and even a kind of zealous regard for liberty and great economic principles will easily provide a cover, if need be, for the true goal. It hardly needs to be said that maintaining a formidable army continually employed in foreign wars must be the indispensable complement to this system. The point must be reached where the state is composed of nothing but proletarians, a few millionaires, and soldiers.

Montesquieu: Continue.

Machiavelli: So much for the domestic policy of the state. As for foreign policy, revolutionary ferment, which is suppressed in one's own country, should be incited throughout Europe. Two important advantages result. The turmoil bred of liberalism abroad will excuse its repression at home. Moreover, because you can easily promote either order or chaos in foreign countries, you will command their respect. The main thing is to infiltrate the seats of power and foment cabinet intrigues. In this way, European politics becomes so entangled that you can manipulate, by turns, any country with which you deal. Don't think that this duplicity, if it is well carried out, could eventually work against the sovereign. Alexander VI practiced nothing but deception in his diplomacy, yet he always succeeded, so well possessed was he of the wiles of the fox.* But in what is today called *official language*, a strikingly different approach must be taken. Here, you cannot affect too great a display of the spirit of integrity and goodwill. Given

---

* *The Prince* XVII.

that people see only the surface of things, the sovereign who knows how to act in this way will gain a reputation for probity.

Whenever there is any domestic turmoil, the prince must be in a position to respond with a foreign adventure. Whenever revolution is imminent, with a general war. But in politics, words must never correspond with deeds. So in these different circumstances, the prince must be clever enough to disguise his true designs. He must always appear to yield to the power of opinion while he executes what he has secretly contrived.

To sum up the whole scheme: within the state, revolution is contained by the fear of anarchy, bankruptcy, and more generally, by general war.

In the quick sketch I've given you, you can already see the crucial role that the art of rhetoric is called upon to play in modern politics. As you will see, I don't minimize the importance of the press and I know how to use the public rostrum when needed. You must be able to employ all the weapons against your adversaries that they use against you. Rather than rely on the violent power of the "demos," I would recur to the principles of right, in order to turn its arcane subtleties into resources of power. When decisions are made that might appear unjust or reckless, it is essential to know how to couch them in fine phrases, to adorn them with the most elevated principles of morality and right.

As you see, I have in mind an idea of power that is far from barbaric. On the contrary, power must draw to itself all the strengths and talents of that civilization where it finds itself. It must surround itself with journalists, lawyers, administrators, and men of experience, with people who know all the hidden mysteries, all the essential springs of social life, people who can speak all languages and who have studied man in all situations. They must be recruited wherever they are found, for these people perform extraordinary services by virtue of the ingenious ways they apply their talents to politics. In addition, it must have a multitude of economists, bankers, industrialists, capitalists, planners, millionaires, for everything ultimately can be reduced to numbers.

Assume for a moment that I have at my disposal the various intellectual and material resources that I have just outlined to you. Now, give me any nation—do you hear—any nation whatsoever! In *The Spirit of the Laws*, you regard it as an essential maxim *not to disturb the character of a nation,*[*] that is, if you want to preserve its original vitality. Well, I wouldn't even need twenty years to transform utterly the most indomitable European character and to render it as docile under tyranny as the debased people of Asia.

Montesquieu: While amusing yourself in this way, you have just added a chapter to *The Prince*. Whatever your doctrines, I won't debate them. I will only make one observation. It is clear that you have not upheld your end of the bargain. The use of any of these means presupposes absolute power, and I have asked you

---

[*] *The Spirit of the Laws* XIX 5.

explicitly how you could obtain it in political societies that rest on liberal institutions.

Machiavelli: Your observation is perfectly correct and I don't intend to dodge it. This was only a preface.

Montesquieu: I ask you to deal with a state based on representative institutions, a monarchy or a republic, a nation with a long experience of liberty. I ask you how, from there, you could return to absolute power.

Machiavelli: Nothing could be easier.

Montesquieu: Shall we see?

Second Part

Eighth Dialogue

Machiavelli: Hypothetically, let me take the most difficult case, a state constituted as a republic. With a monarchy, the task would be much too easy. I choose a republic, because with such a form of government, I will encounter what seems an insurmountable obstacle as far as ideas, mores, and laws go. Is such a case all right with you? Give me a state of any size, large or small. I assume it to be endowed with all the institutions that guarantee liberty. But I want to put to you this one question. Do you think the ruling power is beyond subversion or what is today known as a coup d'état?

Montesquieu: Certainly not. But at least you will agree with me that such an enterprise would be singularly difficult in contemporary political societies as presently organized.

Machiavelli: Why? Aren't such societies, like all societies throughout history, a prey to factions? Isn't civil war latent in all societies, subject to parties and rival claimants to power?

Montesquieu: I admit the possibility. But it won't take too much to keep you from drawing the wrong conclusions. Nowadays usurpers face great dangers and are repugnant to modern mores. They do not succeed very frequently and certainly don't have the significance you appear to want to lend them. Changing who governs does not lead to a change in institutions. A pretender may disturb the state. O.K. And I grant that his party may triumph. But power is in other hands. That's all. Public right and the institutional basis of power stay intact. That is the crucial thing for me.

Machiavelli: Can you really be so deluded?

Montesquieu: Show me the contrary.

Machiavelli: Do you grant that an armed enterprise directed against established authority might momentarily be successful?

Montesquieu: Yes.

Machiavelli: You have to appreciate exactly where I stand at this moment. For the time being, I have suppressed all power other than my own. The institutions still left standing present no real obstacle to me. It's all pure form. In fact, my will would face no real resistance. The Romans coined such a beautiful term for the extralegal position I hold—dictatorship—connoting both power and energy. That is to say that at this moment I can do as I wish. I am legislator, executive, judge, and as head of the army, I'm firmly in the saddle, so to speak.

Keep this in mind. In the circumstances, my triumph was due to the support of a faction. That means that this could only have been brought off in response to ongoing internal strife. Let me venture to pinpoint its causes: either a conflict between the aristocracy and the people or between the people and the propertied classes. This is the deepest and perhaps most salient source of social discord. It manifests itself in a cacophony of ideas and opinions, from contradictory pressure groups and interests, as happens in all states where liberty is momentarily unleashed. Political elements of all kinds make their class interest felt. Present are remnants of previously victorious but now vanquished parties, unbridled ambitions, burning greed, implacable hatreds. There are men of every opinion and doctrine—those that would restore former regimes, demagogues, anarchists, and utopians, all acting out of devotion to their cause and equally at work in trying to overthrow the existing order. What are we to conclude from such a situation? Two things. First, the country feels a great need for tranquillity and will refuse nothing to whatever power can provide it. Second, given these partisan divisions, there is no real locus of power or rather only one—the people.

I am a former pretender, now victorious. Assume that I have a great historical name capable of capturing the imagination of the masses. Like Pisistratus, Caesar, even Nero, I find my support in the people. That is as elementary as the *ABC*'s for every usurper. With them is found the blind power that enables the usurper to do anything with impunity and authority, using a name to cover everything. See how the people really care about your legal fictions and your constitutional guarantees!

At the center of factional dispute, I have induced silence. And now I'll show you what I will do.

Perhaps you remember the rules I set down in *The Prince* regarding the preservation of conquered territories. The usurper of a state is in a position analogous to that of a conqueror. He is forced to remake everything, to dissolve the state, to destroy the city, and to change the customary practices of right and wrong.

That is the goal. But in modern times, you can only get there by indirect routes and roundabout ways, by employing clever schemes, and eschewing violence, as much as possible. I won't destroy institutions directly; rather, one by one, I will secretly tamper with each of their mechanisms. In this way I will by turns rig the operation of the judicial branch, voting, the press, individual liberties, and education.

Beyond constitutional law, I would pass a whole new set of ordinary laws that would not expressly abrogate old ones but would first blunt their influence and then completely overshadow them. These are my general ideas. Now you will see in detail how I would put them into practice.

Montesquieu: If only you were still in the gardens of Rucellai, Machiavelli, discoursing on such lofty precepts. How regrettable that posterity can't hear you!

Machiavelli: Rest assured. All this is in *The Prince*, for those who know how to read.

Montesquieu: All right. It's the day after your coup d'état. What are you going to do now?

Machiavelli: One big thing, then one very little thing.

Montesquieu: How about the big one first?

Machiavelli: Taking over power after a violent coup is not enough. In general, factions do not readily accept their defeat. An accurate reading of the usurper has yet to be made. A test of wills will follow. There will be armed uprisings against him. The moment has come to subject the entire city to a kind of terror that causes the most intrepid souls to shrink back.

Montesquieu: What are you up to? You told me that your rule repudiates bloodbaths.

Machiavelli: There is no place here for false humanity. Society is menaced. We've arrived at a point where its defense is legitimate. What looks like an excess of harshness and even cruelty will prevent new bloodletting down the line. You needn't ask about the details. Terror must enter their souls so that fear softens their characters.

Montesquieu: Yes, I remember what you said in *The Prince* when you recount how Borgia staged his cynical execution in Cesena.* You are ever the same.

Machiavelli: No, no, as you'll see later. I only act this way out of necessity. It pains me.

Montesquieu: Then who will actually spill this blood?

Machiavelli: The army—that great arbiter of justice, whose hand never dishonors its victims! There are two things of the greatest consequence that follow

---

* *The Prince* VII.

from the army's handling of repression. One, it will find itself forever alienated from the civilian population that it so indiscriminately punished. Two, it will bind its fate to the fate of its leader with indissoluble ties.

Montesquieu: And you don't think that you'll be implicated in all this bloodletting?

Machiavelli: No. In any case, the people see the sovereign as above such things. The excesses of soldiers are not always easily contained. The generals and ministers who carried out my orders will be held responsible. I can assure you they will be fanatically devoted to me, for they know full well what would await them after me.

Montesquieu: So that's your first act as sovereign! Now shall we see the second?

Machiavelli: I don't know whether you have fully appreciated in politics how much power lies in little things. After doing what I just told you I'd do, I'd issue a great quantity of new currency, and upon each coin my image would be stamped.

Montesquieu: But given far graver affairs of state that you have to sort out, this would be frivolous.

Machiavelli: You think so? That's because you never held power. Having the human profile stamped upon coins is the clearest sign of power. At first, the proud will be consumed with anger, but people will get used to it. The very enemies who oppose my power will be forced to carry my portrait around in their purses. It is quite certain that little by little everyone will eventually learn to smile upon those features that are everywhere stamped on the material tokens of their joy. From the day that my image appears on coins, I am king.

Montesquieu: These are rather novel conceits, I confess. But haven't you forgotten that modern peoples are inclined to give themselves constitutions that guarantee their rights? Given that the origin of your power is force, plus the measures you said you would immediately take, you still find yourself in the presence of a fundamental charter whose principles, regulations, and provisions are completely contrary to your maxims of government.

Machiavelli: I'll enact another constitution. That's all.

Montesquieu: And you don't think that will raise other difficulties?

Machiavelli: What difficulty could there be? For the time being, there is no other will, no other power than mine, and the popular element of the regime serves as the basis of my action.

Montesquieu: That's true. However, I have one reservation. According to what you have just told me, I imagine that your constitution will not be a monument to liberty. Do you think a single crisis, a single display of timely violence, is sufficient to rob a nation of all its rights, all its achievements, all its institutions, all the principles under which it has been accustomed to live?

Machiavelli: Please! Not so fast. As I told you a moment ago, peoples, like men, are more impressed by appearances than reality. This notion lights the way in politics and I would scrupulously adhere to it. Please tell me the principles you prize most highly and I'll show you that they don't inconvenience me as much as you think.

Montesquieu: What are you going to do with them?

Machiavelli: Don't be timid. Name them.

Montesquieu: I admit my reluctance.

Machiavelli: Very well. I will remind you of them myself. No doubt, you would have mentioned the principle of the separation of powers, freedom of speech and the press, religious liberty, and personal rights. You might also have mentioned the right of association, equality before the law, the inviolability of personal property and the home, the right to petition, no taxation without representation, punishments proportionate to crimes, the prohibition against *ex post facto* laws. Is this enough or do you want still more?

Montesquieu: I think it's more than enough, Machiavelli, to encumber your government.

Machiavelli: That's where you're wrong, so much so that I see no problem with proclaiming these principles myself. If you want, I will even put them into the preamble of my constitution.

Montesquieu: You have already shown that you are a great magician.

Machiavelli: Nothing to do with magic—only political savoir faire.

Montesquieu: Having inscribed these principles at the head your constitution, how can you avoid putting them into practice?

Machiavelli: Ah! Let's be precise. I told you that I would proclaim these principles but I did not tell you that I would inscribe them, nor even that I would expressly enumerate them.

Montesquieu: What do you mean?

Machiavelli: I would stay away from any specification of rights. I would merely declare to the people my recognition and support for the great principles of modern right.

Montesquieu: The significance of this escapes me.

Machiavelli: You will see how important it is. If I were to spell out these rights, my freedom to act would be restricted by those so specified. And I don't want that. By not specifying them, I appear to grant them all, and yet I grant none explicitly. This will later allow me to make an exception of those I may judge dangerous.

Montesquieu: I understand.

Machiavelli: Moreover, strictly speaking, some of these principles belong to the domain of political and constitutional right and others under civil rights. Herein is a distinction that must always guide the exercise of absolute power. People are most attached to their civil rights. These I will not touch, if possible. In this way, at least one part of my program will be fulfilled.

Montesquieu: And what about political rights?

Machiavelli: In *The Prince*, I set down a maxim, the truth of which is still relevant. "If the prince leaves the people's possessions and honor alone, they will always be content. Then he has only to worry about the pretensions of a small number of malcontents against whom he will easily prevail." That is my answer to your question.

Montesquieu: Strictly speaking, your response is not wholly satisfying. Someone could claim that political rights are also possessions, that respect for them is crucial to the people's sense of honor, and that interfering with them is tantamount to interfering with their possessions as well as their sense of dignity. Someone might additionally claim that respect for both civil and political rights is mutually dependent. If the citizens are today deprived of political liberty, what guarantee is there tomorrow that they will not be deprived of individual liberty? If their liberty is assailed today, that tomorrow their property will not come under attack?

Machiavelli: You seem to have gotten yourself a bit worked up over your argument. But I think you will also come to see how exaggerated its importance is. You seem to think that modern peoples thirst for liberty. Can you imagine a time when the people no longer desire liberty? Is it possible for princes to be more passionately committed to it than the people? The societies that you've described are so incredibly lax that individuals live only in the narrow sphere of their egoism and material interests. If you asked most people, you'd find the same response everywhere. "What does politics have to do with me? What does liberty matter to me? Aren't all governments the same? Doesn't a government have to defend itself?"

Moreover, note well that it is not only the people who speak this way. It is the middle class, industrialists, the educated, the rich, the men of letters—all those who are in a position to appreciate your lofty doctrines of public right. They will thank me. They will cry out that I have saved them, and that the people are mere children, incapable of directing their own lives. Hey, nations have a kind of hidden love for vigorous and powerful geniuses as long as they demonstrate skillful deception. With respect to all those violent acts marked by duplicity, admiration will outweigh condemnation and people will say: "It's not right, but so what? It's shrewd, well calculated, and smoothly executed."

Montesquieu: Are you about to return to a discussion of the essence of your doctrines?

Machiavelli: No. We're now ready for their application and I would have been farther along if you hadn't caused me to digress. Let's continue.

Ninth Dialogue

Montesquieu: You were speaking of the day after you established a constitution without the consent of the nation.

Machiavelli: Just a minute now. I never said that I would go so far in offending traditional opinion. I am fully aware of its power.

Montesquieu: Really?

Machiavelli: I'm quite serious.

Montesquieu: Do you expect to unite the nation behind *the new modes and orders* you are proposing?

Machiavelli: Certainly. Does that surprise you? I will go you one better. I will start by having my coup against the state ratified by popular vote. In a carefully crafted message to the people, I will show that we were in a crisis situation. I have totally broken with the past to save them. I want what they want. People are free to condemn or vindicate me by their vote.

Montesquieu: Free under the threat of terror and armed force.

Machiavelli: I will be acclaimed.

Montesquieu: I believe it so.

Machiavelli: I have turned the popular vote into an instrument of my power and it will become the very foundation of my government. I will expand suffrage by abolishing the poll tax and class-based qualifications. With this simple step, the groundwork of absolutism will be laid.

Montesquieu: Yes. And at the same time you move to destroy the solidarity among families, debase the vote, and cancel out more enlightened voices with the weight of numbers that are turned into a blind power subject to your will.

Machiavelli: What I achieve represents real progress to which all the peoples of Europe today aspire. I bring about universal suffrage as Washington did in the United States. It will be put into play right away when I submit my constitution to its authority.

Montesquieu: What! Are you going to have it debated in constituent assemblies or ratifying conventions?

Machiavelli: Oh! I beg you. Leave your eighteenth century ideas out of it. They are already dated.

Montesquieu: Very well. Will the ratification of your constitution be debated? How will its main articles be discussed?

Machiavelli: But I don't intend them to be discussed at all. I believe I've already told you that.

Montesquieu: I'm only pointing out the implications of principles you were eager to adopt. You spoke of the United States of America. I don't know if you are a new Washington, but what is certain is that the present Constitution of the United States was discussed, deliberated, and voted upon by the representatives of the nation.

Machiavelli: For goodness sake. Let's not confuse times, places, and peoples. We are in Europe. My constitution is presented *en bloc*. It is accepted *en bloc*.

Montesquieu: But such a step doesn't fool anyone in the least. Voting under these conditions, how can the people know what they are doing and to what extent they are bound?

Machiavelli: And where have you ever seen a constitution truly worthy of its name and truly lasting that has ever been the product of popular deliberation? A constitution must issue, fully elaborated, from the head of a single man or it is only a work doomed to disappear. It will necessarily bear the mark of all the petty opinions that presided at its drafting and lack consistency, coherence, and practical force.

Once again, a constitution can only be the work of a single man. Things have never happened otherwise, as the histories of all the founders of empire testify— Sesostris, Solon, Lycurgus, Charlemagne, Frederick II, Peter the First, for example.

Montesquieu: You are about to expound upon a chapter from one of your disciples

Machiavelli: Who?

Montesquieu: Joseph de Maistre. Some general points you make are not without merit but I find them inapplicable here. Listening to you, I have the impression of someone who is about to lead a people out of chaos and the extremely benighted times that marked their origins. You don't seem to remember that according to our working hypothesis, the nation has reached the pinnacle of civilization, public right is well established, and well-ordered institutions are functioning.

Machiavelli: I'm not saying anything different. However, you will see that I don't need utterly to destroy your institutions to reach my goal. All I need to do is modify their organizational structure and to change their relations to each other.

Montesquieu: Explain.

Machiavelli: A little while ago you gave me a discourse on constitutional law. I intend to put it to use. Moreover, contrary to what might be generally thought in Europe, I am not completely unacquainted with all these ideas of seesaw politics. You could find some of them in my discourses on Titus Livy. But let's return to the matter at hand. A moment ago you remarked, reasonably enough, that government powers in the parliamentary states of Europe were almost everywhere similarly distributed. The government consists of bodies whose interrelations are regulated by constitutional procedures.

Therein, we inevitably find a cabinet, a Senate, a legislative body, a Council of State, and a court of appeal. They may operate under different names but they have virtually the same functions. I will spare you all needless elaboration of the respective mechanisms of these powers whose workings you have deciphered better than me. It is obvious that each of them corresponds to an essential function of government. Notice that it is the function I consider essential, not the institution. Thus, there must be an executive power, a conserving power, a law-making power, a regulatory power—of this there is no doubt.

Montesquieu: But if I understand you, these various powers are really one in your eyes and you are going to give them all to one man by doing away with public institutions.

Machiavelli: Once again, you're wrong. It could not be done without danger, especially in your country, given the fanatical support that reigns there for what you call the principles of '89. But please listen to me carefully. In statics, moving the fulcrum causes a change in the direction of the forces. In mechanics, changing the location of a spring causes a change in the machine's movement. And yet, it appears to be the same apparatus, the same mechanism. Likewise in physiology, character traits manifest themselves as a function of internal organs. If the organ's functioning is altered, the character changes. And so, the various institutions that we have just mentioned perform functions in the governmental structure similar to vital organs in the human body. I will tamper with internal chemistry. External features will not be touched but the political complexion of the state will change, nonetheless. Do you see what I'm getting at?

Montesquieu: It's not that difficult. You needn't be so circumspect. You keep the names but the thing itself is gutted. That is what Augustus did in Rome when he destroyed the Republic. There continued to be a consulate, praetorship, censorship, tribunate, as always, but there were no longer consuls, praetors, censors, or tribunes.

Machiavelli: You have to admit that worse models could be chosen. Anything is possible in politics if public prejudices are flattered and respect for appearances is maintained.

Montesquieu: Let's not lapse back into generalities. Get to work. I'm following you.

Machiavelli: Don't forget that each thing I do is grounded in certain personal convictions. As I see it, your parliamentary governments are only schools for quarreling, centers of sterile conflict that sap the creative energy of nations, doomed to impotence by public debate and the press. Consequently, I feel no remorse. I proceed from an elevated point of view and my goal justifies my deeds.

I substitute practical reason for abstract theory and follow the experience of the ages and the examples of men of genius who have done great things using the same means. I begin by restoring the vital conditions of power.

My first reform immediately impinges upon the claim you made for ministerial responsibility. In centralized countries, like yours, for example, public opinion instinctively holds the chief of state responsible for everything, good as well as bad. To inscribe at the beginning of your charter that the sovereign is not responsible is to contradict what public sentiment holds true and to promulgate a fiction that will never survive the noise of revolution.

I begin by striking out of my constitution the principle of ministerial responsibility. The sovereign that my constitution establishes will have sole responsibility before the people.

Montesquieu: No beating about the bush here.

Machiavelli: As you explained your parliamentary system, the representatives of the nation draft the bills alone or with the executive. Well, that is the source of the gravest abuses. In such a scheme, a deputy can take the place of the government at any time and propose poorly researched and badly considered bills. Why with parliamentary initiation of bills, the lower chamber could overthrow the government whenever it wanted. I strike parliamentary initiative from my constitution. The sovereign alone may propose laws.

Montesquieu: If your intention is to arrive at absolute power, I see you are taking the best route. In a state where the initiation of laws belongs only to the sovereign, he becomes the sole legislator to a great degree. But before you go any further down that road, I want to raise one objection. You want to establish yourself upon rock, but I see you building on sand.

Machiavelli: How so?

Montesquieu: Haven't you taken universal manhood suffrage as the basis of your power?

Machiavelli: Certainly.

Montesquieu: Then you are only the agent of the people, in whom alone true sovereignty resides, and serve at its pleasure. You thought that you could make this principle serve your authority. But don't you see that you can be overthrown whenever the people so desire? Moreover, you declared that you alone are responsible. Do you expect to rule like an angel? Try as you will but you will still be blamed for everything bad that might happen and you will disappear at the first crisis.

Machiavelli: You're getting ahead of yourself. Your objection is a bit premature. But I will answer you now, since you are forcing the issue. You are quite mistaken if you think I haven't anticipated this objection. If my power is threatened, it could only be because of factions. I am protected against them by two basic prerogatives that I have placed in my constitution: the right of appeal to the people and the right to place the country in a state of emergency. I am head of the army. All coercive power is in my hands. The first sign of insurrection would find my bayonets taking the measure of the resistance. And I would find at the polls a new consecration of my authority.

Montesquieu: Your arguments are unassailable. But, I beg you, let's return to the legislative body that you've installed. I still see some complications. You have taken away parliamentary initiative from this Assembly. But it still retains the right to vote on bills that you propose there. Certainly you don't intend that this right be exercised, do you?

Machiavelli: You are more untrusting than I am. I swear I don't see anything inconvenient in this. With only myself able to propose laws, I don't have to fear any threat to my power. I hold the key to the tabernacle. Besides, as I said before, it is part of my plan to allow institutions to exist in appearance. But I have to say that I don't intend to allow the Assembly what you call the right of amendment. Obviously, to allow the exercise of such a power would enable the legislator to change the purpose and spirit of any of my laws. The law doesn't exist that cannot be diverted from its original purpose and made susceptible to a variety of interpretations. The law is accepted or rejected—no other alternative.

Montesquieu: But that's all that's needed to overthrow you. This could be accomplished if the Assembly were to systematically reject all your bills or merely refuse to vote taxes.

Machiavelli: You know perfectly well that things can't happen that way. Any chamber whatsoever that would so boldly shackle the course of public affairs would commit suicide. Besides, I have a thousand ways to neutralize the power of such an Assembly. I could reduce the number of representatives by half, thereby halving the political passions I would have to contend with. I could reserve to myself the right to name the presiding officers in the legislative bodies. Instead of permanent sessions, I could reduce the tenure of the Assembly to a few months. Above all, I could do something of very great importance that, I'm told, is already being put into practice. I would abolish the unpaid status of legislative service. I would have the deputies receive an emolument. Their service should be salaried to some extent. I regard this innovation as the surest way of attaching the representatives of the nation to my power. I don't need to elaborate. Its usefulness is fairly self-evident. I might add that as head of the executive branch, I have the right to convoke and to dissolve the legislative body and, in cases of dissolution, I would wait a long time before convoking a new one. I perfectly well understand that it would be dangerous if the legislative Assembly remained independent of my power. But rest assured. We will soon encounter other practices that will tie it to me. Are you satisfied with these constitutional details? Do you want more?

Montesquieu: That is hardly necessary. You can now proceed to the organization of the Senate.

Machiavelli: I see that you have clearly understood that it represents the principal element in my designs, the keystone of my constitution.

Montesquieu: I really don't know what else you need to do because from this point on I regard you as complete master of the state.

Machiavelli: So you say. But in reality, sovereignty could not be established on such frail foundations. At the side of the sovereign must be found bodies of individuals that remain impressive by virtue of brilliant titles, respectability, and the personal illustriousness of those who compose them. It is not good for the sovereign himself to be constantly active, always to reveal his hand. He must be able, when necessary, to hide his acts under the authority of great magistracies that surround the throne.

Montesquieu: It is easy to see that this is the role for which the Senate and Council of State are destined.

Machiavelli: Nothing escapes you.

Montesquieu: You speak of the throne. I see that you are king, while a moment ago we were in a republic. This is quite a leap.

Machiavelli: It's beneath the illustrious French publicist to ask me to pause over such petty details. When I have all power in my hands, the exact time that I proclaim myself king is but a matter of expediency. Before or after having promulgated my constitution—it doesn't matter—I will be king.

Montesquieu: Let's assume what you say is true for the moment. We need to return to the organization of the Senate to see if what you say can possibly be borne out.

Tenth Dialogue

Machiavelli: Given the exhaustive studies you had to make in order to write your memorable work on *The Causes of the Greatness of the Romans and Their Decline*, you could not have failed to notice the role that the Senate played in relation to the Emperors, beginning with the reign of Augustus.

Montesquieu: If you will allow me to say so, this is a matter that historical research has not yet completely clarified. This much is certain. Until the last days of the Republic, the Roman Senate was an autonomous institution vested with great privileges and having independent powers. That was the secret of its influence, the reason why its political traditions took such deep hold, and how greatness would be stamped onto the Republic. But from Augustus on, the Senate was nothing more than a tool in the hands of the emperors. Yet, it is not clear how they proceeded finally in stripping it of its power.

Machiavelli: My motive in returning you to this period of the Empire is not to clarify this point in history. This question doesn't interest me. All I wanted to say is that the Senate, as I see it, should play a political role vis-à-vis the prince analogous to that of the Roman Senate in the times that followed the fall of the Republic.

Montesquieu: All right. But in that epoch laws were no longer voted on in the popular forums, but were made by decree of *senatus consultum*. Is that what you want?

Machiavelli: Not at all. That would hardly be in conformity with modern principles of constitutional right.

Montesquieu: Your scruples in this regard deserve profound gratitude!

Machiavelli: I have no need of such procedures in order to decree what seems to me necessary. You understand that I fill in the details of legislation. In addition, my decrees have the force of law.

Montesquieu: It's true that you had forgotten to mention this point, though it is hardly insignificant. But then I don't see why you keep a Senate.

Machiavelli: Playing an exalted role in the constitutional system, its direct intervention should be reserved for grave situations only, for example, if it were necessary to amend the organic law or if sovereignty were threatened.

Montesquieu: You speak ever more like a prophet. You relish setting the stage for what's to come.

Machiavelli: Up to now, the constitutions your modern disciples have given the people fixated on the idea of foreseeing every eventuality and regulating everything in advance. I am not prone to such an error. I would not want to confine myself within strict boundaries. I would only spell out what is impossible to leave uncertain. I would have a fairly large opening for change. Then, in serious crises, there might be some other alternative to the disastrous expedient of revolution.

Montesquieu: These words shine with prudence.

Machiavelli: And as for the power of the Senate, I would put in my constitution the following provision. "The Senate shall act by *senatus consultum* in all matters that have not been specifically provided for in the constitution and which are necessary for its continued existence. It shall define the meaning of articles of the constitution that are open to various interpretations. It will have the power of judicial review to determine the constitutionality of all acts referred to it by the government or though grievances filed as petitions by the people. It may draft measures in the national interest. It may propose amendments to the constitution which will be enacted by *senatus consultum*."

Montesquieu: All this is quite nice. We have here a truly Roman Senate. I'll make only a few comments on your constitution. I gather it will be written in a vague and ambiguous language since you say that you will be able to predetermine the meaning of constitutional provisions.

Machiavelli: No. But everything must be anticipated.

Montesquieu: I thought your principle in such matters was the opposite, to avoid trying to anticipate and regulate every contingency.

Machiavelli: My illustrious interlocutor has not haunted the palace of Themis without profit nor has he donned the cap of president of a court of justice in vain. My words have had no other meaning than this: it is necessary to anticipate what is essential.

Montesquieu: Pray tell, I beg you, does your Senate, interpreter and guardian of the fundamental law, have any power of its own?

Machiavelli: Certainly not.

Montesquieu: Anything the Senate does will actually be done by you?

Machiavelli: I'm not saying anything different.

Montesquieu: It will be you, not the Senate, who actually interprets the constitution, reverses precedent, and overturns law.

Machiavelli: I don't claim to deny these things.

Montesquieu: Then that means that you reserve for yourself the right to undo what you have done, to take away what you have given, and to change your constitution for better or worse or even make it disappear altogether if you judge it necessary. I will not prejudge the intentions or motive that might lead you to act in various circumstances. I only ask you where one may find even the weakest safeguards for citizens in the vast field of arbitrary power. Above all, how could they ever be brought to endure such a situation?

Machiavelli: I see I've hit a sensitive nerve in you again. Rest assured. I would not bring about any change in the fundamental principles of my constitution without submitting these amendments to the approval of the people through popular vote in a referendum.

Montesquieu: But you would still be the judge of whether or not the amendment you propose is of such fundamental importance that it must be submitted to the people for their approval. However, you concede that amendments are to be ratified by a plebiscite and not made by a decree or *senatus consultum*. Will your constitutional amendments be publicly debated? Will they be submitted to conventions for deliberations?

Machiavelli: Decidedly not. If ever conventions were allowed to debate constitutional provisions, nothing could prevent the people from taking hold of the whole constitution and exercising their right to pass everything under review. The next day there would be revolution in the streets.

Montesquieu: At least you are consistent. So these constitutional amendments are presented as a whole, accepted as a whole?

Machiavelli: Indeed. In no other way.

Montesquieu: Well, I think we can now proceed to the organization of the Council of State.

Machiavelli: You really do direct the discussion of such matters skillfully, in the exacting manner of a presiding judge in a sovereign court. I forgot to tell you that I salary the Senate as I did the legislature.

Montesquieu: That's understood.

Machiavelli: I needn't add that I also reserve the right to nominate the president and vice-president of this august body. Concerning the Council of State, I will be briefer. Modern institutions offer such powerful tools for centralizing policy-making that it is almost impossible to make use of them without exercising sovereign authority.

According to principles you yourself laid down, what in fact is the Council of State? It represents the interests of state and, through its rule-making prerogatives, brings a considerable amount of power into the hands of the prince. Its powers are quasi-discretionary and its regulations can substitute for actual laws, when so desired.

I've heard it said that the Council of State in your country is, in addition, invested with a special prerogative even more extraordinary. I am told on good authority that on questions before ordinary courts it can lay claim, by right of review, to all litigation that it deems to have an administrative character. Thus, in a nutshell, what I find so extraordinary in this prerogative is that the courts are relieved of their jurisdiction when faced with an administrative writ removing the case and referring it to the Council of State for decision.

Now, once again, what is the Council of State? Has it power of its own? Is it independent of the sovereign? Not at all. It is only a drafting committee. When the Council of State issues a rule, it is at the behest of the sovereign. When it judges a case, it follows the sovereign's will, or, as you say nowadays, the administration's. The administration is both party and judge in its own case. Do you know anything more formidable than that? Do you think that it takes a lot to establish absolute power in states where everything is so well organized under an institution like this?

Montesquieu: I must admit that your comments are apropos. But, granting that, the Council of State is an excellent institution in itself. Nothing could be easier for its proper functioning than to insulate it from political pressure. Undoubtedly, this is not what you will do.

Machiavelli: Indeed. I will preserve political control wherever I find it. I will restore it wherever it is lacking by strengthening the political ties that I consider indispensable.

You see, we haven't been idling along. There you have it. I have just presented you my constitution in finished form.

Montesquieu: Already?

Machiavelli: A small number of artfully arranged mechanisms are sufficient to change completely how power operates. This part of my plan is complete.

Montesquieu: I thought that you would address yourself to the court of appeals.

Machiavelli: It would be better to postpone what I have to say about it.

Montesquieu: It's true that if we add up all the powers in your hands, you might feel some satisfaction.

Let's summarize: You make law, first—by proposals to the legislature; second—by decrees; third—by *senatus consultum*; fourth—through rules; fifth—by writ of Council of State; sixth—by ministerial regulations; seventh—and finally—by coup d'états.

Machiavelli: You don't seem to be aware that the most difficult task still remains.

Montesquieu: I really doubt it.

Machiavelli: Then you haven't taken sufficient notice of the fact that my constitution was silent concerning a bunch of traditional rights that would be incompatible with the new order I have just founded. For example, freedom of the press, the right of association, judicial independence, voting, the right of electing municipal officers by commune, the right to form a militia and many other things that will have to disappear or be changed radically.

Montesquieu: But haven't you implicitly recognized all these rights by formally recognizing those principles from which they are derived?

Machiavelli: I told you I recognize no principle or right in particular. Moreover, the measures that I will adopt are only exceptions to the rule.

Montesquieu: That's right. Exceptions that prove the rule.

Machiavelli: To succeed I must choose my moment well, for a missed opportunity may ruin everything. In *The Prince* I penned a maxim that could serve as a rule of thumb. "The usurper of a state must carry out all the harsh deeds security requires all at once so that he will not have to come back to them. Later, he will no longer be able to oppose his subjects either in good or bad times. If you have to act in bad times, once fortune is opposed to you, you're no longer in a position to do it. If in good times, your subjects will not tolerate a change they believe to be coerced."

On the very next day after my constitution takes effect, I will issue a series of decrees with the force of law that will do away with these liberties and rights, whose exercise may prove dangerous, in a single stroke.

Montesquieu: Indeed, you've chosen your moment well. The country is still terrorized by your coup d'état. As for your constitution, nothing will be denied you, since you could take everything. As for your decrees, there is nothing to grant you, since you ask for nothing and take everything.

Machiavelli: You do have a way with words.

Montesquieu: You'll admit, however, that my words come more easily than your actions. Despite your strong hand and your steady eye, I confess to having some trouble believing that the country will not rise up with a second coup d'état, awaiting you in the wings.

Machiavelli: The country will willingly close its eyes, for according to my working hypothesis, it is tired of strife and longs to settle down, like the desert sands after the shower that follows a storm.

Montesquieu: What beautiful metaphors. It's too much!

Machiavelli: But I hasten to assure you that the liberties I suppress I shall formally promise to restore after factional strife has been quieted.

Montesquieu: I suspect that we will wait forever.

Machiavelli: It's possible.

Montesquieu: It's certain, for your maxims allow the prince to break his word when it's in his interest.

Machiavelli: Don't jump to conclusions. You will see how I'll make use of this promise. Soon, I will take it upon myself to pass for the most liberal man in my kingdom.

Montesquieu: Now that's a surprise for which I am unprepared. But in the meantime, you directly suppress all liberties.

Machiavelli: "Directly" is not in the statesman's vocabulary. I directly suppress nothing. Here the fox's mantle must cover the lion's skin. What's the use of political maneuvering if it can't attain the desired goal by devious ways, when straight ones are inadequate? The form of my system is now in place. Its animating forces have been readied. Nothing remains but to set it in motion. But to do this I must have a delicate hand. It is here that prudence is recommended to the prince in putting into place all the artifices of government and legislation.

Montesquieu: I see the argument is entering a new phase. I am ready to hear you out.

Eleventh Dialogue

Machiavelli: You very reasonably observed in *The Spirit of the Laws* that liberty is a word to which many different meanings are attached. I am told that the following proposition can be found in your book. "Liberty is the right to do what the laws permit."* The definition is apt and I strongly agree with it. And I can assure you that my laws will permit only what is necessary. Their essential spirit will soon become clear. Where would you like to begin?

Montesquieu: I would not be averse to seeing how you will protect yourself from the press.

Machiavelli: Indeed, you have put your finger on the most delicate part of my task. I have in mind a plan for handling this problem whose design is both momentous and subtle. Fortunately, here I have a little elbowroom. I cut and prune with confidence so that my acts will not provoke any reaction.

Montesquieu: Why? Pray tell.

Machiavelli: In most parliamentary systems, the press has a knack of making itself hated. Why? Because it always finds itself in the service of violent, selfish, narrow passions. It is adversarial by nature. It is venal, unjust, without magnanimity and patriotism. Finally, and above all, the role it plays can never be made clear to the great mass of men.

Montesquieu: Oh, if you're looking for grievances against the press, it doesn't take too much to find a great many of them. But if you are asking about its proper role, that's another thing. Quite simply, it prevents the exercise of arbitrary power. It forces the depositories of public authority to govern constitutionally. It obliges them to be honest, restrained and respectful of constitutional practices in relations among themselves and with others. Finally, to make a long story short, it gives to anyone who is oppressed the means to voice one's grievances and be heard. Much can be pardoned in an institution that, despite so many abuses, serves so many crucial purposes.

---

* *The Spirit of the Laws* XI 3.

Machiavelli: Yes, I am familiar with such theoretical claims on its behalf, but try to make them understood by the masses. Consider the number of those who really care about the press's fortunes and you'll see what I mean.

Montesquieu: So you might as well go on to how in practice you will *muzzle* it. I believe that's the appropriate word.

Machiavelli: That's it. Moreover, it's not only journalism that I intend to control.

Montesquieu: All printing then.

Machiavelli: You're resorting to irony.

Montesquieu: Next, I suspect that even irony will be censored, given the curbs you'll bring to free expression.

Machiavelli: There's no defense against such refined wit. But you understand quite well that it wouldn't be worth the effort to escape the attacks of the press if I had to suffer those in books.

Montesquieu: All right, let's begin with the press.

Machiavelli: Any notion about suppressing newspapers purely and simply would be very imprudent. It is always dangerous to violate popular sentiments. Instead, I would change the details of certain laws and the modifications would appear to be motivated simply by solicitude for public morality and order.

I would declare that in the future no newspaper would be allowed to operate without governmental authorization. There's the way to nip evil in the bud. It's not hard to see that only those organs devoted to the government will receive authorization in the future.

Montesquieu: But since you raise these points, let me just say that the spirit of a newspaper is a function of the personnel on its editorial board. How will you prevent editorial boards from being hostile to your power?

Machiavelli: The problem you raise is really a paltry one. The choice is ultimately up to me not to authorize any new newspaper, if I so wish. But I have other schemes, as you'll see. You ask me how I would neutralize a hostile editorial board? It's very simple, really. I will stipulate that governmental authorization is also necessary for all changes in editorial personnel, from editors-in-chief to managing editors.

Montesquieu: But the old established newspapers—those inveterate enemies of your government whose editorial board won't change—will speak out.

Machiavelli: Just hold on. All newspapers, present and future, can be brought under certain fiscal controls to curb their enterprises. I will impose upon political newspapers what is today known as a stamp tax and a surety. The newspaper business will soon be barely profitable and thanks to the imposition of these measures, it will only be embarked upon warily.

Montesquieu: This is not an adequate solution for you. Political parties are not concerned with profits.

Machiavelli: Don't get so worked up. I have something to shut them up. Here come the repressive measures. There are states in Europe where suits against the press are brought before juries. I know of no more deplorable measure than this, for it means that the pettiest journalistic drivel may stir up a controversy. The crimes of the press are very hard to pinpoint. A writer can disguise his attacks in such varied and subtle ways that it is not even possible to bring clear charges before the courts. The courts will always be empowered to act. That goes without saying. But, ordinarily, this repressive power must be exercised administratively.

Montesquieu: Then there will be crimes that won't be within the province of the courts to judge, or rather, you will strike with two hands—judicially and administratively.

Machiavelli: How awful! Such solicitude for a few nasty and spiteful journalists who make a point of attacking and denigrating everything. They act no differently toward governments than armed bandits toward travelers on their journeys. Give a little leeway and they constantly put themselves above the law. What if we took a little of this leeway away?

Montesquieu: They are the only ones you will repress?

Machiavelli: I can't promise that, for these people are like the heads of the Hydra of Lerna. If you cut off ten of them, fifty more sprout up. I lay the blame primarily on newspapers that are scandalmongers. I would have them consider the following speech. "I could suppress all of you. I haven't yet done so but I can. I'll let you live, on one condition, that you don't try to block my progress or discredit my power. I don't want to have to summon you every day before the courts or to be constantly resorting to the law to curb your infractions. Even more, I don't want an army of censors looking into the day before what you are going to publish the next day. You have pens, so write! But keep this in mind. I reserve to myself or my agents the right to judge when I am being attacked. No subtleties. I'll know when you attack me. And you will be made aware of it in return. In such a matter, I will take justice into my own hands, but I won't act precipitously. We must come to a certain understanding. I shall warn you once or twice but the third time you will be suppressed."

Montesquieu: I am struck by the fact that your scheme isn't limited to curbing the journalist but it strikes at the newspaper itself, whose ruin affects the interests and groups behind it.

Machiavelli: Let them find some other outlet. They won't be bothered. As I told you, my administration will impartially impose those sentences handed down by the courts. Two convictions in one year will inevitably lead to the suppression of the newspaper. I would not stop there. By decree or law, I would also say to newspapers the following. "Keep to your proper concerns and do not hope to stir public opinion by commentaries on the debates that take place within my government. I forbid you to report on them. I even forbid you to report on judicial proceedings that deal with the press. You must no longer expect to move the public mind by what purports to be news gathered by outside sources. The publication of false news, in good or bad faith, will be punished by jail."

Montesquieu: That seems a bit harsh. In the final analysis, newspapers have nothing else to sustain them but what comes from such newsgathering, it being too dangerous to engage in political commentary directly. To require that each news story published by a newspaper be true seems quite unreasonable to me, for in most cases the newspaper will not be able to defend its veracity with absolute certainty, and even when circumstantially certain that the story is true, hard evidence may be lacking.

Machiavelli: They will think twice before stirring up public opinion, as they should.

Montesquieu: But there's another problem. You may have eliminated opposition from the domestic press but you may still find opposition in the foreign press. All kinds of discontent and hatred will be inscribed on the doors of your kingdom. Newspapers and inflammatory writings will hurtle across your borders.

Machiavelli: Here you touch upon a point that I intend to regulate in the most rigorous manner, because the foreign press is indeed very dangerous. First, the introduction or circulation in the kingdom of any unauthorized newspapers or writings will be punished with imprisonment, and the punishment will be sufficiently severe to stifle the desire. Next, those of my subjects convicted of having written against the government while abroad will be investigated and punished when they return. It is truly reprehensible to write against one's government when abroad.

Montesquieu: That depends. But the foreign press in bordering states will speak out.

Machiavelli: You think so? We are assuming that I rule a large kingdom. The small states on my border will be kept in constant fear, I assure you. I will make them pass laws that will prosecute their own citizens for attacks on my government by the press or otherwise.

Montesquieu: I see I was right when I said in *The Spirit of the Laws* that the areas surrounding a despot must be laid waste. Civilization must not be allowed to penetrate. I'm sure that your subjects will be kept from knowing their own history. As Benjamin Constant once said, you will make your kingdom into an island where what happens in Europe will not be known, and the capital will be made into another island where what happens in the provinces will not be known.

Machiavelli: I don't want my kingdom to be disturbed by rumors from abroad. How will news of the outside world be conveyed? By a small number of agencies that will filter information sent from the four corners of the world. So, these agencies have to be bribed, and from then on the only news they transmit will be under the control of the government.

Montesquieu: That's quite enough. You can now proceed to how you would police books.

Machiavelli: This is less a concern of mine. At a time when newspapers have proliferated so dramatically, books are hardly read any more. But I in no way intend to leave the door open. In the first place, I will require those who choose for a profession that of printer, editor, or bookseller to have a license. That is to say, government authorization will always be revocable, either directly or after a judicial hearing.

Montesquieu: But then all these businessmen will only be like public officials. The instruments of thought will become the instruments of power.

Machiavelli: I shouldn't think you'd complain, for this is how things were in your time under parliaments. Old customs should be preserved when they are good. But let's return to fiscal measures. I shall hit books with the stamp tax already imposed on newspapers or rather I shall impose a heavier stamp tax on books that do not have a certain number of pages. For example, a book that does not have two or three hundred pages is not really a book. It is a pamphlet. I think you grasp the advantages of this scheme. On the one hand, the tax will considerably reduce the great number of these little books, which are like an extended form of journalism. On the other hand, I force those who want to escape the stamp tax to embark upon long and expensive compositions that will barely sell and scarcely be read in that form. Today, there are hardly any but a few devils that have the conscience to write books. They will give it up. Taxes will discourage literary pretensions and criminal law will make the publishing industry itself more amenable, for I shall make the publisher and printer criminally responsible for what their books contain. If there are writers daring enough to write works against the government, it is imperative that they find no one to publish them. Such salutary intimidation will resurrect censorship, but by indirect means. Government could not itself exercise such a power because of the discredit into which this preventive measure has fallen. Before bringing out new works, printers and publishers will confer. They will scout what is available and bring out books that respond to popular demand. Through them, the government can always remain well informed about publications that are being prepared against it. Prior restraint of such publications can be invoked and their authors may be handed over to the courts.

Montesquieu: You told me that you would not touch civil rights. You don't seem to realize you have just struck a blow against free enterprise. Property rights are involved here and will disappear in turn.

Machiavelli: These are mere words.

Montesquieu: Then you have finished with the press?

Machiavelli: Oh, not yet!

Montesquieu: What's left?

Machiavelli: The other half of the job.

Twelfth Dialogue

Machiavelli: So far, I've only shown you the "defensive strategy" I would pursue with regard to this power. But I now must make clear how I will use this institution to augment my power. I dare say that, to this day, no government has conceived of anything as bold as what I am about to describe. Since it is almost always because of the press that governments in parliamentary countries are brought down, my scheme envisions neutralizing the press by the press itself. Because journalism wields such great power, do you know what my government will do? It will become like them. It will be journalism incarnate.

Montesquieu: Truly, you constantly amaze me. You offer me an ever-changing panorama of things to consider. I confess that I'm curious to see how you will go about putting this novel project into effect.

Machiavelli: It taxes the imagination much less than you think. I shall count the number of newspapers that represent what you call the "opposition." If there are ten in this category, I shall have twenty pro-government. If twenty, I shall have forty. If forty, eighty. You will recall that I have reserved myself the power to authorize the creation of new political journals. Surely, by now, it's obvious how I will make use of it.

Montesquieu: Indeed, it's all quite simple.

Machiavelli: Not quite as simple as you might think. However, the public at large must not suspect this tactic or the scheme would miscarry and public opinion would forsake those that openly defend my policies.

I shall divide the newspapers devoted to my cause into three or four categories. In the first group, I will put a certain number of newspapers that will adopt the official line of things in a straightforward way. They will defend my acts unreservedly. I hasten to say that these are not the ones that will have the most influence on public opinion. In the second group, I will gather another host of newspapers whose character will be less orthodox and whose mission will be to rally to my power that mass of lukewarm and indifferent men who accept the established order without reservation but whose political religion extends no farther than this.

In the following categories of newspapers, the most powerful support for my power will be found. Here, the official or quasi-official slant on things is totally absent, but only on the surface, of course. Even these newspapers will be tied to my government, visibly, in some instances, and invisibly, in others. I won't venture to say how many there will be, since I expect a loyal organ in every camp, in every party. I shall have an aristocratic organ in the party of aristocrats, a republican organ in the republican party, a revolutionary organ in the party of revolution, an anarchistic organ, if need be, in the party of anarchists. Like the god Vishnu, my press will have a hundred arms, and these arms will stretch out their hands throughout the country delicately giving form to all manner of opinion. Everyone will belong to my party without knowing it. Those who think they are speaking the language of their party will be acting for mine. Those who think they are marching under their own banner will be marching under mine.

Montesquieu: Are these ideas possible or only wild fantasies? They make the head swim.

Machiavelli: Steady yourself. We're not finished yet.

Montesquieu: I'm only wondering how you will be capable of leading and rallying all these troops of propagandists secretly enlisted to your government.

Machiavelli: You must consider it an organizational matter only. For example, I will set up under the title of Division of Printing and the Press a center to coordinate action. It is from here that instructions will be sought and commands will issue. As it so happens, those wholly in on the secret of this scheme will witness something bizarre. Newspapers devoted to my government will attack me, cry out, and stir up controversy about me.

Montesquieu: That is beyond me. I'm not following you.

Machiavelli: It's not all that difficult. Let it be well understood that neither the foundations nor the principles of my government will ever be attacked by the newspapers I'm talking about. They will only give voice to polemical nitpicking and will be an in-house opposition operating within the narrowest limits.

Montesquieu: So what's the use of all this?

Machiavelli: That's a rather naive question. The advantages are quite considerable in themselves. But beyond them, most people will come to be heard saying something like the following. "This regime lets anyone speak his mind. It is unjustly attacked. But instead of clamping down, which it might do, it puts up with these things and is tolerant." Another no less important result will be to elicit observations like the following. "See the extent to which the foundations of this government and its principles command the respect of everyone. Here, newspapers are allowed the greatest freedom of speech and yet they never attack the established institutions. They stand above unjust accusations born of passion. Even the enemies of the government cannot help but render them homage."

Montesquieu: That, I swear, is truly machiavellian.

Machiavelli: I am greatly honored but I haven't yet mentioned the best things. Such newspapers, secretly devoted to my cause, allow me to shape public opinion the way I want on all questions of domestic or foreign policy. I can stimulate the imagination of my people or put them to sleep. I can reassure or disconcert them. I can take either side of an issue and present one or the other as true or false. Depending on circumstances, I can admit to something as a fact or deny it. In such a way, I plumb public opinion and assess whatever reaction I provoke. I try out schemes and plans and make decisions on impulse in order to launch what you call in France "trial balloons." I am free to fight against my enemies without ever compromising my power. After making these newspapers speak, I can force them to make the strongest possible retractions. I elicit public favor for certain decisions. I can incite enthusiasm or hold it back. I always have my finger on the pulse of the public. Unconsciously, it reflects my personal feelings on things. Sometimes it expresses astonishment at finding itself so consistently in agreement with its sovereign. It will be said that I am a man of the people, that there is a secret and mysterious sympathy that unites me with their will.

Montesquieu: In theory, these various schemes seem to be perfectly conceived. However, I offer one more observation, though I do so tentatively this time. You abandon China as a model in this regard and the silence that prevails there. But if you allow your troops of newspapers to fake opposition in order to advance your designs, I truly don't see very clearly how you can prevent the non-affiliated newspapers from mounting a real attack on you, after figuring out the game you're playing. Don't you think that eventually they will lift some of the veils that cover so many machinations? When they figure out the secret of this comedy, how can you keep them from laughing? It all appears to me a squalid joke.

Machiavelli: Not at all. I tell you I've spent a great deal of my time here examining the strong and weak points of these schemes. I am quite well informed about the conduct of the press in parliamentary countries. Surely you are aware that journalism is a kind of freemasonry. Those who live by it are all more or less attached to one another by bonds of professional discretion. Like ancient auguries, they do not easily divulge the secret of their oracles.

They would gain nothing by betraying one another since most of them have skeletons in their closets. I agree that it is fairly likely that in the heart of the capital city, among a certain class of people, these things will not stay a mystery. But such things will not be suspected anywhere else. The overwhelming majority of the nation will proceed along the track I have laid out for it with the utmost trust.

What does it matter if in the capital a certain group may be aware of the artifices my journalism employs. Its most potent influence is reserved for the provinces. The climate of opinion will always be favorable to me there, and each of my schemes will carry the day. The provincial press will belong to me completely. No contradictions or discussion is tolerated. From the administrative center where I shall sit, the order will be transmitted to the governor of each province to make the newspapers speak out in a particular way on a given matter. At the same time, the whole country will come under the same influence. A particular impulse will be transmitted and felt long before the capital is aware of it. You see that opinion in the capital does not preoccupy me. It may indeed find itself enveloped by opinion emanating from the provinces and running behind trends, if need be, without their even knowing it.

Montesquieu: I wanted to raise one last objection. But your train of thought is so powerful and sweeping that you have made me lose my own. A certain number of independent newspapers still exist. It's well nigh impossible for them to debate political questions, but they will be able to attack you over matters of administration. Your officers will not be perfect. Achieving absolute power brings in its train a number of abuses for which the sovereign himself may not be responsible. But all those acts of your agents that affect the private interests of your subjects will make you vulnerable. Complaints will be heard. Your agents will be attacked. You will necessarily be held responsible and public esteem for you will gradually erode.

Machiavelli: I don't fear that.

Montesquieu: It is true that you have so multiplied the means of repression that you only have to choose among them.

Machiavelli: That's not what I had in mind. I don't want to have to resort to repression constantly. A simple decree is enough to put an end to all discussion on a subject related to my administration.

Montesquieu: And what form will it take?

Machiavelli: I shall require newspapers to give front-page coverage to the corrections sent them by the government. Agents of my government will hand them memoranda that will lay the matter out in no uncertain terms. "You have said such and such, but what you say is not exactly true. You have allowed yourself to voice such and such a criticism, but you have been unfair, acted improperly, and are mistaken. Consider yourself notified." As you can understand, this is a rebuke that is fair and open.

Montesquieu: Of course there will be no reply.

Machiavelli: Obviously not. Discussion will be closed.

Montesquieu: So you will always have the last word and without resorting to violence. Very ingenious. You phrased it very well a moment ago when you said your government would be journalism incarnate.

Machiavelli: Just as I don't want the country to be stirred up by rumors coming from abroad, I don't want it to be set off by rumors from within, even those passed on by word of mouth. If there is some strange case of suicide, some shady financial dealings, some malfeasance by a public official, I shall forbid the newspapers to speak of it. Silence about such things, rather than noising them about, is more respectful of public decency.

Montesquieu: All the while, you yourself will be making use of journalism with a vengeance?

Machiavelli: It's quite essential. Today, it's a law of survival for any government to make effective use of the press in all its forms. It's very strange, but true. And so I will be involved in this medium well beyond what you may imagine.

To understand all the ramifications of my scheme, you have to see how I will use statements in my press to prepare the ground for official political acts. Suppose I want to resolve some problem in domestic or foreign affairs. For several months, each of my newspapers will play upon the public mind in their own fashion and then recommend a course of action. One fine morning, this course of action is officially adopted. You know with what care and ingenious circumspection official documents must be drafted in important matters. The problem in such cases is to give a certain amount of satisfaction to all parties. Therefore, each of my newspapers, according to its particular slant, will try to persuade each party that an adopted course of action favors it most. Things not explicitly stated in official documents can be implied through interpretation. The official newspapers will openly expand upon what appears only by allusion. Democratic and revolutionary newspapers will trumpet what they read into it. Meanwhile, as dispute rages and my acts are given the most diverse interpretations, my government always reserves the right to answer once and for all. "You are mistaken regarding my intentions. You have misread my declarations. I only meant to say this or that." What is key is never to be forced to contradict yourself.

Montesquieu: What! After what you've just told me, you can make such a claim?

Machiavelli: Certainly. And your astonishment proves that you have not understood me. It is a very important matter that words be consistent when acts cannot. Do you think the masses can judge whether logic guides its government? It's enough to tell them so. I want the various phases of my policies to be presented as the development of a single thought linked to an unchangeable goal. Every event, whether foreseen or unforeseen, will appear to be a cleverly intended result of policy. Changes of direction will be presented as different responses to the same problem, different roads leading to the same destination, various means to an identical solution, a goal unremittingly pursued despite obstacles. The most recent event will be presented as the logical culmination of all the others.

Montesquieu: Truly, you are to be admired. What strength of mind! What deeds!

Machiavelli: Every day my newspapers will be filled with official speeches and reports, referring to ministers and the sovereign. I am not forgetting that we live at a time of faith in human industry to solve all the problems of society. It is a time that is preoccupied with improving the lot of the working classes. I would devote myself all the more to such matters as a welcome outlet for channeling the energies of domestic politics. People in southern climes need to see the government constantly busy. The masses consent to be inactive, but on one condition—that those who govern them provide a spectacle of incessant, feverish activity. The masses constantly want to be distracted by novelties, surprises, and dramatic moves. Perhaps it seems bizarre, but once again, that's the way it is.

I would assiduously pursue what all this implies. Therefore, with regard to industry, the arts, and even administrative matters, I would commission studies calling for all manner of projects, plans, schemes, changes, reshuffling, and improvements. Reports of such things in the press would overshadow proposals coming from the most numerous and innovative publicists. It is said that political economy is a fertile field in your country. Well, I would leave nothing to be invented, published, or even said by thinkers, utopians, and the most enthused intellectual hacks of your schools. The welfare of the people would be the single and invariable object of my public utterances. Whether I speak or have my ministers or my writers speak for me, all subjects relating to the greatness of the country, its prosperity, the majesty of its mission and destiny would never be exhausted. The exalted principles of modern right, the great questions that stir humanity would find constant expression. My writings will breathe the spirit of the most enthusiastic, universal liberalism. Western peoples love the oriental style. Therefore, all my official speeches, all my proclamations would be filled with exalted and scintillating images, always stated in the most high-sounding way. People do not like atheistic governments. Therefore, in my dealings with the public, I would never fail to present my acts as falling under Divine Providence, while subtly tying my fate to that of the country.

I would like the acts I take during my reign to be compared constantly to those of past governments. This would be the best way to accentuate my benefactions and elicit the gratitude they deserve.

It will be very important to cast the mistakes of those who preceded me into relief. This will demonstrate my capacity to avoid the same. In such a way, a kind of antipathy, indeed an ineradicable aversion, will be attached to the regimes I succeed.

I would give a certain number of my newspapers the task of constantly exalting the glory of my reign while holding other governments responsible for the shortcomings of European politics. Moreover, I would want a great many of these eulogies to seem to be only an echo of foreign newspapers. I would reprint articles paying homage to the brilliance of my policies, whether deserved or not. In addition, I would have certain newspapers sold abroad. Their support of me would be all the more persuasive as I would allow a tincture of opposition on certain small points.

I am not unaware of the need of outlets for the public spirit. Intellectual activity closed off at one point will necessarily manifest itself at another. For that reason, I have no fears in seeing the nation engage itself in all manner of speculation—theoretical and practical—regarding industrial life.

Moreover, outside of politics, I assure you I would be a very good prince. Philosophical and religious questions would be debated undisturbed. In such matters, freedom of conscience becomes a sort of obsession. This tendency need not be opposed. It couldn't be done without danger anyway. In the most civilized countries of Europe, the invention of printing has given rise to a foolish and mad kind of writing that stops just short of pornography. It's a grave disease that knows no bounds. But, sad to say, it is better not to restrain it, so that this rage to write that possesses your parliamentary democracies may be satisfied to a certain extent.

This pestilential writing whose speech cannot be stopped issues from the platitudinous writers and men who dominate journalism. It will not fail to create a repellant contrast to the dignity of the language that will issue from the throne and the lively and picturesque arguments that will subtly defend my power in all its manifestations. Now you understand why I wanted to surround the prince with this swarm of publicists, bureaucrats, lawyers, businessmen, and judges. They are essential for drafting this mass of official communications. Its impact on men's minds would be very potent.

In brief, that is the broad outline of my regime's regulation of the press.

Montesquieu: Then are you finished with it?

Machiavelli: Yes, regretfully, for I have been much briefer than I should. But our time is limited. We have to proceed quickly.

Thirteenth Dialogue

Montesquieu: You've put me through an emotional ringer. You have at your disposal such a wealth of resources! You put forward such novel ideas! There is poetry in all this—a kind of sinister beauty worthy of a modern Byron. The dramatic talent of the author of *The Mandragola* is again on display here.

Machiavelli: Do you think so, Monsieur de Secondat? Your irony hints at a lack of self-assurance. You are not certain that these things are not possible.

Montesquieu: If you're concerned about what I think, I tell you I'm waiting for the upshot to all this.

Machiavelli: I'm not quite there yet.

Montesquieu: So, go on.

Machiavelli: I await your orders.

Montesquieu: Your first moves have seen you enact a formidable set of laws governing the press. You have extinguished all voices except your own. Factions stand mute before you. Don't you fear anything from conspiracies?

Machiavelli: No, for I wouldn't have been very far-sighted if I didn't disarm them all. All it would take would be a single swat from the back of my hand.

Montesquieu: How so?

Machiavelli: I would start with hundreds of deportations—all those who greeted my coming to power with gun in hand. In Italy, Germany, and France, I am told that secret societies recruit the lawless individuals who conspire against established governments. In my country, the dens where such sinister threads of conspiracy are woven into plots will be found out. I shall break them like spiders' webs.

Montesquieu: And after that?

Machiavelli: The act of organizing a secret society or of being affiliated with one will be severely punished.

Montesquieu: That's fine for the future. But what about societies already in existence?

Machiavelli: In the name of public safety, I will expel all those notorious for having been members. Those beyond my reach will remain subject to constant harassment. I will pass a law that will allow the government administratively to deport anyone who has been affiliated with such societies.

Montesquieu: That is to say, injudiciously deported.

Machiavelli: Why do you say "injudiciously?" Administrative decisions can be judicious, can't they? Rest assured. There will be little pity for factions. In countries continually agitated by civil discord, peace must be implacably restored. If domestic tranquility must claim a certain number of victims, the price will be paid. Afterward, the imposing presence of the commander is so formidable that no one will make an attempt on his life. After having covered Italy in blood, Sulla could appear again in Rome as an ordinary citizen. No one would dare touch a hair on his head.

Montesquieu: I see we are in a period filled with terrible executions. I am reticent about making any comment. Yet, it seems to me you could be less harsh and still achieve your ends.

Machiavelli: If an appeal were made to my mercy, I would look into it. Confidentially, some of the tough provisions I write into law are there to intimidate and will remain so, as long as I am not forced to use them otherwise.

Montesquieu: That's what you mean by "simply to intimidate?" Nevertheless, your nod to mercy does reassure me somewhat. Really, if any mortal heard you, there would be moments when you chill his blood.

Machiavelli: Why? I lived very near to the time of Duke of Valentinois whose historic reputation for terror was well deserved. He did have his ruthless moments. However, I assure you that once the necessity for executions had passed, he was a rather good-natured fellow. The same could be said of almost all absolute monarchs. Deep down, they are filled with goodwill, especially toward the disadvantaged.

Montesquieu: I'm not sure whether or not I like you better in your outbursts of rage. Your gentleness is even more frightening for me. You've abolished secret societies. Let's get back to the matter at hand.

Machiavelli: Don't go so fast. That I didn't do. You've confused things on this point.

Montesquieu: What? How so?

Machiavelli: I have suppressed secret societies of a certain ilk. I am speaking of those whose machinations would escape the surveillance of my government. But I have no intention of depriving myself of a useful channel of information and a means to influence affairs that can be considerable, if cleverly used.

Montesquieu: What are you thinking of in this connection?

Machiavelli: As I see it, I could give to a certain number of these societies a kind of legal existence or, rather, I could put them all under a single organization whose chief I would name. Then I would be in a position to control the various revolutionary elements in the country. These societies are made up of people from every nation, every class, and every social rank. I will be privy to the most obscure political intrigues. It will be like an auxiliary unit of my police. I will speak further about them in a short while.

The underground world of secret societies is filled with empty-heads who don't concern me in the least. But they can take directions. They represent a force that can be put in motion. If there is a commotion somewhere, it is my hand that sets it going. If a plot is hatched, I am the instigator. I am the head conspirator.

Montesquieu: And you think these bands of democrats, republicans, anarchists, and terrorists will let you come into their midst and break bread with them? What makes you think that those who want to throw off all forms of human domination will accept a guide who, you might say, is nothing but a master!

Machiavelli: O Montesquieu. You don't realize how impotent and even stupid most of these European demagogues are. These tigers have the souls of sheep. They're airheads. All you have to do to be accepted by them is speak their language. Moreover, almost all their ideas have an incredible affinity with the doctrines of absolute power. They dream of the gathering of individuals into a symbolic unity. They demand the complete realization of equality, which can only be brought about by power wielded by a single person. You see, even here I am the headmaster of their school! And besides, I have to say they have no choice. Secret societies exist under the conditions I have just laid down or they don't exist at all.

Montesquieu: The finale of *sic volo sic jubeo* does not have to wait long with you. I acknowledge you are definitely well protected against conspiracies.

Machiavelli: Yes, and it is important to underline the fact that the law will not allow gatherings or meetings in excess of a certain number of people.

Montesquieu: How many?

Machiavelli: Why are you concerned with such details? All right, gatherings of more than fifteen or twenty people will not be allowed.

Montesquieu: What! Friends numbering more than that won't be able to dine together?

Machiavelli: I clearly see how worked up you're getting by this outrage to Gallic conviviality. All right, they may dine together, for my reign will not be as savage as you think. But on one condition. Politics is not to be discussed.

Montesquieu: Can they talk about literature?

Machiavelli: Yes, but only if literature is not used as the pretext for a political assembly. It is possible not to discuss a word of politics at a banquet. But a banquet itself may assume the character of a demonstration and be so understood by the public. That must not happen.

Montesquieu: Alas! Such a regime makes it difficult for citizens to breathe without offending the government.

Machiavelli: That's not correct. Only the factious will suffer from these restrictions. No one else will feel them.

It goes without saying that I am not talking here about acts of rebellion against my power, nor attempts whose aim is to overthrow my rule. Nor am I talking about attacks on the person of the prince or acts that question his authority or institutions. These are true crimes that are rightfully suppressed by procedures common to all legal orders. Legislation will anticipate all such acts. They would be punished in my kingdom according to various degrees of seriousness. The laws will be clearly framed in such a way to prevent the least injury, whether direct or indirect, to the established order of things.

Montesquieu: I take you at your word in this matter and will not inquire into your methods. Still, it's not enough to enact draconian legislation. A judge must be found who is willing to apply it. This poses a bit of a problem.

Machiavelli: There's no problem.

Montesquieu: Are you going to destroy the judicial system?

Machiavelli: I destroy nothing. I modify and innovate.

Montesquieu: Then do you plan to set up military courts, summary courts, and, finally, courts of special jurisdiction?

Machiavelli: No.

Montesquieu: Then what are you going to do?

Machiavelli: First, you should realize that I feel no need to decree a great number of harsh measures that I must then enforce. Many already exist and they are still in force. All good governments, free or absolute, republican or monarchic, face the same difficulties. In moments of crises, they are forced to resort to harsh laws. Some of these remain in vigor and others have grown weak after the necessities that occasioned their birth disappear. Both kinds must be used. With regard to the latter, remember that they haven't been explicitly abrogated. Prudence dictated their enactment and they are perfectly defensible. The return of abuses they first prevented necessarily brings them back into application. In this way, the government seems merely to be doing what good administration requires. And this is often the case.

You see that it is only a question of giving the courts a little fine-tuning. This is always an easy matter in centralized countries where the judiciary stays in direct contact with the administrative machinery under the authority of the government ministry responsible for it.

Implementation of the new laws made under my reign, most of which will have been promulgated as small decrees, will not likely be so easy. In countries where judges serve for life, there may be resistance to direct meddling by the government when it comes to interpreting the law.

But I think I have found a very ingenious and simple scheme, which appears as totally legal. Although it challenges the principle of life tenure for the bench, it will be seen as correcting the most unfortunate consequences of that principle. I shall issue a decree that will require judges who reach a certain age to retire. I don't doubt that here again I will have popular sentiment on my side. It is pitiable to see, as so frequently happens, a judge who is called upon to decide the highest and most difficult questions of law fall into a state of debilitating senility.

Montesquieu: Allow me a word here. I have some ideas on this subject. What you present as the fact of the matter is completely belied by experience. Men whose lives entail a continued exercise of the mind do not suffer a weakening of intelligence, as you would have it. If I may say so, this is the privilege granted those whose primary pursuit is thinking. If the faculties fail with age in the case of a few judges, they are preserved among the greater number. Their powers of thought continually augment. There is no need to replace them. Death inevitably and naturally brings vacancies to their ranks. But even if there were as many examples of senility as you claim, it would be a thousand times better, in the interest of sound justice, to suffer this drawback than to accept your remedy.

Machiavelli: I have other reasons for this remedy that are proof against your objections.

Montesquieu: Reasons of state?

Machiavelli: Perhaps. Be assured of one thing. In cases that are purely civil, judges will not deviate from the letter of the law any more than they did before.

Montesquieu: I think I see what you're driving at. If I correctly read what you just said, you will give judges a certain flexibility when it comes to political matters.

Machiavelli: I won't. They must do their duty and side with power. In politics, public order requires it. It would be the worst of all worlds if the sovereign were exposed to the seditious decisions of a court. These might be seized upon by the whole country and used against the government. To what purpose was silence imposed on the press if the voice of the people can make itself heard in the decisions of the courts?

Montesquieu: Though it seems a modest change, your appointment scheme has far-reaching consequences. This is why you attach such importance to it.

Machaivelli: You're right. It effectively eradicates that spirit of resistance, that esprit de corps, which is always dangerous in judicial bodies that have preserved the memory of past governments and display a devotion that may border on worship. It brings to them new elements whose influences are all favorable to the spirit that animates my reign. Every year twenty, thirty, or forty posts in the judiciary will open up due to retirement. This means that the entire personnel of the judicial system can be reshuffled from top to bottom every six months. You understand that a single vacancy may lead to fifty new appointments by the successive upward movement of the holders of lower positions. Imagine what happens when there are thirty or forty vacancies at the same time. The collective spirit formed by prior professional attachments evaporates and greater solicitude for the present government is created because of the large number of positions at its disposal. There are young men ambitious to advance whose careers are not blocked by the life tenure of those who are ahead of them. They know that the government prizes law and order. The country, too. They serve both when they do what is called for on such questions.

Montesquieu: Unless people are incredibly blind, you will be accused of infecting the judiciary with a competitive spirit fatal to judicial bodies. I shall not elaborate on the consequences for I don't think that will stop you.

Machiavelli: I don't expect to escape criticism. It matters little to me, provided it doesn't reach my ears. In any case, I would consistently keep to a policy that sees my decisions as irrevocable in spite of any grumbling. A prince who acts in this way is always sure to win respect for his force of character

Fourteenth Dialogue

Machiavelli: I have told you many times already, and I repeat it once more, that I don't need to create and reorganize everything. I find in existing institutions a great many of the instruments of my power. Do you know what sovereign immunity is?

Montesquieu: Yes, unfortunately for you. Without setting out to do so, I spoil a surprise that you would have been happy to spring on me with all your dramatic flair.

Machiavelli: What do you have in mind?

Montesquieu: I'm thinking of what you seem to want to talk about and what's true at least in France. Traditionally, exceptions to this practice have been countenanced under certain circumstances. But this legal recourse must be modified, if not completely abrogated, in a regime where sovereign immunity is recognized.

Machiavelli: I find you quite amenable on this point. Put simply, your ideas on this subject support one of the most tyrannical practices in the world. What! When individuals are wronged by government agents performing their duties and bring them before the courts, judges must answer them thus: "You have no legal recourse here. The doors of the court are closed. Go to the ministry for authorization to prosecute its officials." Such rigid conformity to legal process is a veritable denial of justice. How often will the government authorize such prosecutions?

Montesquieu: What are you complaining about? This would seem to suit your purposes very well.

Machiavelli: I told you that only to point out that in states where judicial procedure encounters such obstacles, a government does not have much to fear from the courts. In others, it is always as a temporary expedient that exceptions are inserted into the law. But when circumstances change, the exceptions remain, as they should. When order returns, they are not inconvenient; only when it is disturbed are they necessary.

There is another modern institution that serves the purposes of the central power no less effectively. I am speaking of the creation of that great magistracy attached to the courts that you call the Public Ministry. It was formerly called, much more accurately, the Ministry of the King, because this office holder is essentially removable and his power revocable at the discretion of the prince. I hardly need to describe the influence this magistrate has on the courts near where he is seated. It is considerable. Keep all of this in mind. Now I am going to speak of the Supreme Court of appeals, which I have avoiding speaking about, but which plays a considerable role in the administration of justice.

The Supreme Court of appeals is more than a judicial body. In some ways, it is a fourth branch in the state because it has the last word in determining the meaning of the law. So I will repeat what I believe I have already said with respect to the Senate and the legislative Assembly. If a court of justice were completely independent of the government, it could overthrow it at will by virtue of its powers and almost total discretion in matters of constitutional interpretation. In the name of liberty, all the court would have to do is systematically limit or expand those provisions of the law that regulate the exercise of political rights.

Montesquieu: Apparently you are going to demand it do the opposite.

Machiavelli: I won't demand anything. It will do what is appropriate all by itself. The various ploys I mentioned a short time ago will bring their respective influences to bear here. The nearer a judge is to power, the more power controls him. The conservative spirit of my reign will concentrate here to the highest degree. In their deliberations, the police power will receive an interpretation so favorable to my power that I will be relieved of a multitude of restrictive measures that otherwise would be necessary.

Montesquieu: Hearing you, someone would think that the laws are subject to the most fantastic interpretations. Aren't the laws written with clarity and precision? Do they lend themselves to the expansions and contractions that you imply?

Machiavelli: Surely the author of *The Spirit of the Laws*, the experienced judge who authored so many excellent decisions, does not need me to teach him about jurisprudence. There is no text, however clear, that is not susceptible to the most contrary interpretations, even in matters purely of civil law.

But please keep in mind that we are talking about political matters here. Now it is a common practice of legislators in all times to adopt elastic wording in many of their provisions. This allows them to adjust for various circumstances that cover all cases and allow exceptions that would have been imprudent to specify more precisely.

I am perfectly well aware that I must furnish you some examples, for without them what I am proposing would appear too conjectural to you. While speaking of sovereign immunity, you said that the common practice of making exceptions to the law must be changed in a free country.

Well, suppose that a certain law exists in the state that I govern and suppose that it has been changed somewhat. Thus, I am supposing that before my time a law had been promulgated that in electoral matters permitted the prosecution of government agents without the authorization of the Council of State.

The question is presented under my reign that has, as you know, introduced great changes in public right. Someone wants to prosecute an official before the courts on an electoral matter. The public prosecutor gets up and says: "The privilege that is claimed no longer exists today. It is no longer compatible with current institutions. The old law that dispensed with the authorization of the Council of State in such a case has been tacitly abrogated." The courts respond yes or no and finally the debate is brought before the Supreme Court of appeals. It defines public right on this point in the following manner. "The old law is tacitly abrogated. The authorization of the Council of State is necessary to prosecute public officials, even in electoral matters."

Here is another more specific example borrowed from the regulation of the press. I am told that in France there was a law that required, under penal sanction, that anyone making a living by distributing and peddling published materials must have a license. This license was to be furnished by a public official in charge of the general administration of a province. The law sought to regulate peddling as its main goal and to subject it to strict surveillance. Let us suppose that the text of the provision declares: "All distributors and peddlers must be furnished with an authorized license."

Well, in the event that the matter came before it, the Supreme Court of appeals could say: "It is not only the regulation of an occupation that the law had in view. It meant to cover any distribution or peddling per se." Consequently, the author of a piece of writing or a book who delivers even a single copy of his work, without prior authorization, (even if nominally complementary and not for sale), is engaged in an act of distributing and peddling. As a result, he falls under the penal provisions."

You immediately see what results from such an interpretation. Instead of a simple exercise of the police power, you have a law regulating freedom of the press and restricting the right to publish one's thoughts.

Montesquieu: You've certainly got what it takes to be a jurist.

Machiavelli: It's a must. How are governments overthrown today? Through legal distinctions and the subtleties of constitutional law, put to the task of opposing the ruling power by all available means, tools, and contrivances not prohibited by law. Do you expect the ruling power not to use these legal stratagems against the opposition, when they use them so relentlessly against the ruling power? Then the contest would not be equal. It would be impossible to mount any resistance. It would be necessary to abdicate.

Montesquieu: So many dangers stand in your way. It would be a miracle if you could anticipate them all. The courts are not bound by previous decisions. Jurisprudence will leave you with many lawsuits on your hands. People with justiciable claims will not tire of knocking on the doors of courts asking for different interpretations.

Machiavelli: In the beginning, it's possible. But when a certain number of decisions have definitively settled the law, the opening that existed before will close and the source of lawsuits will dry up. Public opinion would become so tame that total reliance would be placed on the official opinions of the government for the meaning of the law.

Montesquieu: How so?

Machiavelli: At certain moments, when there is a good reason to fear that some controversy may arise over some point of law, the government will declare as an advisory opinion that the law applies to this or that situation or that the law extends to this or that case.

Montesquieu: But these are merely declarations that in no way bind the courts.

Machiavelli: Nevertheless, coming from a government as powerful as the one I have organized, these declarations will have very great authority for and influence over courts of justice. They will be particularly effective in controlling individual petitions and, in many cases, not to say always, they will forestall annoying lawsuits, which won't even be filed.

Montesquieu: As you proceed, I see that your government becomes more and more tutelary. This is judicial behavior that is almost patriarchal in spirit. In effect, such paternal solicitude demonstrated in so many ingenious ways must be acknowledged.

Machiavelli: So you have been brought to admit that I stand quite distant from the barbarous methods of government that you seemed to ascribe to me at the beginning of our conversation. You see that violence plays no role in all this. I take my stand where everyone does today, on right.

Montesquieu: On the right of the strongest.

Machiavelli: The right that gains obedience is always the right of the strongest. I know of no exception to this rule.

Fifteenth Dialogue

Montesquieu: We have covered a vast amount of ground in our discussion and you seem to have an answer for just about everything. But I feel compelled to tell you that you've got a long way to go before convincing me that you can hold onto power for very long. The thing that most astonished me was your intention to base your power on universal suffrage. I know of nothing more fickle. Please tell me if I am understanding you correctly. You told me you would be king, right?

Machiavelli: That's right, king.

Montesquieu: Elected for life, or a hereditary monarch?

Machiavelli: I would be king in the strict sense of the word—a hereditary monarch whose crown would pass to the first-born male. Women would never occupy my place.

Montesquieu: Not a very gallant attitude.

Machiavelli: Let me point out that it is the tradition of the French and Salic monarchy that I am following here.

Montesquieu: How will you be able to establish a hereditary line, given a democratic right to vote like that in the United States? Can you tell me this?

Machiavelli: Certainly.

Montesquieu: Come on now! Do you expect the will of future generations to be bound to such a principle?

Machiavelli: Yes.

Montesquieu: For the moment, though, I would like to know how you would square suffrage with the appointment of public officials.

Machiavelli: Which public officials? In monarchies, you know full well, the government appoints officials at all levels.

Montesquieu: That depends. Generally, administrators at the local level are chosen by local inhabitants, even in monarchic governments.

Machiavelli: A simple law can change that. In the future, such officials will be appointed by the government.

Montesquieu: Will you also appoint the nation's representatives?

Machiavelli: You know that is not possible.

Montesquieu: That's a real pity. If suffrage is left free, and you fail to contrive the outcome of elections, a popularly elected Assembly, under the influence of various parties, will soon be filled with deputies hostile to your power.

Machiavelli: But I have no earthly intention of leaving suffrage free.

Montesquieu: I expected as much. What then do you propose to do?

Machiavelli: One thing is extremely important. Those who wish to represent the country must be attached to the government. I will have all candidates swear a solemn oath. I don't mean an oath to the nation, in the manner of your revolutionaries of 1789. I want an oath of fidelity sworn to the prince himself and to his constitution.

Montesquieu: If you have no compunction about violating your political oaths, how do you expect others to be more scrupulous in this regard?

Machiavelli: I rely very little on the political conscience of men. Rather, I put my stock on the power of public opinion. No one will dare disgrace himself by being openly false to his sworn word. Let me underscore the fact that the oath I require will precede elections rather than follow them. Under such circumstances, the commitment to serve me would have to precede any vote gathering.

Henceforward, the government will have to possess the means to resist the opposition and prevent it from drawing away its supporters. At election time, the parties customarily proclaim their candidates and submit their lists to the government. I shall reciprocate by declaring my candidates and placing their names before the parties.

Montesquieu: If you didn't have a monopoly on power, the odious way you deal with the opposition would alone spark resistance. By offering open competition, you invite retaliation.

Machiavelli: I intend to have the agents of my government, from the lowest to the highest rank, actively involved in making sure that only my candidates are elected.

Montesquieu: In light of what you said before, that is something entirely to be expected.

Machiavelli: "The laws establishing suffrage are fundamental, likewise how suffrage is apportioned and how ballots are cast."* The smallest details of the electoral laws are of utmost importance.

Montesquieu: Sometimes I don't recognize what I've said when it comes from your mouth. It seems to me that what you just quoted was meant to apply to democratic governments.

Machiavelli: Most certainly. But you have seen already that the essence of policy entails reliance on the people. Although I wear a crown, my avowed and true goal is to represent them. Trustee of all delegated powers, I am alone their true representative, after all. What I will, they will. What I do, they do. Consequently, it is absolutely imperative that elections not afford factions the opportunity to subvert all that I—backed by armed might—personify.

So, I have found other ways to counter their efforts. Take, for example, the law that forbids public assemblies. Naturally, it will be applied to political conventions. In this way, parties will not be able to gather together and draw up platforms.

Montesquieu: Why do you always emphasize parties? For all your talk about them, isn't your real policy directed toward frustrating the will of the voters? After all, parties are only groups of voters. If the voters are prevented from meeting and open debate, how can they ever vote intelligently?

Machiavelli: You show a certain naiveté when it comes to political passions and their infinite adaptability and cunning in circumventing prohibitions. But don't worry about the voters. Those with "politically correct" dispositions will always know who to vote for.

Besides, I let toleration work to my advantage. Not only will I allow groups to gather in support of my candidates, I will go so far as to close my eyes to the activities of several popular candidates who loudly proclaim the cause of liberty. However, let me add that those who cry the loudest will be my own.

Montesquieu: And how will you regulate suffrage?

Machiavelli: Let me first outline my policy as far as the vote in the countryside goes. I don't want people to cast their votes in populated areas. There they can be infected with the spirit of opposition commonly found in towns and cities, which follow the lead of the capital. I want voting by commune. The benefits of this arrangement, so deceptively simple, will nevertheless be considerable.

Montesquieu: Your intentions are obvious. The rural vote will divide itself among insignificant local personalities, or, for want of familiar names, will fall

---

* *The Spirit of the Laws* II 2 and following.

back on candidates nominated by your government. I seriously doubt that this arrangement will bring many able or talented men to office.

Machiavelli: Public order has less need of men of talent than men devoted to the government. Great ability belongs to the person who sits on the throne and those gathered around it. Elsewhere it is useless, maybe even harmful, for it can only find expression in measures against authority.

Montesquieu: Your maxims cut like a sword. I have no argument against you. Rather, I ask you please to elaborate further on how you would regulate elections.

Machiavelli: For reasons you can well appreciate, I am opposed to proportional representation. It distorts elections by allowing for coalitions among men of diverse principles. I will draw up a number of electoral districts from larger administrative units, from which a single deputy may be elected. Thus, each voter will be able to mark only one name on his ballot.

In addition, I must be able to neutralize the opposition in districts where it has too much influence. For example, suppose that in a previous election the majority in a given district had opposed me. Suppose that there is again good reason to anticipate opposition to the government's candidate. Nothing could be easier to remedy. If this district has only a small population, I simply redraw it and put it into a neighboring district where opposition voices will be drowned out and where enthusiasm for its cause is dissipated. On the other hand, if the hostile district has a fairly large population, it can be divided into several smaller districts. They are then annexed to neighboring districts, where the opposition is completely submerged.

I am skipping a wealth of detail directed to the same general end. For example, when necessary, I could divide electoral districts in ways to allow for more administrative control. I could have municipal officers, whose appointment depends on the government, preside over the functioning of these districts.

Montesquieu: I am taken aback by the fact that you are not advocating something that was reportedly once employed in the time of Leo X. I am referring to having election supervisors rig the results.

Machiavelli: That might prove a tad difficult today. Such a practice would have to be conducted with the utmost prudence. Besides, a skillful government has so many other resources at its disposal! It's not necessary directly to purchase votes. Groups of people can be made to vote the way you want by plying them with government contracts, here promising a port, there promising to buy something, at another place promising to build a canal. Conversely, cities and towns that oppose my government get nothing.

Montesquieu: I don't want to discredit the brilliance of these schemes, but aren't you afraid of opening yourself to the charge that you are at one time a corrupter of popular will and at another its oppressor? Don't you fear compromising your power by constantly engaging in struggles where it is always so directly committed? The least success in contests against your candidates will be a shining victory for the opposition and a rebuff to your government. I am frequently struck by something quite unnerving in your policy. It seems that you are constantly required to succeed in all your endeavors, or suffer something catastrophic.

Machiavelli: Such language smacks of fear. Let me reassure you. I have come so far and have succeeded in so many things that I can't possibly feel threatened by such infinitely small things. For true political men, Bossuet's grain of sand will not tip the scale. I am so entrenched that I could weather the storm, without danger. The paltry administrative inconveniences that you mention are of no significance. Besides, I don't claim to be perfect. I know quite well that mistakes will be made. Certainly, now and then, some cases of corruption and scandal will surface. What can I do? Will that destroy or even jeopardize in any way the rest of my project? It is less important to avoid committing mistakes than to assume responsibility for them with alacrity and a proper attitude that silences critics. Even if the opposition succeeds in insinuating some local dissidents into my Assembly, what does it matter to me? I am not like others who make no allowances for the necessities of their times.

One of my great principles is to set things against themselves. Just as I use the press against the press, I would use oratory to counter oratory. I would have as many men as I needed with prepared speeches, capable of speaking several hours non-stop. The essential thing is to have a solid majority behind you and a presiding officer who can be trusted. There is a special art in conducting debates and summoning votes. But do I need all these parliamentary tricks? In my Assembly, I will control nineteen out of twenty men, all of whom will follow my instructions. In the meantime, I would pull the strings of a sham opposition, clandestinely enlisted to my cause. Anyone may then declaim ever so nobly. Their words would as easily penetrate the ears of my deputies as wind through a keyhole. Now do you want me to speak of the Senate?

Montesquieu: Having studied Caligula's reign, I can imagine what is in store.

Sixteenth Dialogue

Montesquieu: One of the striking features of your politics is the annihilation of parties and the destruction of other collective forces. Your program has not failed in this regard. However, I see around you certain things that you have not dealt with, for example, the clergy, universities, the bar, the national militia, and business corporations. It seems to me there is more than one dangerous element in all that.

Machiavelli: I can't say everything at once. Let's consider the national militia so that I won't have to be concerned with it anymore. One of my first acts would have to be its dissolution. A citizen militia cannot be reconciled with the existence of a professional army. Unlike regulars, citizens in arms are liable to be fractious at any given moment.

And this matter does pose some difficulties. A national guard may be a useless institution but it is nonetheless very popular. In military states, it appeals to the puerile instincts in certain bourgeois circles. It may be anomalous and ridiculous but it brings together a taste for soldierly pomp and certain commercial mores. It is based on an inoffensive prejudice that would be inconvenient to counter. The prince must never appear to have interests opposed to those of the city, which believes its security is guaranteed by arming its inhabitants.

Montesquieu: But I thought you dissolved the militia?

Machiavelli: I dissolved it in order to reorganize it on other foundations. It is essential to put it under the command of certain civil authorities and to remove from it the prerogative of electing its leaders. Furthermore, I will tolerate its existence only in places convenient for me. I reserve the right to dissolve it again and to reorganize it on still other foundations, if circumstances so require. I have nothing more to tell you on this matter.

As for universities, the way that things are now handled is just about fine for me. You are aware that these great bodies of learning are no longer organized as they were. I'm told that they have almost everywhere lost their former autonomy. They are no longer anything but institutions in the service of public interests, financially governed by the state.

As I've said more than once, where we find the state, there we find the prince. The moral orientation of public institutions is in his hands. His agents mold the spirit of the youth. The government appoints the head of the teaching corps and its staff in their respective capacities. They are tied to it. They are dependent on it. And this is all that's needed. Here or there, we might find some vestiges of independence in some public school or academy. But it is easy to bring it back under central control and direction. All that is needed is a new regulation or a simple ministerial decree. I don't have to elaborate on every detail of what could be done. However, before leaving this subject, I must tell you that I regard it as very important to proscribe studies of constitutional law in the teaching of public right.

Montesquieu: Indeed, there are reasons enough for that.

Machiavelli: My reasons are actually very simple. I don't want young people who leave the schools to be mindlessly concerned with politics so that at eighteen years of age they are wrapped up in writing constitutions as they would tragic poetry. Such instruction can only twist the mind of the young and prematurely initiate them into matters that are beyond the limits of their intelligence. With these poorly digested and badly understood notions, we would not be educating real statesmen but utopians, whose rash thoughts would eventually be translated into rash actions.

The generations born under my reign must be raised to respect established institutions and to love the prince. To this end, I would make fairly ingenious use of the controls I would have over the curriculum. In general, I believe that the schools make a big mistake in neglecting contemporary history. It is at least as essential to know one's own times as it is that of Pericles. I want the history of my reign to be taught in the schools while I'm still alive. In such a way, a new prince finds his way into the hearts of a generation.

Montesquieu: Of course, such history would be one big defense of all your acts.

Machiavelli: Obviously I would not have myself denigrated. I would also try to undermine private education, which could not be directly proscribed. I could do this through the state universities. These would contain cadres of professors that would utilize their time outside the classroom to propagate convenient doctrines. I would have them offer courses in all the important cities that anyone could attend. In such a way, I would spread the government's influence and further indoctrination.

Montesquieu: In other words, you would co-opt even the last vestiges of independent thinking.

Machiavelli: I wouldn't co-opt anything at all.

Montesquieu: Would you allow professors other than your own to diffuse learning in the same way, without license, degrees, or authorization?

Machiavelli: What? You want me to sanction "clubs"?

Montesquieu: No, but let's go on to another subject.

Machiavelli: The safety of the government depends on a multitude of regulatory measures. Among my concerns, you were right to draw attention to the legal profession. Yet, regulation of this profession would get me involved where it is not necessary. Here I am dealing with civil matters and my rule of thumb is to show as much restraint as possible. In states that have a professional organization of lawyers, litigants regard the independence of the bar as a guarantee inseparable from the right of a public trial, whether it concerns a matter of honor, money, or life. It will be very rare when I intervene in such things. Public opinion would be alarmed by the inevitable cries that would be raised by the whole legal profession. Yet, I know that this body will be a source of influence constantly hostile to my power. You know better than I, Montesquieu, that this profession fosters cold and stubborn temperaments when it comes to matters of principle and minds whose tendency is to hold the acts of government to strict legality. Lawyers do not have as developed a sense of social necessity as a judge does. He sees the law from too close and in ways too narrow to have an accurate conception, while the judge....

Montesquieu: Spare me your pleadings.

Machiavelli: I don't for moment forget that I am before a descendant of those great magistrates who backed the cause of the French monarchy with so much brilliance.

Montesquieu: And who rarely submitted to pressure on verdicts that would violate the laws of the state.

Machiavelli: That is why they ended up bringing down the state itself. I don't want my courts of justice to be parliaments, nor do I want lawyers, under the immunities of the robe, to engage in politics. The greatest man of the century, to whom your country had the honor of giving birth, said: "*I wish that the tongue of a lawyer who speaks evil of the government could be cut out.*" Because modern mores are softer, I would not go so far.

At the first opportune moment, I would do one simple thing. While doing nothing at all to infringe on the independence of the profession, I will decree that lawyers be enlisted in the ranks of their profession by the sovereign himself. Providing a rationale for my decree will not be too difficult. I will merely point out to potential litigants that this procedure better guarantees their rights than when the profession, with all its cross-pressures, recruits its own members.

Montesquieu: It is only too obvious that even the most execrable measures can be given the color of reason. But let's see what you do with respect to the clergy. That is one institution that is only remotely dependent on the state. It is a spiritual power whose seat is located somewhere other than the fatherland. I know of nothing that threatens your power more than authority that speaks in the name of heaven but whose roots penetrate the entire earth. Remember that the Christian teaching is a teaching of liberty. I know that the state has strictly segregated religious authority from worldly politics. I also know that the words of preachers are limited to terms found in the Gospels. But the message that emanates—of otherworldly ideals—will prove the stumbling block to political materialism. It is this book, at once so humble and subdued, that alone destroyed the Roman Empire, Caesarism, and its power. Nations that avow Christianity will always escape despotism, for Christianity elevates man's dignity and places him beyond the reach of despotism. It develops moral strength over which human power has no sway.* Beware of the priest. He depends only on God. His influence is everywhere—in the sanctuary, the family, and the schools. You can exert no influence on him. His priorities are not yours. He obeys a constitution that is beyond both your laws and sword. If you reign over a Catholic nation and have the clergy for an enemy, you will be brought down sooner or later, even if the people are nominally behind you.

Machiavelli: I don't know why you make such apostles of liberty out of priests. I am unaware of such a role either in ancient or modern times. I have always found the priesthood to be a natural support for absolute power.

The act of founding may have caused me to make concessions to the democratic spirit of the age and to look to universal suffrage as the basis of my power. But I hope that you realize that these things are only artifices demanded by the times. I also claim the privilege of divine right. I am no less a king by the grace of God. It is only natural for the clergy to support me, for we share the same principle of authority. However, if the clergy itself grows fractious, if it takes advantage of its position to conspire against my government....

Montesquieu: Yes?

Machiavelli: You seem to think the church is so influential! Do you know how unpopular it has made itself in several avowedly Catholic states? In France, for example, the press has so disparaged it in the eyes of the masses that its apostolic mission has been rendered impossible. If I were king of France, do you know what I could do, if I so chose?

Montesquieu: What?

Machiavelli: I could provoke a schism in the Church and sever all bonds that tie the clergy to the Court of Rome. That is the real Gordian knot. I would have my press, publicists, and political men all declaim as follows: "Christianity is independent of Catholicism. Catholicism forbids what Christianity permits. The civil independence of the clergy and its submission to the Court of Rome are purely Catholic doctrines that constantly threaten the security of the state. Those loyal

---

* *The Spirit of the Laws* XXIV 1 and following.

to the kingdom must not have a foreign prince for a spiritual leader. This is to leave the internal order of the regime to the discretion of a power that can turn hostile at any given moment. This hierarchy of things, dating from the Middle Ages, is tantamount to the tutelage of the people and keeps them in their infancy. It cannot be reconciled with the virile genius of modern civilization, with its enlightenment and independence. Why seek in Rome for a spiritual leader? Why can't the sovereign also be pontiff?"

The liberal press especially could be made to spread such a message. Moreover, it is highly likely that the masses would gladly listen.

Montesquieu: If you dared to attempt such a project, you would quickly learn of the awesome power of Catholicism, even among nations where it seems weakened.*

Machiavelli: Attempt it, Great God! On bended knee, I ask forgiveness of our Divine Master for having laid out such a sacrilegious doctrine, so infused with the hatred of the Church. But God, Who is also the source of earthly power, does not forbid the prince to defend himself from the encroachment of the clergy. In fact, the clergy transgresses against the precepts of the Gospel when it shows itself insubordinate to the prince. The roots of priestly conspiracies are hidden. By going to the Court of Rome, I would find the way to stop them before they grow.

Montesquieu: How?

Machiavelli: I would have only to point out to the Holy See the moral condition of my people, chaffing under the yoke of the Church, aspiring to break loose, capable of further fracturing Catholic unity, and throwing itself behind the Greek or Protestant schism in the Church.

Montesquieu: Threats instead of action!

Machiavelli: Montesquieu, you're way off the mark. You fail to understand the respect I have for the papal throne! My only role and mission as a Catholic sovereign would be to become the defender of the Church. You are aware that today the temporal power of the Church is threatened by the anti-religious zeal and ambitions of countries north of Italy. Well, I would say to Saint Peter that it is my mission and duty to support and save him from his enemies. In return, I would ask him not to attack me but rather to lend me the support of his moral influence. This would not be too much to ask when I risk my popularity in defense of a cause so thoroughly discredited today in the eyes of the so-called European democracies.

---

* *The Spirit of the Laws* XXV 12.

These risks would not deter me. I would check the encroachment of neighboring states against the Holy See. If, unfortunately, the Pope were attacked and chased from the Papal States (as has already happened), my bayonets alone would restore and maintain him there, as long as I live.

Montesquieu: This would really be a masterstroke. If you could keep a garrison in Rome, you would almost be able to rule the Holy See, as if it were some province of your kingdom.

Machiavelli: Do you think that after rendering such a service to the papacy that the Pope would refuse to lend his support to my power or to come anoint me in my capital, if need be? Are there no such historic precedents?

Montesquieu: There is nothing that history has not seen. But what if, instead of finding in the chair of Saint Peter a Borgia or a Dubois, as you seem to expect, you find a pope who would counter your intrigues and brave your anger? What would you do then?

Machiavelli: Under the pretext of defending the Papacy's temporal power, I would resolve to bring about its downfall.

Montesquieu: Your genius cannot be denied.

Seventeenth Dialogue

Montesquieu: I said that you have a certain genius. It really takes something of the sort to conceive and execute so many extraordinary things. I now have a better understanding of the god Vishnu in Indian folklore. Like the Indian idol, you have a hundred arms, and each of your fingers can trip a switch. Granting that nothing is beyond your reach, are you able to see everything that's taking place?

Machiavelli: Yes. My police force will be so vast that in the heart of my kingdom one half the populace will be watching the other half. Permit me to elaborate a bit on how my police force will be organized.

Montesquieu: Proceed.

Machiavelli: The Ministry of the Police that I set up will be the most important of my ministries. It will bring under centralized control a multitude of tasks that have as much to do with foreign as with domestic affairs.

Montesquieu: But if you do that, your subjects will immediately see that they are caught in a horrible net.

Machiavelli: If this ministry is disliked, I will abolish it and rename it the Ministry of State, if you wish. Besides, in the other ministries, I will organize bureaus with similar functions, most of which will be secretly integrated into what are today called the Ministry of the Interior and the Ministry of Foreign Affairs. As far as this latter department goes, I am not for the moment concerned with diplomacy but only with ways to insure myself against factions at home and abroad. When it comes to security, most monarchs find themselves in similar straits. They would very likely further my projects for an international police force designed to promote our mutual security. I don't doubt for a minute that I could pull such a thing off.

I would then break down my cadres of international police into certain subgroups. First, there would be men who are well off, bon-vivants, planted in foreign courts, whose job would be to keep me informed of the intrigues of princes and exiled pretenders to my crown. Next, I would have a set of revolutionary refugees to serve—for a price, of course—as my conduit into the affairs of obscure rabble-rousers. I would set up political journals, publishing houses, and bookstores in all the great capitals, secretly subsidized to follow at close hand the movements in current thought.

Montesquieu: Your policy is no longer directed at factions in your kingdom. You will end up conspiring against the very soul of humanity.

Machiavelli: You know that big talk doesn't really frighten me. I want every political man in league with foreigners to be observed and continually tracked until he returns to my kingdom. Here he will be immediately incarcerated to prevent a continuation of any such activities. To better infiltrate revolutionary intrigues, I have in mind a scheme that I think rather clever.

Montesquieu: Good God, what could that be?

Machiavelli: I would have a prince of my house, directly in line for my throne, play the role of a malcontent. In posing as a liberal and a critic of my rule, he would rally to his side, and thereby expose, those in the upper echelons of my kingdom who might conceivably engage in some rabble-rousing. Privy to foreign and domestic intrigues, this prince would play the lead role in an elaborate play that would end by informing on such unsuspecting dupes.

Montesquieu: What! You would have a prince of your own house engage in activities of police work?

Machiavelli: Why not? I know reigning princes who, in exile, have served on the staff of the secret police.

Montesquieu: I will hear you out, Machiavelli, but only to put an end to this frightful wager.

Machiavelli: Don't be indignant, Monsieur de Montesquieu. In *The Spirit of the Laws* you called me a great man.*

Montesquieu: I've paid dearly for such words. My punishment is listening to you. From now on, we can do without so many sordid details.

Machiavelli: As for domestic affairs, I will be forced to reestablish the *cabinet noir*.

Montesquieu: Go on.

Machiavelli: Your best kings have made use of it. The privacy of the mails must not serve to shelter conspiracies.

Montesquieu: Come clean. The merest whiff of conspiracy scares you, doesn't it?

---

* *The Spirit of the Laws* VI 5.

Machiavelli: You're wrong. There will be conspiracies under my reign. Some are even a necessity.

Montesquieu: Come again?

Machiavelli: There might be some genuine conspiracies, but I am not talking about them. I can assure you that there will also be some sham conspiracies. At certain opportune times, when the prince's popularity is on the decline, they can be an excellent way of arousing the people's sympathy. The public can be intimidated and the prince can, if need be, procure the harsh measures he wants or put into effect those already at hand. These contrived conspiracies, which of course must be employed cautiously, have yet another use. They can lead to the discovery of real conspiracies. Blanket investigations can be undertaken into anything suspect.

Nothing is more precious than the life of the sovereign and many pains must be taken to guarantee it. He must be surrounded by countless bodyguards. But his secret service must be rather skillfully disguised so that the sovereign does not seem afraid when he shows himself in public. I am told that in Europe such precautions were so perfected that a prince could go out in public like an ordinary individual and seemingly stroll heedlessly through the crowds, while actually being surrounded by two or three thousand of his protectors.

I intend to have my police infiltrate all ranks of society. There will be no private room or gathering place, no drawing room or intimate setting where an eavesdropper is not found to take in what is said at any hour. For those experienced at it, it is astonishingly easy to get men to inform on each other. The techniques of observation and analysis developed by professional cadres of the secret police are more astonishing yet. You have no idea of the range of their tricks and disguises. Instinct, patience, and imperturbability combine with a certain passion for these sorts of things. The ranks of the profession are made up of men from all sectors of society who are brought together by a—how shall I put it—a kind of love of the art.

Montesquieu: Let's keep the curtain closed on such things!

Machiavelli: You get no argument from me on this score. Ruling does indeed involve terrifying, dark secrets. I'll spare you some of the more frightening ones. The way the system is organized, I will be so completely informed that I would be able to tolerate certain genuine intrigues because I would have the power to suppress them anytime I wanted.

Montesquieu: Why would you even consider tolerating them?

Machiavelli: In European states, the absolute monarch must not use force indiscriminately. There are always certain underground activities that need some operating room before they reveal themselves and can be dealt with. Public opinion must not be aroused for just any reason of state security. Consider also that political parties, reduced to impotence, are often not content merely to grouse and remonstrate. To deprive them even of an outlet for their cantankerous minds would be a great mistake. Here and there, their complaints will be heard in books and newspapers. The government will be attacked by innuendo in some public speeches or in court, as the defense makes it summation. Under various pretexts, they will undertake small-scale demonstrations to voice their grievances. All these things, I assure you, will be timid undertakings, and the public, if made aware of them, will only be tempted to laugh. People will find me quite liberal. I will pass for being too easygoing.

I don't want anyone to utter even a word to the effect that my government is afraid. This is the real reason why I tolerate what, after all, can't really harm me.

Montesquieu: That reminds me. You have left a serious gap in your discussion—something your decrees have not touched upon.

Machiavelli: What?

Montesquieu: You have not dealt with individual rights.

Machiavelli: I won't touch them.

Montesquieu: How so? I don't see how you can square tolerance with your claim to be able to squash anything that you see as threatening. Take a state of emergency, for instance, even a less serious concern that requires immediate preventive detention. How can you proceed in the face of *habeas corpus* laws? Isn't it the case that certain legal formalities and procedural guarantees will stand in your way? Time is lost while the mechanisms of law roll on.

Machiavelli: Wait a minute. When I said I would respect individual liberty, that did not preclude some very useful judicial reforms.

Montesquieu: I knew it.

Machiavelli: Hold on. Don't think you've scored some big point against me. What I have in mind would be the simplest thing in the world to do. In parliamentary countries, who is principally entrusted with overseeing individual liberties?

Montesquieu: It is a judicial tribunal composed of judges whose number and independence guarantee justice.

Machiavelli: That is most surely a defective institution. The slowness of its deliberations robs justice of the celerity and fear necessary to deter wrongdoers.

Montesquieu: What kind of wrongdoers?

Machiavelli: I am speaking of people who commit murders, thefts, crimes, and offenses justiciable as crimes against society. Jurisdiction over such matters must be given the necessary unity and dispatch. I would replace your council with a single judge, charged with overseeing the arrests of criminals.

Montesquieu: But we're not only talking about criminals. By this provision, you threaten the liberty of all citizens. At least draw a distinction between different kinds of crime.

Machiavelli: That is exactly what I don't want to do. Isn't someone who conspires against the government guilty in the same way as someone who commits a felony or misdemeanor? A moment of passion and being without resources can explain certain crimes. But what forces people to be interested in politics? Therefore, I want no distinction between crimes against society and crimes against the state. What is there about the spirit of modern government that leads it to organize different kinds of courts? In my kingdom, no distinction will be made between the insolent journalist and the ordinary thief. They will share the same cell and appear in the same court. The conspirator will share the docket with the forger and the murderer and appear before the same jury. Let me underscore the brilliance of such a reform. Public opinion, seeing the conspirator treated no differently than the common criminal, will begin to blur the two categories of crime. It will end up scorning them equally.

Montesquieu: You are destroying the very grounds of sound moral judgments. I know this means nothing to you. But what surprises me is that you would seem to retain the jury system.

Machiavelli: In centralized states like mine, public officials designate the members of the jury. In cases involving ordinary political offenses, my Minister of Justice will be able, if need be, to convene a panel of judges to deal with such things.

Montesquieu: Your scheme of domestic reforms is up to its task. It is time to go on to other concerns.

Third Part

Eighteenth Dialogue

Montesquieu: Up until now you have been concerned with the structure of your government and the stringent laws necessary to maintain it. That is a considerable undertaking, but you have only just begun. For a sovereign who desires absolute power in a modern European state accustomed to representative institutions, you still have to face the most difficult problem of all.

Machiavelli: And what's that?

Montesquieu: The problem of state finances.

Machiavelli: I've not ignored such things. I remember telling you that everything comes down to knowing how to manipulate numbers.

Montesquieu: That's all well and good. But in this case, the very nature of things will resist you.

Machiavelli: I confess that you take me somewhat aback. I was born in a century extremely backward when it comes to matters of economics and I understand little about such things.

Montesquieu: I'm not too anxious on your behalf. However, let me ask you one thing. I remember having written in *The Spirit of the Laws* that the absolute monarch was compelled, by the principle that informed his government, to impose only small taxes on his subjects.* Will you at least give your subjects the same satisfaction?

Machiavelli: I make no such promise. In truth, I know nothing more questionable than the proposition you have set forth there. How do you expect the trappings of monarchic power and the brilliance and display of a grand court to exist without imposing heavy sacrifices on a nation? Your thesis may be true in Turkey or in Persia, for all I know, for petty, lazy people who would not even have

---

* *The Spirit of the Laws* X 13.

the wherewithal to pay a tax. But in European societies, labor produces a superabundance of wealth that presents itself in various forms—all amenable to taxation. In these countries, the government supports itself through luxury. All public service projects are under central control. All high officials and dignitaries are given great salaries at public expense. Can you really expect someone who is sovereign master of all this to limit himself to modest taxes?

Montesquieu: All right. I accept your premises and will not defend my proposition whose real meaning has seemed to escape you. So, your government will be costly. Evidently it will be more expensive than a representative government.

Machiavelli: That's possible.

Montesquieu: Yes. But here is where you begin to have problems. I know how representative governments provide for their financial needs, but I have no idea of how absolute power, in modern societies, can support itself. If the past is any indication, absolute power could be maintained upon the following conditions: first, the absolute monarch would have to be a military leader. You understand this.

Machiavelli: Yes.

Montesquieu: Moreover, he would have to be a conqueror, for war would be the principal source of those revenues that would keep him in splendor and support his armies. If these expenses were met by taxation, they would crush his subjects, not because he spends less but because he finds his means of support elsewhere. But today, war is no longer profitable. It ruins the conqueror as well as the conquered. Here then is one major source of revenue that escapes you. Taxes remain. But to lay taxes as he wants, the absolute monarch would have to ignore the will of his subjects. In despotic states, a legal fiction is appealed to and this allows such rulers to tax indiscriminately. The sovereign is presumed to possess all the goods of his subject by right. When he expropriates something, he is only taking back what belongs to him. Thus, there is no basis for a claim against him.

Finally, it is in the nature of absolutism that the prince be free to dispose of his tax revenues. His action in this domain is above discussion and control. You have to admit that the defects of despotism are so extreme that it would take a lot ever to return to it.

Even if modern peoples are as indifferent as you say to the loss of their liberties, they are not so when their interests are at stake. And these interests are linked to an economic order far removed from despotism. Financial matters, which resist arbitrary handling, will impinge on your discretion in political matters. You whole reign threatens to collapse on this score.

Machiavelli: I don't see the cause for too much concern about this or any other matter.

Montesquieu: We'll see. Let's come to the point. That taxes are voted upon by the representatives of the nation is the fundamental rule of modern states. Do you or do you not accept this principle?

Machiavelli: Why not?

Montesquieu: Don't be too rash. This principle is the clearest token of a people's sovereignty. Granting them the right to pass taxes is to recognize the right to refuse, limit, or reduce to nothing the power of the prince to act. Ultimately, it is the right to destroy him, if need be.

Machiavelli: You seem very sure of yourself.

Montesquieu: Those who vote taxes are themselves the taxpayers. Their interests are closely bound up with those of the nation. They will be attentive to such matters. You will find these representatives adamant and unaccommodating in appropriating money in the same way that you will find them docile with regard to political liberties.

Machiavelli: Here your argument is demonstrably weak. Please consider a couple of things. In the first place, the nation's representatives are salaried. Even if they are taxpayers, other personal matters can make them malleable when voting tax measures.

Montesquieu: I agree with what your scheme portends. Your remark is to the point.

Machiavelli: You see the disadvantages of looking at things too systematically. The least change, if skillfully made, can change everything. Perhaps what you say is right if I were basing my power on the aristocracy or on the middle classes that could refuse to cooperate with me at any moment. Secondly, I base myself on the proletariat, the bulk of which possess nothing. The costs of supporting the state are hardly borne by them at all. I will arrange it so that they are completely exempt from any burden. The working classes show little concern for fiscal measures, since they are unaffected by them.

Montesquieu: If I've understood you correctly, one thing is clear. The "haves" would be forced to pay because that is the sovereign will of the "have-nots." Because of their poverty and greater numbers, the poor will hold the rich ransom.

Machiavelli: And isn't there something fair in this?

Montesquieu: It isn't even true. In contemporary society, from the economic point of view, there is no rigid demarcation between the rich and the poor. Through labor, the artisan of yesterday can be the bourgeois of tomorrow. You must realize what you are doing by attacking the landed or industrial bourgeoisie.

In reality, you are making it more difficult for someone to emancipate himself through labor. You are holding back a greater number of laborers in the bonds of the proletariat. It is a grave error to believe that the proletariat can profit from attacks on the source of productivity. By impoverishing the "haves" through fiscal measures, you will only be creating an unstable social situation. In time, even the "have-nots" will be totally impoverished.

Machiavelli: These are fine theories. I will counter them with others, just as fine, if you wish.

Montesquieu: Not just yet. You haven't resolved the problem I have posed for you. You have to obtain the wherewithal to meet the expenses of absolute monarchy. It will not be as easy as you think, even with a legislature in which you will have an absolute majority, backed by all the power of the popular mandate with which you are invested. Tell me, for example, how can you make the financial mechanisms of modern states amenable to the exigencies of absolute power? I repeat. The very nature of things will resist you. The civilized people of Europe have regulated their finances with multiple guarantees that are so strict and so jealous that it would be just as hard to raise public revenues arbitrarily as to spend it so.

Machiavelli: Please elaborate and explain this marvelous system.

Montesquieu: It will only take a moment to summarize it. The perfection of the financial system in modern times essentially rests on two fundamental operations: *a system of accountability* and *public access to information*. Herein lies the taxpayers' security. A sovereign may not tamper with such reforms without in effect saying to his subjects: "Things may be in order, but I want disorder and obscurity in the management of public funds. There are multitudes of expenditures I want to undertake without your approval. There are deficits that I want to conceal and revenues I want to disguise or inflate, according to circumstances."

Machiavelli: I like what you're saying here.

Montesquieu: In free industrialized countries, everyone is acquainted with financial management either out of necessity or out of personal or professional interests. Your government could not deceive anyone in these matters.

Machiavelli: Who is talking about deception?

Montesquieu: The whole work of financial management, so vast and complicated, can be reduced to two very simple operations: *appropriations* and *expenditures*.

It is around these two financial poles that so many laws and special regulations gravitate. There is nothing complicated in their objective. It is simply to guarantee that the taxpayer pays only the necessary and duly called for tax and that the government applies public funds only for expenditures approved by the nation.

I will not address myself to what is to be taxed, establishment of a tax rate, or how taxes are to be collected. Nor will I investigate how to guarantee against tax evasion and to instill order and precision into the circulation of public funds. Those are accounting details that I don't need to discuss with you. I only wish to show you how public scrutiny goes hand-in-hand with a system of auditing in well-organized systems of public finance in Europe.

One of the most important innovations was to bring the operations of public financing to light, to make visible the government's use of the public's wealth, the source of its revenues and object of its expenditures. This was achieved by the invention of what is today called the state budget, which is a rough estimate of expected revenues and projected expenses, not over an extended period of time, but each year, for the following year. The essentials of the financial situation may be found there. In a way, the budget also shapes that situation, which is improved or worsened according to its projections. The different ministers prepare the parts of the budget and account for the various programs in their departments. They take the allocations of former budgets as a base for their projections, while introducing certain modifications, additions, or necessary cutbacks. All the requests are brought before a Minister of Finance who synthesizes the disparate elements and presents them to the legislative Assembly what is called a budget plan. This impressive document is published, printed, and reproduced in a thousand newspapers and reveals to all eyes the domestic and foreign policy priorities of the state and its civil, judicial, and military administration. It is examined, discussed, and voted upon by the representatives of the country and put into effect like any other law of the state.

Machiavelli: When it comes to financial matters, I want to express my admiration for the illustrious author of *The Spirit of the Laws*, how he rendered obscure theories into apt formulations and reduced somewhat ambiguous terms to the modern idiom in that great work that made him immortal.

Montesquieu: *The Spirit of the Laws* is not a work on finances.

Machiavelli: Your terseness on this score deserves all the more praise, for you were certainly capable of giving a complete account of the subject. Please continue, I beg you. I am following you with great interest.

Nineteenth Dialogue

Montesquieu: It may be said that the creation of the budgetary system has brought in its train all the other financial reforms that are a feature of all well-regulated political societies.

Thus, from the nature of budgeting itself emerges the rule that expenditures correspond to existing resources. This balance must be openly expressed through demonstrable and certified statistics. To better insure this result and so that the legislators that vote on the provisions are not led astray, recourse has been had to a very prudent measure. The general budget of the state has been divided into two distinct elements: an *expenditure budget* and a *revenue budget*, each of which must be voted separately and passed by its own special law.

In this manner, the legislator is obliged to concentrate on expenditure receipts separately and in turn. His decisions are not influenced in advance by vague notions as to the general balance of revenues and expenditures.

In the final stage, he scrupulously examines, compares, and harmonizes these two elements with a view to a final vote on the general budget.

Machiavelli: All this is very good, but can it be that expenditures are restricted to only what has been voted on by the legislature? Is this possible? Is it in the power of a legislative body so to cripple the executive, to forbid a sovereign to appropriate for unforeseen expenses through certain emergency measures?

Montesquieu: Obviously, you are uncomfortable with such an arrangement. I'm not.

Machiavelli: In states that operate in a constitutional framework, isn't there a provision for a sovereign, by decree, to requisition supplementary or extraordinary appropriations when the legislature is not in session?

Montesquieu: That is so, but on condition that these decrees be passed into law when the legislature reconvenes. Its approval is necessary.

Machiavelli: If I have already committed the money, they will be called upon to ratify a fait accompli. I don't find this so bad.

Montesquieu: That would be the case were it not for other restrictions. The most progressive legislation prohibits the sovereign from acting contrary to the ordinary provisions of the budget, other than by requisitioning supplementary and emergency appropriations. But the expenditure of such appropriations cannot be made without the authorization of the legislature.

Machiavelli: I don't think it would be possible to govern under such restrictions.

Montesquieu: Sure it is. Without curtailing the possible abuses arising from supplementary and emergency appropriations, modern states have thought that legislative control over the budget would be a chimera. After all, they thought, since here is a finite amount of resources, expenditures must somehow also be limited. Political events cannot force financial realities to change from one moment to another. Furthermore, the recess of the legislature would never be so long as to preclude the possibility of an expeditious vote on exceptional expenses.

Reform has gone even farther. When resources are earmarked for a certain purpose, they return to the general fund if they are not used. It was thought that, while staying within general allocated limits, a government should not be able to use the funds for other than its appropriated purpose, to engage in a kind of shell game, where funds are transferred by administrative decree from one department to another. If this were not the case, expressed legislative intent could be circumvented, and, by an ingenious subterfuge, we would return to a situation of arbitrariness.

In this light, what has come to be called *line-item budgeting* has been invented. That is to say, expenditures are broken down into subsidiary accounts that are similar in nature in all departments. For example, subsidiary A will comprise, in all departments, expenditure A, subsidiary B expenditure B, and so on. In this scheme, unspent appropriations must be removed from the accounts of the various departments and reported as surplus revenue for the budget in the following year. It goes without saying that department heads will be held responsible.

These financial guarantees culminate in the establishment of an independent board of auditors that sits permanently, acting as a kind of appeals court, having jurisdiction and auditing powers over all facets of state bookkeeping and the management and use of public funds. It even has the task of pointing out to the administration better ways of financial management from the point of view of both expenses and revenues. This explication should give you some idea of how such an organization would constrain absolute power.

Machiavelli: I confess to still being a bit dumbfounded by this financial excursion. You are taking advantage of my weakness. I told you that I understood very little about such things. But let me assure you. I would have ministers who would know how to turn these arguments around and show the dangers of most of these measures.

Montesquieu: You wouldn't be able to do some of these things yourself?

Machiavelli: Don't get me wrong. The principal concern of my ministers would be to spin out fine theories. As for myself, I will speak of finances as a statesman rather than an accountant. There is one thing you are inclined to forget. Of all things that concern politics, financial matters are most amenable to the maxims of *The Prince*. Those states that have budgets organized in detail and kept up to date look to me like those merchants who have perfectly kept books but end up bankrupt. Who has budgets larger than your parliamentary governments? What government is more expensive to run than the democratic government of the United States or the constitutional monarchy of England? It is true that the immense resources of this latter power are placed at the service of the most profound and savvy statecraft.

Montesquieu: You are not speaking to the point. What are you getting at?

Machiavelli: This. The rules that govern financial management on the state level bear no relation to those governing household economics, which seem to serve as your model.

Montesquieu: Are you coming back to that same distinction—between politics and morality?

Machiavelli: In effect, yes. Isn't this universally recognized and practiced? Although much less extreme, didn't such a distinction exist in your time? Didn't you yourself say that when it comes to finances, states permit themselves irregularities that would put the most dissolute sons of well-off families to shame?

Montesquieu: It's true. I did say that. But I would be very surprised if you can draw an argument favorable to your thesis from such a statement.

Machiavelli: I presume you mean that our orientation must be not what is done but what should be done.

Montesquieu: Exactly.

Machiavelli: I answer that it is necessary to will the possible and that what holds universally cannot but be done.

Montesquieu: I agree that this is what experience would teach.

Machiavelli: And I have a sneaking suspicion that if you were even to balance your budget, as you indicate, my government, totally absolute as it is, would be less expensive than yours. But I am not interested in getting into an argument about this. You are completely deceived if you think I feel myself hampered by that system of finance, howsoever perfected, that you have just elaborated. I share with you your enthusiasm for streamlining the process of tax collection and for measures to counter tax evasion. I am delighted at ways to insure accounting accuracy. I am sincere when I say these things. But this plethora of precautions is truly silly if you interpret the real problem as coming from the absolute sovereign dipping his hand into the public till or wanting to manage the public finances alone. Do you think the danger lies here? Once again, so much the better if the funds are collected, move, and circulate with the miraculous precision that you have described. In fact, I expect to adopt all these marvels of accounting, all these splendid financial reforms and have them redound to the splendor of my reign.

Montesquieu: You possess a certain *vis comica.* What I find surprising is that your financial theories are in patent contradiction with what you said in *The Prince,* where you strictly recommend parsimony for the prince, and even avarice.*

Machiavelli: You're wrong to be surprised at such a thing. I recognize that the times have changed. One of my most fundamental principles is to adapt myself to the times. Please, let's go back to what you said about a board of auditors so we can get that out of the way. Is this institution a part of the judicial branch?

Montesquieu: No.

Machiavelli: Then it is a purely administrative body. Let's even presume it to be beyond reproach. There's nothing it can do once it has audited the accounts! Can it prevent appropriations from being voted or expenditures from being made? Its audits tell us no more about the financial state of affairs than the budget. It is a bookkeeper's office, without the ability to oppose, utterly gullible. So let's stop talking about it. I'm not the least bit anxious if such an institution is retained, no matter how efficient you have made it.

Montesquieu: Retain it! Then you plan to tamper with the other features of financial organization?

Machiavelli: You guessed it. After a political coup d'état, doesn't a financial one inevitably follow? Is the exercise of my absolute power to stop short there? What is the magic of your financial institutions that would ward it off? I am like the giant in the fairy tale who was tied down by pygmies while he slept. In getting up, he broke the bonds without having noticed them. The day after I take control of the throne, I won't bother about votes for the budget. It will be decreed extraordinarily. Appropriations will be passed by dictate, which my Council of State will later approve.

Montesquieu: Do you plan to go on like this?

Machiavelli: No. The following year, I will return to legal ways. I've already told you several times that I don't intend to destroy anything directly. There were regulations before me. I will regulate things in my turn. You mentioned

---

* *The Prince* XVI.

that the budget would be voted under two distinct laws. I consider that a bad arrangement. Finances can be better handled when revenues and expenditures are voted at the same time. My government is hardworking. Public deliberations should not squander precious time in useless discussions. Henceforth, budgetary revenues and expenditures will be included under the same law.

Montesquieu: And what about the law that prohibits spending supplementary appropriations other than by a previous vote in the Assembly?

Machiavelli: It is abrogated. You understand the reason very well.

Montesquieu: Yes.

Machiavelli: It is a law that cannot be applied under all circumstances.

Montesquieu: And what about itemized budgeting?

Machiavelli: It can't continue. Expenditures will no longer be voted according to individual line-items in the various ministries, but according to ministry by total expenditures allotted it.

Montesquieu: You are talking about immense sums. Block sums for each ministry gives only the grand total to examine. As far as the public's expenditures go, you have, in effect, thrown away the sieve and are content to have a bottomless barrel.

Machiavelli: That's not quite accurate. I will retain what you call line-items. Expenditures will be in blocks representing distinct elements. They are there to be examined. But ministries will decide expenditures within the blocks and transfers among accounts will be allowed.

Montesquieu: And from one ministry to another?

Machiavelli: I don't go that far. I want to remain within the limits of what is necessary.

Montesquieu: Your moderation is exemplary. Don't you think such innovations will cause financial panic in your country?

Machiavelli: Why would they cause more alarm than other measures?

Montesquieu: Because these touch upon the material interests of everyone.

Machiavelli: The distinctions that you draw are too subtle.

Montesquieu: Too subtle! That's a well-chosen word in this context. Why don't you just say that a country that can't defend itself when it comes to political liberties cannot defend itself when it comes to money?

Machiavelli: What could anyone complain about? In all the essentials, the public's fiscal rights have been preserved. Aren't taxes duly voted and collected?

Aren't expenditures also duly voted? Here, as elsewhere, everything is based on people's votes. My government is certainly not reduced to indigence. The people who acclaim me do not merely tolerate the splendor of my throne. They positively crave it. The people look to a prince for an expression of their power. They really hate only one thing—wealth in their peers.

Montesquieu: Don't try to slip away. You're not finished yet. I want to make you consider budgetary matters a bit further. No matter what you say, the very existence of a budget represents a limit to your power. It may be breached, but only at your peril. It is published. Its elements are known. It stands as a financial barometer of sorts.

Machiavelli: Since you want to, let's get on with it.

Twentieth Dialogue

Machiavelli: The budget represents a kind of limit, you say. Perhaps. But its limit is elastic and can be expanded as far as wanted. I will always act within it, never outside.

Montesquieu: What do you mean?

Machiavelli: Do I have to teach you how things can be handled, even in states that have perfected the art of budgeting? Real art lies in knowing exactly when, by ingenious expedients, to elude limitations that really exist only on paper anyway.

What is the annual budget? Nothing but a provisional measure, a rough survey of principal financial goals. The books aren't closed until account is taken of expenditures that necessarily arise during the year. In your budgeting, there are I don't know how many different kinds of expenditures. These correspond to all types of contingencies and are known as complementary, supplementary, extraordinary, provisional, what have you. Each of these expenditures alone makes up so many more distinct budgets. Now this is the way it happens. Suppose for example that the main budget passed in the beginning of the year totals 800 million. At mid-year, financial realities are no longer in line with first estimates. There is then presented to the Assembly what is called a revised budget that adds 100 million or 150 million to the original estimate. Afterward comes the supplementary budget. It adds 50 or 60 million to it. Finally, there comes a budget to amortize the debt, which adds 15, 20, or 30 million. In short, in terms of the general budget, the total difference is one-third of the anticipated expenditure. The legislature is called to confirm these later figures by vote. In this way, at the end of ten years, the budget can be doubled or tripled.

Montesquieu: I doubt that this increase in expenditures is based on anything you've done to improve the financial situation. Nothing you've hypothesized can occur in states that are not subject to your inanities. But you're not finished yet. Expenditures, after all, must balance with revenues. How will you bring this about?

Machiavelli: It can be said here that everything consists in the art of classifying certain sets of figures and in making use of certain distinctions among different expenditures. Skillfully done, the necessary latitude can be obtained. Thus, for example, the distinction between the ordinary budget and the extraordinary budget can be of great use. *Extraordinary* is a marvelous cover word. Such a budget can be used to help pass what would otherwise be an arguable expenditure or to raise more or less problematical revenues. Assume, for example, that I have 20 million in expenses. It must be met with 20 million in revenue. I have listed among my revenues a war indemnity of 20 million, which will be collected later on. Or again, I have listed an increase of 20 million from the proceeds of certain taxes, but which will be realized only the following year. Examples like these could be multiplied. Such things would take care of the revenue problem. As far as expenditures go, recourse can be had to a contrary procedure. You simply subtract instead of add. For example, the expense of collecting the tax is deducted from expenditures.

Montesquieu: May I ask how all this will be justified?

Machiavelli: I could reasonably maintain that this is not an expense of the state. In a similar way, I could remove from general state expenditures the cost of services to provinces or towns.

Montesquieu: I won't debate any of that. I just want to know what you plan to do with revenues that mask deficits and with the expenditures that you eliminate?

Machiavelli: The essential thing in this regard is to make use of the distinction between the ordinary and extraordinary budgets. Those expenditures that so preoccupy you must be referred to the extraordinary budget.

Montesquieu: But in the end these two budgets are totaled and the sum of expenditures appears.

Machiavelli: On the contrary. They must not be totaled. The ordinary budget is presented alone. The extraordinary budget is presented as an appendix and is handled in a different way.

Montesquieu: How?

Machiavelli: Don't make me get ahead of myself. In the first place, there is a particular way of presenting the budget to disguise rising costs, when the occasion presents itself. The government doesn't exist that isn't required to act like this. There are inexhaustible resources in industrial countries, but, as you pointed out, those countries are sometimes parsimonious and suspicious. They haggle over even the most necessary expenditures. The conduct of financial policy is no different from others. It can't be done openly and aboveboard. Otherwise, it would meet with obstacles all along the way. But in the end, and, thanks to the perfection of budgeting, everything is broken down to be seen and analyzed. If the budget can be made to harbor certain mysteries, it also must bring certain things to light.

Montesquieu: Undoubtedly, you mean for the initiated only. I surmise that you will reduce financial legislation to obscurity and empty formalities as happened with the Romans' judicial procedure at the time of the Twelve Tables. But let's get into this a bit more. If your expenses increase, your resources must increase proportionately. Or do you expect, like Julius Caesar, to find two billion francs in the coffers of the state. Perhaps you intend to discover the Potosi mines?

Machiavelli: You're getting a bit carried away. I will do what all governments do, what makes government itself possible. I will borrow.

Montesquieu: This is what I wanted you to say. Certainly there are but few governments that do not have to borrow. Yet, they resort to such expedients with great caution. It would be immoral and dangerous to weigh down future generations with exorbitant burdens beyond the limits of any foreseeable resource. How are loans made? By issuing notes that support an obligation on the part of the government to pay interest at a rate proportionate to the amount of money lent out. For example, if the loan is 5 percent, the state at the end of twenty years has paid a sum equal to the borrowed capital. At the end of forty years, double that sum. At the end of sixty, triple. Notwithstanding this, there will remain the indebtedness for the full amount of the principal. It follows that if the state adds to its debt indefinitely, without taking any steps to pay it off, it would eventually make it impossible for it to borrow any more or cause it to fall into insolvency. The upshot of all this is easy to grasp and there isn't a country that doesn't recognize it. In this light, modern states wanted to set certain limitations to the increase in taxes. A scheme called a system of amortization was invented. It is truly admirable in its simplicity and mode of execution. A special fund was created whose resources are designed to redeem the debt in successive stages of payments. Every time the state borrows, it must contribute a certain sum of money to a sinking fund for the purpose of extinguishing the newly owed money over a given time period. The government is indirectly limited in such a scheme. This is the source of its ingenuity. Because of the requirements of amortization, the nation, in effect, says to the government: "Borrow if you must, but you must always make provision to fulfill the new obligation you contract in my name." If constantly required to amortize, borrowing will not be undertaken lightly. The nation will authorize only borrowing that is duly amortized.

Machiavelli: Why should I adopt such a scheme, I ask you? Tell me which states have sound amortization laws? Even in England they have been suspended. If we don't find them there, where are we to find them? What is done nowhere can't be done.

Montesquieu: I can assume that you won't have them, then?

Machiavelli: On the contrary. The scheme does have certain advantages. I will have such regulations and will certainly put the funds produced to good use.

When the budget is up for adoption, the money in the sinking fund could, from time to time, be accounted as revenue.

Montesquieu: And when the debt falls due, it will be accounted an expense?

Machiavelli: I can't swear to that. It all depends on circumstances. Of course, I will be very sorry if this financial arrangement does not proceed in an orderly way. My ministers will present the situation in a very dour manner. My God, when it comes to finances, I don't claim that my administration can't be criticized for certain things. But when a case is well presented, many things can be gotten away with. Don't forget that financial management is also to a large degree *a matter for the press.*

Montesquieu: What?

Machiavelli: Didn't you say that the very essence of a budget was the public scrutiny it allows?

Montesquieu: Yes.

Machiavelli: Aren't budgets accompanied by accounts, reports, and official documents of all sorts? What possibilities these public communications lend to the sovereign when he is surrounded by able men! I want my Minister of Finance to be perfectly clear in his use of statistics. Moreover, his literary style must be impeccably lucid.

It's good policy to repeat constantly the truism that "the management of public finances at the present time takes place in broad daylight."

This incontestable statement must be presented in a thousand ways. I want things written like this: "Our accounting system, the fruit of long experience, is distinguished by the clarity and verifiability of its procedures. It hinders abuses and allows no one, from the petty bureaucrat to *the chief of state himself,* to divert the most miniscule sum from its destination or to put it to improper use."

Or, take your own words. How might they be improved upon? It could be said that: "The excellence of the economic system rests on two foundations—*a system of accountability* and *public access to information.* By auditing and overseeing financial management, we make it impossible for even the most miniscule sums to enter the public coffers from the hands of the taxpayer and from there be transferred from one account to another. It will not be passed into the hands of state creditors without guaranteeing the legitimacy of its collection, the regularity of its movement, and the legitimacy of its use. We will see to it that the funds are audited by responsible officials, judicially overseen by irremovable judges, and finally sanctioned and accounted for by the legislature."

Montesquieu: O Machiavelli, you ridicule everything. But your ridicule has something hellish in it!

Machiavelli: You are forgetting where we are.

Montesquieu: You would defy heaven itself.

Machiavelli: Only God can fathom the heart.

Montesquieu: Shall we get back to the matter at hand?

Machiavelli: At the beginning of the fiscal year, the Comptroller of Finances will declare: "Up until now, nothing changes the estimates of the current budget. Without being overly optimistic, there are very good reasons to hope that, for the first time in many years, the budget, despite borrowings, will show no deficit. Such an enviable state of affairs, obtained in exceptionally difficult times, is the best indication that the increase in national income has not slowed."

Do you think that's well phrased enough?

Montesquieu: Go on.

Machiavelli: At this point, debt management, which you mentioned a short while back, will be addressed in the following terms. "Plans to pay off the debt will be carried out soon. If what is projected in this regard actually comes to pass, if the revenues of the state continue to increase, it is not impossible that, in the budget five years hence, the public debt will be liquidated because of a surplus of revenue."

Montesquieu: These are long-term hopes. But what if, after having promised to work out some schedule of debt cancellation, nothing is accomplished? What will you say?

Machiavelli: It will be said that the moment was not propitious. It will be necessary to wait a little longer. It is possible to go even further—respectable economists contest the real efficiency of sinking fund schemes. You must know about these theories. I can recall them for you.

Montesquieu: It's not necessary.

Machiavelli: These theories can be published in non-official journals, until they insinuate themselves into the public's consciousness and are finally openly avowed.

Montesquieu: What are you saying now? Earlier you had recognized the efficiency of amortization and exalted its benefits.

Machiavelli: But don't the fundamentals of all science change? Mustn't an enlightened government be open to the advances made in economics in this century?

Montesquieu: Nothing displays more effrontery. We'll leave aside debt management. After having been unable to keep any of your promises, when you find yourself overrun by expenses, after having predicted a surplus of revenue, what will you say?

Machiavelli: If need be, our state of affairs will be boldly acknowledged. This frankness does honor to a government and moves the people when it emanates from a mighty power. But on another level, my Minister of Finance will try to strip away all significance from statistics that indicate increasing expenses. He will say what is true: "When it comes to finances, experience demonstrates that a certain amount of overspending is not as serious as thought. New resources ordinarily arise in the course of a year, notably in the proceeds from this or that tax. In addition, a considerable portion of appropriations, not put to use, will be impounded."

Montesquieu: Will that ever happen?

Machiavelli: When it comes to finances, you know that there are certain cut-and-dried terms, stereotypic phrases, that have a great effect on the public, calm it and reassure it.

Thus, while artfully presenting this or that liability, something like the following is said. *"There is nothing exorbitant about this figure. It is not out of the ordinary. It conforms to preceding budget requests. Figures that later bear on our outstanding debt are very encouraging."* There is a bunch of similar expressions that I won't mention because there are other more important artifices to which I must call your attention.

First, in all official documents, it is necessary to insist on the theme of prosperity, increasing productivity, commercial activity, and a *constantly rising standard of living.*

The taxpayer is less affected by any imbalance in the budget when he is told such things. So magical is the effect of official documents on the mind of bourgeois blockheads that these things can be repeated ad nauseum without their ever challenging them. When the budget falls out of balance and, the following year, the public mind must be prepared for a certain shortfall, you have merely to publish an advance report to the effect that *next year the deficit won't be nearly so high.*

If the deficit proves lower than predicted, it will be presented as a real triumph. If higher, you merely say: *"The deficit is greater than predicted but was even more the preceding year.* On the whole, the situation is better. Less has been spent, although the circumstances have been particularly trying—war, scarcity, epidemics, unforeseen shortages of certain essentials, etc. But next year, increasing revenues will, in all probability, allow us to attain the long-desired goal of solvency. The debt will be reduced and *the budget correctly balanced.* Progress can be expected to continue. Barring extraordinary events, a balanced budget will be customary in our public finances as it is now our standard."

Montesquieu: This is high comedy. The standard will be customary indeed! It will never be attained. There will always be some extraordinary circumstance, some war, or some essential shortage somewhere.

Machiavelli: I'm not so sure there will be such crises. What is certain is that I will be the standard bearer of the nation's honor.

Montesquieu: That's the least you could do. If you win glory, that's no cause for rejoicing. In your hands, honor is only a means to power.

Twenty-First Dialogue

Machiavelli: I fear you have some prejudice against borrowing. It is a very useful practice in a number of ways. Whole families are made dependent on the government. Individuals are given an excellent investment opportunity. Contemporary economics recognizes that far from impoverishing the state, public debts enrich it. Allow me to explain how.

Montesquieu: That's not necessary. I am familiar with such theories. Because you are always speaking of borrowing and never repaying, I first would like to know to whom you will ask for such capital and for what purpose.

Machiavelli: Foreign wars are a great help in providing a rationale. For a large state to undertake a war, it might take about five hundred or six hundred million francs. Only one-half to two-thirds of such a sum need be spent. The rest finds its way into the treasury for domestic expenditures.

Montesquieu: Five hundred or six hundred million francs, you say! Where are these modern-day bankers who would loan a sum that, by itself, might equal the total wealth of certain states?

Machiavelli: You mean to say that you haven't gotten beyond such rudimentary notions of borrowing! Don't take offense but you are still in the dark ages of finance. We no longer borrow from bankers.

Montesquieu: From whom, then?

Machiavelli: When you are dealing with money merchants, you are dealing with a small number of people who frustrate competition by combining to insure high interest rates. It is far better to address yourself to all your subjects, the rich, the poor, artisans, manufacturers, anyone who has a coin at his disposal. The public is called upon to underwrite the debt. So that everyone may purchase government securities, they can be sold in very small shares, for ten francs up to a million, or even for five francs up to a hundred thousand. Shortly after the shares are issued, rumor has it that their value is rising and that they are going fast. Word spreads and there is a rush from all sides to purchase them. Things are at a fever pitch. In a few days the coffers of the treasury are overflowing. So much money comes in that places can't be found for it. Nevertheless, arrangements are made for accepting it, for if demand outstrips the supply of outstanding securities, it is then possible really to impress public opinion.

Montesquieu: How?

Machiavelli: Those who acted too late are given their money back. This is played up big in the press and orchestrated with dramatic flair. You may have to give back as much as two to three million. Judge for yourself how great an effect this will have on the public mind.

Montesquieu: As far as I can see, this trust is alloyed with an unbridled spirit of speculation. I've heard this scheme spoken about. But somehow everything that comes from you has a sinister and underhanded air. Be that as it may, you now have your hands full of money, but....

Machiavelli: I would have even more than you think. In modern nations, there are great banking institutions capable of directly lending the state one hundred to two hundred million francs at prime rates. Large cities can also make loans. In these states, there are other financial institutions such a savings banks and agencies to administer health plans and retirement funds. Normally, the state requires that their funds, which are immense (sometimes ranging from five hundred to six hundred million francs), be deposited in the public treasury, where they mix with the general fund, usually in return for small interest to the depositors.

Moreover, the government can raise money exactly like bankers. They issue readily negotiable bonds for a sum of two or three hundred million francs—negotiable I.O.U.'s, so to speak, which are quickly bought up before they fall due.

Montesquieu: Let me stop you here. You speak only of borrowing and these I.O.U.'s. Are you never concerned about paying back what you have borrowed?

Machiavelli: Let me remind you that the state's land can also be sold, if need be.

Montesquieu: Ah. Now you are beginning to sell yourself. Do you have any other way of financing your loans?

Machiavelli: I suppose it is about time I told you how debts are dealt with.

Montesquieu: You say *how debts are dealt with*. I wish you would be more precise.

Machiavelli: I use this expression because I think it is precise. Debts cannot always be paid off, but they do have to be dealt with. The vigor implied in the phrase is quite apt, for debts, like a formidable enemy, must "be dealt with."

Montesquieu: Well, how would you then "deal with them?"

Machiavelli: There are several ways. First, there is taxation.

Montesquieu: That is to say that the debts will be used to pay off the debts.

Machiavelli: You are speaking to me as an economist, not as a financier. What is valid for the one may not be for the other. With the proceeds from a tax, debts can be paid off. I know that taxes cause complaining. If resistance is met, I will try a different one or I might still be able to employ the same tax under a different name. You know that there is great art in filling the loopholes of what can be taxed.

Montesquieu: I imagine that you will soon find and fill them all.

Machiavelli: There are other things that can be done. There is what is called conversion.

Montesquieu: What's that?

Machiavelli: Conversion applies to the consolidated debt, that is, debt that accrues from the state issuing bonds. For example, bondholders can be told something like this: "Until today, I paid you 5 percent on your money, now I intend to only pay 4.5 percent or 4 percent. Agree to this change or immediately take back only the principal that you have lent me.

Montesquieu: But if the money is really given back, the procedure is not wholly dishonest.

Machiavelli: If they ask for it, it will be given back. But very few so situated would do so. Holders of such bonds are creatures of habit. Their funds are invested in the first place because they have confidence in the state. They prefer less interest and a secure investment. If everyone were to demand his money, it is obvious that the treasury would be in a fix. This never happens. In this way, several hundreds of millions of debt can be cancelled.

Montesquieu: Extracting such loans, no matter how it is defended, is an immoral expedient that always destroys public confidence.

Machiavelli: You don't know stockholders.

Here is another scheme that might be tried to finance the public debt. A short while ago I spoke to you of certain other funds, like savings accounts, that were at the state's disposal. The state is required to pay interest for the use of such monies, except when such investments are immediately redeemed. If, after managing such funds over a long period of time, the state cannot pay off these contributors, it can refinance such debt, postponing its due date.

Montesquieu: In effect, the state says to its depositors that temporarily it does not have the money it owes. It merely issues a new certificate of indebtedness.

Machiavelli: Exactly. It can refinance all its uncovered debts in just the same way—treasury bonds, debts owed to municipalities and banks. This applies to all debts that form a part of what is rather picturesquely called "the floating debt," that is, debts that have no fixed basis and which mature in the more or less distant future.

Montesquieu: These are strange ways of paying off the public debt.

Machiavelli: How can you blame me if I am only doing what others do?

Montesquieu: For sure, if everyone in fact does it, how can we hold Machiavelli blameworthy?

Machiavelli: I am only telling you a fraction of the schemes that could be employed. Far from dreading a policy that sees the national debt increase and constantly refinanced, I would want the entire public fortune tied to government bonds. I would have it so that cities, towns, and public authorities convert all their real estate and liquid capital into bonds. It is in the interest of my dynasty to promote these financial measures. Every last cent in my kingdom would depend on my continued existence.

Montesquieu: Isn't all this somehow fatally flawed? Aren't you directly bent on ruining yourself through ruining the state? Large bond markets exist in all countries of Europe, but backed by prudence, wisdom, and the probity of the government. The way you arrange your finances, your bonds would be spurned in foreign markets, and they would fall to the lowest value in those of your kingdom.

Machiavelli: What you say is just plain wrong. A glorious government like mine would enjoy great credit abroad. And vigor would overcome apprehensions at home. Moreover, I would not want the credit of my state to depend on the exaggerated fears of the most insignificant brokers. I would dominate the stock and bond market through the market itself.

Montesquieu: What now?

Machiavelli: I would have mammoth banking institutions ostensibly chartered to lend money to industrial enterprises but whose real purpose would be to bolster my bonds. These financial giants would be able to manipulate the markets at will. They would be able to sell four hundred or five hundred million francs worth of securities at any given moment. They could also relieve pressure on the markets by buying an equal amount of securities. What do you think of such a scheme?

Montesquieu: Your ministers, favorites, and mistresses will reap big profits through such institutions. Apparently, you will let your administration use state secrets to play in the money markets.

Machiavelli: What on earth are you saying?

Montesquieu: How else do you justify these institutions? You have used theory to obscure the real nature of your government. But in practice, it is all too evident. Your government will be unique in history. It will never be slandered.

Machiavelli: If anyone in my kingdom were to do so, he would disappear as if struck by a thunderbolt.

Montesquieu: Admittedly, it is difficult to argue with thunderbolts. You're really quite fortunate to have them in your arsenal. Are we finished with finances?

Machiavelli: Yes.

Montesquieu: It's quickly getting late.

Fourth Part

Twenty-Second Dialogue

Montesquieu: Before listening to you, I didn't really know about either *the spirit of the laws* or *the spirit of finances*. I am in your debt for having taught me both. You hold in your hands the greatest power in modern times—money. You can get nearly as much of it as you want. With such prodigious resources, you will undoubtedly do great things. It is finally the time to demonstrate *that good can come from evil.*

Machiavelli: That's exactly what I intend to demonstrate.

Montesquieu: Well, let's see.

Machiavelli: First, the greatest of my benefactions will be to bestow domestic peace upon my people. During my reign, malevolent passions are suppressed. *The good are encouraged and the wicked tremble!* To a country previously torn by factions, I bring liberty, dignity, and strength.

Montesquieu: Having changed so many other things, have you come so far as to change the meaning of words?

Machiavelli: Liberty does not mean license, any more than dignity and strength mean insurrection and disorder. My empire, peaceful at home, will be glorious abroad.

Montesquieu: How?

Machiavelli: I shall wage war in the four corners of the world. I shall cross the Alps, like Hannibal. I shall fight in India like Alexander, in Libya like Scipio. I shall go from the Atlas to the Taurus, from the shores of the Ganges to the Mississippi, from the Mississippi to the river Amur. The Great Wall of China will fall at the sound of my name. In Jerusalem, my victorious legions will defend the tomb of the Savior. In Rome, the vicar of Jesus Christ. In Peru, my legions will trample the dust of the Incas; in Egypt, the ashes of Sesostris; in Mesopotamia, those of Nebuchadnezzar. As the descendant of Caesar, Augustus, and

Charlemagne, I will avenge the defeat of Varus on the shores of the Danube; the rout of Cannes on the shores of the Adige; the Norman outrages on the Baltic.

Montesquieu: Please. Stop a moment and think. You're not up to avenging the defeats of all the military leaders of history. Of Louis XIV, Boileau once said: *Great king cease your conquering or I cease writing.* I won't even compare you to Louis because it wouldn't do you justice. I grant that no hero of antiquity or modern times could rank with you.

But that's not the question. War in itself is an evil and in your hands it serves to maintain a still greater evil—servitude. But where in all this is the good that you promised to bring about?

Machiavelli: I'm not being evasive here. Glory is itself a great good. It is the most formidable asset. All other assets accrue to the sovereign who has glory. He is the terror of neighboring states and the arbiter of Europe. Whatever you might say about the worthlessness of victories, strength never abdicates its rights, and therefore this sovereign's power prevails and is invincible. Someone may pretend that wars are fought for ideals and make a display of disinterestedness, but one fine day he ends up seizing a coveted province and imposing tribute on the conquered.

Montesquieu: But in a world such as you describe, when the opportunity offers itself, such action is perfectly all right. Otherwise the military profession would be exceedingly foolish.

Machiavelli: Exactly! See, our ideas are beginning to come a bit closer together.

Montesquieu: Yes, like the Atlas and the Taurus. Let's see the other great features of your reign.

Machiavelli: I'm not as disdainful as you seem to be of likening my reign to that of Louis XIV. I would have more than one trait in common with that monarch. Like him, I would erect gigantic buildings. However, my ambition would outstrip his and that of the most celebrated potentates. I would want to show the people that a monument whose construction used to require centuries could be built by me in a few years. The palaces of my predecessors would fall under the wrecker's ball in order to raise them again in new, modernized forms. I would destroy entire cities in order to reconstruct them according to more regular plans and to obtain beautiful views. You can't imagine the extent to which buildings attach people to monarchs. It could be said that they easily forgive destruction of their laws provided that they are built houses. Moreover, you will see in a moment that building projects serve several particularly important objectives.

Montesquieu: After buildings, what will you do?

Machiavelli: You're going pretty fast. The number of great actions is not limitless. From the time of Sesostrus, to Louis XIV, to Peter the First, haven't the two principal marks of great reigns always been war and buildings?

Montesquieu: True, but still there have existed absolute sovereigns who were concerned with providing good laws, improving morals, and introducing simplicity and decency. Some were concerned with financial regulations and a well-structured economy and intended to leave a legacy of order, peace, lasting institutions—sometimes, even liberty.

Machiavelli: Oh! All that will be accomplished. You yourself see something good in absolute sovereigns.

Montesquieu: Alas! Not very much. But try to prove the contrary. Tell me of the good you'll do.

Machiavelli: I would prodigiously stimulate the spirit of enterprise. My reign would be one of commerce. I would launch speculation upon a new and hitherto unknown course. My administration would unfetter certain restrictions. I would free a number of industries from regulation. Butchers, bakers, and theatrical impressarios would be free.

Montesquieu: Free to do what?

Machiavelli: Free to bake bread, free to sell meat, free to put on theatrical productions without official permission.

Montesquieu: I don't see what's such a big deal about that. Free enterprise is a right taken for granted among modern peoples. Don't you have anything better to teach me?

Machiavelli: The people's lot in life would be my constant concern. My government would find them work.

Montesquieu: It would be better to let the people find work for themselves. Political power does not have the right to make a play for popularity with its subject's money. The public revenues are a collective contribution that must be used only for the general welfare. When the working classes habitually rely on the state, they degenerate. They lose their energy, their vitality, and their intellectual skills. Being paid by the state casts them into a kind of servitude from which they cannot rise except by destroying the state itself. Your building projects will consume enormous sums in nonproductive expenditures. They make capital scarce, kill small industry, and destroy credit for lower levels of society. Starvation is the consequence of all your schemes. Economize and you can build later. Govern with moderation and justice, restrict the scope of your government as far as possible, and the people will have nothing to ask of you because it will have no need of you.

Machiavelli: What cold indifference you show to the wretchedness of the people! The principles of my government are quite different. My heart goes out to the most insignificant of our poor, suffering creatures. I am indignant when I see the few rich procure pleasures beyond the reach of the many. I will do everything I can to ameliorate the material conditions of workers, laborers, and those who are bent under the weight of social necessity.

Montesquieu: Very well, then begin by giving them the funds you reserve for the salaries of your great dignitaries, your ministers, your emissaries and ambassadors. Retain for them the largess that you thoughtlessly lavish on your pages, courtesans, and mistresses.

Better yet, dispose of those sovereign trappings whose sight is an affront to the equality of men. Rid yourself of the titles of Majesty, Highness, and Excellency that pierce the ears of the proud like steel. Call yourself protector, like Cromwell, but follow the Acts of the Apostles. Go live in the cottage of the poor, like Alfred the Great. Sleep in hospitals and stretch out on the bed of the diseased like the saintly Louis. It's too easy to perform acts of evangelic charity when one's life is spent on sumptuous couches with beautiful women, when, upon going to bed and arising, great personages are eager to help you into or out of your shirt. Be a father of a family and not a despot, a patriarch and not a prince.

If this role does not suit you, be the leader of a democratic republic. Grant liberty. Infuse it into the public mind if that's your inclination. Be Lycurgus, be Agesilaus, be Gracchus. But I don't see the value of this slack civilization where everyone bows and becomes pale in the presence of the prince, where all minds are cast in the same mold and all souls are made uniform. I can understand aspiring to reign over men but not automatons.

Machiavelli: What an overwhelming flood of eloquence. Governments are overturned by such talk.

Montesquieu: Alas! You have but one concern—preserving yourself. It is a simple matter to put your love of the public good to the test. The people who elected you would only have to express its will by asking you to descend from the throne in the name of the state's salvation. Then it would be obvious to all.

Machiavelli: What a bizarre request! Obviously, it's for its own good that I would oppose such a request.

Montesquieu: What do you know about the public good? If the people are above you, by what right do you subordinate their will to yours? If you are freely accepted by the people, even if their choice is dictated by necessity and not justice, why do you place so much faith in force and nothing in reason? I count you among those rulers who last but for a day.

Machiavelli: A day! I will reign my whole life and my descendants perhaps after me. I have revealed my political, economic, and financial system. Do you want to know the final way by which I will sink the roots of my dynasty into the depths of the earth?

Montesquieu: No.

Machiavelli: You refuse to listen to me. You are vanquished—you, your principles, your school, and your country.

Montesquieu: Since you insist, speak, but let this conversation be the last.

Twenty-Third Dialogue

Machiavelli: I won't respond to any of your oratorical outbursts. Rhetorical excesses are out of place here. Isn't it madness to say to a sovereign: "Would you please descend from your throne for the happiness of the people?" Moreover, to say to him: "Since you are a creature of popular will, abide by changes in the public mood. Be willing to have your fate publicly debated." Is this conceivable? Isn't self-defense the first law of every constituted power, not only out of self-interest, but also in the interest of the people it governs? Haven't I paid the greatest possible homage to modern principles of equality? After all, isn't a government based on universal suffrage the expression of the will of the greatest number? You will tell me this principle is destructive of public liberties. What can I do about it? When this principle has penetrated the public mind, do you know how to uproot it? And if it can't be uprooted, do you know how to realize it in the great European societies of today other than by a single man? You are too strict regarding the ways of governing. Show me some other way executive power can be employed. If there is no alternative to absolute power, tell me how it can escape certain drawbacks that necessarily follow from its principle.

No, I am not a Saint Vincent de Paul. My subjects need not an evangelic soul, but a strong arm. I am not an Agesilaus, a Lycurgus, or a Gracchus because I am dealing neither with Spartans nor Romans. I am in the midst of voluptuous societies, where a passion for pleasure and war go hand in hand, where people, transported by power and sensuality, no longer recognize divine authority, paternal authority, or religious restrictions. Did I create the world in which I live? I am as I am because it would disintegrate even more quickly if it were left to itself. I control this society through its vices because it only presents me with vices. If it had virtues, I would employ them.

Some austere and principled individuals criticize my power. But can they fail to recognize the real services I provide them, my genius, and even my grandeur?

I am the revolutionary arm, the sword that counters a sense of destruction that is in the air. I harness the mad forces that are, at end, driven by brute instincts, ravishing all in their path under the veneer of principle. If I discipline these forces, if I stop their spread in my country, if only for a century, would I not deserve to be honored? Couldn't I even claim the gratitude of European states that turn their eyes toward me as toward Osiris, who alone has the power to captivate these frenzied masses? Look up to the man who bears on his countenance the fatal mark of human destiny and bow down before him.

Montesquieu: Avenging angel, grandson of Tamerlane, though you reduce the people to Helots, you can't prevent free souls from rising somewhere. They will defy you, and their contempt would suffice to preserve those rights of the human conscience that God has rendered invisible.

Machiavelli: God protects the strong.

Montesquieu: Please, forge the last links of the chain you have been fashioning. Forge them together firmly. Use anvil and hammer. You can do anything. God protects you. He himself guides your fate.

Machiavelli: It's hard for me to understand the animus behind your words. Am I really so harsh when I embrace, not violence, but self-effacement as my political end? Rest assured then, I bring you more than one unexpected consolation. Just let me take a few more precautions that I think are necessary for my security. Enveloped with the protection they afford me, you will see that a prince has nothing to fear from events.

Whatever you say, our writings have more than one thing in common. I think that a person who wishes to be a complete despot cannot dispense with reading you. So, it was well said in *The Spirit of the Laws* that an absolute monarch must have a large praetorian guard.* That's good advice. I shall follow it. My guard will be about one-third of the effective strength of the army. I am a great advocate of conscription, which is one of the finest inventions of the French genius. But I believe that this practice must be perfected. I shall try to keep under arms the greatest possible number of those who have completed compulsory service. I think this can be done by clamping down on the buying and selling of military obligations, a practice that occurs in many states, even in France. I would suppress this hideous practice as it is now conducted. I myself would honestly engage in it by establishing a monopoly and creating a military endowment fund out of its proceeds. Those who would want to devote themselves exclusively to a military career would then be lured by money to serve and to continue in the service.

Montesquieu: For all intents and purposes, you want to establish a kind of mercenary force within your country!

Machiavelli: Yes, partisan spite might say something like that. But my suggestion is motivated only by the good of the people and also by an additional interest in my own preservation—very legitimate—that constitutes the common good of my subjects.

---

* *The Spirit of the Laws* X 15.

Let's go on to other subjects. You may be surprised that I am going to return to the subject of building. I warned you that we would come back to it. You'll see the political motive behind the vast system of building that I undertook. I will put an economic theory into practice that has had disastrous consequences in certain European states. This theory looks to providing permanent work for the working classes. My reign promises them a salary indefinitely. If I die, and my system is abandoned, no more work. The people would strike and mount an assault on the richer classes. Open revolt follows. Productivity would nosedive, debts would be canceled, and insurrection would spread to neighboring states. Europe would be aflame. I pause. Wouldn't the privileged classes, which quite naturally fear for their fortunes, closely join ranks with the working classes to maintain either my person or my dynasty? Additionally, wouldn't the great powers join together to support me out of a shared interest in a tranquil Europe?

As you can see, this subject of building, which appears so trivial, is really of colossal importance. Given the ends this policy serves, sacrifices must not be spared. Have you noticed that almost all my political reforms simultaneously serve economic goals? This is the case once again. I will set up a fund for public works, endowed with several hundred million francs that will stimulate construction all over my kingdom. You must have guessed my objective. It will provide me with a worker's *Jacquerie* and be turned into another army that I need against factions. But this proletarian mass that I control must not turn against me if some day they are without bread. The building projects themselves will guard against this. You see, it is characteristic of my plans that each simultaneously serves multiple purposes. The worker who builds for me will also build the means of defense that I need against him. Without knowing it, he drives himself from the center of the city proper where his presence disturbs me. He makes the success of street revolutions forever impossible. The upshot of these great building projects is actually to restrict the area where the artisan lives. He will be confined to suburbs because of a rise in the cost of living, due to an increase in rents. He will soon be forced to abandon even these. It will be almost impossible for those who live by daily labor to be able to live in my capital except in the outskirts. As a result, it will be impossible for insurrections to take place. It is only in neighborhoods bordering the seat of government that insurrection can take place. Of course this means that there will be an immense working population around the capital that can be fearsome if its anger is provoked. But the renovations that I would undertake would all be conceived according to a strategic plan, that is to say, they would allow for great avenues down which cannon could move from one end to the other. The ends of these great avenues would be linked to barracks and fortresses, full of arms, soldiers, and munitions. My successor would have to be an imbecilic dotard or a child in order to allow his being brought down by an insurrection. At the wave of his hand, a whiff of gunpowder could sweep the streets clear up to twenty leagues from the capital. But the blood that flows in my veins burns with vitality, and my race possesses all the signs of strength. Are you listening to me?

Montesquieu: Yes.

Machiavelli: You do understand that I don't intend to make daily life difficult for the working population of the capital. I face a problem here, of course. But, the abundant resources at my government's disposal suggest a solution. It is to build vast cities for the common people where housing would be low priced and where the masses would find themselves united as in vast families.

Montesquieu: Traps!

Machiavelli: Oh! This denigrating mindset, this implacable partisan hatred doesn't miss a chance to run down my institutions. What you say will be repeated. So what? If this tool doesn't succeed, another will be found.

I must not abandon this subject of building projects without mentioning what might appear as a quite insignificant detail. But is there anything insignificant in politics? The many edifices that I construct must bear testimony to my fame—emblems, symbols, bas reliefs, and sculptures that call to mind certain subjects germane to my history. My coat of arms and my initials must ornament everything. In one place, there will be angels supporting my crown. Farther on, statues of justice and wisdom will bear my initials. These are matters of utmost importance.

Through symbols and emblems, the person of the sovereign is always present. One lives with him, his memory, and his thought. As continually falling drops of water dissolve even granite, so the sentiment of absolute sovereignty seeps into even the most rebellious spirits. For the same reason, I want my statue, my bust, and my portraits to be in all public buildings, especially in courtrooms. I want to be represented in royal costume or on horseback.

Montesquieu: Alongside the image of Christ.

Machiavelli: Certainly not, but facing him, for sovereign power is a reflection of divine power. In such a way, my image will be associated with that of providence and justice.

Montesquieu: Justice itself must wear your livery. You are not a Christian, but a Greek Byzantine emperor.

Machiavelli: I am a Roman, Catholic, and Apostolic emperor. For the same reasons as those just mentioned, I want my name, the royal name, to be given to public buildings of all sorts—Royal Tribune, Royal Court, Royal Academy, Royal Legislative Body, Royal Senate, Royal Council of State. As often as possible, the same designation will be given to bureaucrats, agents, and the official personnel who surround the government—King's Lieutenant, King's Archbishop, King's Jester, King's Judge, King's Lawyer. Finally, the word "royal" will be a sign of power for those men or things that bear it. Only my birthday will be a national and not a royal holiday. In addition, as far as possible, the streets, public places, and squares should bear the names which recall the historical events of my reign. Anyone that follows these prescriptions, even a Caligula or a Nero, is certain to impress himself into the memory of peoples and to transmit his fame to the most distant centuries.

I still have so much to say, but I must limit myself. *Who could say everything without a deadly boredom?* I come now to small matters. I am sorry for these things are perhaps not worthy of your attention, but, for me, they are vital.

It is said that the bureaucracy is a scourge of monarchic government. I don't believe it. Bureaucrats are thousands of servants who are naturally attached to the existing order of things. I have an army of soldiers, an army of judges, an army of workers. I want an army of government employees.

Montesquieu: You no longer take the trouble to justify anything.

Machiavelli: Do I have time?

Montesquieu: No, go on.

Machiavelli: In states that have been monarchies, and they all have been at least once, I have discovered a veritable frenzy for braid and ribbons. These things cost the prince almost nothing. He can make people happy and, even better, loyal with pieces of cloth and baubles of silver or gold. Really, it would take little for me to decorate everyone who requests it. A decorated man is a bought man. I would make these decorations tokens of devotion that enthuse my subjects. I really believe that I could buy off nine-tenths of my kingdom for this price. I would thereby satisfy as far as I could the egalitarian instincts of the nation. But mark this well. The more a nation as a whole prizes equality, the more individuals themselves have a passion for distinction. It would be a sorry commentary on my ruling skills not to take advantage of this course of action. Therefore, far from getting rid of titles, as you advised me, I would multiply them as I would honors. I want the etiquette of Louis XIV restored at my court, the domestic hierarchy of Constantine, austere diplomatic formality, and impressive ceremoniousness. Those are infallible ways to govern the minds of the masses. In the midst of all this, the sovereign appears as a god.

I am assured that in states that appear to embrace democratic ideas, the former monarchic nobility has lost nothing of its prestige. My chamberlains would be gentlemen of the oldest stock. Many ancient names would certainly be extinct. But by virtue of my absolute power, I would revive them through titles. At my court, the greatest names of history since Charlemagne would be found.

These ideas might appear bizarre to you, but I can assure you that they will do more for the consolidation of my dynasty than the wisest laws. Worship of the prince is a kind of religion and his worship, like all other religions, involves contradictions and mysteries beyond reason.* Each of my acts, howsoever seemingly incomprehensible, proceeds from a calculation whose sole aim is my security and that of my dynasty. Moreover, as I say in *The Prince*, the really difficult thing is to acquire power, but it is easy to preserve it. Basically, all that is needed is to eliminate whatever harms it and introduce whatever protects it. The essential feature of my politics, as you can see, has been to make myself indispensable.☐ I have destroyed as many intermediary powers as was necessary so that nothing could proceed without me, so that the very enemies of my power tremble at the thought of overturning it.

What remains for me to do is merely develop the moral premises inherent in my institutions. My reign is a reign of pleasure. Surely you won't forbid me to cheer my people by games and festivals. This will help soften manners. It cannot hide the fact that money is the predominant concern of the century. The people's needs have doubled. Luxury ruins families. Everywhere material pleasures are sought. A sovereign would have to be out of touch with his times not to know how to turn to his advantage this universal passion for money and this sensual ardor that today consumes men. Misery squeezes them as if caught in a vice. Luxury inspires them. Lasciviousness drives them. Ambition devours them. They are mine. But if I speak in this way, at bottom it is the interest of my people that guides me. Yes, I shall make good emerge from evil. I shall exploit materialism for the sake of harmony and civilization. I shall extinguish the political passions of men by placating their ambitions, covetousness, and material needs. I intend to have for servants of my reign those who, under previous governments, made the most noise about liberty. The most austere virtues are like Gioconda's wife. All that is necessary is always to double the price of defeat. Those who will turn down money will not turn down honors. Those who will turn down honors will not turn down money. In seeing those who are believed to be most pure fall one by one, public opinion will grow so weak that it will end up abdicating completely. Really, what cause will there be for complaint? I will be harsh only in what relates to politics. This passion alone will be suppressed. I will even secretly favor other passions by a thousand secret channels open to absolute power.

Montesquieu: Having destroyed the political conscience of men, you are about to destroy their moral conscience. You have killed society, now you murder man. Would to God that your words were heard on earth. They would strike ears as the most brilliant refutation of your own doctrines.

Machiavelli: Let me finish.

---

* *The Spirit of the Laws* XXV 2.
☐ *The Prince* IX.

Twenty-Fourth Dialogue

Machiavelli: I have only to sketch certain particulars concerning my way of acting and certain character traits that give my government its final countenance.

In the first place, I want my scheme to be impenetrable even to those who are closest to me. In this regard, I would be like Alexander VI and the Duke of Valentinois. There was a saying about Alexander VI at the court of Rome, "that he never did what he said," and about the Duke of Valentinois, "that he never said what he did." I will reveal my plans only when I issue the order for their execution and I would give my orders only at the last moment. Borgia never did it any other way. His ministers themselves knew nothing and everyone around him was always kept guessing. I have a hunter's patience. When I see my prey, I look away from it, and when it is in my reach, I turn suddenly and pounce on it before it has time to utter a cry.

You would not believe what prestige such a power of dissimulation gives a prince. When it is combined with rigorous action, he is enveloped in a superstitious reverence. His counselors ask themselves in hushed tones what he will think of next. The people place confidence only in him. To them, he personifies providence whose ways are inscrutable. When the people see him pass, they are prompted by an instinctive fear to wonder what his nod could mean. Neighboring states are constantly in fear and shower him with signs of deference because they never know from one day to the next if some enterprise is about to be launched against them.

Montesquieu: You maintain power over your people by keeping them under foot. However, if you deceive the states with which you deal in the same way you deceive your subjects, their combined strength will soon wipe you out.

Machiavelli: You're getting me off the track. I'm only concerned here with domestic politics, but if you want to know one of the principal ways to check the combined hatred of foreigners, here it is. It's understood that I reign over a powerful kingdom. Among neighboring states, I would search out a large country in decline that aspires to rise again. Through some general war, I would raise it to its former greatness, as has happened to Sweden and Prussia, and might one day happen to Germany or Italy. This country would thrive only at my sufferance, would only be an emanation of my being, and would provide me with 300,000 more men against armed Europe for as long as I live.

Montesquieu: And what about the safety of your state? You have raised a rival power on your borders that will sooner or later be an enemy.

Machiavelli: I look to my own preservation first and foremost.

Montesquieu: Then you are not even concerned about the future destiny of your kingdom?

Machiavelli: Who said that? When I provide for my own welfare, am I not providing for the welfare of my kingdom?

Montesquieu: The sketch of your royal countenance is becoming more and more clear. I want to see it in finished form.

Machiavelli: Then please don't interrupt me.

A prince, no matter how intelligent, won't always find the necessary spiritual resources within himself. One of the greatest talents of a statesman consists in making use of advice from those around him. Brilliant opinions are often found in his entourage. Therefore, I would call my council together very often. I would have it debate the most important questions in my presence. When the sovereign distrusts his own instincts or does not have rhetorical skills to disguise his true thought, he must remain silent or speak only to provoke further discussion. When a council is well chosen, the correct course of action for a given situation is almost always formulated in one way or another. A member of the council who had tentatively offered his opinion might be quite astonished the next day to see him take it up and act on it.

You can see in my institutions and my actions the attention I always pay to creating certain effects. It's as important in words as well as deeds. The real test of this skill is to create belief in one's sincerity when one is full of deceit. My schemes will not only be impenetrable; my words will always signify the opposite of what they seem to indicate. Only the initiated will be able to penetrate the meaning of certain words that from time to time I will utter on high. When I say: my *reign stands for peace*, it means there will be war. When I make a *moral* appeal, it means that I am going to use force. Are you listening to me?

Montesquieu: Yes.

Machiavelli: You have seen that my press has a hundred voices that speak constantly of the grandeur of my reign and of the enthusiasm of my subjects for their sovereign. At the same time, it puts in the mouths of the people the opinions and ideas, and even the forms of speech by which they communicate them. You have also seen that my ministers constantly impress the public with incontestable evidence of their accomplishments. As for me, I will rarely speak— perhaps only once a year, and now and then on great occasions. Each of my appearances would then be welcomed as an event, not only in my kingdom but also throughout Europe. A prince whose power is based on democratic foundations must craft his language in a popular idiom. If need be, he must not shrink from speaking like a demagogue, for, after all, he represents the people and must have their passions. When the occasion warrants, he must show proper solicitude, indulge in certain flatteries and certain demonstrations of sensibility. It matters little that these techniques appear base or puerile in the eyes of the world. The people will not look so closely, and the sought-after effect will be produced.

In my book, I advise the prince to take for a model some great man from the past in whose footsteps he must follow insofar as possible.* Even today, these imitations of historical figures have a great effect on the masses. Such a prince is enlarged in their imagination. In his lifetime, he is granted that place which posterity is reserving for him. Besides, in the history of great men are found comparisons, useful hints, and sometimes even identical situations from which valuable lessons can be drawn. All great political lessons are contained in history. When a prince finds a great man to whom he is somewhat analogous, he can do still more. You know that people love a prince to have a cultivated mind, a taste for letters, even to have talent himself. Well, the prince could not put his leisure to better use than by writing, say, the history of the great man of the past whom he has taken for a model. An austere philosophy might condemn such things as frivolous. When the sovereign is strong, he is excused. Such pursuits even give him an indefinable attractiveness.

Moreover, certain weaknesses, and even certain vices, serve the prince as much as virtues. You have already seen the truth of these observations in the use that I have sometimes had to make of duplicity and violence. For example, it should not be believed that the vindictive character of the sovereign harms him. Quite the contrary. While it is often opportune to employ clemency or magnanimity, at certain moments, his anger must be brought to bear in a terrifying manner. Man is the image of God, and the Divinity avails Himself of severe blows as well as mercy. When I have decided to destroy my enemies I will crush them until there remains nothing but dust. Men avenge only slight injuries. They are powerless against great ones.[□] That's what I assert in my book. The prince has only to choose the instruments of his wrath. He will always find judges ready to sacrifice their consciences to his projects of vengeance or hatred.

Have no fear that the people will ever be roused by the blows I deliver. First, they like to feel a strong arm in command. Next, they naturally hate what is elevated and instinctively rejoice when what is above them is struck down. And yet, perhaps you are not aware how quickly people forget.

In the early Roman Empire, Tacitus reports that victims welcomed torture with an inexplicable joy. You do understand that nothing similar happens in modern times. Manners have become quite soft. So now quite light punishments

---

* *The Prince* XIV.

[□] *The Prince* III.

are sufficient—proscription, imprisonment, and the forfeiture of certain civil rights is all that is needed. To achieve sovereign power, it is true that blood had to be spilt and many rights violated. I repeat that all this will be forgotten. The smallest gesture of the prince, acts of good will on the part of his ministers or his agents, will be welcomed with expressions of the greatest gratitude.

If one must punish with an unyielding vigor, it is necessary to be prompt and generous with rewards. This I would never fail to do. Whoever renders a service to my government would be rewarded on the very next day. Positions, distinctions, and the greatest honors would constitute a hierarchy of rank for those who effectively carry out my policy. In the army, in the courts, in all public posts, advancement would be calculated according to the extent of agreement with and the degree of zeal for my government. You are silent.

Montesquieu: Continue.

Machiavelli: I return to a consideration of certain vices and even certain eccentricities that I think are necessary for the prince. Handling power is an awesome task. However skilled a sovereign may be, however penetrating his sight, and however vigorous his resolve, fortune still plays a role in his existence. He has to be superstitious. Don't think that this is of no consequence. In the life of the prince, there are situations so difficult and moments so grave that human prudence no longer suffices. In those instances, decisions are almost a matter of rolling dice. The course of action I recommend and would follow in crises is to line yourself up with famous historical dates and appropriate anniversaries, placing this or that bold decision under the auspices of a day when a victory was won or a surprise attack successfully carried out. I must tell you about another great advantage in being superstitious. People identify with this turn of mind. These attempts at playing to destiny often bear fruit and they must also be employed when success is certain. The people, which only judges by results, gets used to believing that there is a correspondence between each of the sovereign's acts and certain celestial signs, that historical coincidences force the hand of fortune.

Montesquieu: When you come right down to it, you are a gambler.

Machiavelli: Yes, I have unheard-of good fortune. And I have such a sure hand and so fertile a brain that fortune has no role to play.

Montesquieu: Since you are portraying yourself fully, you must still have other vices or other virtues to show off.

Machiavelli: I hope that you'll pardon licentiousness. A sovereign can put the passion for women to use much more than you might imagine. Henry IV owed a part of his popularity to his incontinence. Men are so made that they are pleased to find this penchant in those who govern them. Indulging in moral improprieties has been fashionable in all times, a gallant trait in which the prince must outdo his peers, as he outdoes his soldiers before the enemy. These are French ideas and I don't think that they will prove too offensive to the author of *The Persian Letters*. I don't want to carry such vulgar considerations too far. However, I can't dispense with telling you that the most substantial benefit from the prince's behavior is to win the sympathy of the more beautiful half of his subjects.

Montesquieu: You're not going to compose madrigals, are you?

Machiavelli: One can be serious and gallant. You yourself provide the proof. I will not retreat from my proposition. The influence of women on the public mind is considerable. For political reasons, the prince is condemned to be attentive to women, even if basically he cares little for it. But such a case will be rare.

I can assure you that if I carefully follow the rules I have just outlined there will be little concern about liberty in my kingdom. The people will have a vigorous sovereign, lusty, full of the spirit of chivalry, and adroit in all athletics. He will be loved. Austere people will not be able to do anything about it. They will be swept up in the wave. What's more, nonconformists will be proscribed and isolated. People will put no trust in their character or in their disinterestedness. They will be thought malcontents who want to be bought off. If once or twice I show no favor to a certain talent, it will be spurned everywhere. Consciences will be casually tread upon. But basically, I would be a moral prince. Certain limits must be set up. I will respect the public's sense of shame when it shows it wants to be respected. I will remain unblemished in all this, for the odious aspects of administration will be assigned to others. The worst that might be said of me is that I am a good prince with a bad entourage, but that I want the good, genuinely want it, and will always do it when it is pointed out to me.

If you only knew how easy it is to govern when one has absolute power. There is no opposition and no resistance. I have the luxury of time to carry out my plans and to correct my mistakes. Facing no opposition, I can devote myself to the happiness of the people, which is my constant concern. I can assure you that boredom will not exist in my kingdom. A thousand different objects will constantly occupy people's minds. I shall spread before the people the spectacle of my lavish trappings and the display of my court. Grand ceremonies will be orchestrated. I shall lay out gardens. I shall entertain kings. I shall attract ambassadors from the remotest lands. At times, there will be rumors of war. At other times, talk will concentrate on complicated matters of diplomacy for months on end. I shall even go so far as to satisfy the obsession for liberty. The wars that will occur in my reign will be undertaken in the name of the liberty of men and the independence of nations. And while people are acclaiming me along the way, I will secretly whisper in the ears of absolute monarchs: Have no fear. I am with you. I wear a crown like you and I'm anxious to keep it. *I embrace European liberty but only to stifle it.*

Perhaps there does exist one thing that could compromise my fortunes—the day when all sides recognize my politics as disingenuous and that all my acts are a product of calculation.

Montesquieu: Who will be so blind not to see that?

Machiavelli: My people as a whole, except for a few coteries of little consequence. Besides, compared to them, I have brought into being around me a formidable school of political men. You can't believe the extent to which Machiavellianism is contagious and how easy many of its precepts are to follow. In all branches of government there will be veritable miniature Machiavellis, who will trick, dissimulate, and lie with an imperturbable sangfroid. Truth will not be able to come to light anywhere.

Montesquieu: As I see it, Machiavelli, you have been jesting from beginning to end in this conversation and I regard your irony in this regard as your most impressive achievement.

Machiavelli: Irony! You are quite mistaken if you think so. Don't you see that I have spoken candidly and that it is the terrible violence of the truth that colors my account? And you see that as irony!

Montesquieu: Surely, you've finished.

Machiavelli: Not yet.

Montesquieu: Then finish.

Twenty-Fifth Dialogue

Machiavelli: I shall reign for ten years under these conditions without changing anything in my legal code. Success is assured only at this price. Nothing, I repeat, absolutely nothing must make me change during this period. The cover of the cauldron must be made of iron and lead. During this time, the work of destroying factious spirits is carried out. Perhaps you believe the people are unhappy and that they complain. Ah! I could be held to account if that were so. But when the springs are most tightly coiled and when I weigh most heavily on the chests of my people, here is what will be said: "We only got what we deserved. Let's put up with it."

Montesquieu: You are quite blind if you construe that as a defense of your reign and if you don't understand these utterances as indicating a powerful longing for the past. Those stoic words foretell the day of your downfall.

Machiavelli: Your words disturb me. O.K. The time has come to uncoil the springs. I am going to grant liberties.

Montesquieu: Oppression by you, even granting all its excesses, is a thousand times better. Your people will respond: "Keep what you have taken."

Machiavelli: Ah! I clearly see an implacable partisan hatred at play here. It concedes nothing to its adversaries—nothing. It doesn't even acknowledge benefits.

Montesquieu: No, Machiavelli. I grant you nothing, nothing! The immolated victim receives no benefits from his executioner.

Machiavelli: Ah! How easily I can read the minds of my enemies in this regard. They flatter themselves in hoping that the coiled energies that I have compressed will sooner or later launch me into space. The fools! They will really understand me only in the end. In politics, the slightest pretext of danger can serve to play into the greatest possible repression. And such pretexts will be found.

Surely, I won't grant significant liberties, but you have to grasp the extent to which absolutism has already penetrated the public mind. I bet that at the first mention of these liberties, dreadful rumors will circulate about me. My ministers and counselors will cry out that I have abandoned the rudder, that all is lost. I shall be implored in the name of the state and the country not to grant them. The people will say: "What's he thinking about? His genius is no longer in evidence and he's losing his grip." The lukewarm will say: "He's finished." Those who are full of hate will say: "He's dead."

Montesquieu: And they will be right. A modern writer has spoken a great truth: "Do you want to ravish men of their rights? One must do nothing by halves. What is left them will be used to reclaim what has been stolen. The hand that is left free frees the other from its chains."

Machiavelli: That's a fine thought and very true. I know that I am quite vulnerable. You have to see that you treat me unjustly, for I love liberty more than is said. A short while ago you asked me if I could act disinterestedly and sacrifice myself for my people by relinquishing the throne, if need be. You now have my answer. I could relinquish it as a martyr.

Montesquieu: You're growing quite soft. What liberties would you grant?

Machiavelli: On the first day of each year I would allow my legislature to express its wishes to me in a petition.

Montesquieu: But since the great majority of the lower chamber is devoted to you, what will you receive but thanks and tokens of admiration and love?

Machiavelli: Well, yes, but aren't these tokens genuine?

Montesquieu: That's the only liberty you'll grant?

Machiavelli: But this first concession is significant, whatever you may say. However, I will not rest there. In Europe today, there is a movement of thought away from centralization, not among the masses but among the enlightened classes. I shall decentralize. That is to say, I shall give my provincial governors the right to settle many of the petty local questions that used to be handled by my ministers.

Montesquieu: You only make tyranny more unpalatable if the local level counts for nothing.

Machiavelli: Behold the dangerous impatience of those who clamor for reform. Prudent steps must be taken along the path of liberty. However, I shall go one step further. I'll grant commercial liberties.

Montesquieu: You have already mentioned them.

Machiavelli: Industrial matters always concern me. I don't want it said that my laws are set against the people and prevent them from providing for their own subsistence. It is for this reason that I will present to the legislature laws whose purpose is to soften some of the more prohibitive provisions regarding the right of association. Moreover, my tolerant government will make this measure superfluous. Finally, given that we must remain armed, nothing will be changed in the law except its wording. Today there are deputies in the legislature who readily lend themselves to these innocuous stratagems.

Montesquieu: Is that all?

Machiavelli: Yes, but it's a lot, too much, perhaps. But I think I can rest assured. My army is enthusiastic; my courts are faithful; and my penal institutions function with the regularity and precision of all those powerful machines invented by modern science.

Montesquieu: So, you won't alter the laws regarding the press?

Machiavelli: You don't really expect that?

Montesquieu: Local legislation?

Machiavelli: Impossible.

Montesquieu: Voting matters?

Machiavelli: No.

Montesquieu: You won't alter the organization of the Senate or the legislature, change your domestic or foreign policy, or your economic and financial system?

Machiavelli: I shall only alter what I've mentioned. In a nutshell, I leave the period of terror behind and embark upon the path of tolerance. I can do this safely. I could even grant real liberties. You'd have to be completely bereft of political intelligence not to see that by this time my legislation has borne fruit. I've done what I said I would do. The character of the nation has changed. The trivial rights that I have granted are for me yardsticks by which I measure the depth of change. Everything is done. Everything is accomplished. Resistance is no longer possible. There is no more danger. None! And yet, I've given nothing away. You've said just as much. This is the effectual truth.

Montesquieu: Hurry up and finish, Machiavelli. May my spirit never encounter you again and may God erase from my memory the last trace of what I've just heard!

Machiavelli: Take care, Montesquieu. Before this moment lapses into eternity, you will anxiously try to trace my steps and the memory of this conversation will torment your soul eternally.

Montesquieu: Speak!

Machiavelli: All right, let's go on. You're acquainted with everything I've done. By means of these concessions to the liberal spirit of my time, I have disarmed partisan hatred.

Montesquieu: Ah! You continue to wear this hypocritical mask that has covered unspeakable crimes. Do you want me to leave this eternal darkness and to heap reproaches on you! Ah! Machiavelli. Your previous teaching had not degraded humanity to this extent! You did not conspire against conscience. You had not thought to so degrade the human soul that the Divine Creator Himself would no longer recognize it.

Machiavelli: True, I surpass even myself.

Montesquieu: Get out of here! Do not prolong this conversation another moment.

Machiavelli: Before those tumultuous souls over there have reached this dark ravine that separates us from them, I will have finished and you will not see me any more and will call for me in vain.

Montesquieu: Finish then. That will be expiation for the temerity that I've shown in accepting this unholy wager.

Machiavelli: Ah! Liberty! Behold the force with which you possess a few souls although the people despise you and console themselves with baubles. Let me illustrate with a very short anecdote. Dion relates that the Roman people were indignant toward Augustus because of certain very harsh laws that he had made. But as soon as he had the actor Piladus recalled and the seditious were banished from the city, discontent ceased.

There is my anecdote. Now here is the conclusion of an author whose eminence makes him worthy of citation. "Such a people feels tyranny more keenly when an actor is banished than when it is deprived of the protection of the laws."* Do you know who wrote that?

Montesquieu: It doesn't matter!

Machiavelli: Then you realize that you wrote it. I'm surrounded by base souls. What can I do about it? During my reign there will be no dearth of actors and they would have to behave quite badly for me to banish them.

Montesquieu: I don't know if you have quoted my words exactly. But here is a quotation I can vouch for. It will forever give the lie to your slanders against the people. "The character of the prince contributes as much to liberty as laws. Just as the laws can make men out of beasts and beasts out of men, so can the prince. If he loves free souls, he will have subjects. If he loves base souls, he will have slaves."□

That's my response and if I had to add anything to this quotation today, I

---

* *The Spirit of the Laws* XIX 2.
□ *The Spirit of the Laws* XII 27.

would say: "When public integrity is banished from the midst of courts, and when corruption flaunts itself indecently, it only penetrates the hearts of those near a bad prince. The love of virtue continues to live in the hearts of the people and the power of this principle is so great that if the bad prince disappears, it is in the very nature of things for integrity and liberty simultaneously to return to the operation of government."

Machiavelli: That is well said and quite straightforward. There's only one flaw in it. In the mind and soul of my people, I personify virtue. Even more, I personify *liberty* and also revolution, progress, the modern spirit, finally, all that is best at the core of contemporary civilization. I don't say that I shall be respected or loved, but I do say that I will be revered and adored. If I so wished, I could have monuments raised to me because I exert a fatal attraction for the masses. In your country, Louis XVI was guillotined, although he only desired the good of the people and wanted it with all the conviction and ardor of a genuinely honest soul. Several years before, monuments were raised to Louis XIV who cared less for the people than the least of his mistresses. He, with a slight nod of the head, would mow down the rabble while shooting dice with Lauzun. But I am more formidable than Louis XIV because my reign rests on popular foundations. I am Washington, Henry IV, Saint Louis, Charles the Wise. I select the kings you consider best in order to humor you. I am simultaneously king of Egypt and Asia. I am pharaoh; I am Cyrus; I am Alexander; I am Sardanapolus. When I pass by, I exalt the soul of the people. People run deliriously in my train. I am an object of idolatry. The father points me out to his son. The mother invokes my name in her prayers. The girl looks at me, sighs, and thinks that if only I might glance at her, perchance, she could lie for a moment in my bed. When the unfortunate are oppressed, they say: *if only the king knew.* When someone seeks revenge or hopes for help, they say: *the king will understand.* Moreover, I am never approached but when my hands are full of gold. It is true that there are those in my entourage who are harsh and violent and occasionally deserve a flogging. But things are necessarily so. Their hateful and spiteful character, their base cupidity, their debaucheries, their shameless prodigality, and their crass avarice provide a striking contrast with the sweetness of my character, my unpretentious demeanor, and my inexhaustible generosity. I tell you that my name will be invoked as if I were a god. When there are hailstorms, droughts, and fires, I rush up and the people throw themselves at my feet. They would bear me to heaven in their arms if God gave them wings.

Montesquieu: All of which would not prevent you from mowing them down at the faintest sign of resistance.

Machiavelli: That's true, but love does not exist without fear.

Montesquieu: Is this frightful fantasy finished?

Machiavelli: A fantasy! Ah! Montesquieu! How disillusioned you are! Tear up *The Spirit of the Laws*. Ask God to grant you oblivion as your eternal reward. Behold in full the terrible truth that you have already glimpsed. There is nothing fantastic in what I have just told you.

Montesquieu: What are you about to tell me?

Machiavelli: What I have just described—this mass of monstrous things before which the spirit recoils in fright, this work that only hell itself could accomplish—all this is done, exists and is prospering in the light of day, at this very hour, in that place on the globe that you have recently departed.

Montesquieu: Where?

Machiavelli: No. That would mean inflicting a second death on you.

Montesquieu: Ah! Speak, in the name of heaven!

Machiavelli: Well....

Montesquieu: What?

Machiavelli: The hour is past! Don't you see that the whirlwind is carrying me away?

Montesquieu: Machiavelli!

Machiavelli: Look! Do you recognize these souls passing nearby with their hands covering their eyes? It is they who were the glory and envy of the whole world. They are petitioning God on behalf of their fatherland!...

Montesquieu: Eternal God, what have you permitted!...

COMMENTARY

Part I

The Machiavelli-Montesquieu Debate

Chapter One

THE ESSENTIAL DIFFERENCES BETWEEN
MACHIAVELLI AND MONTESQUIEU

The *Dialogue in Hell* consists of four major parts. Part one contains the first seven dialogues. In the last of these, Machiavelli gives a "quick sketch" of his revolutionary regime. It is a fitting preface to the rest of the *Dialogue* as a whole, which elaborates the essential elements of a new despotism in detail. The present chapter will comment on the first three dialogues. The next chapter will comment on the remaining dialogues of Part One. Before turning to this textual analysis, a brief summary of the movement of the argument in Part One is in order.

In the first two Dialogues, Machiavelli and Montesquieu respectively present the fundamental principles of their political philosophies. This concludes with Machiavelli's assertion that despotism is an eternal possibility and Montesquieu's contrary assertion that the progress of history since his interlocutor's death has rendered despotism obsolete. The Third Dialogue begins a more elaborate discussion of Montesquieu's political science which is designed to counter the concentration of power that is the necessary and perhaps sufficient condition of tyranny. By the end of the Third Dialogue, we are made aware of a certain gap, not in Machiavelli's knowledge of history, but in that of Montesquieu, who is largely unaware of certain critical events since his own death. His ignorance of what had happened since 1847 crucially changes the whole direction of his conversation with Machiavelli. If we count the Seventh Dialogue as prefatory, this occurs literally in the center of Part One.

The next chapter of this study is devoted to a commentary on the Fourth through the Seventh Dialogues and begins with Machiavelli's initial assault on the political system just elaborated by Montesquieu. The Sixth Dialogue concludes in a "wager". Montesquieu is confident that his regime is proof against "Machiavellian" despotism, while Machiavelli claims that he can found such a regime, even granting liberal institutions and the most enlightened political conditions.

In the rest of the *Dialogue in Hell*, Machiavelli redeems his bet by describing a new political founding that supplants the liberal regime of Montesquieu. He proves the eternal possibilty of despotism but in the element of a totally new un-

derstanding of political things—what later chapters will show as essentially derived from the "Doctrine of Saint-Simon." A new political science and conception of history emerges in Machiavelli's discourse and it can be understood as
the counterpart of Montesquieu's political science, as elaborated in Part One.

The Encounter

The First Dialogue opens with an impressive demonstration of Machiavelli's
dialectical skill. He expresses his elation at finding Montesquieu, whom he has
assiduously sought out. To converse with "great men' whose "names have resounded throughout the universe" is more than ample compensation for the loss
of earthly existence which, in Machiavelli's case, proved so burdensome in
many particulars. Of all "illustrious persons," he would rather meet no one more
than "the great Montesquieu."

In repeating the epithet "great," Machiavelli returns the compliment of the illustrious author of *The Spirit of the Laws* who had indeed referred to the Florentine philosopher in that work as a "great man."[1] Montesquieu reacts to such a
seemingly gracious greeting with reserve. It is perhaps less an indication of Machiavelli's true feelings and more an example of "the language of courts" he put
to use as a Florentine diplomat. The fact that Montesquieu does not warm up to
this original entreaty is an indication of a quite understandable suspiciousness in
the face of such an enigmatic and ill-reputed personage.

It is a disconsolate Montesquieu that Machiavelli greets. The position in
which Montesquieu finds himself apparently has robbed him of former pleasures, chiefly glory. "The name 'great' belongs to no one here, O Machiavelli,"
he states with sighing resignation. Indeed, Montesquieu is so disconsolate that
he risks a breach of good manners. He denies greatness, not only to himself, but
also to anyone else in this hell, thereby in effect retracting the compliment he
paid Machiavelli while alive. He is somewhat surprised that Machiavelli could
relish a conversation under such circumstances, when there is nothing to exchange but "anguish and regrets." To say the least, Montesquieu does not share
Machiavelli's enthusiasm for any conversation.

Far from being a mere exercise in courtliness and engaging flattery, Machiavelli's greeting has served to sound out his interlocutor's frame of mind. Machiavelli learns that Montesquieu is not an eager conversationalist and that steps
must be taken to turn this reluctance around, if they are to profit in any way
from their encounter. He first must know the deeper causes of Montesquieu's
"anguish," and the question he frames is delicately designed to encourage a
fuller revelation of his interlocutor on this score. In a little while, we learn that
Machiavelli's knowledge of history is up-to-date, while Montesquieu is crucially
ignorant of the happenings since 1847. Nothing he has learned, apparently, has

prepared him for what follows this momentous date. Hidden from Montesquieu is the revolutionary breakdown of society, and the knowledge of what this imports directly bears on the question of the possibilities for despotism that becomes the substance of their conversation. The point is that Machiavelli initially masks in optimism his distressing knowledge of what has come to pass in contemporary Europe. He tests his interlocutor by asking how it is that such a renowned "philosopher" and "statesman" could speak so disconsolately. But before Montesquieu can answer, Machiavelli indicates, speaking for himself at least, that Montesquieu's attitude is groundless in either case.

To true philosophers, the passing of earthly existence, which Montesquieu regrets so much, is of little account. The truth of things, what really matters to such men, is deathless, and present circumstances offer certain advantages in its pursuit that are unavailable to mere mortals. Here, in the "domain of pure reason," a person may converse with the great minds of the past. Furthermore, one may meditate upon the affairs of the world, an engaging "spectacle to contemplate," "full of marvels," as related by the deceased who have descended to this hell. And such "marvels" are far from disquieting. Rather, they bespeak the unfolding "lessons of history" that vindicate "human rights." Insofar as the goal of the statesman is to secure these rights, Machiavelli shows Montesquieu that he especially should not be disconsolate or despairing. Moreover, since even "the void of death" could not break all the ties that attach us to earth, Montesquieu's statesmanlike role in history as "legislator of nations" is still acknowledged. For advancing the political art and so ameliorating the lot of his fellow man, no one so blessed by posterity can wait more confidently for final judgment.

Why then such "anguish and regrets" on Montesquieu's part? By implication, it must be for other than purely philosophical reasons or disinterested concern for mortals, in whose happiness he does not share at present. He seems to regret his loss of glory and personal celebrity, the full measure of which attaches to earthly existence. It certainly "belongs to no one here," where all are reduced by death to a miserable existence in this peculiar hell. In any case, a frank admission of such regrets would be unbecoming, smacking too much of human pride and vanity. Montesquieu does not like being put into a position of inferiority to Machiavelli, who appears more genuinely disinterested. However, it is the concern with glory that is uppermost in the Montesquieu's mind. He wonders how someone like Machiavelli, apparently so capable of lofty concerns and sentiments, can support the infamy of his reputation—what he facetiously calls "immense renown."

Montesquieu's response is noteworthy in a number of respects. Machiavelli has spoken, for his part, on the nature of present existence in a manner that invites commentary from his interlocutor. Given his expressed unhappiness, we might expect Montesquieu, for his part, to criticize the edifying picture of hell just described for him. Disembodied existence precludes material pleasures. But even the merits of the philosophic life, praised by Machiavelli, might appear questionable in such circumstances. The imminence of divine judgment might overshadow any pursuits, including the pleasures of the mind.

Moreover, had Montesquieu known of the most recent events in France, he would have questioned straight away the sanguine view of history that seemingly provides such edifying and interesting material for Machiavelli's contemplation. Yet, as we shall see, he essentially accepts this perspective and believes that history is inexorably moving toward the universal fulfillment of human rights. Montesquieu appears not only singularly complacent, he is perhaps not sufficiently philosophic. At least he lacks the dogged earnestness of his interlocutor in his search for conversation and enlightenment. He rests confident of his knowledge and sure in his faith in history. Machiavelli will address him accordingly.

In any event, we get neither the "philosophic" nor the "political" discussion Machiavelli tried to elicit. Instead, Machiavelli is called to justify himself. Their conversation cannot take place in any meaningful way if Machiavelli is in fact as his reputation depicts him. Montesquieu's suspiciousness must be dissipated. As we shall see, Machiavelli gets his philosophic and political dialogue. He turns what ostensibly begins as a personal defense into a testing of Montesquieu's deepest and dearest convictions and thereby cleverly succeeds in revealing his interlocutor more than himself.

The exchange to this point can be summarized as follows. Montesquieu has returned the courtly compliment of Machiavelli that opens their conversation with one that is caustically facetious. He hides his own desire for recognition and real regret at his loss of the world by feigning to admire Machiavelli's "modesty" in the face of his "immense renown." The subject suddenly changes from Montesquieu's fame to Machiavelli's infamy as "compliments" come to be understood by both as veiling barbed reproaches. Before Montesquieu might have to answer to loving reputation and the worldy trappings of glory and success too much, he accuses Machiavelli of shameless disregard of reputation that had him promoting despotism while truckling with tyrants. Machiavelli's "modesty" is really brazenness and his "renown" infamy.

Machiavelli begins his defense by himself attacking his interlocutor for a vulgar view which, full of "blind prejudice," makes the name Machiavelli synonymous with evil. Judging like "the crowd," he would hold Machiavelli responsible for all tyrannies. Far from truckling with tyrants, Machiavelli presents himself as having put his life, fortune, and honor on the line in defense of his fatherland and the advance of republicanism there. He even suffered torture at the hands of the Medici for remaining true to his cause. He expects a better judgment from the "great French publicist" while, as a last recourse, he appeals to Providence to correct the injustices he has suffered.[2]

Such an appeal is calculated to affect the Frenchman, who is shown in the *Dialogue* to be a staunch patriot himself. Montesquieu admits that the dichotomy between Machiavelli's life and thought has always been a puzzle to him.

How can the "servant of a republic" be the founder of a school that would "justify tyrannies' most heinous crimes?" he asks in sincere consternation.

Since the topic is broached, Machiavelli will give a most pleasing answer to Montesquieu. It confirms the view Montesquieu would like to hold of the Florentine, while it separates him from Machiavelli's "vulgar accusers." Montesquieu assumes he belongs among those who "know" Machiavelli's life and have "attentively read" his works. In fact he takes at face value what is only hypothetically offered as a defense. He mistakenly sees as candid a response that appeals to his vanity in confirming his own opinions regarding the "true" Machiavelli and his superiority to those who judge like "the crowd."

"What if I told you that the book was only the product of a diplomat's imagination?" Machiavelli asks. He goes on to explain that the book was never meant for publication. Therefore, the infamy it gained him was undeserved and unfortunate. Moreover, he indicates that in depicting political conditions in sixteenth century Italy, he was merely reflecting the standards of the times, not eternal maxims for politics—a line of defense that is not even complete when Montesquieu interrupts to congratulate him for such a frank avowal. In fact, this is what Montesquieu thought all along but it does Machiavelli "honor" to hear him dissociate his "real" self from the thoughts contained in *The Prince.* The politics of the times had "clouded" his "exalted mind." The book can be seen as the reflections of a diplomat, and should not be judged by the rigors of philosophy or political science. The skeptical regard of Montesquieu vanishes. He now can enthusiastically enter a conversation with one so maligned and misunderstood. At the precise moment Montesquieu opens up, Machiavelli retracts what Montesquieu found so pleasing and reassuring.

The Fundamentals of Machiavellian Thought

Machiavelli now attacks not only the vulgar conception of himself but also the more learned one espoused by Montesquieu and others, who have declared their confidence in having understood the Florentine. Far from a personalized account with limited historical applicability, his thinking is based on eternal truths, Machiavelli now forthrightly claims. Rejecting dialectics and the ancient philosophic approach identified with Socrates, he claims to join his interlocutor in putting forth a systematic account of human things, deduced from certain principles that are based on hard "facts," however unpleasant. Particular attention should be paid to Machiavelli at this point, which comes before the full measure of his interlocutor has been taken. The tack of the conversation changes in light of certain of Montesquieu's limitations, which are not yet known.

In what is perhaps his most forthright description of his intention, Machiavelli claims that his "only crime" was "to speak the truth to peoples as I did to kings"—not the "moral truth" or "the truth as it should be," but the "political truth" as "it is and always will be." Machiavellianism, the paternity of which is attributed to Machiavelli, is actually "grounded in the human heart." Machiavelli is only the objective analyst of what later came to be known as "Machiavellianism." He cannot be held as its cause. In fact, "Machiavellianism preceded Machiavelli," as a long list of practitioners of the Machiavellian arts attests. Of course, it also succeeds Machiavelli. However, *The Prince* could not teach to such types anything that they already didn't know by the practices of power. They are no different from those that preceded *The Prince* and have all acted in remarkably similar fashions.

Such a statement is a sufficient response to the charges of his more vulgar detractors and their moral condemnation of his thought. He did not intend to depict "moral truths" nor did he intend, in the manner of ancient philosophy, to investigate "how things should be." His was the effectual truth of political matters, something which is eternally true. Therefore, his thought cannot be so easily dismissed as the product of a particular era. The Machiavellianism he describes, because it is inscribed in the human heart, has its practitioners throughout human history. And the most recent past, known to Machiavelli but hidden from Montesquieu, finds his teaching on despotism once again relevant.

According to Machiavelli, his political teaching is based on modern science which, he implies at the end of the First Dialogue, is also the animating spirit of Montesquieu in his works. Therefore, it makes as much sense to reproach Machiavelli for seeking the effectual truth of politics as the physicist for seeking the physical cause of falling bodies that harm us. It is not unlike blaming "the doctor," he continues, "for describing diseases, the chemist for cataloguing poisons, the moralist for portraying vice, and the historian for writing history."

Though admittedly not gifted in argument,[3] Joly's Montesquieu would like to protest the evident fallacy of such an analogy, given the thrust of Machiavelli's teaching in works that he supposedly "attentively read." Despite his disavowal of more vulgar critics, Montesquieu here shares with them a moral condemnation of Machiavelli for communicating to states through his works "how to distill" political poison. According to this view, Machiavelli seeks evil in order to propagate it, not to cure it. However, if we take Machiavelli literally at his word here, he seems to present himself in Montesquieu's camp as an enemy of despotism and in patent conflict with *The Prince*, at least as Montesquieu here interprets it. By his analogy with the medical art, Machiavelli condemns despotism as an evil, a malady of the political system as is heart disease, for example, to the bodily system. Machiavelli does not correct Montesquieu's understanding in this regard but merely rebukes him for not having understood his thought "in its entirety."

Given Montesquieu's "incomplete" understanding of Machiavelli, it is curious that Machiavelli does not take steps to enlighten his interlocutor at this time about the "full" meaning of his thought. This has the desired effect of provoking

Montesquieu to a further revelation of himself and to an articulation of his own political principles in the Second Dialogue. Machiavelli succeeds in engaging Montesquieu in the serious discussion he was previously reluctant to enter and effectively lays the groundwork for their fateful wager by encouraging Montesquieu to believe not only in the moral rectitude of his position but its unassailable character, as well.

Machiavelli states that his own system is "unshakable" because it is based on an "eternal truth." It is a "fact" that Machiavelli does not even feel compelled to demonstrate that "the evil instinct in man is more powerful than the good." Because man is "more attracted by evil than by good," it follows that "fear and force have more sway over him than reason." In such a bleak description of human nature, the prospects for despotism are enhanced. "All men seek domination and no one would not be a tyrant," if he honestly followed his inclinations. Still, the picture is curiously qualified immediately after such a blanket statement. "All, *or nearly all*, are ready to sacrifice another's rights to their own interests."

As the qualification seems to indicate, Machiavelli has been intentionally provocative to this point. He does in fact recognize the force for good in man, though he thinks the inclination to evil is much stronger. He apparently thinks that "some" at least might be willing to sacrifice their interests for the rights of others. Shortly, in what appears to be a blanket critique of liberty, he claims that in certain "regions of Europe," people are incapable of moderation in its exercise. Are there other "regions" where liberty suits its people? Liberty's degeneration into license again prompts a rather qualified praise for despotism. Is it not a better alternative than anarchy?

Beyond the shocking way in which Machiavelli expresses himself, there is perhaps not so great a distance between the Machiavelli of the *Dialogue* and this Montesquieu, after all. Certain aspects of the Montesquieuan system are compatible with what Machiavelli here states as his own teaching. It would not be incorrect to characterize that system as intending to build upon certain general human proclivities to effect a more common good, while leaving scope and encouragement for man's better instincts, if only found in the few. Accordingly, Montesquieu's teaching might be viewed as "Machiavellianism come of age"— a prudent and less shocking application of similar principles. "If I am not mistaken," Machiavelli asks, "aren't a number of these ideas found in *The Spirit of the Laws*?"[4]

As in certain passages of *The Prince*, Joly's Machiavelli returns to the beginnings of society to discover the real operative principles of politics. He eschews considerations of transcendent "ends" or any "abstract" standard by which to judge political life as ineffectual guides that distort political life as it really is. "I have taken societies as they are," Machiavelli states, "and have laid down rules accordingly." Violence and deceit might be considered evil "in the abstract," he continues. However, such acts cannot be judged good or evil in themselves. The standard we should bring to bear is whether or not they promote what is "useful and necessary" to political life. And it is the necessity "to live" that "dominates states as it does individuals." In fact, "good," understood as Montesquieu understands it, "can come from evil." Furthermore, as the most brilliant societies of the world have issued from despotism, it might be argued that "one attains good through evil." In sum, "the end justifies the means" and we shower great men with glory who effectively act by this maxim in the founding of their countries.

Given the self-seeking nature of "these ravenous beasts we call men," force is always a recurrent necessity for ruling and maintaining order. Political crises, the real focus of Machiavelli's discussion, might be said to require a return to "the origins of society" where "brutal and unrestrained force prevails." In this light, law is "still force," but "institutionalized" and softened by "certain forms." Machiavelli, who consults history and not abstract standards, finds in force the fundamental ground of politics. "Everywhere force precedes right," and is its precondition. The brute fact of force may be compared with the idea of "justice,"—a mere "word"—"infinitely vague" whose application to the political conduct of rulers, though admittedly relevant, is demonstrably contingent and therefore "extremely limited."

The limits of justice are most clearly discerned in relations among nations, whose lupine practices reveal the fundamental role of force. Such limits also hold, covertly, regarding the relation of the ruler to the people, whose self-regarding and "ravenous" nature is a constant threat to authority. When unrestrained by the prince, the masses inevitably lead society to "dissolution" and "the brink of destruction." Indeed, there is no real distinction between internal and external enemies. Therefore, the "force and cunning" that we applaud in one sphere cannot legitimately be condemned in the other. Rather than following the requirements of any abstract standard in this regard, we might arrive at the truth of what Machiavelli says by contemplating what is implied in the praise of the Caesarian leaders in history, whose "heavy hands were placed more often on the hilts of their swords than on the charters of their states."

"Have you ever seen a single state conduct itself according to the principles that govern private morality?" Machiavelli asks Montesquieu. What obtains in the real world remains the standard for Machiavelli and this is what prompts such a rhetorical question. The vulgar criticisms of *The Prince* that judge politics by other principles amount to nothing more than "childish" reproaches. Indeed, a politics guided by "private morality" is not only ineffective, it also brings disaster, for the necessities of political life—unless addressed with cunning and force—will sooner or later make themselves felt.

As a final provocation to Montesquieu, Machiavelli retracts the patriotic statements he had earlier made in his defense and which proved so pleasing to Montesquieu. He defends the justice of despotism for a country that lacked the capacity "to conceive and respect the conditions of free life." He thereby disavows his lifelong efforts on behalf of a republican cause. Having confessed his failure in his life's enterprise, he cleverly ends the First Dialogue with praise of Montesquieu as the "legislator of nations." Montesquieu is moved by this praise to a fuller articulation of his own political principles, which, in his lifetime, brought him the celebrity and practical influence that escaped Machiavelli.

Montesquieu's Correction of Machiavelli

Montesquieu initially responds to Machiavelli with confident condescension. In effect, this restatement of Machiavellianism is "old hat." There is really nothing "new" in all this. Machiavelli's menacing posture, which Montesquieu sees as intending to shock him, appears farcical. To this point, Machiavelli's discourse has been less than "philosophic," according to Montesquieu. Indeed, if the conversation is to continue in any meaningful way, it must be raised to a higher theoretical level where the ultimate "principles" of what Machiavelli says regarding the foundations of political life are investigated and understood in a more rigorous and consistent fashion.

Montesquieu charges that Machiavelli is not a great theoretician, implying that he, the poor debater, is. Machiavelli is "above all a political man," more impressed by "facts" than "ideas." According to the Frenchman, *The Prince* is unlike *The Spirit of the Laws* in having no universally applicable political teaching. As Machiavelli earlier stated, *The Prince* is more a chronicle of sixteenth century Italy, the value of which is limited, though revealingly depicted by one who was an active participant in the politics of his time.

Machiavelli expresses little patience with considerations of what transcends this world and the effectual workings of its politics. Accordingly, Montesquieu stresses the realism of his position even as he challenges Machiavelli's views on the utter irrelevance of morality for politics. What will make it possible for Montesquieu to bring decency and realism together is the argument that the world has changed. The horizon of *The Prince* is no longer adequate for modern times. "Eternal truths" cannot be derived from what applies only to a given moment in a long historical process. According to Montesquieu, Machiavellianism is passé, even granting that it could ever be theoretically justified. Indeed, a look to the real world confirms its irrelevance.

According to Montesquieu, the Machiavellian position, just articulated, grants "no place" to "morals, religion, or justice." This reduces political life, what is in fact unique to human beings, to the animal world. For this reason, the role of "force and cunning," the two words ever on Machiavelli's tongue, receives preponderate influence in what could more accurately be called the law of the jungle. Montesquieu does not quibble with the fact that "force plays a great role in human affairs" and that "cunning is a prerequisite for statesmen." This "needs no demonstration." He rather questions the exclusive part Machiavelli reserves for them in politics.

The more "theoretical" Montesquieu would caution the "practical" Machiavelli to be cognizant of certain fundamental principles that are inextricably involved in any discussion of the foundations of political life. If he intended to "set up violence as a principle and cunning as a maxim of government," we in effect lose contact with the human world and enter the animal world where "justice" does give way to "brute force." Not even Machiavelli goes so far in such a crude reductionism. If he does not recognize the question of justice as central to politics, he does recognize a distinction between "good and evil" as relevant to the political realm and human affairs. From a moral point of view, the problem is that the relationship between "good" and "evil" is much more ambiguous than most people realize or admit.

According to Machiavelli, "good can come from evil." This is revealed most fully in the investigation of political origins, for these show the roots of morality to lie in immorality. As Machiavelli puts it, the ground of "justice" lies in its "negation"—force. But Montesquieu is not content with this simple point and intends to explore this assertion in a more rigorous fashion. This will bring into better focus certain presumptions behind the Machiaellian political view that Montesquieu now claims to be not only inapplicable to the present day but without theoretical foundations.

According to Montesquieu, a political teaching that would sanction any act—including corruption, violence, or murder, just because it is deemed "necessary," "useful," or "advantageous"—is untenable. Principles that could guide political life cannot be derived from such a position. Indeed, a society could not even be constituted, let alone maintained, among individuals who always acted selfishly. If Machiavelli were consistent, he would have to admit as much.

In fact, what Machiavelli permits the rulers, he forbids in the ruled. What is a "virtue" for the one is a "crime" for the other. Machiavelli's "morality" is the "morality" of the strong, or rather, it is the view that the strong, by virtue of their station, are exempt from morality insofar as it is embodied in certain rules, both written and unwritten, that guide the weak or many. Therefore, Machiavellianism, properly understood, applies narrowly and only to the few. Any "maxims" derived from his teaching must be understood accordingly and not, as Montesquieu says, as universally applicable "principles."

According to Montesquieu, the "force" that Machiavelli sees as the basis of society is but an "exception in the conduct of orderly societies." It is not called into play as part of the ordinary operation of society but is confined to the ruler's discretion at truly exceptional and dire moments. Montesquieu himself does recognize overriding "reasons of state" but not in the manner of Machiavelli, who sees in them broad sanction for rulers to act outside the dictates of justice. He refuses to follow the Machiavellian line of reasoning that "posits as the basis of society that which destroys it."

A closer examination of these extreme moments indicates that precisely when rulers are forced to violate the ordinary rules of society, the spirit of justice is invoked. "Even the most arbitrary powers are obliged to seek sanction in considerations foreign to the theory of force." The extreme situation in fact does not reveal the naked datum of interest, of which Machiavelli speaks, but the continued relevance of moral ends, considerations of the common good (if not the explicit rules that normally apply), that alone can guide and redeem any legitimate application of force.

The pursuit of Machiavellian self-interest by princes or peoples leads to crimes that spell the dissolution of society. Montesquieu, on the other hand, does not expose himself to such consequences when he gives justice as the basis of society. As a more cogent examination of the extreme situation reveals, justice is an "idea" that "sets limits" beyond which state interest "must not pass"—if rule is to endure and in fact avoid the very degeneration of society which, according to Machiavelli, only despotic force can arrest.

Montesquieu's defense of morality is made in the name of the "self-preservation" of society, that is, the same grounds on which Machiavelli rests his theory of force. To neglect the dictates of justice is tantamount to introducing "civil war" into "the bosom of society." Machiavelli does not serve the principle of order in exempting princes from a morality that necessarily guides the behavior of private citizens. Furthermore, there is nothing "doubtful or obscure" about its precepts. "They are written into all religions and are imprinted in luminous characters in the conscience of man." This is the "pure source" from which civil, political, economic, and international law must flow.

Just as there can be nothing obscure in the violence of despotism, there is likewise nothing obscure in the requirements of morality. The prince's violation of what holds universally and clearly thus has important consequences for political rule. "Stop deceiving yourself," Montesquieu adjures. "Each act of usurpation by the prince in the public domain authorizes a similar infraction where the subject is concerned. Each act of political treason engenders the same in society at large. Each act of violence in high places legitimates one in low." Contradicting Machiavelli, Montesquieu concludes by categorically asserting that "princes cannot permit themselves what private morality does not permit."

Machiavelli is not only being logically inconsistent in offering as a "principle" of politics what applies only narrowly to princes. He offers as "maxims" for political action what in fact destroys the order of society he seeks to preserve. In concerning himself only with "facts" that apply in the real wold, Machiavelli claimed to be scientific in his approach to politics. Montesquieu, however, can claim that it is really he who is faithful to the spirit of modern thought that Machiavelli pioneered. His conclusion about morality and politics is based exclusively on logic and empirical evidence that avoids the abstract theorizing that characterized pre-modern thought.

It becomes increasingly clear that historicist presumptions are the basis of Montesquieu's view of Machiavelli. For all of Machiavelli's claims for himself as embracing the spirit of modern thought, his defense of princely politics bespeaks a defense of an historical order, pivotal indeed for the evolution of modernity, but historically dated from Montesquieu's later and more inclusive perspective on the character of man's development. In a gentlemanly but still condescending manner, Montesquieu exonerates the sanguinary views of his interlocutor as due to limitations of history, not of mind.

As an apologist for the princely politics of his time, Machiavelli speaks from a point of view where the necessity of order often predominated over the ordinary rules of justice. Machiavelli admires "great men," who presided over such moments and stamped their personality on whole epochs. Through personal rule, they wielded the force necessary to bring order out of chaos. On the other hand, Montesquieu admires "great institutions only." These are the by-product of the progress of reason which has slowly changed the character of history and politics to the point where order is guaranteed only in the advance of justice and the popular cause. "As enlightenment has spread among the diverse peoples of Europe, justice has been substituted for force in theory and practice."

To Machiavelli, Montesquieu's concern for justice bespeaks the vestiges of ancient theory. Being guided by such lights inevitably leads to practices that are antithetical to the political necessity that always operates on human society and is neglected at our common peril. For Montesquieu, the institutions he admires have rationalized society and terminated the era of great men whose contributions to society are much more ambiguous than Machiavelli would want to admit. Their Machiavellian practices might be exonerated in certain instances during Machiavelli's own time. They now have been effectively neutralized by a new political science that has sought, through the complex play of institutions, a more effective organization of political society than the strictly hierarchical arrangements of the past.

According to Montesquieu, the fate of whole peoples is no longer tied to the personality of a given individual. Man has advanced as history has advanced and such a tutelage that formerly existed is no longer appropriate to his present condition. Therefore, Montesquieu tells Machiavelli, "if you could say in your time that despotism was a necessary evil, you could not say so today." So powerful is the hold of reason and so irreversible is the progress of history that "among the principal peoples of Europe, despotism has become impossible." At the beginning of this Dialogue, Montesquieu had attributed to Machiavelli a crude reductionist view of man. His own view is one that moves in an opposite direction and speaks of man's *perfectibility*, not in a transcendent image of ancient philosophy, but "in fact," as empirically verified by the progressive march of history.

Because of his faith in history, Montesquieu can be more sanguine and tolerant in the face of "crimes committed in the name of liberty." The anarchy that was a constant political possibility for Machiavelli indicated to him the eternal possibility for despotism. Popular uprisings are no longer anathema for Montesquieu but may serve history in its transition to a higher stage of development.[5] In more enlightened times, such turmoil bespeaks the changed character of the people and it marks the distance from the despotism that reigns in the Orient, "where people doze peacefully in the degradation of slavery." In the next Dialogue, Montesquieu explains his own contribution to enlightened politics and the advance of political science.

The opening of the Third Dialogue reminds the reader of the eerie context of the conversation as well as its precariousness. Montesquieu is protective of his interlocutor lest they be separated in the continual migration of souls that marks this hell. It is perhaps a measure of his interest and confidence at this particular point that he is so solicitous that his conversation with Machiavelli continues. Nothing that Machiavelli has said has shaken him and he probably relishes the thought of besting him in their evolving dispute. Such solicitude also bespeaks the skill of Machiavelli in so sedulously engaging such a reluctant interlocutor to the conversation he wanted.

Later in the very same Dialogue, we learn that Montesquieu has passed most of his time in hell with people from the ancient world. He has only recently come into contact with modern souls and these have "arrived from the distant corners of the universe." They have not been very informative about the most recent happenings in Europe and France, matters close to Montersquieu's heart.

Montesquieu's Political Teaching

Montesquieu is anxious to defend his statement about the utter impossibility of despotism taking root in modern times—which is certainly his most provocative proposition. This naturally leads to a discussion of his own formidable contributions to a political science that designs the institutions of government in such a way as to counter despotic ambitions. "If anything can alleviate my anxiety in the hours before the Last Judgment, it is the thought that my time on earth had something to do with this great emancipation," he states. Machiavelli has succeeded in having his conversation with Montesquieu by turning his interlocutor's thoughts away from his unhappy lot here in hell to "sweeter" ruminations, namely, the beneficent role he played in furthering the emancipation of man.

Machiavellli asserts that he is fully conversant with the thought of Montesquieu in his most famous work. However, he sees a discrepancy between what the Montesquieu of *The Spirit of the Laws* says and what the Montesquieu who stands before him says with respect to the present impossibility of despotism. If Montesquieu has accused Machiavelli of being less than rigorous in his pretensions to science, Machiavelli, in turn, accuses Montesquieu of loose talk in "overstating the implications of principles found in *The Spirit of the Laws*. According to Machiavelli, who has apparently taken great pains to come to know the thought contained in Montesquieu's books, the teaching of *The Spirit of the Laws* is not so sanguine about the meager prospects for despotism.

In his own defense, Montesquieu claims to have "avoided elaborating long theories" in *The Spirit of the Laws*, a book known for its terse but elegant style. What he currently holds is not at all at odds with that work and can easily be deduced "from the principles there posited." Moreover, he adds, what he has subsequently learned in hell prior to his encounter with Machiavelli has reinforced his optimism. Presumably, the modern men "from the most remote corners of the world" have not been untouched by several of his ideas, nor have they been immune to the general movement of history. He will not go so far as to say that despotism is now incompatible with the conditions of all peoples but it is emphatically so in most of the western part of Europe, including France, where enlightenment has settled the politics of a formerly turbulent country. Of course, Montesquieu's optimism would be tested and his theories modified were he aware of the latest happenings in his own land.

Machiavelli, who is not at all ignorant in this regard, immediately suspects the deficiency of Montesquieu's historical knowledge, which, by his probing, stands fully revealed at the end of this Dialogue. Given the conditions that now characterize France, Montesquieu's optimism is comprehensible only in light of his crucial ignorance. The course of Machiavelli's conversation with Montesquieu is profoundly altered by this revelation.

For his part, Montesquieu remains unperturbed in the face of a lacuna of only fifteen years (1847-1864).[6] Such a period of time is not long enough to change the direction of history and so alter the prospects for despotism in enlightened Europe. In fact, "centuries are necessary to change the principles and forms of government under which people have been accustomed to live." Given modern developments and the change in the character of peoples that has occurred subsequent to the era of Machiavelli, "the doctrines of Machiavelli certainly would not be the ones that triumph" in the short span of years in the most recent past.

Montesquieu is given ample opportunity to elaborate the principles and forms of government that attain in enlightened times. He iterates the fact that it is to institutions, not to men, that we owe progress in "liberty and morals." "All the good, indeed all the bad, which redounds to man in society, necessarily depends on the correct or incorrect ordering of institutions." This is immensely important in understanding the development of civilization, he avers. The "political ills" man endures are a function of "theoretical and practical ignorance." Their "cure" lies in "enlightenment," primarily in education of the people as to their rights and the "fundamental principles of organizing political power." The reason for Montesquieu's optimism is grounded in his belief in the power of reason to affect history in bringing about the progressive betterment of man's condition.

Montesquieu is emphatic in distinguishing the spirit of his political science from that of "those deplorable reformers who claim to found societies on a purely rational basis." He approves of the "fine words of Solon" and speaks, like the great ancient founder, only of the "the most perfect institutions that people are able to support." The organization of political society is not made in a vacuum but is fully consonant with the "climate, habits, customs, and even prejudices" that form the people. Contrary to what Machiavelli thinks, the prudence so evident in the eminent author of *The Spirit of the Laws* is not abandoned to any exaggerated hopes or claims, nor is it based on any hypothetical or abstract application of reason unguided by the conditions of time or place.

Montesquieu's idea of progress can best be appreciated against the backdrop of Machiavelli's own time, which, Montesquieu intimates, fundamentally limits and defines the views of his interlocutor. Machiavelli was born "at the end of the Middle Ages," which was only the first dawning of modern times, a period that was "still quite infected with barbarism." Anarchy and despotism were but two sides of the same coin, a product of the theoretical and practical ignorance in which nations had been for so long for want of principles that *The Spirit of the Laws* refined into a science. The growing influence of such a work guaranteed the spread of reason in Europe and beyond.

In Machiavelli's time, "sovereignty rested solely in the person of the prince," who had at his disposition the unlimited exercise of absolute authority. All power was concentrated in the hands of an individual who considered himself "a preordained divinity" to whom "the human race was delivered." This thinking gave rise to an arbitrary rule that could only be tyrannical. The precariousness of a social order based on such foundations invited anarchy from a populace which could so easily be dispossessed of their "goods," "rights," and very "persons." Liberties and public rights that did exist were fragile and rested on the better motives of some rulers, the spirit of moderation among certain kings, or their fear of angering the people.

Indeed, anarchy, pure and simple, defined the world of Machiavelli. It existed in a most barbarous manner among nations where "kingdoms were the prey of conquerors." But it also existed within states and manifested itself in the wars of sovereigns with their vassals, often claiming whole cities, the seeds of civilization, as victim. These were bold and tumultuous times, replete with "intrepid commanders, men of iron, and audacious geniuses," that could appeal to the artistic imagination if not to any refined moral sensibilities. And this, according to Montesquieu, is what explains the lively, brazen character of *The Prince*.[7]

Today, sovereignty is understood differently. An assertion of its prerogatives no longer finds such violent expression. It is based on the principle of equality, an idea perhaps strangely new to the ears of Machiavelli. People now "regard themselves as the arbiters of their destinies." The strictly stratified society of the Middle Ages which separates subjects from rulers in the manner of men from gods has been replaced by one which, "in theory and practice," has destroyed "privilege and aristocracy." In contrast to "the principle of sovereignty" that "rested solely in the person of the prince," allusion is made to a different notion of sovereignty—popular sovereignty, the proper understanding of which and what it entails will shortly become the main point of contention.

The advance of the principle of equality can be traced from the "beginnings" when institutions and laws were traditional, primitive, and narrowly conceived. First, "personal rights were secured by civil laws." Gained by the "ancestral blood," these changed the status of subject to citizen, according to each individual the same privileges and immunities vis-á-vis one another. What measure of protection and tranquility that the citizen gained thereby was succeeded by advances in "public right." Developments in international law, hardly known to Machiavelli, today "regulates the relations among nations as civil law regulates the relations of subjects in each nation." Unlike Machiavelli's time, conquerors are no longer permitted to despoil the property of the conquered. Beyond such minimal guarantees, treaties and conventions further refine relations among nations and define areas of rights and mutual interest.

A rational politics sees perhaps its greatest advance in the establishment of constitutions, which in turn exhibit their own progressive refinements. It is this later development that orders affairs between the people and their rulers and establishes modern political right on a firm basis. "The person of the prince ceases to be confounded with the notion of the state." The source of sovereignty is transferred to the "very heart of the nation." This allows the people to determine as is convenient a whole new distribution and arrangement of powers between the prince and other political bodies.

Montesquieu does not need to elaborate the details of his political science, embodied in the constitutional regimes of France and England, to such "an illustrious statesman." In simple terms, it features a separation and balance of essential governmental powers. Government is institutionally divided according to function into three branches that are endowed with the interest and power to resist each other's encroachments. The "blending of powers," which formerly permitted princes to "make tyrannical laws and to execute them tyrannically," is thereby thwarted. In brief, government is made responsive to the people. This solves the "primary problem" and the foremost political question by determining the issue of ultimate sovereignty. Secondarily, the operations of government are so arranged that possible abuses of power are frustrated—"mechanistically"—through checks upon each other. This assumes that the government, which the people ultimately control, also controls itself in its daily operations.

It is the nature of human beings, from considerations of pride and insecurity, to seek an extension of their power. Montesquieu shares the realistic views of Machiavelli in wanting to build upon this most basic human proclivity in his system of government and use such anti-social dispositions to the advantage of society as a whole. In his political science, we might dispense with a too precarious reliance on the better motives of rulers to serve the interests of the ruled. Power will be limited by erecting effective countervailing power.

According to Montesquieu, "at all times" and no matter what the political regime, society "is always governed by laws." Therefore, it is in the way "the laws are made" that are found all the guarantees of the citizens. Here, Montesquieu effectively reverses the Machiavellian dictum that "the end justifies the means." The "means," that is, the formal procedure of lawmaking in the well-founded regime, is itself in large measure determinative of the "ends," the protection of the rights of the individual.

The principle of the separation of powers, by which "internal public right was created," is actually a very sophisticated device to ensure that laws are framed, executed, and judged by separate institutions or powers and according to recognized procedures. In such a system of government, the private interest of a given group or individual, whose motives are always suspect, cannot find effective means to fulfillment. Because he has the means to effect his own personal will, the individual who makes the law and judges in his own case can be suspected of partiality. For this reason, the lawmaking function is divorced from that of judging. On the other hand, the executive may rightfully enforce the law but only in accord with legislation duly passed by the proper lawmaking body. Conversely, the legislature may pronounce the law in general terms but cannot arbitrarily punish or benefit an individual. Security for the individual is thus presumed in the very arrangement and operation of the different powers of government. This has an important influence on political behavior. A tranquillity of spirit is bred in the citizenry at large when it perceives its rights to be safeguarded by the due process of law. This conduces to a moderate and civil politics that was formerly preserved through moral appeals and a severe civic education.

Montesquieu's scheme is meant to correct a political problem that Enlightenment science rendered difficult. In former times, reverence for the law was assured by an appeal to divine sanctions, whose authority was premised in the myths of the founding or, as in later Christian times, the divine right of kings. The advance of secular philosophy precludes recourse to such precepts and supports in modern liberal regimes, where the "human all too human" character of the law is evident in its very origins and daily administration. Nevertheless, an abiding respect for the law emerges from Montesquieu's political science in its capacity to guarantee the law's impartiality. The operative principle behind Montesquieu's political science—"that no one is higher than the law"—endows the constitution and statutes, duly passed by the people, with legitimacy, if not sanctity. In modern times, the claim of the law over the individual approximates the hold it had over man in ancient polities where "the conditions of free government were admirably understood." [8]

The prudence of Montesquieu is again demonstrated in his suspicion of not only princely ambitions at odds with the people but in unmediated popular rule.

Though ultimate sovereignty rests with the people through their duly elected representatives, the popular assembly itself is properly tempered and controlled through its relations with the other institutions of government. The regime is envisioned as "mixed." Aristocratic, monarchic, and democratic elements are given expression in the various branches of government and in a "happy compromise," some of the strengths of the three forms of government are combined at once. The proper balance of these elements depends on circumstance and can be applied "in a thousand ways according to the temperament of the people."

Given the establishment of enlightened government, liberty and progress are further assured by a free press—the public voice. This is not only for the important watchdog purposes it serves. It also reflects a fundamental Enlightenment premise that posits a harmony between matters of the mind and the interests of society. To their mutual benefit, reason is allowed access to society. The hostility of politics to reason marks the barbarism of the past and is the hallmark of despotism that would resist its humanizing influence. In contrast, openness to reason is the very "essence of free countries." A free press helps establish and maintain an informed and vigilant citizenry, upon which ultimate authority rests. The vestiges of primitive thought and fear are eliminated through the spread of reason and, with them, the violent behavior they often inspire. Technological advances—the fruits of Enlightenment science—further communications among the citizenry and eradicate backwardness. The exchange of ideas and goods is facilitated, increasing the easy interactions among peoples and their common ties. The people come to share a common purpose in the material advance of society and the defense of individual rights. It was thought that they would act wisely, drawn to an elevated view of their self-interest by a free and responsible press.

The success of the Enlightenment project in the advanced states of Europe makes it increasingly difficult for other countries to preserve themselves from its influence. The ideas of the former are imported with their trade. This promotes the unity of peoples that religions had formerly separated. There seems to be nothing in Enlightenment science that prevents the universal application of its principles. Machiavelli sees Montesquieu as proposing England's experience as "a universal panacea," given his statement that it has "the only practicable mode of government given the ideas of modern civilization."

Notes

1. Montesquieu refers to Machiavelli as "ce grand homme" in the *The Spirit of the Laws* VI 5. He is mentioned again at XXIX 19 in a short chapter "Of Legislators." There he is grouped with Aristotle, Plato, More, and Harrington. The tone of the chapter is critical. Passion and prejudice infect the minds of even the grandest lawgivers. Machiavelli stands for criticism for being "full of his idol, the Duke of Valentinois."

2. Undoubtedly, there is poignancy to the fate that the real Machiavelli suffered and Joly gives it its due. The author of the "Memoir of Machiavelli" that introduces the Bohn Library Edition of the Florentine's writings pushes this poignancy to a melodramatic extreme. He speaks of the return of the Medici after the fall of the Republic that Machiavelli served. A conspiracy against the Medici caused Machiavelli to fall under suspicion.

> Fear and suspicion followed the secretary into retirement, and when in the course of the following year (1513), an extensive conspiracy against the Medici was accidently discovered, he was immediately arrested and put to the torture which was at that time indiscriminately employed under all Italian governments in examining persons accused of state crimes. Six shocks of the cord were inflicted on Machiavelli with fruitless cruelty, and not a word escaped him in the bitterness of his agony that could be wrested into a confession of guilt, or serve as an accusation of others. Unable to convict him, they could still torment; and, accordingly, buried in the depths of a loathsome dungeon, his lacerated body closely bound with chains, and his mind distracted by the cries of mercy and the degradation that reached him from every side, he was left to the long torture of solitude and suspense. Here also his fortitude remained unshaken, and his noble power of patient endurance baffled the snares of his adversaries and wearied their malignity.

The text continues in the same vein. If this were not Machiavelli, the account might be worthy of entry into John Henry Newman's *Lives of the Saints*. We might paraphrase what was once said about St. Neot, who is memorialized in the pages of Newman's book. "This is all, and perhaps more than all" that is known about the "blessed" life of Machiavelli. See the "Memoir of Machiavelli" in *The History of Florence Togethyer with The Prince and Various Other Historical Tracts*, ed. H. B. Bohn (London: George Bell & Sons, 1906) xiv.

3. What Albert Sorel asserts about Montesquieu accords with what Joly says here. Montesquieu "did not consider himself an orator" nor "suited to formal speech-making." And this was perhaps linked to the disdain he felt, not for the law, for sure, but the practice of law as it was conducted in his time. I want to make the following point. It seems that here, as elsewhere, Joly took pains in fleshing out even small details in the portraits he fashioned of the two philosophers.

Montesquieu considered his bashfulness "the scourge of his life." He often put up with bores and the things they said in order to escape having discussion with them. Still, this was the man that France was to make its "favorite." See Alber Sorel, *Montesquieu*, tr. Melvile B. Anderson and Edward Flayfair Anderson (Port Washington, N.Y.: Kennikat Press, 1969) 12ff.

4. Machiavelli implies that the Encyclopedists as well as the author of *The Persian Letters* are kindred spirits belonging to the same "school" which others call "immoral." If

he is implying that the *Persian Letters* shocks certain proprieties, he might have also cited, with even better reason, Montesquieu's *Temple of Gnidos*.

5. Jefferson and his American progeny share the same perspective: "the tree of liberty is watered by the blood of patriots," is it not? What we today in Asia call "people power" is benignly viewed as helping history to bring more enlightened political and economic arrangements to peoples victimized by rapacious and petty tyrants. Indeed, this violent turmoil—even lapses of legality—are to be forgiven. They bespeak the changed character of these peoples and their receptivity to new political developments. As Machiavelli cautions, though, things might not be so simple nor the end so happy.

6. A short period of years, can, of course, radically change the direction of history. Think only of 1914-1917. Who, standing at the cusp of the nineteenth and twentieth centuries and basking in the optimism of that moment, could have predicted the catastrophes to fall? This is a sufficient response to those today who see a global order benignly falling into place. Extrapolating from statistics of trade and commerce, they mistakenly put economics before politics and therefore blind themselves to other less sanguine possibilities. Who can so blithely believe that there are no more jokers in history's cards? Is it not much more likely that, after the Cold War, the deck has just been reshuffled?

7. Montesquieu here gives voice to a common conception of Machiavelli, that is to say, that he can be explained by his times. He is a kind of artist, in perhaps the greatest "age of art." Essentially, *The Prince* is his portrait of the times and it is painted in the boldest and most lively colors. In chapter 9, I will argue why this interpretation of Machiavelli is inadequate. Meanwhile, what are we to make of the author of *The Spirit of the Laws* in the movingly intimate way he concludes the Preface to his great work?

> When I have seen what so many great men in France, in England, and in Germany, have said before me, I have been lost in admiration. But I have not lost my courage. I have said with Correggio, "And I also am a painter."

Indeed, he too is an artist. And he painted on the broadest of canvases, it might be added. In the gallery of the "greats," he also deserves recognition. Those who want to delve deeper in Montesqueieu's views on art, especially Renaissance art, should consult his *Essay on Taste* and *Mes Pensées*, esp. XII.

8. The case of Richard Nixon shows that, until most recently, it used to have the power of even removing presidents from power.

Chapter Two

AN ELABORATION OF THE RESPECTIVE POLITICAL TEACHINGS

In the Fourth Dialogue, the central Dialogue of Part One, Machiavelli begins a critique of Montesquieuan political science as well as the deeper philosophic and historic convictions upon which it is based. Machiavelli raises the key issues that are the substance of their debate in the rest of this Part. This immediately serves to further define the respective views of the two interlocutors as it ultimately deals in matters that reverberate throughout the rest of Joly's work.

According to Machiavelli, Montesquieu has failed to reckon with an "irresistible movement of history that tears societies today loose from their old traditions." This makes illusory any hopes of universalizing the experience of England and making the constitutional regime a "panacea" for all states. Within two hundred years, the theories of the division of powers among the three branches of government will be no more than "a memory," something "antiquated and obsolete" as arcane to men of the future as obscure Aristotelean doctrines are to us today.[1]

Why Montesquieuan Thought Is Obsolete

Machiavelli, like Montesquieu, sees history as moving to a new world order. It may be likened to the momentous advance of modernity, the furthest reaches of which are attained in the Enlightenment age that shapes and is shaped by Montesquieu, over the order of the Middle Ages dominated by Aristotle. Implicitly, Machiavelli reverses the accusation of Montesquieu against Machiavellianism—that it is limited by a specific historic horizon. Speaking from a point of view even more advanced than that of the Enlightenment's most illustrious figure, Machiavelli sees the eternal truth of Machiavellianism once again vindicated in a new age of despots.

Machiavelli begins his attack with what Montesquieu says are longstanding reproaches against liberal government, voiced by reactionaries that benefited from the old order of things. Again, nothing much is new in what Machiavelli says. His is a standard critique of the liberal system.

Machiavelli implies that the separation of powers system, which "confines" three powers to distinct departments and balances them off against one another in an intricate political mechanism, is overly abstract and perhaps a misapplication of a principle of physics to human realms. Strictly viewed, the balance of power "ideal," if in fact achieved, would render government inoperative. Were government to function "perfectly," there would be nothing but exhausting stalemates. The theoretical foundations of Montesquieu's constitution is in conflict with the vigor he also intended for a government that is designed to act in the people's interest.

As Montesquieu explained his "mixed regime," the institutions of government represent various social groups and interests, none of which is motivated by the interest of the whole. The "balance of power" among such institutions is inherently precarious, as it involves mutually antagonistic forces that, individually at least, seek their own play at the expense of the system's equilibrium. It is as if the system would be plagued by inaction where it is not subject to dissolution.

In theory, the press serves to reestablish equilibrium in the system by counteracting the disintegrative forces of faction. It elevates discourse in speaking for the common good. It sets the tone and standard of public discussion and forces the competing interests at least to justify themselves in more disinterested terms. In actual practice, Machiavelli charges, the press foments further discord by "discrediting" all authority. In effect, it gives "arms to all parties" and turns the public forum into an "arena."

According to Machiavelli, the operation of such a political system makes it most difficult to maintain peace and order among the competing interests and segments of society. Dissolution is also threatened in a more fundamental way by a more radical social cleavage. This separates those groups with a direct role and clear stake in the prevailing order from those masses of people "whose poverty chains them to their work in the same way that slavery did in former times." Montesquieu speaks of the great movement of history and the blessings it has brought in its train. It has in fact resulted in the triumph of only a small minority, whose privileges, wrought by the chance workings of new social and economic forces, are not appreciably different from those enjoyed by the nobility of medieval times, distinguished by birth.

For "huge numbers," the vaunted "rights" of the liberal order are only academic—"a bitter irony of fate," of which the law permits their ideal enjoyment and necessity refuses their active exercise. "Parliamentary conventions" make no difference to tangible happiness, which logically seeks outlet in a despotism that can appease their real wants while satisfying their feelings of envy. According to Montesquieu, however, liberal society's declaration of rights, which Machiavelli sees as cruelly abstract for the majority of people, does have important consequences that he fails to appreciate. It is of no little importance "for those very people destined by birth to the most humble conditions" that they share in a common dignity by virtue of citizenship in such a society. Moral sentiments are attached to the regime of liberty which recognizes the self-worth of individuals. Citizens there are "no less strongly" attached to such regimes by more material interests.

Machiavelli is simply wrong to liken the privileged of such a society to an "aristocracy of birth" and the lot of the proletariat to slavery. It is a far more dynamic and fluid society than Machiavelli realizes where "the law recognizes no privileged classes and where careers are open to individual enterprise." The "ideal" rights that Machiavelli criticizes have concrete consequences. The various fortunes of individuals are by and large a manifestation of their exercise and a vindication of the protection that such a society affords the different faculties of men.

Machiavelli sums up Montesquieu's arguments and gives a perfectly fine understanding of the design of his government. We come to realize that perhaps Montesquieuan political science is "old hat" for Machiavelli. "On the surface, the society appears monarchical, but at bottom everything is democratic, for in reality there are no barriers between classes and work is the means to all fortunes." The balance of power mechanism requires artfulness in its adjustment that perhaps makes any close analogy with physics unfair. To counter the natural strength of the popular element, the other elements must be reinforced to achieve proper equilibrium. This involves certain property qualifications conferring electoral rights, using the power of opinion to back men of merit, and taking advantage of the proper strengths of the corresponding powers—all to dilute and counteract the power of the popular body. The prestige of grand manners and the brilliance of superior rank is played up and respected. Tradition, the memory of all great historical events, and the celebration of greatness, is guarded.

The Incipient Anarchy in Modern Principles

Having secured an admission from Montesquieu that he can at least understand thoughts he doesn't agree with, Machiavelli accuses Montesquieu of not appreciating the full consequences of his own principles. These bring in their train the reign of force and not the reign of reason he projects. In particular, Machiavelli has in mind the principle of popular sovereignty. Adumbrated earlier in their discussion, such a notion of sovereignty was offered as an alternative to the principle of "divine right" upon which rested the princely politics of Machiavelli's time. In broaching such a topic, Machiavelli attempts to make explicit a matter that goes to the heart of their discussion as well as *The Spirit of the Laws* itself, which he believes is intentionally vague on this point.

The "prudent, politic Montesquieu" did not spell out the doctrine of popular sovereignty in *The Spirit of the Laws*. But, mimicking Montesquieu of only a few moments ago, Machiavelli states that "certain things follow implicitly from the principles" he set down there. Despite Montesquieu's disavowal of any association with "radical reformers," the affinity of his doctrines with Rousseau's *Social Contract* and revolutionary theory of the general will is unmistakable, at least according to Machiavelli.

The French revolutionaries based themselves on such theories when they wrote that "a constitution can only be a free compact among equals." Inspired by such thought, the people took direct possession of all powers that had been recognized as only ultimately and indirectly residing in them. The year 1793 demonstrates how the people asserted their sovereignty "by severing the head of the king." Making a litter of all their "rights," they cast their lot, out of delirium and weariness, to "the first soldier of fortune they came across."

Under the full sway of the principle of popular sovereignty, all the latent forces of the masses are marshaled, spelling "death" to parliamentary government. The intricate mechanism of the balance of power is too fragile and is overwhelmed by an irresistible force that is not in its control. Deference to tradition and the respect for forms that is critical to the workings of enlightened government disappears in the Machiavellian portrait of the modern masses. Ominously, the renewed activation of their power, in a repeat of '93, augurs a more virulent anarchy as well as a more extreme form of despotism as the fate of contemporary man.

Machiavelli says as much to Montesquieu in delineating the course of history in France since the principle of popular sovereignty made itself felt in the Revolution. Aristocratic monarchy was in too flagrant contradiction with the democratic thrust of history. It had to vanish in the "conflagration of 1830, as the government of 1830, in its own right...." Machiavelli concludes his historic discourse with a tantalizing allusion to the Revolution of 1848. The July Monarchy was attacked as a "pious fraud" in presenting itself as a popularly grounded kingship. After a revolutionary moment, a brief return to republican government was finally supplanted by the "democratic despotism" of the Empire that presented itself, as we shall see, as the authoritative fulfillment of popular will.

Machiavelli here seems to present a cyclical view of history as an alternative to Montesquieu's linear and progressive view. The "inevitable path" of nations that have popular sovereignty as their animating principle is to engender a demagoguery that leads to anarchy and finally to despotism. Since despotism is barbarity to Montesquieu, the people, it seems, "return to barbarism via civilization"—a process that runs directly counter to the forces of history as Montesquieu sees them.

Despotism is not only an eternal possibility. According to Machiavelli, it seems to be an inevitable occurrence. The popular excesses and licentiousness that accompany the degeneration of popular rule demand a return to authoritarianism. The history of France manifests a cyclical passage through the extremes of popular and despotic rule. Enlightenment politics, personified by Montesquieu, has perhaps only broadened out this cycle and temporarily slowed its revolutionary turn toward despotism. But as the *Dialogue* augurs, this may finally lead to a precipitous return to a more profound and extensive tyranny.

From still other points of view, despotism is the only form of government that is appropriate to the social conditions of modern people. According to Machiavelli, ancient polities, above all, provide the proper soil for liberty. There, citizen concerns came to the fore, as manual labor was assigned to slaves. The fires of patriotism burned in ancient souls and found outlet in external war that preserved internal peace in uniting all in a common enterprise of overriding urgency and importance. The conflict that moderns experience between their worldly and religious engagements was unknown to the ancients. The dictates of morality were neither conflicting nor vague.[2] A civil religion, rich in ceremony, held sway over the minds and imaginations of men and reinforced their political education. Self-rule was possible because a stern morality guaranteed against its abuse.

Machiavelli sees despotism as the destiny of modern peoples because the social conditions that preserved liberty are currently absent. Christianity has tamed the martial spirit and eradicated the institution of slavery, perhaps forever. Materialism and atheism have usurped its place and cosmopolitanism has replaced patriotism. Liberty has existed even into the Christian era but in smaller, more austere republics. The scale of modern society, moreover, is immense and open to diverse influences that conflict with the dictates of citizen virtue. Politics vacillates between impassioned fanaticism and cold indifference, both of which can be exploited by the clever despot.

Material interests demonstrably do not attach people to liberty, as Montesquieu says. The dispossessed are motivated only by hatred and envy of the propertied, who resort to force to maintain themselves. Under such conditions, patriotism suffocates and "morality can no longer be guaranteed except by repressive laws." Modern societies, "veritable colossuses with feet of clay," require extreme centralization where all movements of individuals can be minutely regulated. A return to Caesarism is in order, as Machiavelli ends his discussion with a most provocative praise of administrative despotism as most fitting the requirements of the time.

When Machiavelli talks so authoritatively about the state of contemporary morals, Montesquieu wonders if he is speaking hypothetically. He remains convinced that a look to history would produce evidence decidedly on the side of his theories. In the previous Dialogue, Machiavelli spoke from the example of France, bringing the beloved fatherland of Montesquieu to the fore. For the sake of argument, they may continue to use France as the touchstone of their conversation.[3]

Montesquieu is far from reluctant to agree, for it is precisely in France that the picture Machiavelli has drawn is least applicable. "The home of great ideas and passions" leaves no room for the "sinister doctrines" of Machiavelli. Privy to a new political doctrine, (of which more will be said later in discussing the ideological core of the Napoleonic revolution), Machiavelli would add that France is perhaps not only noteworthy for a still vibrant legacy of ideas, it is also "a field of experiment" devoted to political theories more ominous than imagined.

Such a cryptic illusion to new doctrines is beyond Montesquieu who cannot conceive of an experiment advancing despotism that could take root in contemporary Europe. Even where pure monarchy has been preserved from the influences of liberal institutions, in Turkey and Russia, for example, we may detect, at least in the "internal changes taking place in the heart" of this latter power, "intimations of an approaching transformation." In the final analysis, the forces for change favor the transformation of oriental despotism into liberal polities and not the contrary process which, Machiavelli asserts, needs less than a century to work itself out fully.

The Historical Basis of Montesquieu's Optimism

Montesquieu states why he thinks such a prediction absurd. He imputes such gross errors to a mistaken conception of history, a way of thinking common to the medieval horizon that still included Machiavelli's world. He warns Machiavelli against drawing false inferences from the use of certain historic analogies. For Machiavelli, it seems, the course of French history from the anarchy following the French Revolution to the institution of the despotism of Napoleon I is being repeated in contemporary France. Accordingly, the assault on the settlement of 1830 might be likened to that of 1793 for having failed to reconcile the principle of monarchic legitimacy with popular liberty. Machiavelli's fondness for such analogies stems from his cyclical view of history which seeks enlightened guidance for the present in the study of similar situations in the past.

According to Montesquieu, however, we "must beware of taking what is contingent for universal laws" and of transforming what is particular to certain times and places into general rules. Contrary to Machiavelli, each historical situation is unique and specific to time and place. Despotism and force is not an absolute historical necessity but more an "accident" in an historical process beyond the comprehension of one whose understanding is essentially limited by the Middle Ages.

Despotism "has played a transitional role in history." The cyclical view of history cannot account for a broader and more fundamental historical tendency toward "progress" and perfection—what is truly inevitable and irreversible as "a foreordained social law." For sure, despotism has occurred at times in the past "as a consequence of social upheavals." But it is impermissible to conclude from this that it will definitively solve the "crises of modern times," as Machiavelli sees them. Rather, the general tendency of history reveals our astonishing capacity to better our condition. Montesquieu has not been sufficiently impressed by the proportions of the historic crisis that Machiavelli has intimated. As rational beings, we have been granted powers commensurate to the evils we find and this applies to the problems identified by Machiavelli as defining modern life.

Collectively, we are participants in a divine drama guided by "Eternal Wisdom," which reveals itself in history through the thought of the "great historic thinker." The Montesquieuean teaching holds to an idealist, progressive view of history. Ultimately, its movement is a necessary consequence of the movement in ideas, which are made concrete in the political world as they are "translated into fact." His essential optimism can be traced to the powers of reason and its capacity to shape history. It is based on a faith in the working out of a plan of an "Eternal Wisdom" that providentially guides the destiny of man. Indeed, Montesquieu sees himself as a key figure in the unfolding historic drama as the thinker who stands at the pinnacle of the Enlightenment. It is his theories—"translated into fact"—that define the modern epoch as the era of constitutional government, bringing an end to the era of princely politics.

Machiavelli implies that Montesquieu is overly optimistic about the powers of reason to change the limits that define our condition. A society may in fact survive a certain crisis but one day it must "die." Political regimes, too, are mortal and subject to life cycles similar to that of man. It therefore follows that infinite progress and indeed perfection are beyond the possible. We are limited by a more fundamental reality that is Machiavelli's guide in his efforts to propound a truly realistic teaching—one that discounts any reliance on "faith," even in the secularized way it is rendered in Montesquieu's teaching.

Machiavelli's short but poignant reminder of the mortality of all human things leaves Montesquieu nonplussed. He once again warns against placing oneself at "the extreme," in the manner of Machiavelli, who takes political crisis as the starting point of his theories. Moreover, he seizes upon the "organic" analogy of Machiavelli to elaborate upon his view of the historic process. According to Montesquieu, "societies never die in the process of generation." The "death" of societies is only apparent; their vital forces give rise to more sturdy progeny before they pass from existence. "In this way, the various peoples of Europe have been successively transformed from a feudal to a monarchic system and from a pure monarchy to a constitutional regime."

One cannot derive valid maxims from "analogies" between such epochs because, no matter how related in certain particulars, they each have their own essential personality or character. Machiavelli seems to equate all epochs and this flies in the face of historic diversity as well as a more fundamental tendency toward progress. In sum, the demands for order that can be satisfied at one moment only by despotism do not hold in the context of later epochs. Despotism, where relevant to the historic process, does not hold in the less than extreme situation, nor, certainly, in the context of the present time.

Montesuieu claims to catch Machiavelli in a contradiction. How can Machiavelli, who posits the eternal necessity for despotism, praise liberty "in certain times and places?" Montesquieu's praise of liberty is without qualification. Breathing the air of liberty, whether in ancient or modern times, strengthens the soul and elevates the character of citizens. Liberty is not a poison for political life but its strongest regimen. Contrary to Machiavelli, then, despotism is not a historical necessity, but a transitional phase, an evanescent moment in the historical process. On the other hand, liberty is not only appropriate to certain brief moments in ancient and some modern times, but precisely to contemporary times, where the institutional operation of government is specifically designed to secure its blessings as its chief end.

With Montesquieu, we might wonder at the Florentine's inconsistency as he acknowledges his interlocutor's deft sallies. His position as to despotism, qualified by a praise of liberty, is put to question. At this point, he changes the conversation once again to the topic of popular sovereignty, the full thrust of which he feels Montesquieu is escaping by the tangential matters they are now considering. Once again, however, the question of the "real" Machiavelli presents itself, especially with regard to liberty.

Machiavelli confesses he is anxious to see how the "sober" Montesquieu will deal with the principle of popular sovereignty, a "specter" that haunts his theories. He asks point blank and in accusatorial tones whether or not it is part of his system: "Do you or do you not accept it?" For reasons that shortly will become clear, Montesquieu admits that he cannot answer such a question "posed in such terms." But before answering, he would like to remind Machiavelli of his writings and the character of his mission. Being a "philosopher who proceeded so prudently in his quest for the truth," he takes great umbrage with a former accusation leveled by Machiavelli that associates his name with the "iniquities of the French Revolution."

How Machiavelli understands that great upheaval is key to his thinking about the prospects for despotism. By implication, the historical cycle that saw the popular cause degenerate into Napoleonic despotism is being repeated in France. It is interesting to note that Montesquieu asserts the centrality of those very same events to his own political theories. "I saw into all the practical consequences" that would emerge from this event. Fully conscious of a new Napoleonic Empire, Machiavelli has a fundamentally different perspective from Montesquieu, who saw in his science the definitive antidote to revolutionary excesses.[4]

The Revolution & Montesquieu's Constructive Role in History

According to Montesquieu, the case of the French Revolution is the clearest vindication of his theories in demonstrating the preeminent role of reason in history. In his view, the French Revolution was a transitional phase in the historic process that, no matter how violent or despotic, served "to sweep away the ancient forms of monarchical government." But "while imprudent innovators directly attacked the foundations of authority and unknowingly prepared a momentous catastrophe," Montesquieu single-mindedly applied himself "to the study of free governments to discover the fundamental principles upon which they rest." He was acting more in the capacity of "statesman" than "philosopher" in seeking to teach his country how to govern itself rather than "calling into question the very principle of authority."

The task that Montesquieu gave himself was constructive, not destructive. Though both apparently are historically necessary, it is the constructive task that endures, at least according to the optimistic view of Montesquieu. The moment that follows the French Revolution sets for Montesquieu a different historic project in a different historic context, shaped by different needs and circumstances. The principle of popular sovereignty is legitimately voiced in the moment "of intellectual ferment" that prepared the revolution and opened the way for Montesquieu's teaching. However, the direct application of that principle in the context of the ordinary operations of government would be tantamount to social and political dynamite.

Indeed, if political life and liberty are to endure, "calling into question the very principle of authority" must be deflected and popular will moderated by measures requisite to stability. This is why Montesquieu is so circumspect in answering Machiavelli's blunt question. The liberty of which Montesquieu speaks is an "ordered liberty" and his institutions are designed to secure its blessings.

Montesquieu prefers the term "national sovereignty" to "popular sovereignty" to designate the principle that informs his government. "National sovereignty" comprehends the existence of groups, including "the more enlightened classes of society," which deserve protection for the contribution they uniquely bring to a diverse, productive, and plural nation. According to "this idea," sovereignty is not determined by direct recourse to the authority of the people. This is the politics of the French Revolution that leads to violent disorder. What is involved here is a "crucial distinction" between a "pure democracy and one that is representative."

In Montesquieu's understanding, the people's will is refined by representation. Lawmakers are insulated from the immediate pressures of the people and are given an opportunity to resolve the interests of competing groups from broader and more informed perspectives. While the franchise assures the people that their representatives will be responsive to their particular interests, a too frequent recourse to elections would impinge upon the freedom of representatives to pursue a greater collective good that alone can dissolve more debilitating parochial conflicts.

Representation allows for the extension of republican regimes. This gives to such societies a character different from that envisioned by Rousseau and from that attained in ancient polities. The very size of such regimes, embracing myriad social groupings, is an obstacle to despotic ambitions that would be hard pressed to centralize and control such disparate elements. Furthermore, a certain moderation is brought to the law-making process where the emphasis is put upon the art of compromise between groups and coalition building to achieve the consensus that majority rule requires. The real challenge to Machiavelli is to establish despotism in just such a regime—a large, modern nation, with representative institutions.

The Restraining Function of Religion

Moreover, even the notion of "national sovereignty" is not absolute but only "relative." An understanding of sovereignty that recognizes only human authority is a "profoundly subversive idea" likened to the "materialistic and atheistic doctrine that set the French Revolution on its bloody course." According to Montesquieu, "it's not quite correct to say that nations are absolute masters of their destinies, for their sovereign master is God Himself, and they can never be beyond His power." If they did indeed possess absolute sovereignty, in principle they could do anything, including what transgresses God's eternal design and justice. "Who would dare go so far?"

We know already that Montesquieu is at least equally opposed to the contrary principle—divine right. This is "no less a deadly principle" leading through obscurantism to the same conclusion—despotism. However, in contrast to the febrile societies that issue from the notion of popular sovereignty, "divine right" logically favors societies such as that of India. The people there are separated into castes and turned into a "herd of slaves," led "by the hand of priests and trembling under the rod of the master." It cannot be otherwise when the sovereign "is the very representative of God on earth," having "complete power over the human beings under his sway."

According to Montesquieu, "furious partisan conflict" has been waged over the legitimacy of these two extreme positions. "Some cry: no divine authority; others: no human authority!" Yet, Montesquieu himself ventures to side with neither camp in an attempt to moderate the deepest source of party strife in modern regimes. He aligns himself with a "Supreme Providence" which places the real truth "between a divine right that does not include man in its considerations and a human right that does not include God." He concludes: "nations, like individuals, are free in the hands of God." That is, "they possess all rights and all powers provided they are exercised in accord with the rules of eternal justice."

Montesquieu's formulation in this regard is curious. However, his endeavor to preserve the vitality of the tension between the realms of divine and human authority relies on logic similar to what informs his division of power theory. Moreover, as we shall make clear later on, the religious question it raises from the political point of view touches upon perhaps the most fundamental level of Joly's work and the Machiavellian revolution that follows in succeeding parts of the *Dialogue*.

According to the position Montesquieu stakes out, there are clear moral limitations to the expression of popular will, beyond any institutional safeguards. Legitimacy seems to exist only in recognition of the principles of both divine and human authority, without admitting to one exclusively. To submit entirely to divine authority effectively entails the submission to a vicar of God. This brings about the capitulation of personal autonomy and puts our political rights in jeopardy. To accede solely to human authority, as expressed in the radical notion of popular sovereignty, would by a different path culminate in despotic rule, necessary to restore order and to carry out popular dictates. This leads to outrages that God condemns. It reduces the civilizing influences of His commandments and loosens the hold of the universal claims of conscience, where, Montesquieu earlier claimed, is found the source of all morality and law.

Montesquieu clearly intends to leave a rather broad scope for permissible human action, while attacking the extreme positions of those that feed party strife and seek tyrannical means to implement their policies. The one group may be designated the party of reaction for adhering to principles, discredited by modern science, that find their greatest influence in former eras. They are the ones who shout: "no human authority!" They are opposed in turn by by another group, the revolutionary party of secular thought that shouts: "no divine authority!" This group would eradicate all vestiges of religious influence, oblivious to its positive social benefits and the deeper levels of truth it addresses.

The Montesquiean position clearly calls for the overthrow of tyrannical power, whether it is the priest or the politician who wields it, the ayatollah or the shah, as it were. But short of wide extremes and manifest abuses from these quarters, toleration is appropriate. This is in recognition of the inexact and flexible lines of worldly and other-worldly authority and the sense of the importance of each to a moderate politics and a civil existence. Speaking as a "practical legislator," as "a statesman more than philosopher," and as "a jurist more than a theologian," Montesquieu tries to compromise the differences between parties by encouraging a politic sense of toleration. This serves a dual purpose. It conduces to a forebearing temperament appropriate to liberty and a plural nation while it also counters moral fanaticism, whether bred from religion or the claims of secularism.

Machiavelli had characterized the souls of ancient men as steeped in the severe virtues that preserved liberty and an independent polis. Such stout virtues were rigorously guarded in a closed society supported by impressive religious convictions. The conflicts between the claims of religion and politics either did not exist in the polis as today or were greatly mitigated. Joly's Montesquieu implies that in the modern soul the universal and dual claims of an earthly and otherworldly morality work to broaden the moral horizon and soften sensibilities. At the same time, the tension between worldly and heavenly authority in modern regimes restrains the tyrannical tendencies emanating from one source or the other as they affect politics.

Joly's Montesquieu suggests that the countervailing powers he wants to erect in his system of government and within society are appropriate to the two most fundamental sources of authority, whose vital tension he wants to preserve. This reflects the spirit of the liberal regime in its suspicion of authority, per se, which, no matter what the source, requires checks and balances. It also prepares us for the most radical feature of Machiavelli's politics as it is described in the rest of the *Dialogue*.

We are anticipating ourselves somewhat when we describe his revolution as aiming at the merging of the sources of both secular and religious authority, in a single person, a new ruler, who is as much a religious as a political founder. This thoroughly modern prince seeks to eradicate the fundamental source of party strife by responding to the claims of both reactionaries and secularists. Far from a thinker limited by the horizon of the Middle Ages, Machiavelli will call for a new political religion that answers to the deep psychological needs of individuals in the party of reaction as it provides the solid basis for a new social order. Fully consistent with certain strains of modern thought, this new understanding of things will win the party of revolution to the prince's side in the advance of a social agenda they favor. In a new "civil religion," unity is restored to the soul of modern man as it existed in antiquity, but at the price of a new and potentially universal form of despotism that remains our task to describe more fully later on.

Faced with the ambiguities of Montesquieu's position, Machiavelli declares that he would like to come to some definite conclusions and "to determine exactly what follows" from what Montesquieu just said about the authority of God over men. Machiavelli exposes the heterodox character of Montesquieu's position by citing written authority. According to Biblical text, "God makes kings." Nothing could be more clearly contrary to the Montesquieuan position or more succinct in supporting "divine right."

Montesquieu accuses Machiavelli of casuistry, perfectly in keeping with parts of *The Prince*. Contrary to Machiavelli, he appeals to logic and cites other Biblical text to make his case. The political sovereignty that God sanctions as part of His design of things does not extend to any and all sovereigns, who are charged with reigning according to His design and ruling according to His laws.

It is not, as Machiavelli implies, that the fact of rule is sufficient for God's investiture. "God did not will that the most sacrilegious reigns could invoke His sanction and that the vilest tyrannies could claim His ordination." Indeed, if it were as Machiavelli claims, "we would have to bow down before Nero as well as Titus, before Caligula as well as Vespasian." Though Machiavelli may well return Montesquieu's charge of bending Scripture to his own advantage, he does not choose to pursue such a tack.

Popular Sovereignty, Again

Machiavelli abstracts from Montesquieuan political science as it has been described for him. He is not interested in those forms of government that give most effective determination of national will, according to time and place, but what in a more fundamental way gives any form of government its legitimacy. For the moment, he would like to force Montesquieu to "the extreme situation" he so prudently avoids by considering how in fact legitimate human authority comes into being. He finally has Montesquieu admit that it is "the free will of the people" that "gives rise to sovereign power." In the final analysis, even in kingships, it is the people who ultimately dispose of sovereignty.

In words reminiscent of the American Declaration of Independence, to hold otherwise would be an outrage against "a truth of pure common sense," self-evident at least for right-thinking or enlightened men, however foreign to one who lived so close to the Middle Ages. Everywhere that sovereign power is established justly, that is, "other than by invasion or conquest," it came into being by "the free will of the people" by "means of election." This holds for ancient times as well as the Middle Ages and includes the case of France where, as with kingships elsewhere, heredity became the substitute for election—a legitimate conferral of authority by the people in deference to tradition and the brilliant services of a single family.

In other words, government is rightly established by the consent of the governed, by election or tacitly. It is a "fact" to which we constantly return in revolutionary times and which is always invoked for the "consecration" of new powers. According to Montesquieu, "consent" is the fundamental principle of legitimacy, prior and preexisting. But unlike former times, it "has been explicitly recognized only recently in certain constitutions of modern states."

While rightful authority may take any form of government congruent with the will of the people and their particular circumstances, modern regimes informed by enlightened institutions clearly exhibit an appreciable advance over former times. Government is not so liable to abuse in a broadly representative regime where the principle of consent is more explicitly realized in the ordinary operations of government. The people need not, as in former times, resort to revolution for the redress of grievances that can be corrected through the due process of law.

According to Machiavelli, if the people have a right to establish the form of government that they want, then there is nothing that prevents them from changing it. Therefore, just as they may choose their masters, they may, by caprice, overthrow them. It is not a regime of order and liberty that follows from such doctrines as much as "an era marked by continual revolutions." Machiavelli accuses Montesquieu of assuming the infallibility of the people in their choice of both good government and political institutions. But are not the people, being mere mortals, "prone to passion, error, and injustice?"

In denying the validity of consent, as expounded by Montesquieu, Machiavelli in turn is accused of denying the universal experience of history and what can be discerned as the basis for all legitimate revolutions and governments. The perversity of such a position and the denial of a "fact" that "could not have been otherwise since time immemorial," effectively returns man to the situation of accepting the most odious governments as his fated dispensation.

According to Montesquieu, oblivious to the events of 1848, an era of revolution is not forthcoming. The people may in fact legitimately overthrow their governments. But such a right is perhaps more important in reserve than in actual exercise. Revolutions will not be undertaken for light and transient reasons but only "in extreme cases and for just cause." Self-interest and morality, it seems, militate against an easy turn to such a course. Yet, the legitimate invocation of such a right keeps leaders properly chastened so as to obviate the necessity of its actual exercise.

Moreover, we need not await God's judgment to pass on our transgressions. A breach of justice on a matter so consequential is not without its own punishment. "They will be punished with the scourge of discord, anarchy, and despotism itself." Yet, in mentioning "despotism," Montesquieu does not recognize it as the inevitable upshot of the right to revolution. Such an inference, drawn by Machiavelli, is really not "worthy" of his "great intelligence." As Montesquieu stated earlier, one must not confuse "the right with an abuse that may or may not result from its exercise."

In fact, "God has granted peoples neither the power nor the will to change so radically those forms of government essential to their existence." The people as a whole are slow and obstinate and this favors conservatism and tradition. The violent overthrow of the ancient traditions and institutions that are integral to their definition as a people is exceptional. Montesquieu once again reverts to an organic metaphor to seal his point. "In political societies, as with all organic beings, the very nature of things limits the range of freedom."

Moreover, in addition to the natural conservatism of men are historic forces that militate against the possibility of a return to "an era marked by continual revolutions." According to Montesquieu, the influence of modern ideas will make men even less disposed to violence and revolution. The modern character has softened for various reasons, not least of which is the influence of industrial production. This has changed the mode of acquisition from slavery and warfare to a common enterprise that multiplies the ties of society in all directions as it shatters its rigid stratification. It is difficult to conceive a centralized despotism that could succeed in controlling such a diverse and complex social organization. The temper of the times could not be more remote from the force and fear that traditionally characterized regimes. According to Montesquieu, the proper soil for liberty is not Athens or Rome but the modern age, previously condemned by Machiavelli for its materialism and atheism. Montesquieu endeavors to show that these are superficial critiques and obscure more fundamental truths about the character of modern industrial society.

Modern Materialism, Rightly Understood

In modern societies, what may contemptuously be dismissed as "materialistic" is really not at all at odds with liberty. The productive wealth of a nation is crucially linked to economic liberty which, in turn, is crucially linked to political liberty. Montesquieu says that "industry cannot do without liberty and is itself only a manifestation of liberty." Furthermore, economic liberty necessarily gives rise to political liberty, so that it can be said that the most advanced industrial societies are also the freest."[5]

The free scope that is allowed economic activity is essential to maximize productivity. A rich and prosperous society not only accords with the desires of individual citizens, including the working class, but with the desires of the government. The rulers and ruled share a common interest in preserving a free and vital private sphere as the condition of abundance. Machiavelli vastly overstates the revolutionary potential of the working classes, whose self-interest is bound to maintaining the order by which they themselves can better their lot. "Industry is the archenemy of revolutions, for without social order, it perishes and the vital sap that sustains modern peoples is halted."

Moreover, the society Montesquieu is describing, far from being atheistic, is advancing ideas the source of which lies in the Christian faith. According to Montesquieu, "societies that live by means of work, exchange, and credit are essentially Christian, for all such powerful and varied forms of industry are basically applications of several great moral ideas derived from Christianity"— despite all appearances to the contrary. The anathema placed on slavery stems from the Christian recognition of man's essential equality before God. This led to new social developments and required a fundamentally different arrangement of productive forces than what obtained in the rigidly stratified and martial city-states of antiquity.

Several "great moral ideas stemming from Christianity are evident in even more subtle ways in such regimes. Once thought perilous to the soul, enterprise became elevated in Christianity as it evolved through its Protestant variant. The worldly duties of the elect found their proper virtues in diligence, thrift, sobriety, and prudence—the same traits that promised commercial success and are given full scope for development in societies that live by "work, exchange, and credit." Borrowing from an organic metaphor that appears in the Fifth Dialogue, we might say that the Christian religion spawns the capitalist ethos. But the former continues to endow the latter with its vital force even as the parent creed seems to expire. In the same Dialogue, Montesquieu had claimed that there existed a certain tension between our worldly and otherworldly responsibilities that served to restrain each other's extremist tendencies. He now argues that they also mutually reinforce each other in a moral sphere that they have come to share.

With the end of the Sixth Dialogue, Machiavelli has finally succeeded in distilling the essence of Montesquieu's teaching. Popular sovereignty, understood as the consent of the governed, comes to light as the only just basis of government. It is discovered at the bottom of all revolutions as a fundamental right upon which all legitimate forms of government are erected. At the same time, Machiavelli has left undisturbed his interlocutor's opinion of himself and his infamous teachings. He poses as the defender of divine right and reinforces the image of a man born at the dawn of modernity but still tainted by the influence of the Middle Ages.

Dramatically, the Sixth Dialogue ends by setting down the conditions for the their "wager." Montesquieu cedes nothing to his interlocutor and Machiavelli demands no more. He must establish despotism in the most advanced and enlightened state, as Montesquieu has in fact described it.

The Sixth Dialogue, which seems to end inconclusively insofar as the theoretical dispute goes, in fact sets the stage for the rest of the conversation. Montesquieu sees himself as the architect of a political order that has set man on the path of liberation. Machiavelli is about to introduce new modes and orders. As he does, Montesquieu's confidence in himself and the constitutional era over which he presides disintegrates. He is forced to abandon his stereotyped view of the Florentine and to confront his teaching again, this time, presumably, with the deadly seriousness it deserves.

Notes

1. Machiavelli claims that Montesquieu has been captivated or seduced by England and has universalized its particular experience. Later, in the face of Machiavelli's cyclical view of history, Montesquieu cautions against letting one era or historic example guide our understanding of present reality.

2. The best treatment of the point Machiavelli here makes in fact is made by Montesquieu in his discussion of education and his comparison of ancients and moderns on this

score. See Montesquieu, *The Spirit of the Laws* IV 4. Private education in ancient times reinforced public or civic education. In modern times, however, private education, or the education received from one's family, in being dominated by religion, leads in conflicting directions from what was required by civic education.

3. France is described as the most civilized nation in Europe and least amenable to the portrait of modern times drawn by Machiavelli. Before the century ends, France will have returned to conditions similar to oriental despotisms, according to Machiavelli.

4. The Fifth Dialogue concludes the discussion of the subject of popular sovereignty and it contains the most frequent references to religious themes. In the Montesquieuan scheme of things, religion is the ultimate safeguard for preventing an abuse of the people's right to sovereignty. Much will be said about this later.

5. Montesquieu offers his portrait of modern times as a definitive response to that offered by Machiavelli in the Fourth Dialogue.This effectively ends the debate in Part One. In the next dialogue, the last of this part, Machiavelli gives in rapid outline a realistic portrait of modern times and the wholly new form of despotism that exists in France. At the end of the *Dialogue* as a whole, he gives in "rapid outline" a sketch of Napoleon III.

Parenthetically, the coupling of economic development with political liberty is accepted as a "truism" today. Things may be more complicated than this. Political liberty may be a rarer plant than commonly thought. It also needs constant attention and nurturing.

Part II

The New Machiavellian Founding

Chapter Three

THE POLITICAL REVOLUTION I

The undermining of the liberal regime proceeds in an orderly fashion in Part Two of the *Dialogue*. Since Machiavelli is largely free at this point to develop the discussion as he wants, particular attention will be devoted to the way in which the discussion evolves. Joly is indeed a fine student of the works of Machiavelli and well-versed in their spirit. We have noted Konrad Heiden's appreciation for Joly's mastery of the Machiavellian teaching but we would also suggest a certain artful imitation of his way of writing. The *Dialogue*'s subtitle is "Machiavellian Politics in the Nineteenth Century" and some of the intricacies found in the Florentine's presentation of his political teaching can be found in Joly's work, as well.

Part Two contains ten Dialogues. The first Dialogue (the Eighth) begins with a discussion of the coup that brings the despot to power. What follows is how that power is made secure. The next two Dialogues (the Ninth and Tenth) deal with the "reform" Machiavelli will bring to the legislative and executive branches. This is followed by more Dialogues (the Eleventh and Twelfth) on the very important subject of the press. The first explains how the despot will defend himself against the press's attacks and gain control over the sources of information. The second describes how he will put it to use within his regime. This is followed, after an interruption, by a discussion of the judiciary, to which Machiavelli again devotes the major part of two Dialogues (the Fourteenth and Fifteenth). What is discussed in this section leads naturally to such a topic and allows Machiavelli to complete his reform of the three branches of government.

After the institutions of government have been discussed, Machiavelli turns his attack to society and important social groupings that present obstacles to despotism. The Fifteenth Dialogue addresses itself to political parties and the undermining of the political process. The freedom of association, guaranteed in a liberal system, encourages the formation of parties that organize and promote various social causes and interests. The next Dialogue (the Sixteenth) deals with other social groups, less conspicuously political but nevertheless important for their political effects. These include the militia, universities, the bar of law, and the clergy.

This last Dialogue deals largely with the police. It proceeds on a new plane at the end, but only, in the words of Montesquieu, to fill "a serious gap" left in the discussion of the judiciary.[1] It is through the police that ultimate social control will be effected. We anticipate the great importance of this topic in the broader scheme of Machiavelli's attack on society. The present chapter will comment upon the Eighth through the Eleventh Dialogue. The next chapter will begin with the Twelfth Dialogue, the end of which culminates at the dramatic heart of Joly's work. It will then proceed to a commentary on the rest of Part Two in the next chapter.

An example of the Machiavellian care with which Joly has constructed his work is revealed by the following consideration. The center of Part Two divides at the beginning of the Thirteenth Dialogue. Precisely at this point Montesquieu intervenes to break the order of the discussion, which has been proceeding by discussions involving pairs of Dialogues. The center of Part Two, which describes the political teaching of the *Dialogue*, is a short discourse separated from the topic of the two preceding Dialogues—the press, and that of the Dialogue following—the judiciary. It is a discussion of conspiracies. One is tempted to say that Joly understands the real core of the Machiavellian teaching to be its teaching on conspiracies.

Even more remarkable is the fact that the entire *Dialogue in Hell* also has its center at this very same place. There are twenty-five Dialogues in the whole work that divides at the beginning of the Thirteenth Dialogue, that is to say, at this same discussion of conspiracies—a theme of vast importance to Machiavelli's *The Prince* as well as *The Discourses*. Through the complex organization of the text, itself "meaningful" in a careful writer, we are given some preliminary evidence that we are perhaps in the presence of an uncommon student of the real Machiavelli. Joly shows an awareness not only of the darker Machiavellian themes but of an intricate way of writing that he broadly imitates, out of certain prudential considerations, and even in details of his text. It is an awareness of this way of writing that allows him to perceive different levels to Machiavelli's character and teaching, the true appreciation of which he endeavors to convey in the portrait of the philosopher given in the *Dialogue*.

Part Two of *The Dialogue in Hell* could be roughly characterized as describing a situation that begins in violence and ends in domestic peace, later declared the great good of Machiavellian politics. It shows how Machiavelli deals with the institutional obstacles to the consolidation of power he finds upon assuming the seat of rule. It then enters upon an important interlude, a discussion of the press, from which it ascends to the peak of the work. At that peak, there is a discussion of the propaganda offensive that can be launched through manipulation of the press. This is the most brilliant section of the work, as Jean-François Revel has sensed.[2] It prepares, finally, a teaching on conspiracies, a theme of the piece that has great resonance which will be touched upon throughout the commentary.

The teaching on conspiracies is actually out of order. Machiavelli intimates that, if not for Montesquieu's interruption at the end of the Thirteenth Dialogue, he would consider the topic to be more appropriate to his latter discussion of the police. In fact, the conspiracy discussion is resumed in the "appropriate place" in the last Dialogue of this part. Thus, Machiavelli's treatment of conspiracies envelops the second half of Part Two and has been prematurely taken up, literally to be put at the center of the work. A fuller discussion of Machiavelli's and Joly's way of writing will await a later chapter and the analysis of the *Dialogue*'s drama.

The second part of the *Dialogue in Hell* opens with the Eighth Dialogue where Machiavelli establishes certain ground rules for their "wager."[3] They will take as their hypothesis "a state constituted as a republic" and "endowed with all the institutions that guarantee liberty." Machiavelli assumes what he understands to be the most difficult case to prove his theories. It is a regime where resistance to despotism is most extreme and where, to all appearances, ideas, customs, and laws are least amenable to his project. Such a "hypothetical" case could indeed be France, specifically described in just such a manner by Montesquieu in a previous Dialogue. In any event, Machiavelli generously offers to take as his test case the Montesquieuan regime par excellence. Tactically, the granting of such a large concession at the outset makes it difficult for Montesquieu to quibble over small points later on.

Given such ground rules, we come to see why Joly thought the illustrious Montesquieu and the infamous Machiavelli appropriate interlocutors and adversaries for this dialogue in hell. Montesquieu presents the modern political teaching that is most profoundly "anti-Machiavel," insofar as the Machiavellian teaching is understood as the teaching of political tyranny. Montesquieu's early confidence in the face of Machiavelli's attack, and certainly some of the concessions he later grants him, stem from the fact that he thinks he has anticipated the threats of Machiavellianism. The anti-Machiavellian design for Montesquieu's regime is understood by its architect to be based on the accumulated wisdom of the ages. We are thus meant to see in its subversion the consummate test of tyranny and its most artful demonstration.

A "Hypothetical" Coup d' Etat

Montesquieu seemingly grants very little to Machiavell in agreeing with him that such a state is not immune to a successful coup d'etat. As Machiavelli points out, the opportunity for such a takeover is latent in "factions" that prey upon regimes throughout history and threaten society with divisiveness and breakdown. In fact, the factional threat is perhaps even more pronounced in a large, diverse, and plural nation where different groups proliferate and are free to organize in promotion of their interests. As Montesquieu himself admits, the elements of "civil war" are latent in party conflict and it is often the case that pretenders to rule kindle such conflagrations.

However, Montesquieu goes on, a successful coup would be singularly difficult in a modern, enlightened society. Given "modern mores" and deference to law, usurpers face "great dangers" and their success would be exceedingly rare. Moreover, they don't have the significance that Machiavelli attaches to them. A pretender might install his faction in rule. Yet, "power is in other hands. That's all."

Without overthrowing the political system altogether, the successful usurper find himself constrained by institutions beyond his control. "Public right and the institutional basis of power stay intact" and that is the "crucial thing" for Montesquieu. He grants to Machiavelli that dangerous factions can arise and be manipulated by the unscrupulous in securing power. However, he requires a further argument from Machiavelli that despotism can succeed usurpation without in turn provoking a popular counterrevolution.

Machiavelli describes the social conditions that favor the success of "an armed enterprise," which, for the sake of argument, Montesquieu grants as a distant if real possibility. Again, such a state of affairs, offered as a hypothetical case, in fact describes the actual conditions of France as it existed in the atmosphere of 1848.

> [Social discord] manifests itself in a cacophony of ideas and opinions, from contradictory pressure groups and interests, as happens in all states where liberty is momentarily unleashed. Political elements of all kinds make their class interests felt. Present are remnants of previously victorious but now vanquished parties, unbridled ambitions, burning greed, implacable hatreds. There are men of every opinion and doctrine—those who would restore former regimes, demagogues, anarchists, and utopians, all acting out of devotion to his cause and equally at work in trying to overthrow the existing order.

In sum, it is a political society more fractious than Montesquieu might well imagine and has nothing in common with the more regularized conflict of interest groups that characterize healthy liberal regimes. Its revolutionary symptoms can be read in the general anarchy of ideas, reflecting a yet more fundamental internal conflict between the privileged classes and the people. This is the deepest and perhaps most salient source of social discord. The diverse parties that create this impression of general anarchy can agree only in their opposition to the established order which is perceived by the bourgeoisie and the aristocracy as failing to protect their privileges and by the people as frustrating their desires.

In Part One of the *Dialogue*, Machiavelli contended that the need for order had primacy over the desire for liberty, "a secondary idea." The new prince will play to this need, now felt universally, in the breakdown of society. He will triumph in the vanguard of that faction which, because of its privileges, has most to lose in the drift toward anarchy. But he will direct his energies toward harnessing the popular forces that threaten to overwhelm a society, so divided, by their strength and numbers. His course is determined by two considerations. "First, the country feels a great need for tranquillity and will refuse nothing to whatever power can provide it. Second, given these partisan divisions, there is no real locus of power or rather only one—the people."

The appeal to the people will cover all necessary acts and their cause will supply "the blind power" behind his authority. The people in fact care nothing for the "legal fictions" that are the basis of Montesquieu's constitutional guarantees. The institutions still standing after the coup present no real obstacle to his power. They are purely formal, parchment barriers to the dictatorial force he has assumed.

For the moment, there is no power except his own. "I am legislator, executive, judge, and as head of the army, I'm firmly in the saddle, so to speak." He is himself a victorious pretender. In less than subtle reference to Louis Napoleon and his illustrious uncle, he will assume the name of a great man in history, "capable of capturing the imagination of the masses."

Enjoying a momentary respite from the discord of factions, the new prince will proceed according to advice found in *The Prince*, a book that contains all one has to know "for those who know how to read." His situation is not unlike that of a conqueror "forced to remake everything," even to changing the prevailing customs of the people.[4] However, modern times require him to eschew naked violence as far as possible and to move by indirection and cunning. He will not dismantle institutions but will "secretly tamper with each of their mechanisms." A new spirit will infect old laws. Without their outright abrogation, their hold gradually slips away. Following these generalities, he then proceeds to particular acts.

He will undertake "one big thing" and then "one little thing" on the day after his successful coup. The "big thing" Machiavelli's prince will do is to crush the factions that have opposed him. The insecurity of his position requires immediate eradication of serious opposition as well as a demonstration of strength to intimidate others that might want to test the usurper. He will unleash a terror that will cause "the most intrepid souls to shrink back." This is no time for temporizing or "false humanity." This terror is demanded to preserve the order of society itself.

Apparently, the modern prince does not wholly repudiate bloodshed. What is important is that it be employed well so that its use may be effectively circumscribed. Above all, Machiavelli implies, the prince must avoid a reputation for cruelty. Though circumstances would exonerate him, he nevertheless is visibly pained by the measures that necessity force upon him.

The prince takes great precautions to avoid the odium of the people, which belonged to Agathocles, by having others dispense his harsh justice. He pursues a clever policy that will at once make sure of his control over the armed forces at the same time that he covertly works through them as the agents of his repression. When an army punishes, it "never dishonors its victims." A public execution, skillfully managed by the armed forces, can impress the community with a sense of urgency without outraging its sense of justice.[5] Moreover, the odium of such acts will be attached to the prince's overzealous agents in the military, who are presumed to act without the knowledge or countenancing of the prince. Isolated in its actions, the army will in turn bind itself ever closer to the prince.

As Montesquieu points out, the prince's actions are not unlike those of Borgia in Cesena. The clever prince might profitably imitate him in sacrificing the willing accomplice and agent of his commands in a public execution, when his services are no longer needed. A violently grotesque demonstration of princely displeasure softens his subjects' character through fear while it satisfies their thirst for vengeance. It also endears them to the prince, their real tormentor, who is received as their liberator. The skillful use of terror is aptly illustrated in such an anecdote. Quickly and definitively applied, it will "prevent new bloodletting down the line." Moreover, the "image" of De Orco vividly introduces the theme of mass conditioning, a subject that gets immediately developed and is constantly amplified in Machiavelli's discourse.[6]

The "second thing" Machiavelli will do is mint a great amount of currency stamped with his visage. Given the urgent political problems he faces, he is accused of indulging in puerile vainglory. Machiavelli emphatically denies the charge, however. "From the day that my image appears on coins, I am king," he retorts. In fact, such currency multiplies the presence of the living ruler who insinuates himself in the daily matters of exchange among people in a modern commercial society. He assumes an honor normally reserved for dead national heroes, replacing the mottoes and abstract symbols of the republic with the new ruler's portrait.

Montesquieu initially misses the full significance of Machiavelli's action. Vulnerable in modern times are those staunch souls, "proud spirits," whose dignity rests on a noble indifference to material things and their blandishments. Even the enemies that opposed the prince's coup "will be forced to carry his portrait in their purses" and, "little by little," they will be forced, like everyone else, to associate him "with the material tokens of their joy."

In issuing such currency, Machiavelli intends an act of hubris to dazzle the proud, the ranks from which arise future rivals to his power. Not only will everyone, including the spirited, be obliged to carry the tyrant's image in their pockets, their eyes will also see the stamp of his "image" in a monumental architecture, of which more will be said later. In reducing the pretensions of the proud, Machiavelli gives a preliminary indication of how they will be undermined. He will ply society with material satisfactions to erode any independence of spirit. Finally, the proud, too, begin to smile on his countenance as the tyrant is deemed their active benefactor.

The real threat of the materialist mentality to the future of free institutions is not its effect on the people at large but those proud and spirited souls that would be the watchdogs of the people's liberties. The continued vitality of liberal society seems to rest on cultivating these characters and finding a noble outlet for their passions, turning a prideful, self-regarding posture toward concern for the common good. In the "two things" that Machiavelli will do after the coup, we have the key to Machiavellian politics. The able use of fear and love, of intimidation and benefaction, is directed toward controlling and pleasing the many and undermining that spirited group of people that pose the strongest threat to his regime.

If successful in reducing that spirited group, the prince will effectively homogenize society. It will assume the uniform character and taste of the masses of people, that, by virtue of an extended franchise, will rise to a politically dominant position. In effect, the class that sets the tone for society is seduced or isolated and can provide no counterpoise to popular passions. This prepares the way for the prince who can then, by various techniques, further shape society to conform to the mass desires that favor his despotic rule.

Still, "the two things" Machiavelli will do after his coup do not speak to what really concerns Montesquieu. The prince will continue to operate within the context of "a fundamental charter whose principles, regulations, and provisions are completely contrary" to *The Prince*'s "maxims of government." A third thing he has neglected to mention will be to "enact another constitution. That's all." There really is no difficulty in such a step, Machiavelli asserts. "For the time being, there is no other will, no other power than mine, and the popular element of the regime serves as the basis of my action."

Montesquieu imagines quite correctly that this new constitution "will not be a monument to liberty." However, he does not see how the momentary opportunity that crisis offers the prince as sufficient "to rob a nation of all its rights" and "all the principles under which it has been accustomed to live." Machiavelli not only names these principles, presumably so embarrassing to the prince, but will go so far as to include them in the preamble of his constitution. Being more attached to "appearances than reality," the people will be mollified and rest content with a mere declaration of his backing for "the great principles of modern right." He must be especially careful, however, not to enumerate them specifically within that document as in a bill of rights. This would restrict his "freedom to act" by holding him precisely accountable to certain standards of behavior. He prefers only to seem to accord all rights, while not specifically according any.

Montesquieu thinks such a ploy presumes too little of the people. They are attached to liberty as to a sacred patrimony and see in its defense the only surety for their lives and possessions. To the contrary, Machiavelli sees even in modern people nothing that would change his opinion expressed in *The Prince*: "The governed will always be content with the prince, so long as he touches neither their possessions or honor. And from that time on he has only to combat the pretensions of small numbers of malcontents, whom he can easily finish off."[7]

He presumes a freer rein for the prince when it comes to questions of constitutional principles such as "separation of powers." These are matters beyond the people's comprehension and concern. He will, however, be more scrupulous with respect to "civil rights," to which "the people are most attached." Moreover, those who can comprehend such principles are hostile to the ends they serve. The literati join the classes of the privileged in making known "a kind of hidden love for vigorous and powerful geniuses." The people do not "thirst for liberty." Nor are the educated few enamored of popular institutions that discount their influence. They rest contemptuous of a regime oriented by "interests" that concern them little.

Plebiscitory Democracy

Montesquieu assumes that Machiavelli's constitution will be foisted upon the people "without the consent of the nation." In fact, Machiavelli has no intention to so offend "traditional opinion." He must iterate his conformity with such ideas and will even go one better than Montesquieu in their direction. The nation will not only be involved with the new prince in the preparation of a fundamental charter but directly so. Accordingly, the people will be immediately called upon to ratify the coup "by popular vote." There is no question about the outcome. All are pleased by his reign's promise of general peace as well as by the benefits it promises to bring to each group individually.

Moreover, the prince sees himself as bringing about what all the peoples of Europe ardently aspire to. Universal manhood suffrage is decreed before such ratification takes place. The "poll tax and class-based qualifications" will be abolished. As Montesquieu quickly points out, such a step is far from progressive. It intends to reduce the influence of the enlightened few so that the prince may, by dint of raw "numbers," justify his usurpation and begin to harness the "blind power" of the people to his will. Absolutism will be set up in a single stroke as popular will becomes the very base of his government.

In Part One, Montesquieu held that constitutional rule was the most historically advanced regime precisely because its institutions gave soundest expression to the fundamental principle of popular sovereignty. In the rule Machiavelli begins to describe, that principle finds even more direct expression in a plebiscite called to ratify the constitution submitted by the prince. As Machiavelli insisted in his discussion of political origins, we indeed find "brute force" as the fundamental reality. But it is masked by certain "forms" congruent with the times and the democratic thrust of history.[8]

Machiavelli claims to be not unlike a Washington in establishing universal manhood suffrage for his nation. But as Montesquieu points out, Americans were not called upon to ratify their constitution directly. Rather, it was "discussed, deliberated, and voted upon by the representatives of the nation" in numerous assemblies. Machiavelli sarcastically ridicules Montesquieu's reproof as belonging to "eighteenth century" ideas, wholly out of step with "modern times."

Mimicking criticisms formerly made by Montesquieu, Machiavelli implies that it is not he who suffers from certain antiquated notions. "For goodness sake. Let's not confuse times, places, and peoples. My constitution is presented *en bloc*. It is accepted *en bloc*." The specific articles of its text will not be formally debated and discussed. In associating himself with Washington, the new prince has no intention of founding a republic in the manner of the United States. Rather, he invokes Washington's name as one who stood in the vanguard of the people, properly reflecting the spirit of time and place.

Ratified at large, in a plebiscite and not in conventions, the new constitution will retain a singleness of design and purpose that is requisite to a strong and enduring rule. "A constitution must issue, fully elaborated, from the head of a single man or it is only a work doomed to disappear," wracked by the dissensions of the various parties that presided at its composition. A look to history, to the examples of Sesostris, Solon, Lycurgus, Charlemagne, Frederick II, Peter I confirms his contention. In moving from the example of Washington to such figures, Machiavelli reveals his real ambitions for his prince to be imperial and not in the mold of Montesquieuan or Washingtonian liberalism.

Montesquieu objects to Machiavelli's comparison with these great historic founders. The situation he is facing is not at all comparable to the situation they faced. They were bringing new modes and orders to benighted peoples while the premise of their discussion has been an enlightened regime and a civilized people where public right is well established, and well-ordered institutions are functioning.

Machiavelli does not propose destroying Montesquieu's institutions to consolidate power in a single person, as his interlocutor presumes. Through his study of Rome and Titus-Livy, he is not unfamiliar with mixed regimes and even the "seesaw politics" described as uniquely belonging to the parliamentary states of Europe. What he has found is that certain powers belong to any government, if not a specific institution. Thus, it is necessary that there be an executive, legislative, judicial, and regulatory power somewhere. In a modern state, these might find themselves dispersed among a cabinet, Senate, Assembly, Council of State, and Court of Cassation.

Machiavelli does not want to shock political sensibilities, particularly where lip service is still paid to "the principles of 89," by overthrowing such institutions. Moreover, since the functions they serve are essential anyway, he will let them stand. Again, mimicking Montesquieu and his penchant for mechanistic metaphors, Machiavelli indicates the spirit of his reform. "Please listen to me carefully. In statics, moving the fulcrum causes a change in the direction of forces. In mechanics, changing the location of a spring causes a change in the machine's movement. And yet, it appears to be the same apparatus, the same mechanism." Machiavelli will proceed accordingly and will not change the overall machinery of the constitutional regime. Only the inner workings and internal springs will be rearranged.

In coupling his talk of imperial ambition with the republican institutions described by Titus-Livy, Machiavelli has subtly introduced the experience of Rome as background to the discussion of the present founding. Montesquieu correctly sees the spirit of reform introduced by the new prince as imitating that of Augustus when he destroyed the Republic. The "names" of institutions stay the same while their purposes are redirected. The leitmotif of the Roman experience, introduced by Joly on the title page of the *Dialogue* itself, surfaces most obviously at this point, as Machiavelli acknowledges Augustus as an appropriate "model" for his founding.

Machiavelli harkens to "the experience of the ages" to demonstrate the eternal relevance of living genius for "greatness" in rule. He intends to contrast such an understanding with the impersonal and systemic politics of Montesquieuan parliamentary government. His scheme represents nothing more than "schools for quarreling" and "centers of sterile conflict." "Public debate and the press" condemn such governments to "impotence."

While Montesquieu wants to hedge in vaulting ambition in the name of rational politics, Machiavelli wants to give it latitude for its vast designs. He appeals to a restoration of vital powers as wielded by one of the few "men of genius" that history ordains to lead. The despot claims to proceed from an elevated point of view and means his reforms to be seen in the light of the exasperating stalemates and respective turbulence that can infect parliamentary government.

Legislative and Administrative Reform

Having heard Machiavelli elaborate upon the general spirit of his reforms, Montesquieu demands his interlocutor stop talking in "generalities" in order to come to some precise conclusions. Machiavelli then announces his "first reform." He will abrogate ministerial responsibility. The sovereign will accept direct responsibility for all that occurs in his administration. Machiavelli reasons that the people attribute such responsibility anyway. To accept total responsibility is therefore in accord with public sentiment and is more in keeping with the magnanimity he would like to convey in his person. It would thus further his direct rapport with the people.

Machiavelli then turns to the most popular branch of government. Parliamentary initiative in introducing legislation runs counter to the personal responsibility of the prince. It is, of course, ultimately threatening to despotic rule in permitting the lawmaker to "take the place of the government." Accordingly, Machiavelli denies to all but the sovereign the right to propose laws, a step that Montesquieu sees in turn as effectively setting him up "as the sole legislator."

Still, it would seem, the prince finds himself in tight straits. Universal suffrage, Machiavelli admits, is the sole basis of his rule. Yet, if the prince is solely responsible for the actions of his government, it is inconceivable that he would survive even the first crisis. Contingencies that require unpopular steps threaten the foundations of his rule. Ultimately, a new majority of representatives in the Assembly may bring down the prince without recourse to violence.

Machiavelli reminds Montesquieu that the constitution has reserved certain dictatorial powers for the prince in emergency situations. As head of the armed forces, he has the entire public force in his hands to meet insurrections. He may also petition the people directly through the plebiscite were he to encounter too much intransigence even within his "reformed" Assembly. As a matter of fact, Montesquieu's reservations come too soon. Machiavelli has barely begun to list his scheme of reform for the Assembly and the rest of his government's institutions, all of which intend to wed popular will with autocracy.

Beyond denying lawmakers legislative initiative, Machiavelli also denies them the right to change laws once submitted to them. Their deliberations are confined to voting a measure either up or down, without compromise. Such then is the beginning of his intention to "reinvigorate" politics.

The employment of any extraordinary constitutional power would be truly exceptional, since control over the rules of the Assembly would seemingly suffice to effect the sovereign's will. The size of the body will be reduced, allowing leadership to exert effective discipline. The leadership is appointed by the sovereign and not elected by the membership. Machiavelli would then reduce the length of the legislative session, which denigrates that body and increases reliance on executive prerogatives and decrees. Any popular agitation that might find voice in the Assembly can be quickly silenced as the sovereign assumes the power of convoking and proroguing the legislature.

Above all, he "would abolish the unpaid status of legislative service." The implication is that, henceforth, bribery, more or less covert, will be one of the more efficacious means of promoting public policy. A truly independent legislature, drawn from the leisured and more enlightened segments of society, will at once be more democratic and more malleable. In sum, there are multiple ways of neutralizing the power of the Assembly.

For Montesquieu, the subversion of the Assembly would seemingly suffice to establish the prince's supremacy. But "in reality, sovereignty could not be established on such frail foundations." At the end of the Ninth Dialogue and before he turns to the "reform" of the Senate, Machiavelli indicates more generally how power comes to be exerted within a nominally popular regime.

He will leave Montesquieu's form of government intact but will shift the base of power from the Legislature proper to the Judiciary, which, by a change in the appointment process, is tied to executive will. Ultimate sovereignty for the prince may derive from the plebiscite, but real authority within the frame of government moves in a contrary direction, away from nominally popular institutions, until it concentrates and reaches its proper locus at the throne, where all meaningful action is determined.

At the end of the Ninth Dialogue, Montesquieu accuses Machiavelli of acting like a king while at least according to the ground rules of their discussion, they are in a republic. According to Machiavelli, however, the "exact time" he proclaims himself king is "just a matter of expediency." In fact, the discussion of the Senate that opens the next Dialogue reveals the prince, in action, making the transition from a republican past to an imperial future.

The Tenth Dialogue continues the discussion of Rome with reference to Montesquieu's "memorable work" *The Causes of the Greatness of the Romans and Their Decline.*[9] Specifically, Machivaelli asks the author of such "exhaustive studies" to discourse for a moment on the role of Senate under Augustus. Montesquieu declares that "until the last days of the Republic," the Roman Senate was "an autonomous institution vested with great privileges" and powers. Its independence, revered through long tradition, was key to "the greatness it stamped on the Republic." It is not clear by what means the Emperors succeeded "finally in stripping it of its power." In any case, it became nothing more than "a tool in the hands of the Emperors."

Machiavelli declares that his Senate will play a political role "analogous to the Roman Senate in the times that followed the fall of the Republic." It is always necessary for the prince to cover his actions with respected authority. "At the side of the prince must be found bodies of individuals that remain impressive by virtue of brilliant titles, respectability, and the personal illustriousness of those who compose them." The imposing stature of the Senate will fill this need and is "the keystone" in Machiavelli's constitution.

Continuing his scholarly commentary, Montesquieu indicates that the Senate during the Empire made law by *senatus-consultum.* Machiavelli abjures such a power in his regime as foreign to modern times. Besides, the new prince has himself such decree-making powers. The real power of his Senate is reserved for the most solemn occasions, as guardian of the fundamental law.

According to Machiavelli, modern theories have tried to anticipate everything in their constitutional schemes of government. Machiavelli "is not prone to such an error," which would so circumscribe his powers. To perpetuate his rule, his constitution must have ample means to adapt to change. "Then, in serious crises there might be some other alternative to the disastrous expedient of revolution." The Senate will propose amendments by *senatus-consultum* to the fundamental law. In the manner of "a truly Roman Senate," as Montesquieu says, it will be able to judge statutes and ultimately define the meaning of individual constitutional articles.[10]

Machiavelli denies that his constitution will be vaguely drawn and subject to disputes that dilute reverence for it. If everything cannot be anticipated, everything "essential" must be. He will not constrict himself and be subject to contingencies by strictly limiting the means to amendment and thereby the survival of his power. On the other hand, he will see to all that is essential to the preservation of that power in any circumstance.

Pressed by Montesquieu, Machiavelli admits that the Senate will have no real power of its own. Theoretically, it may so amend the constitution "as to make it disappear altogether" if the prince judges it expedient. Montesquieu charges that the people will not stand for such a deception. But, exactly as in the adoption of the constitution itself, the people in plebiscite will be called upon to ratify any constitutional change *en bloc*. Dissidence will be controlled because, ultimately, the people as a whole will be made a party to any changes. The despotic design that is advanced in such constitutional changes will be cloaked in concerns for making the popular will effective.

Machiavelli will be "briefer" about the Council of State, a powerful tool of centralization, ready at hand. This is the proper rule-making body. Moreover, at its discretion, it may remove from the courts any matter of an administrative character it prefers to decide, thereby effectively making itself "both party and judge in its own case." As the body that drafts the laws, it is merely an adjunct of the prince. And he will exert the tightest "political control." Like the Senate, its eminence will lend prestige to what are the plots and maneuverings of the prince.

With the discussion of the Council of State, Machiavelli has presented his constitution "in finished form," except for the discussion of judicial matters, which Machiavelli would rather postpone until later. Montesquieu proceeds to "add up" the prince's powers, equating them with the numerous lawmaking functions he has taken upon himself. These effectively extend legal power into properly legislative and judicial grounds and find for their legitimacy popular sanction in the plebiscite.

It is agreed that the powers are indeed formidable. For Montesquieu, we will recall, the primary political question relates to how the laws are made. For all intents and purposes, it is the prince alone who makes laws, directly, and when convenient, indirectly. Montesquieu sees the "most difficult" part of Machiavelli's task in establishing despotism as already accomplished. He grants too much at this point, at least according to Machiavelli, whose political art enters a more delicate phase. Machiavelli turns to a mass of subsidiary rights, which follow implicitly from constitutional rule, but which are wholly "incompatible with the new order" of things. These include the freedom of the press, the right of association, the independence of judges, the right of suffrage, periodic elections, the institution of the civil guard—topics that receive due treatment eventually

At the outset, Machiavelli will admit only the rights that are convenient for him. None follow necessarily or in "principle." In fact, the "day after" his constitution takes effect, "a series of decrees" will abrogate all the rights and liberties that might prove dangerous. In acting in such a way, Machiavelli is applying a maxim of *The Prince* to contemporary times.

The successful innovator will undertake reform not in a piecemeal fashion but all at once. The essentially conservative nature of the people will endure a sudden and definitive change more readily than a series of changes that constantly strain patience. In effect, the constitution they are asked to adopt—*en bloc*—fulfills the prince's prescription.[11] Furthermore, any harsh measure will be decreed forthwith, since from that point on the prince will become progressively more tolerant. The liberties he is forced to repress are solemnly promised restoration after "the storm" abates. Soon he will take it upon himself "to pass for the most liberal man" in the kingdom.

"In the meantime," Montesquieu assumes, he will "directly suppress all liberties." Machiavelli objects to the word "directly." The successful innovator must be as much "fox" as "lion." This reference to *The Prince*[12] indicates to Montesquieu that Machiavelli is about to enter a "new phase" in his teaching.

Controlling the Press

The next two Dialogues are devoted to a discussion of journalism and the press, a topic chosen by Montesquieu after the outline of the constitution is finished. Machiavelli avers the shrewdness of Montesquieu in turning the discussion to what he calls "the most delicate part of my task." In fact, Machiavelli clearly warms to a topic that displays his Machiavellian arts in the most impressive manner by detailing a project that is "both momentous and subtle."

The discussion approaches the heart of Machiavelli's teaching. It concludes literally at the end of the Twelfth Dialogue where Machiavelli delivers the longest uninterrupted statements in the work to this point. Dramatically, the silence of Montesquieu in so deferring to Machiavelli contrasts sharply with his captious criticisms and repeated interruptions at the beginning of this discussion. It is testimony to Machiavelli's dialectical skill that he so changes Montesquieu's grudging recognition to an unabashed admiration for his artfulness and the power of his mind.

His discussion outlines the uses to which his press will be put and presents a scheme unprecedented in its vision. "No government has conceived of anything as bold" as what he is about to describe. The most dazzling part of Machiavelli's teaching, it represents one of the earliest analyses of modern political propaganda and the enormous potential it holds for shaping the masses to tyranny. The use to which it will be put is much more than Montesquieu can possibly imagine. Montesquieu comes to realize Machiavelli's ultimate intention is to transform "the instrument of thought" into "instruments of power" wielded by he prince.

A reminder of *The Prince* might prove fruitful to introduce the section on propaganda. *The Prince* advises the political innovator to use his own arms and not those of another, as one is more secure and less dependent in the use of what is one's own.[13] According to Montesquieu in Joly's *Dialogue*, the modern arm par excellence against tyranny is the press. In effect, Machiavelli illustrates in this section how he would appropriate the weapon of his adversaries as his own. In the Eleventh Dialogue, Machiavelli shows how he will in fact, through various schemes, defend himself against the press's attack. This is "the defensive part," so to speak, of the regulations he would impose on the press. Next, he will make Montesquieu understand how he will employ this institution to his own advantage.

In the Eleventh Dialogue, Machiavelli first indicates how he will deal with newspapers, then how he will deal with other publications. We shall see that he intends to assume control over all sources of thought within his regime. Two sections are devoted to newspapers. One concerns the regulations governing domestic news and the other concerning the steps that will be taken to control even the foreign press. He thus intends to control and use information arising from beyond his borders or, when not convenient, at least to neutralize its effects.

Machiavelli admits that he is entering a task that requires finesse. If he decided to suppress newspapers outright, he would imprudently shock public sensibilities that are always dangerous to oppose openly. He will proceed by indirect means in an attempt to "muzzle" the press, not suppress it. Still, he indicates that such a task is simplified by the way it conducts itself in parliamentary governments.

In a scathing critique, Machiavelli alludes to the peculiar knack of the press "of making itself hated." Among other things, it is "mercenary," not unlike any other enterprise for profit. Its character is formed accordingly as it appeals to prejudice and a disparaging leveling that finds popular favor. Being in the service of "violent, selfish, and narrow passions," it is a "public voice" but for narrowly interested groups. For such reasons, it often fails to attain the larger view that justifies its freedom. It often stands rightly accused, as the Anglo-Saxon press of today, of being "unjust," "operating without magnanimity and patriotism." Joly would agree that there is much truth in a view that famously saw the journalistic corps as "effete," "impudent," and "snobbish."[14]

Montesquieu is aware of all these "grievances against the press." In fact, it is easy enough to amass a great many more. Yet, its crucial role in liberal regimes cannot be denied. The fate of free governments, by its very nature, is tied to public opinion that the press forms. It forces the depositories of public authority to govern constitutionally. It obliges them to be honest, restrained, and respectful of constitutional practices in relations among themselves and with regard to others. Finally, "it gives to anyone who is oppressed the means to voice grievances and be heard." To adequately perform its function, it needs freedom from state control and restrictions. It stands, so to speak, virtually unchecked among the system of checks and balances it surveys. It has no direct government power and it is granted these prerogatives in deference to the role it plays in the grander design of free government. "Much can be pardoned in an institution that, despite so many abuses, serves so many crucial ends."

According to Machiavelli, however, the "masses" are utterly incapable of understanding that grander design and what it implies for them. He is freer than Montesquieu realizes to meet its manifest "abuses" through certain measures, each of which cumulatively acts to reconstruct the press's role in the context of the new regime and to actively shape thought to its requirements. The importance of its role is perhaps even more magnified in the Machiavellian scheme. By direct and indirect means, the new prince attempts to move public opinion beyond the clash of narrow interests which the press serves to what in the Twelfth Dialogue is revealed as a new collective consciousness united behind a new historic leader.

Machiavelli begins by announcing that all future newspapers will be thoroughly reviewed by the government prior to being authorized to operate. This is not an adequate safeguard to protect the prince, Montesquieu points out, as even licensed newspapers can become antagonistic later on. "The spirit of newspapers" emantes from its board of editors. It guides the thought of reporters and shapes the newspaper's stance on a variety of complex matters. In response to Montesquieu, Machiavelli will authorize any changes in editorial personnel, subsequent to a newspaper's licensing.[15] As with government institutions, he intends to undermine the press by tampering with "its internal mechanisms." As Montesquieu again points out, such measures do not prevent old newspapers with hostile editorial boards from speaking out. We shall see how such ripostes disappear as the scope of Machiavelli's design overwhelms him.

To undermine present newspapers and discourage any antagonistic new publications, Machiavelli will continue his indirect assault. All newspapers will be subject to a stamp tax and a surety of future solvency. As profit-making operations, newspapers are vulnerable to economic disincentives that, if rigorous enough, will drive even established newspapers out of business. In any event, if such newspapers do in fact become too expensive, they will likely be the luxury of the well-to-do, that is, the classes least prone to incendiary politics.

We thus have the first instance of policy goals indirectly effected through the taxing power, a technique that promises wider application, given the nature of modern finance described in the subsequent part of the *Dialogue*. By such measures, the prince can reduce the number of hostile newspapers while, we shall shortly see, he takes other steps to proliferate friendly enterprises. Nevertheless, Montesquieu objects, all measures to this point do not affect the publications of political parties and other associations. These are not profit-making ventures. However, Machiavelli has something "to shut them up" and introduces measures that are blatantly more repressive.

He criticizes the jury system as it exists in several states of Europe, particularly as a proceeding to handle the "misdemeanors" of the press. It is a "deplorable measure" that often ends up enflaming opinion it seeks to quell by providing a forum for dissident views. Machiavelli has respect for the cleverness of journalists whose subtle way of writing vouches for a nimble intelligence beyond the reach of the common juror. "A writer can disguise his attacks in such varied and subtle ways that it is not even possible to bring clear charges before the courts." Machiavelli therefore suggests that such offenses be handled by an administrative proceeding, conducted without the same regard to formal procedures that attain in regular judicial proceedings.

Again, the prince's goal will be achieved by indirect means, through threats and intimidation wherever possible. In the text, the new prince speaks in his own voice, underscoring his personal solicitude for such matters. He will not suppress any writer without cause and tries to make such "restraint" appear commendable. He explains that more aggressive steps would be counterproductive anyway. He likens the corps of journalists to the head of Hydra—"if you cut off ten of them, fifty more grow."

Knowing the penchant for writing in the now literate times of Europe, he actually encourages newsmen in their writing endeavors. "I don't want to summon you everyday before the courts" or be constantly relying on the law to curb infractions. "Even more, I don't want an army of censors looking into the day before what you are going to publish the next day." Nevertheless, the activities of recalcitrant troublemakers will be closely monitored. After a few warnings, certain things will simply not be tolerated. They may write, by all means, but "no subtleties" and nothing that will obstruct the prince or diminish his power. He alone will judge such things.

As Montesquieu points out, the journalist is not the target in all this. The ultimate object of the prince is not so much to be rid of certain noisome newspapermen, "nasty and spiteful journalists" who "constantly put themselves above the law." It is rather to strike at the association and the cause a newspaper serves. Two convictions in one year will automatically bring about the suppression of the newspaper.

Machiavelli lists other restrictions that might find application. He will forbid verbatim reporting of chamber debates and judicial proceedings. The publication of "false" news, whether in good or bad faith, might be penalized by the reporter's incarceration. Nor will the reporter be allowed to pass on news from abroad in an effort to escape personal responsibility. The prince ultimately determines the "veracity" of matters that pertain to him. This is as it should be and will give pause to newsmen who often lack material proof for "news" that is really only their personal convictions.

Montesquieu grants that the prince may secure himself against the domestic press by such measures. He then draws Machiavaelli's attention to the foreign press, ostensibly beyond the prince's control but which still might hold him accountable before world opinion. Machiavelli proposes the most rigorous punishment of those who distribute news items from unauthorized foreign sources. "First, the introduction or circulation in the kingdom of any unauthorized newspapers or writings will be punished with imprisonment, and the punishment will be sufficiently severe to stifle the desire." Furthermore, "those of my subjects convicted of having written against the government while abroad will be investigated and punished when they return."[16]

Assuming he governs a large kingdom, the small states on the border will be sufficiently intimidated to curb their own press in what regards him and to extradite agitators. According to *The Spirit of the Laws*, "the areas surrounding a despot must be laid waste." The modern despot also will not stop short in taking all steps necessary to prevent the penetration of civilization. The prince might try to seduce opinion-makers in foreign countries responsible for disseminating information entering his realm. Machiavelli quotes Benjamin Constant in describing the actions of his prince. He will make "his kingdom into an island where what happens in Europe will not be known, and the capital will be made into another island where what happens in the provinces will not be known."[17]

Having apparently satisfied Montesquieu with regard to his control of the press, Machiavelli next turns to how he will control other publications. In fact, control would be even easier as their production involves different enterprises. The publishing industry can be crippled by attacking the printer, the editor, or the bookseller, all of whom will be regulated by the government. Taxes will be particularly steep on small tracts that deal with political themes. "I shall impose a heavier stamp tax on books that do not have a certain number of pages." In what is a comment on modern tastes, Machiavelli declares that steep taxes on long and expensive texts are not necessary. There is no will to write them and certainly no inclination on the part of the masses, otherwise diverted, to read them.

"Today, there are hardly any but a few devils that have the conscience to write books." Economic considerations will discourage "literary pretensions" while "criminal law" will discourage printing. "If there are writers daring enough to write books against the government, they must not be able to find anyone to publish them."

Indirect censorship will be employed to exert pressure, not so much on the author, as on the publisher. Timid types will simply refuse to deal with certain material. Moreover, through the surveillance of printers and publishers, the government can procure subject matters prior to its distribution and sale. Unlike newspapers, prior restraint is not disavowed as the ultimate method of control.

Where Montesquieu assumes that Machiavelli is already well fortified against the press, Machiavelli declares that he has completed only one half of his project. What remains, the subject of the Twelfth Dialogue, is how Machiavelli will use the press against itself, followed by a discussion of how Machiavelli will employ it for propaganda purposes. In effect, Machiavelli intends his government to absorb the function of journalism in order to project the information and thought it wishes.

Notes

1. The gap that needs filling in concerns individual liberties, police powers, and the judiciary.

2. See Revel's Preface to the *Dialogue aux Enfers*, xviiff.

3. Toward the beginning of the Eighth Dialogue, Montesquieu remarks that their discussion here would find the perfect setting in "the gardens of Rucellai." This was the setting for Machiavelli's dialogue on the *Art of War*. Fabrizio Colonna (Machiavelli?) engages in conversation with the amiable and capable Cosimo Rucellai. He comments on some rare plants that the garden contains. The plants were favored by their Roman ancestors and Cosimo's grandfather, a Renaissance enthusiast of ancient things, planted them. Fabrizio comments that it's too bad that the enthusiasm for the past attaches to such trivial things. The discussion then turns to the way their Roman ancestors conducted war. This passing reference to Rucellai is another example of the effort Joly makes to embellish his *Dialogue* with details relevant to the lives of his interlocutors. Montesquieu is also intimating that they are discussing dark themes that should not be spoken of openly.

4. See *The Prince*, V and VI for reference to the proper conduct of one who has recently acquired rule. That text is meant to give a "general idea" of how the prince will proceed. What follows are the details of how he will conform to *The Prince*'s prescriptions in a modern setting. "For those who know how to read," all is contained in *The Prince*, Machiavelli claims, giving a dig to Montesquieu. Remember that Montesquieu considers himself as among those who truly understand Machiavelli. Here Machiavelli is indeed not saying anything "new."

5. Reference to Agathocles occurs in *The Prince* VIII. It is interesting that in addition to a reputation for cruelty, Agathocles affronted the prevailing religious sentiments of his time. The actions of Machiavelli's prince in the *Dialogue* should be kept in mind in this regard.

6. See *Prince* VII for references to the Remirro de Orco episode.

7. The different character of the nobility and the populace is the focus of discussion in *The Prince* IX. Joly quotes from there. Joly's Machiavelli is very attentive to that "noble" class of "spirited men" and what it implies for politics. He returns often to this theme in the course of his discourse.

8. Nazi apologists, who saw the Second Empire as a precursor to the Third Reich, especially admired the way Napoleon periodically used the plebiscite to justify his dictatorship.

9. Machiavelli's treatment of Rome is a source of inspiration for Montesquieu's "memorable work." David Lowenthal, in his Introduction to Montesquieu's *Consideration of the Causes of the Greatness of the Romans and their Decline* (Ithaca, N.Y.: Cornell University Press, 1965) 1, begins his discussion of Montesquieu's book by asserting how formidable the influences of the *Discourses* was upon it. When Joly's Machiavelli praises the author of the *Considerations*, it is genuine. The two "adversaries" might again be trading sincere compliments. Joly's Machiavelli has already remarked on the similarity of certain of Montesquieu's ideas to his own. Throughout the *Dialogue*, Joly often refers to common ground shared by the two disputants.

10. The irony is that while Montesquieu speaks of a "truly Roman Senate," a parody of the Napoleonic constitution is being discussed.

11. See *The Prince* VIII.

12. The infamous phrase appears in *The Prince* XVIII.

13. See *The Prince* VI which is entitled "Of New Dominions Which Have Been Acquired By One's Own Arms and Ability."

14. Spiro Agnew's famous characterization of journalists was in fact coined by a then obscure journalist. Remember, too, that Joly made his living as a journalist and a government aide.

15. Vladmir Putin is probably the most notorious practitioner today of Machiavellian arts here described.

16. It is remarkable that Joly foresaw all the dangers he was running in publishing his work. The first publisher he approached, a Frenchman, was indeed a "timid soul" and refused to print Joly's work, having divined its true target—Napoleon III. Joly then sought publication in Brussels. Joly here indicates some of the reasons why he wrote the tract he did. Among other things, it conforms to prevailing literary tastes. What is said about the character of contemporary authors, the reading public, and the secret police is no doubt meant to shed light on Joly's endeavors in the *Dialogue*. The design and intention of Joly's work gets fuller elaboration in chapter 9.

17. Cf. *The Spirit of the Laws* V 14. Montesquieu there writes that a despotic state is "happiest when it can look upon itself as the only one in the world, when it is environed with deserts, and separated from those people whom they call barbarians. Since it cannot depend on the militia, it is proper that it should destroy a part of itself."

Chapter Four

THE POLITICAL REVOLUTION II

Machiavelli may belittle journalists but he doesn't "the press." Indeed, it is because of the press that governments fall in parliamentary regimes. Because "journalism wields such great power," his government will turn journalist itself. It will become "journalism incarnate" in actively shaping thought to what will be presented as an historic rule. "No government has conceived of anything as bold as what I am about to describe," he declares.

In the Eleventh Dialogue, Machiavelli listed the steps he would take to contain the press in an effort to reduce and control any hostility emanating from such quarters. The tools he employs are many and impressive but useful for what has a limited purpose in the overall scheme of things. In the Twelfth Dialogue, Machiavelli shows how he will expand the role of the press in his regime in proliferating newspapers and other means of communication. This will provide the proper outlet for the vanity that stands behind the penchant for writing in modern times.

He intends to enlist the most talented writers of his generation to his cause and plays upon their secret predilections for power. The prince himself, we shall see, has no mean pretensions in the field of letters and moves freely among men of ideas. He bestows honors and other recognition on otherwise disaffected intellectuals to reconcile them to the new political order. They are capable of projecting the prince's rule in proper terms, while their art embellishes his reign with monuments to its spirit. In such literate times, they are essential allies of the prince and key to the success of its political project.

His more important allies will speak from their favored positions and will give voice to the loftiness of princely sentiments. Their defense of the prince's policies will be projected against the background of the narrow self-interested views advanced by the myriad journals found in parliamentary regimes. Ultimately, he intends to convert the press, the freedom of which was to stimulate wide-ranging debate on public policy, to an instrument in service to the prince's regime.

Putting the Press to Use

The new role for the press bespeaks a fine appreciation for the character of modern writing. The prince predicates his own effectiveness in this area precisely upon his understanding of its nature in modern times. He uses the press to create certain impressions that help insinuate certain ideas. He eschews cruder propaganda techniques and prefers to shape rather than force opinions. His scheme is deemed appropriate for the most civilized regime in modern Europe, where, according to Montesquieu, ideas still have the greatest influence.

Machiavelli begins rather simplistically. He will count the number of opposition newspapers in his kingdom and double their number with pro-government journals whose ties to the prince will be covered. Machiavelli's plan gets refined. He will categorizie the newly created journals into several groups. The first group will present the most orthodox views and will appeal to the most fanatic of government partisans. The next group will rally that "mass of lukewarm and indifferent men" whose abiding interest lies in support of public order, regardless of government. These newspapers will reflect the official slant on things but in less demagogic terms.

A more important role is reserved for the remaining categories of newspapers. His personnel will be used to infiltrate parties and other associations to form respectable alternatives to existing journals. To become credible in this capacity, they must downplay official orthodoxy. Once in place, they will proceed to subtly shade opinions. Such journals will be secretly tied to the prince as if by a leading string. Those who work in key positions in the journals ostensibly agitate for their group's concerns, while they are actually employed by the government and serve its purposes.

Finally, every variety of opinion will be absorbed into the government's press and be secretly manipulated. "Like the god Vishnu, my press will have a hundred arms, and these arms will stretch out their hands throughout the country delicately giving form to all manner of opinion." Such a scheme begins to do justice to the presumed sophistication of the populace in succeeding to neutralize inconvenient views while amplifying its own.

The whole enterprise will be secretly controlled and coordinated from one center. What appears under the title of "division of printing and the press" has more in common with a bureau of intelligence. Montesquieu is confounded by the orders that are issued from such an agency. For example, the prince will be attacked. Newspapers devoted to him will "cry out and stir up trouble" for the prince. But never will the principles of his regime or the foundations of his rule be subject to criticism. Noise will be heard but only on peripheral matters. It signifies nothing more than polemical differences.

The benefits to the prince are many. In suffering the attacks he himself has orchestrated, the prince will earn a reputation for great restraint and tolerance. The press will be supposed to have the widest latitude of freedom yet there will never be heard the least doubts about the essentials of the prince's rule. Because of their reputation for being captious, the reporter's silence on such matters will be heard as loud praise.

The description of the scheme to this point, called "truly Machiavellian" by Montesquieu, expounds upon even more noteworthy benefits. Through his corps of journalists, the prince will establish an almost organic rapport with the people. "A secret and mysterious sympathy" unites the prince with the will of the people. The throne will be enveloped in a reverent awe. With the help of government newspapers, he can "plumb public opinion and assess whatever reaction" he provokes. He is free to try out schemes, float trial balloons, incite enthusiasm or hold it back, and attack enemies "without ever compromising" his power.

As a slightly more chastened Montesquieu points out, the sole vulnerability in all this would seem to be the independent newspapers that were in existence prior to the coup and are not affiliated with the government. Machiavelli is confident that his secrets will not reach the public. "Surely you are aware that journalism is a kind of freemasonry. Those who live by it are all more or less attached to one another by bonds of professional discretion." Indeed, "like ancient auguries, they do not easily divulge the secrets of their oracles." But even those privy to such secrets will be intimidated by the more severe measures leveled against potential troublemakers.

The prince does not fear the few sharp reporters in his capital. Any influence they have will be circumscribed and exist only in that city. Gullible provincial types are most susceptible to the prince's propaganda and are among his most fervent supporters. He intends to make use of this situation through the mechanisms of the press that he has just elaborated.

The prince will prepare the ground for his political moves by sending word to his press bureau. A stimulus will be given that spreads throughout the provinces. The capital will be the last affected by a movement that begins in the outer reaches of the kingdom. The capital, in effect, is no longer the activist center of the kingdom and is now reduced to a reactive role. It will run behind trends without even being aware of it.

According to Montesquieu, "absolute power brings in its train a number of abuses for which the sovereign himself may not be responsible," but for which he will be blamed. Even Machiavelli admits that the prince's government "will not be perfect." Moreover, he has assumed sole responsibility for all that happens and will thus, at the very least, lose prestige in the treatment he suffers from certain journalists. Recognizing this vulnerability, Machiavelli does not wish to be put into a position that requires a ceaseless recourse to covert repression. His censure is open. He simply obliges newspapers to print retractions. He will "always have the last word, without resorting to violence."

Machiavelli asserts that his prince will engage in journalism to a much greater extent than imagined. In preparing a political initiative, Machiavelli will have the issue mooted. Directives will be sent out to his political newspapers to promote a course of action. Finally, an official directive will declare policy in a Delphic-like pronouncement. Reacting to what is said, the newspapers will again be in turmoil, each interpreting the prince's statement "according to its particular slant" on things. The prince will then clarify the confusion to which his newspapers have contributed.[1]

This will have a profound impression on the people. All movement in the kingdom will be seen to initiate with the prince. Grand drama will surround his official statements. He is not one to break his silence for trivial reasons. The prince's statement will be solemn and stern, reflecting his august rank and elevation of mind. This will contrast sharply with the noise of the press, as each newspaper reads the prince's statement in light of its own narrow concerns. Where the throne radiates mystery, dignity, and decisiveness, the press in general appears as the source of squabbling and confusion. A host of publicists, the favored of the prince, will step forward as his effective mouthpiece.

Machiavelli intentionally creates the background of confusion that demands the commanding presence of the prince. Without changing its essential character, the press will be put to use in creating the impression of a prince who is indispensable and inhumanly prescient. The prince will present policies that circumstances force him to change as a development of a single thought and a single goal. Words, if not deeds, can be made consistent. All this has a great effect on the masses that must not only admire their leader but treat him as a superior kind of being.

Machiavelli spares no enthusiasm in describing the activities of his official press. Every day the papers will be filled with references to his ministers' reports, projects, and schemes. While docile themselves, the masses, particularly in southern climes,[2] demand an active and energetic government. "Novelties, surprises, and theatrics" will constantly divert their attention. But beyond mere diversion, the prince and his policies will be presented in a certain ideological light that, we shall see in detail later, reflects key elements of the doctrines of Saint-Simon. The people, we are told, do not like anything that smacks of atheism in their governments. He will build upon religious sentiments, not contradict them, and will present his acts as under the protection of Divine Providence.

He may be likened to the medieval prince who, under the dispensation of "divine right," acts as "God's anointed representative on earth." In Part One, Montesquieu had described princes as presuming the persons and property of all their subjects as their own and the domain of their private pleasures. This nineteenth century prince attains to similar power but has as his putative goal the welfare of the people. His utterances will "breathe the spirit of the most enthusiastic, universal liberalism." In matters of commerce, arts, industry, and administration, he will look to all sorts of projects, plans, innovations, and improvements and have his course of action broadcast by the press as aiming at disinterested beneficence.

According to Montesquieu, certain Christian forces shape the development of modern society. This modern prince can be seen as advancing such influences in a secular context through social policies that answer to Christian charity in the relief of man's estate. This is presented as effectively completing the social progress, begun by Christianity, in advancing the lot of the many, a goal that becomes the direct object of social policy. It is not so much in the name of "divine right" as traditionally understood that the new prince acts, but in the name of "history" and the historic process, which is interpreted as tending to the prince's rule as a culminating and providential goal. The people will be encouraged to see human and political problems as having technological solutions, and hopes and energies will be directed accordingly. Technological advances give the masses palpable evidence of progress. The new reading of universal history will reinforce a view, also shared by Montesquieu, which sees this progress as extending to political and moral realms.

In effect, the prince expands on the Enlightenment view of historic progress that Montesquieu emphasized in defending liberalism in Part One but has it culminate in an explicitly authoritarian regime. His regime intends no violence to the principle of popular sovereignty, however. Indeed, in the frequent appeal to plebiscites that installs the prince in power, sanctions his constitution, and ratifies policy decisions, that principle arguably enjoys more direct and relevant application than in the liberal regime, where popular consent is understood to be only tacitly accorded. Shortly, the prince will reveal the techniques available to him to ensure that the exercise of the franchise will not pose any problems for the prince's rule. In purely secular terms—according to the principle of popular sovereignty—the prince gains legitimacy for his reign.

He is not, however, content to ground his rule on the mere voice of the people. To accommodate his dynastic ambitions, popular support must be deepened. His rule, like that in the Middle Ages, seeks some higher justification to enlist the profounder allegiance of the masses. Here the religious elements of the prince's rule are adumbrated in the reintroduction of the principle of divine right, which, in an updated version, once again becomes applicable to legitimate authoritarian rule. They stand more explicitly revealed at the end of the *Dialogue* when the prince emerges as a kind of "living god' and the character of his regime receives final definition

Appeal is made to both secular and religious authority and points to realms that Montesquieu was at great pains in Part One to keep in vital tension. Here they begin to blur and merge in the reign of the new prince as secular rule receives sanctification in quasi-religious terms. In ending that tension, Machiavelli wants to end the deepest source of party strife, earlier identified by Montesquieu as pitting the religious party of reaction against the secular modernists. A religious base is ultimately sought for politics to satisfy the profound need for order in a modern society At the same time, autocratic rule is directed toward technological progress, as espoused by the modernists. Such a regime presents itself as holding forth the greatest hope for ameliorating the lot of the masses, the constant object of the prince's public solicitude and a solid popular base for his regime. It could be characterized as being animated by the Christian teaching of charity, but in a "new" application of this core doctrine to society. An unprecedented consensus of thought is sought on this basis. It has legions of writers and artists at the prince's command to give it expression.

Unlike former times, which attained a consensus on fundamental issues in antiquity and the Middle Ages, thought need not be controlled. He will satisfy the rage for writing and allow philosophic and religious questions to be debated. But, as stated earlier, free inquiry will stop at key elements of his rule. There may be differences of opinion, but as with the scholasticism of the high Middle Ages, it bespeaks a more fundamental harmony of views.

At the end of the Twelfth Dialogue, it is Machiavelli who is anxious that his conversation with Montesquieu continues. His discussion of the press, hastened because of circumstances that threaten their dialogue, has succeeded in giving a "first impression" of the new regime. Montesquieu responds with irony to the evident enthusiasm of Machiavelli. The image Machiavelli conjures of his prince is likened to "poetry" not unworthy of a "Byron." The talents of the author of the *Mandragola* are well displayed. Yet, it is a nervous irony as Montesquieu is "not quite certain that these things are not possible."

Formerly overconfident and complacent, Montesquieu is now uneasy as he gets his first clear premonition of the ultimate designs of the prince. Out of his discomfort, he encourages Machiavelli to finish. Machiavelli wants to press the attack but not lose Montesquieu altogether through his growing exasperation. He therefore yields the initiative to Montesquieu who may choose the topic he wishes. He turns to the subject of conspiracies.

Conspiracies

The discussion of propaganda and conspiracies stand at the heart of Joly's work. Their juxtaposition is not accidental. In the *Dialogue*'s most brilliant section, Machiavelli shows how the prince will publicly present his regime. This is followed by a discussion of the most sinister aspects of his rule—machinations, intrigues, and the subterranean supports that assure the prince's security. The rest of the discussion in Part Two is literally enveloped in the subject of conspiracies as the topic is resumed in his concluding discussion of the police.

Conspiracies have a big role to play in Machiavelli's scheme beyond what Montesquieu initially imagines. Montesquieu is perhaps too easily satisfied by Machiavelli's methods of controlling conspiracies. This prompts Machiavelli to return to the discussion and to elaborate on how he will make crucial use of them. Machiavelli beguiles Montesquieu, whose patience is being tested, by fascinating him with the intricate web of tyranny he spins. Watching his interlocutor operate, he is often as much intrigued as repelled. It is a disposition of mind that persists only so long as he remains convinced that he is merely involved in a theoretical dispute, the "fantasies" of a poet, as it were.

The prince's rule begins with a conspiratorial coup and, in a way, all the prescriptions in Part Two are meant to guarantee against a second such occurrence. Conspiracy is the preoccupation of the prince and in a crucial sense it is the essence of his politics.[3]

Because the prince's constitution and other "reforms" have effectively blocked political paths of change, the most serious obstacle to his security comes from conspiratorial sources. Montesquieu seems to understand this by broaching the matter at this particular time when, after Machiavelli's brilliant discourse on propaganda, he would like to exploit his most obvious vulnerability.

The design of Machiavelli's politics, aside from cultivating the masses, was to take the necessary steps against the fewer but more spirited of his subjects. The people at large are tamed through various benefactions, but force must subdue the latter, at least initially. It is from this group that the danger of conspiracies arises. The more thorough the prince's political control, the more they are forced to extralegal channels and ultimately to resistance in seeking effective political expression.

The prince may "liberalize" his rule, but only when assured that these more spirited individuals have been subdued and no longer pose a serious threat to him. Otherwise, political control requires a concomitant repression and an enormous police apparatus geared to searching out and eradicating conspiracies. But this has its own inherent dangers. Repression that is too thorough will of itself spark broader resistance to his rule. The most important features of the prince's politics are found as much in the prince's public pronouncements and projects as they are in the use of repression, which becomes his most delicate political problem.[4]

Montesquieu had earlier argued in Part One that the "public morality" of the prince cannot escape the strictures that govern "private morality." A rule that begins in violence and which uses violence to stay in power will end violently. Machiavelli gives testimony to the truth of Montesquieu's contention in presenting a public image of the prince in the Twelfth Dialogue that effectively masks the violent steps that follow. It is to be remembered that the new prince "stands for peace." Furthermore, the prince is most anxious to be a popular tyrant and to put himself on a course where repression can be progressively eased. This is one of the chief ends of propaganda, the effectiveness of which will diminish the necessity for harshness.

The topics of propaganda and conspiracies are thus intimately connected in a thematic way as integral components of the prince's policy. As propaganda has its effects, the class of people that would resist his rule will be reduced. Conspirators will be deterred from their projects if convinced that their efforts will find no broader appeal among the growing partisans of the regime. Moreover, the ideological appeal of the prince is directed toward satisfying many that might be among the number of potential revolutionaries. "Almost all their ideas have an incredible affinity with the doctrines of absolute power."

Machiavelli will cleverly use conspiracies so that he can move against conspirators themselves through his police. Harshness can then be focused and concentrated and need not disturb those other elements of society, longing for peace, that are content with his rule, if not its enthusiastic supporters or chief beneficiaries. Machiavelli had stated he would have his prince be "journalism incarnate." Apparently, he is also the regime's arch conspirator. Our discussion of conspiracies will include Machiavelli's discussion in the Eighteenth Dialogue and will give a broad outline of the state's repressive machinery and its use.

Machiavelli states that he will use the moment after his coup to move against secret societies since it is through them that conspirators are recruited. Accordingly, "the act of organizing a secret society or of being affiliated with one will be severely punished." Also, Machiavelli states, "I would start with hundreds of deportations—all those who greeted my coming to power with gun in hand." Any alleged member of a secret society will be tried administratively. There will be little pity for sedition mongers. Peace must be implacably restored.

Montesquieu sees the future as filled with executions. Given the peculiar sensitivity of such a despot to conspiratorial elements, he sees Machiavelli as launching an all-out attack to annihilate any and all seedbeds of dissension. Machiavelli will not proceed down the harsh path predicted by Montesquieu. If rigorous enough at the beginning, future dissidence will be kept to a minimum. He follows Duke Valentinois, who, apart from some "ruthless moments," was "a rather good natured fellow," especially kind to the "disadvantaged," Machiavelli adds facetiously.

Contrary to what Montesquieu thinks, some secret societies must not only be tolerated in his regime, but actively cultivated. Those within these societies are "from every nation, every class, and every social rank." Without their knowing it, the prince will have his allies infiltrate secret societies. This will allow the prince to be "privy to the most obscure intrigues." His ultimate goal would be to subvert their leaders and control them from the throne.

Machiavelli hints at the size of his secret police, an institution so vast "that in the heart of his kingdom one half the populace will be watching the other half." To please Montesquieu, he might change the name of his police to something more euphemistic, such as "ministry of state." He will establish security bureaus in each of his departments. These will survey the offices of government and will be centralized under the prince's direction. This is only the beginning of the "multitude of tasks" that he will assign to what he calls "the most important of my ministries." An enormous secret police will be integrated with the machinery of government. Its activities will extend to the remotest reaches of society and beyond, into international realms.

Machiavelli's police share certain key traits with police in later totalitarian states, not the least of which is its expanded ranks and functions. Integrated into various facets of government, one of its many duties will be to ensure political loyalty. When we recall that the prince's corps of journalists are really involved in intelligence gathering, we begin to see a new social role for police activities that intends to guarantee the orthodoxy of all opinion and behavior in matters essential to the prince. Machiavelli implies that his police will be everywhere. Through it, he will be like the god Vishnu, not only able to "touch everything" but literally to "see everything." However, unlike the police of later totalitarian regimes, its more repressive functions are not meant to spread terror through the populace at large. Rather, it guards its secrecy while choking the seeds of potential resistance.

The prince's object is not to intimidate everyone but only the dangerous. As Machiavelli points out, acceding to "Gallic conviviality" and its garrulous character, "his reign will not be as savage" as Montesquieu thinks. Gatherings of a certain number of people will be permitted. Even literature may be discussed. But, under its cover, people must not promote partisan political goals. In the end, the nature of Machiavelli's secret police is a reflection of the regime's revolutionary objective to arrive at a new historic order, while eschewing a reliance on the force typical of later totalitarian regimes.

The international functions of the police will be diverse. There will be those whose backgrounds allow them easy access to court life in other countries. These are bon vivants who will survey foreign princes and even certain pretenders to his own crown. Next, there will be a cadre whose revolutionary credentials are impeccable. They will penetrate the ranks of more obscure revolutionary circles, both at home and abroad. The prince will also subsidize bookstores, foreign journals, and publishing houses, where political opinions can be more easily monitored. Finally, he will have a prince of his own house seated on the steps of thrones in foreign capitals who "plays the role of the malcontent." He gulls his entourage while informing the prince of the most interesting intrigues hatched abroad.[5]

Domestically, his secret police will infiltrate all levels of society. It is only slightly hyperbolic when Machiavelli states that "there will be no private room or gathering place, no drawing room or intimate setting where an eavesdropper is not found to absorb what is said at any hour." Among other things, Machiavelli's police will survey the mails and will possess the most advanced instruments of espionage. Such things are alluring for the characters that would be attracted to serve in his police, drawn to such activities by "a kind of love of the art," not unlike the fabricators of *The Protocols*, we might add.

Machiavelli reveals other benefits that accrue from his way of handling conspiracies. He confounds Montesquieu by saying that some conspiracies are an absolute necessity. At opportune times, contrived conspiracies can be put into play to rally the people and justify a request for extraordinary powers. Hearings can be called to investigate his sham conspiracy and if they are skillfully handled, the prince "will pass for being too easygoing." Where in fact repression is most thorough, it is most hidden, and the reputation of the prince masks a different reality.

The centrality of conspiracies in Joly's organization of the *Dialogue* reflects what is perhaps the most fundamental preoccupation of the prince. Moreover, in a very real way, much of the prince's activities are at their core conspiratorial—the application of "force and cunning" in league with the secret police. In Part One, where Machiavelli purported to state the essence of his teaching, he implied that the successful prince does not distinguish between domestic and foreign policy. In effect, the spirit of foreign policy, at least in its reliance on "force and cunning," predominates even in domestic policy.

Judicial Reform

Machiavelli concludes his teaching on the techniques of tyrannical rule in Part Two with judicial reforms. Again, the bent of his proposals is directed against conspiracies. He intends to undermine the judicial process and protections afforded the individual that extend to political enemies of the state. Accordingly, the prosecution of cases will be expedited. Arguments will be heard before a single magistrate instead of a panel. The privacy of such proceedings will work to the defendant's disadvantage.

Machiavelli also shows himself a crafty master of judicial proceedings in using them to condition the masses. He will do away with the distinction between misdemeanors of common law and political misdemeanors. He will also do away with specific criminal courts that separate different classes of offenders. "In my kingdom," Machiavelli states, "no distinction will be made between the insolent journalist and the ordinary thief. They will share the same cell and appear in the same court. The conspirator will share the docket with the forger and the murderer and appear before the same jury." Such an innovation will have an effect on public opinion. The people will see "the conspirator treated no differently than the common criminal" and "will begin to blur the two categories of crime" in their mind.

Machiavelli's discussion of conspiracies in the Thirteenth and Seventeenth Dialogues lead in both instances to a discussion of the judiciary because the laws that are necessary to control political enemies eventually will be brought before the courts for their hearing and interpretations. In the Montesquieuan scheme, the judiciary is the ultimate check on the tyrant and the last refuge of the subject. We have already seen how its character begins to change in the new regime founded by Machiavelli.

In general, the judicial branch retains its eminent position. The harsh laws of the prince will be determined with a solicitude for certain "forms." In this regard, Machiavelli is very far from the barbarous processes of government attributed to him at the beginning of his conversation. Indeed, "violence plays no role." Unlike traditional despotism, this regime is premised on respect for due process of law. The prince finds support where every enlightened ruler of today finds it—in the law, not outside it. In fact, Machiavelli feels "no need to decree a great number of harsh laws," as many laws necessary to the prince will already be in force. Without exception, all governments must have laws sufficient to protect the public order. Machiavelli's government is no different. In difficult situations, the prince may not have to pass new laws but only resurrect old ones that have fallen into desuetude.

Machiavelli begins "judiciously" enough with deference to judicial forms. The prince would rather appeal to magistrates on the precedents of existing laws than to have to convince judges of the need to apply harsh and novel acts. Circumstances require the prince to be adaptable to meet extreme situations. The new prince will attain this flexibility moving through the laws, not beyond them. "You see that it is only a question of giving the courts a little fine-tuning." This is always easy in centralized countries where the judiciary stays in direct contact with the administrative machinery.

Machiavelli turn to a "very ingenious and simple scheme" to achieve his ends. In the Montesquieuan system, judges are appointed by the king to life tenure, not elected to the bench. The intent of such a procedure is to remove judicial selection from the pressure of politics and to allow merit to determine the choice of personnel, according to the prince's considered judgment. The judge is not the representative of the people but of the law and he is to act as its living embodiment. Life tenure ensures his independence and conduces to a temperament rich in the prudence that comes with age among men who live by the "continued exercise of the mind."

Machiavelli intends to exploit the prince's appointment power to eradicate the independence of the bench and tie it to despotic rule. He does not advocate anything as crude as court-packing.[6] There will be no wholesale turnover of court personnel nor any revision of judicial operations. In harmony with his other "reforms," he wants to maintain dignity and respect for the bench because, once subverted, it will be a useful tool in his hands. He proposes a single change, justifiable on the grounds of the high esteem in which he holds the judicial branch. He will merely require judges to retire at a certain age to preserve the judiciary from the unseemliness of senility. Public opinion will be on his side.

The repercussions from this small change are great. It plays to the careerist ambitions of sitting and prospective judges. It shatters the esprit de corps and common interest that binds them as a branch of government and introduces divisiveness among men supposedly characterized by the disinterested concern for the law. Machiavelli explains that forced retirement will open many positions that can be filled by the prince. His appointments will set the tone for the judiciary as a whole and shape the behavior of prospective judges as they strive to emulate the favored. Every year, Machiavelli continues, at least twenty and as many as fifty new appointments can be made on the basis of a single vacancy through the successive advancements of those in lower positions. Career interests, especially among the young and ambitious, will keep these justices from ranging too far from the prince's wishes. "In their deliberations, the police power will receive an interpretation so favorable to my power that I will be relieved of a multitude of restrictive measures that otherwise would be necessary."

The rest of this discussion, continued in the Fourteenth Dialogue, may be said to focus on the merits and drawbacks of an active bench. As Machiavelli points out, it is perhaps impossible to keep judicial activities contained. Even the most clearly written law is liable to surprising interpretations. Moreover, the legislature often passes laws with a certain elasticity to accommodate ensuing situations. The potentiality for activism is latent in certain legislation. Once the judiciary as a whole has been rendered subservient through appointment "winnowing," an active judiciary can prove useful to the prince in cloaking despotic will with the respectability of "forms."

Machiavelli gives two such examples involving the court of appeals, apparently taken from actual cases in contemporary France. In an electoral matter the court declares the principle of a "tacit abrogation" of law to escape the potentially embarrassing prosecution of an elected representative. In a matter of concern to the press, "peddling" of publications, restricted under certain police regulations, is extended to even the author of a "pamphlet" who distributes several copies, even as gifts.[7] Thus, "instead of a simple exercise of the police power, you have a law regulating freedom of the press and restricting the right to publish one's thoughts."

Montesquieu claims that when courts are not bound by their own judgments, numerous lawsuits will result from individuals who try to affect policy through judicial petitions. This need not be the case, however, as several determinate decisions on specific matters could definitively discourage what are costly endeavors for any citizen. Declaratory judgments could even preempt inconvenient lawsuits. Montesquieu rightly suspects the general thrust of Machiavelli's policy to place the people under a form of paternalism, a mode of governance far from the lupine practices he first imagined.[8]

Political Reform

Machiavelli freely admits his intention to declare his prince not only king, but hereditary monarch for life with succession going to the first-born male. He continues his pose as a man of the Middle Ages in harkening back to the principle of Salic and Frank monarchic rule. However, he has already declared that his regime will be founded on popular sovereignty. This causes Montesquieu to see

Machiavelli as espousing two incompatible premises. The dynastic ambitions of the founder cannot be built on such unstable foundations. The people need not have recourse to revolution to rid themselves of the prince as they are given the means to deliver themselves in their right to vote.

In Dialogue Fifteen, Machiavelli elabates on the techniques that are available to ensure the "proper" exercise of the franchise and gives a view of his rule strikingly different from medieval notions. Though he wears a crown, his avowed goal is to embody popular will. He is in fact one with the people. "What I will, they will. What I do, they do." He declares himself the "trustee" of all power it has delegated. He is their "true representative."

With this understood, Machiavelli will begin by extending appointment powers where they do not already exist. For example, the prince will appoint the administration of the localities. The franchise will then be exercised only to determine national representatives. Presumably, this is where the sovereign will of the people is voiced anyway and where interesting and important concerns are decided. Therefore, resistance to his restrictions of the franchise to the national legislature would not be forthcoming. Such policy might even pass as enlightened administrative policy.

In avoiding local elections, Machiavelli will keep his citizenry from participating in a too-frequent exercise of their sovereignty. This will prevent the cultivation of certain habits that develop from a vigilant regard for the operations of government. People in the provinces will be taught to look to the centralized administration to solve their collective problems. The prince will focus his energies on the national chamber. In effect, he can secure his reign by making sure of this body by steps that amount to de facto appointment there.

Machiavelli will have candidates swear "a solemn oath" to the person of the prince and not, as in 1789, to the nation. Here begins a more overt effort to accommodate them to personal rule. Fidelity and personal loyalty will once again be elevated in the public's esteem. Such an oath will contrast sharply with republican mottoes of former eras.

According to Machiavelli, "the smallest details of electoral laws are of the utmost importance." He taunts Montesquieu by directly citing the authority of *The Spirit of the Laws* in this regard. "The laws establishing suffrage are fundamental, likewise how suffrage is apportioned and how ballots are cast."[8]

Machiavelli states that he will submit his list of candidates with those of other parties. Here the wisdom of extending his appointment powers comes into play. Within the government itself, Machiavelli will have the built-in support he needs eager to work for the cause of the prince and his party, if for no other reason than personal interest. In the nature of things, the prince's party will be the strongest. Indeed, the prince himself will be seen as the people's most ardent and true representative. Through his control of the press, the prince will have the ears of his subjects as well as a feeling for what they desire.

The relative strength of the prince's party can also be assured by sabotaging opposition parties. Still other ways have been found to paralyze their efforts. Political assemblies will be forbidden and the ban will extend to conventions, thus preventing opposition parties from drawing up platforms and drumming up enthusiasm for shared political goals. Public proclamations for opposition candidates will be tolerated but will be dwarfed by the same proclamation of support for the prince's candidates.

Machiavelli next proceeds to an elaboration of how suffrage will be regulated to his advantage. He will have voting by commune. The vote will then be split among local personages and be attracted to the better-financed and better-known official candidate. His eye is not directed toward men of ability. "Public order has less need of men of talent than men devoted to the government." In effect, "great ability belongs to the person who sits on the throne and those gathered around it." Moreover, elections will be in single-member districts with a plurality vote being sufficient to elect or return the prince's favorite. There will be recourse to "gerrymandering" and districts will be conveniently divided to dissipate the crucial numbers of opposition votes.

Finally, electoral colleges can be influenced. Machiavelli eschews a more blatant form of vote tampering, given other means at his disposal. To Montesquieu's surprise, ballot stuffing, a measure "during the time of Leo X" is not proposed. The controversy it could ignite is dangerous and unseemly and can be avoided, we may presume.[10] Recalcitrant districts can be made amenable through patronage. Contracts and other benefactions may be promised districts if there vote is right. In the discussion of the budget, we shall see the expanded opportunity for such leverage.

Machiavelli admits that, despite such efforts, opposition may emerge. Scandals alone may create vacancies that will be filled by opponents. However, he never claimed that his regime or his representatives would be perfect. From his position of strength, he can admit to faults and thereby appear magnanimous. Moreover, within parliament he will have orators on his side that will anticipate and counter attacks. Legislative business will be controlled by the presiding officials that the prince has appointed and conducted according to his rules.

Social Reforms

Montesquieu next draws attention to certain social groups that are important buffers against tyranny. Unlike parties, the expressed goal of these groups is not directly political but their influence has important consequences for politics. The principles that they serve harmonize well with the liberal design of things. Montesquieu claimed that modern political mores are least receptive to the regime of tyranny. These groups encourage those elements of character that are nourished in a greater community of shared interests and high-minded purposes, independent of the state.

As a political system, Montesquieuan liberalism tried to institute checks and balances internal to the functioning of government so as to frustrate tyranny. These groups provide some of the stronger social checks to a tyrannical project. They are the social supports to the political system that butress the freedom that the system allows. By virtue of freedom, they are allowed to exist, and they in turn endow the regime of freedom with certain strengths.

Montesquieu lists some of these major social groupings: the church, the university, the bar of law, the national militia, and business corporations. The prince's relation to private enterprise is not treated here but can be extrapolated from his discussion of the budget and state finances. The variety and vitality of these groups poses a problem for the prince in his move to centralize control. Montesquieu characterizes Machiavellian politics as trying to annihilate political parties and destroy "other collective forces."

Unlike the disciplined regular army, the citizens' militia is often a fractious group. Machiavelli will dissolve it as currently organized only to reconstruct it on new foundations. He will choose its leaders and determine where it can legally exist. To outlaw such a "useless institution" (or to confiscate its guns, we presume) would be exceedingly unpopular. The people derive a sense of security from its existence, however false, as well as certain "puerile" satisfactions from participating in certain of its exercises.

Machiavelli's approach to higher education shows greater seriousness. Nevertheless, he declares that "the way things are now handled is just about fine" the way it is. He immediately explains himself. "These great bodies of learning are no longer organized as they once were." The state has already encroached upon a large measure of their autonomy and reoriented the direction of learning to the point where they are no longer anything more than the appendage of the state and an extension of its power and influence. His attack on the institutions of higher learning is as much an attack on liberal education itself.

Machiavelli merely furthers recent trends affecting state education. It is only a question of a decree or ministerial order to further the changes he wants. He will assume the prerogative of hiring and promoting the heads and members of the teaching corps. He also assumes control over the curricula. For example, the study of constitutional politics in the teaching of law will be proscribed. He wants to prevent certain false ideas from reaching the youth, who might become as "wrapped up in writing constitutions as they would tragic poetry." Such studies later on will only produce utopians instead of sound statesmen. The changes signal a more or less blatant attempt at indoctrination. "I want the history of my reign to be taught in my schools while I am still alive. In such a way, a new prince finds his way into the hearts of a generation."

Machiavelli will multiply the state schools. He thereby gains a reputation for love of learning while infiltrating the colleges and universities with professors he has appointed. Private education will not be proscribed but will suffer in competition with the state schools. The prince advocates open enrollment and free courses in all the major cities. This will not only dilute educational excellence as traditionally conceived, it will also provide a convenient forum for his indoctrination, as he tries "to co-opt even the last vestiges of independent thinking."

According to Machiavelli, the law profession must also be suborned. "You know better than I, Montesquieu, that this profession fosters cold and stubborn temperaments when it comes to matters of principle and minds whose tendency is to hold the acts of government to strict legality." A rigid emphasis on the formal requirements of law would frustrate the grand designs of the prince, who might be called to account for his illegal ways in a court of justice. However, the people hold the bar of law in high esteem and see its independence as a guarantee of material possessions, life, and honor. Machiavelli's proposal is to have the prince designate the bar while not touching its independence in any other way. Current practices could be discredited as favoring the well-connected over the meritorious. Machiavelli would wean lawyers away from the temptation to engage in certain causes that embarrass the prince by tying their livelihood to his will.

According to Montesquieu, however, the greatest bulwark of liberty is found in the clergy and the propagation of faith. "I know of nothing that threatens your power more," he declares. "The Christian teaching is a teaching of liberty." The spread of Christian influence through the "humble and gentle" Gospels was enough "to destroy the Roman Empire, Caesarism, and its power." Its morality elevates the individual and strengthens the soul, over which human power has no sway. In sum, "nations that avow Christianity will always escape despotism." Assuming the prince rules over such a country, he will be checked by the clergy, whose influence is intimately felt everywhere, emanating from the sanctuary to deeply influence the family and the schools.[11]

Machiavelli denies that the priesthood is as Montesquieu indicates. Pointing to history, in both ancient and modern times, he has found it "to be a natural support for absolute power." The ultimate basis of the prince's authority is no different from its own. The idiom of his public speech, laced with appeals to divine sanction, will find approval from the priestly caste. Machiavelli further denies that the church has influence as wide and deep as Montesquieu claims. The progress of Enlightenment thought has had its effect as it shapes liberal and advanced opinion toward anti-clericalism. Machiavelli would provoke a schism in the Church by appealing to such elements. A break with Rome would be warmly greeted in such quarters and perhaps not broadly resisted by the masses. But, finally, Machiavelli has a keener appreciation for the conservatism of the people—already manifest in his appeal to "divine right"—that he would want to build upon as more solid than liberal opinion and secularism.

Machiavelli intends to radicalize the anti-clerical elements in his regime to impress the clergy and the papacy with the anti-religious fervor with which he must contend. The Pope, already under siege in Italy, would be grateful to the prince for any effort on his part to maintain the status quo in his regime. In coming to the Pontiff's aid with his armies, the prince finally succeeds in attaching him to his person both by gratitude and self-interest. In rising to his defense, he becomes the protector of faith and installs his legions in Rome. These armies might prove useful to intimidate the Pope if his gratitude becomes exhausted. Such a foreign policy will open up options that can be followed according to changing circumstances. He will have the alternative at any time to accede to those liberal elements in his regime, if need be.

In the meantime, the defense of the Pope will be popular with the masses. Again, in pointed reference to Napoleon I, the people might even see the prince anointed in Paris. In such an event, the lingering strength of Christianity and its hold on the public's consciousness would attach itself to such a prince. Machiavelli thereby shows how the Vicar of Rome can be made the servant of the new Caesar, reconciling the tension between secular power and religious authority in the prince's favor. "The secular religion of revolutionary ideology ends up playing the same role that orthodox religion did...Caesaro-Papism is reborn and the interpreter of History becomes the pope-emperor."[12]

We shall see that this theme gets most explicit treatment in the last part of the *Dialogue* and concludes the work as a whole. With Montesquieu, we come slowly to the realization that Machiavelli is describing not merely a change in rule but the most radical and complete of foundings, extending beyond political and into spiritual realms. At the end of the *Dialogue* itself, the portrait of the prince is complete. He seeks God-like status in an Empire that wants universal influence.

Notes

1 Here is the forerunner of our masters of "leaks" and "spin." The "spinning" of economic statistics in manipulating the budget is comically fresh. Napoleon's ministers are specifically cited in Part Three.

2. Machiavelli makes this remark to the thinker who famously focused on considerations of climate to determine what is politically appropriate, or possible.

3. This accords with Marx's analysis of Louis and will be discussed more fully in the last chapter. Rymond Aron has stated that "the maintenance of a kind of conspiracy within the party that controls the state" is one of the essential elements of totalitarianism. It is one on a list of other elements which, "*all of them taken together*" (Aron's emphasis) reveals the "essence" of the phenomonon. See Aron's essay "The Essence of Totalitarianism According to Hannah Arendt" in Daniel J. Mahoney, ed. *In Defense of Political Reason* (Lanham, Md.: Rowman & Littlefield, 1993) 104. It is interesting that all the

elements Aron mentions, except terror, are features of Napoleon's rule. The absence of terror indicates what perhaps made Napoleon's regime more sedulous than twentieth century varieties as well as crucially different.

4. Autocratic regimes of today, threatened by oftentimes violent secret societies, use the whole panoply of repressive techniques so ably described by Joly. His discussion is a worthy introduction to the essential character of certain of these places.

5. This was the role played by Prince Napoleon, cousin of the Emperor, who had widespread connections in opposition circles. His faction, called the Palais Royal Group, was active in working class causes.

6. Unlike FDR's very rare political misstep.

7. The incident he chooses to illustrate his point is significant. Remember, the secret police of the Second Empire saw Joly as indeed the writer of just such a "pamphlet." Parenthetically, it can be noted that Napoleon understood very well the threat from a *samizdat* press.

8. With the discussion of the judiciary, Machiavelli has completed his teaching regarding the formal institutions of government. In the broad sweep of his treatment of the judiciary and the fine details of criminal proceedings, we should bear in mind that Joly himself was a practicing lawyer and observed the justice of the Second Empire from within courtrooms and behind bars.

9. The discussion of suffrage in democracies is found in *The Spirit of the Laws* II 2.

10. An American who has lived through "The Dade County Shad Controversy" and other voting irregularities can appreciate Machiavelli's prudent restraint in this regard.

11. Machiavelli underscores the point by references to *The Spirit of the Laws* XXIV 3. He there memorably writes: "How admirable the religion which, while it seems to have in view the felicity of the other life, continues the happiness of this!"

12. The words are Raymon Aron's again and describe Stalinist totalitarianism. They are perfect in their description of Louis Napoleon, as he appears in the *Dialogue*. They indicate how archetypical the Joly analysis is for the despotic era he saw forthcoming. See Raymond Aron, "The Essence" in *In Defense of Political Reason*, 110.

Chapter Five

THE ECONOMIC REVOLUTION

Part Three consists of four Dialogues, the Eighteenth through the Twenty-First and divides about equally between Machiavelli and Montesquieu. Montesquieu first lays out the teaching of modern finance and budgetary science, which he believes is inimical to despotism. It is followed by Machiavelli's attack and final victory over Montesquieu, who meekly defers to his interlocutor in Part Four and allows him to put the finishing touches on the portrait of tyranny he has drawn.

The drama of the dialogue in Part Three gives us convincing evidence of Machiavelli's absolute control over the movement of the discussion. In successfully handling what Montesquieu perceives as "the most difficult problem of all" for a sovereign who wants to exert absolute power, we suspect Machiavelli's complete control throughout the entire conversation.

The movement of Part Three is not unlike that of the conversation to this point. The debate begins with Montesquieu's emphatic assertions and ends with Machiavelli's victory. Montesquieu begins this section with a display of confidence he has not shown since the beginning of their encounter.

Though *The Spirit of the Laws* is not simply a "financial treatise," it displays a masterful grasp of the science of modern economics that Montesquieu in fact helped formulate in his most famous work.[1] On the basis of such competence, Montesquieu presumes a superiority over Machiavelli and has held this subject matter in reserve as a final obstacle to Machiavelli's goal. It is understood as his "last stand," as it were, from a position he deems unassailable.

Though Machiavelli has accomplished a great deal thus far, "he has only just begun," compared with what remains for him to do. Machiavelli coyly encourages Montesquieu by assuming the defensive and playing to what his adversary deems the real basis of his superiority. A tone of deferential modesty is struck. "I confess that you take me somewhat aback. I was born in a century extremely backward when it comes to matters of economics and I understand very little about such things."

Machiavelli takes the position of student to teacher and allows Montesquieu to expound his doctrines confidently. After his previous rout, Montesquieu would only be too eager to press any advantage he has. Though Machiavelli claims to be extremely backward in economic matters, he shortly will reveal his knowledge as up to date. It includes the "latest theories" and might be said to supercede the liberal understanding in such matters. We eventually come to realize that Machiavelli has maneuvered Montesquieu into a position that will render his defeat all the more resounding and definitive.

Liberal Economics Explained

Montesquieu proceeds as if it were he that was baiting Machiavelli. According to his view of despotic government, the tyrant necessarily rules over a primitive economy and a less than enterprising population. Destitution is the common lot and any wealth that does exist makes its way to the despot's hands. Under such conditions, there is neither the means nor the will for society to generate its own wealth. As *The Spirit of the Laws* indicates, it follows as "a principle" of that government that the despot can impose "only small taxes" on his subjects.[2] To finance their rule, the sovereigns of such societies are forced to plunder others, relying on arms for what industry cannot produce. Having some inkling of Machiavelli's aggressive designs in foreign policy, Montesquieu feigns naiveté when he wonders aloud if his despotism will follow suit. In this case, the subjects of Machiavelli's regime might at least avoid an oppressive taxation. "Will you at least give your subjects the same satisfaction?"

For his part, Machiavelli asserts that there is "nothing more questionable than the proposition" put forth in that particular part of *The Spirit of the Laws*.[3] Montesquieu's theory might be true "in Turkey or in Persia" but he does not intend to rule a satrapy. To say the least, the praise of oriental despotism at the end of the Fifth Dialogue stands qualified. He intends to rule a luxurious European kingdom whose labor economy generates a superfluity of goods and whose government provides a broad range of services.

How could Montesquieu expect him to limit himself to moderate taxes when he has both the opportunity and need to tax on a larger scale? In modern societies, "labor produces a superabundance of wealth that presents itself in various forms—all amenable to taxes." Moreover, luxury is a tool of modern governments. The state undertakes extensive public services. These create posts for functionaries who enjoy great salaries at public expense. An active and munificent rule will prove costly. The main question is how its revenue needs can be met.

Looking to past experience, Montesquieu sees this absolute ruler as forced to warfare to meet the financial needs that cannot be met internally without crushing his subjects. "He would have to be a conqueror, for war would be the principal source of those revenues that would keep him in splendor and support his armies." However, this presents its own problems, not the least of which is the necessity to remain victorious in such foreign undertakings if the despot himself is not to find his wealth confiscated by others. In a sort of vicious circle, the despot turns to war for his finances. But to guarantee his success in war, he needs greater and greater wherewithal.

Moreover, unlike the past, the conduct of war in contemporary times is complicated for an even more substantial reason. Given the destructive power of modern weaponry, large-scale warfare, to which the despot is driven, has become outmoded.[4] The expense of war, for lack of better motives, makes its conduct prohibitive. "War is no longer profitable." There can be no rational incentive for Machiavelli's despot to pursue a course that ends by ruining "the conqueror as well as the conquered." Inevitably, then, revenue must be raised internally, through taxes. It is precisely here that Machiavelli's despot would seem to receive his strongest check.

In despotic states, Montesquieu points out, there exists a "legal fiction" that allows the despot to tax at will. "The sovereign is presumed to possess all the goods of his subject by right." Therefore, when he expropriates something, he is only taking back what belongs to him in the first place. He thus finds little resistance on the part of the people. Legally, at least, there is no recourse.

Modern society is informed by a different understanding of things. Government is instituted to protect subjects who cede to it only those powers necessary for guaranteeing their security and possessions. When modern governments appropriate, they are perceived to be taking private property. This is why such action must be sanctioned by the people, or their representatives, who assure the spending of monies for necessary and agreed-upon common purposes. Far from being based on a "legal fiction," both appropriations and spending follow a "due process of law" premised on "informed" consent and popular control.

To remain absolute, the prince must be free to dispose of the resources procured for him by taxes. His actions are "above discussion and control." This matter is crucial to Machiavelli's rule. If the new prince cannot control finances absolutely, he cannot remain absolute politically. The whole reign "threatens to collapse on this score."

Machiavelli's easy acceptance of popular control over his budget seems to Montesquieu testimony of his interlocutor's naiveté in such matters. In letting the power of the purse stay in the hands of the nation's representatives, Machiavelli has surrendered the most fundamental of powers to the people. "This principle is the clearest token of the people's sovereignty." Giving the people the right to vote taxes means giving them the right "to refuse, limit, or reduce to nothing the power of the prince to act." As Machiavelli stated earlier, the prince will likely find it easier to trifle with the people's liberties than with matters where their material interests are so clearly involved. In sum, their interests are bound to an economic regime antithetical to despotism.[5]

Moreover, "those who vote taxes are taxpayers themselves." Their concern in such matters is inextricable with that of the nation. This conduces to vigilance on the part of representatives who regard such affairs with eyes wide open. The new prince will find the nation's representatives as "adamant and unaccommodating in appropriating money" as he found them "docile with regard to liberties."

Machiavelli makes two points that reveal the weakness of Montesquieu's argument. Dealing with his last point first, Machiavelli points out that, taxpayers or not, the representatives of the nation are salaried. They may be disciplined by the leadership and lose positions of importance, along with their emoluments. They are not disinterested guardians of the nation's purse. Their votes may be assured by making spending decisions they favor. Montesquieu does not deny the validity of Machiavelli's counterarguments. Ultimately, fiscal matters are a question of votes like any other piece of legislation and the prince will have an assured majority within the legislature.

More important, Montesquieu exaggerates his case when he assumes parsimony on the part of an "enlightened" group of citizens as well as an unyielding jealousy over their prerogatives in fiscal matters. He might very well be right if the new prince based his power on the aristocracy or the bourgeoisie. However, the foundations of his rule rests upon "the proletariat, the bulk of which possess nothing." Machiavelli repeats an argument of Part One when he states that, unlike the propertied classes, fiscal niceties do not inform the character, interests, and habits of the working class. Since the "costs of supporting the state are hardly borne by them," he will take further steps so that "they are completely exempt from any burden." In the expanded franchise, he will have the votes to extract necessary revenues by encouraging the predatory instincts of the poor.[6]

Montesquieu very soberly rebukes such a policy. The poor must be made to see their interests as resting with a system that advances their liberation from poverty, not in plundering the sources of wealth. It is a grave error to believe that the proletariat can profit from such attacks. The best promise for the poor lies in encouraging productivity and expanding the base of capital. "By impoverishing the haves through fiscal measures, you will only be creating an unstable social situation. In time, even the have-nots will be totally impoverished." A secure social and political order is a prerequisite for the release of society's productive forces and is ill-served by a mortal class warfare that Machiavelli's policies invite.

Montesquieu apparently is blind to the great concentration of wealth that Machiavelli sees today. "In contemporary society," he states, "there is no rigid line of demarcation between the rich and the poor," at least in any permanent sense. "Through labor, the artisan of yesterday can be the bourgeois of tomorrow." Though he assumes he speaks from the most advanced historical point of view, Montesquieu is perhaps describing the liberal regime in only its nascent stages. He is oblivious to the rapid social changes wrought by industrialization in the interval of years hidden from his view. In any event, Machiavelli indicates that he is fully capable of countering his interlocutor's "pretty theories" with those of his own. In fact, his are presented as more harmonious with the conditions of "contemporary society" and its historic demands. As we shall see, such theories do not contemplate class warfare to bring about the necessary social revolution.

Such a policy would run counter to the conservative instincts of the new prince and the desire for order that is repeatedly demonstrated in the political steps he took in Part Two. All revolutionary change is meticulously veiled and takes place behind the facade of liberal institutions. The prince is a self-declared harbinger of peace and intends to found a dynasty. Such a political project, with no mean pretensions to personal glory, cannot endure on the basis of a politics that appeals to class warfare. By and large, Machiavelli accepts the premises of Montesquieu's arguments.

Machiavelli will show that the productive potential of the modern economy might be augmented tremendously by an expanded and more dynamic role for government that simultaneously serves imperial ambitions and embraces certain welfare policies. In the latter half of Part Three, Machiavelli indicates how he will assume greater control over the resources of society. By exploiting them, he will gain his glory and win over the forgotten masses to his side. This awaits a discussion in Part Four of the *Dialogue* of the grand public works projects he envisions for his reign.

Financial Management

Montesquieu cuts Machiavelli short from elaborating his theories at this moment. He prefers to counter Machiavelli's "two points." Even if Machiavelli were to work from a majority in the legislature, his designs on absolute power would be encumbered by the science of finance that informs "the financial mechanisms" of modern enlightened societies. Like the development of public law, the science of finance has gone through progressive refinements designed to counter the exercise of arbitrary power in state fiscal matters. "In free industrialized countries, everyone is acquainted with financial management either out of necessity or out of personal or professional interests. Your government could not deceive anyone," Montesquieu affirms.

Machiavelli feigns ignorance in order to elicit an elaboration of this science, which Montesquieu gives in summary form. His financial system rests on two foundations: an intricate scheme of accountability that minutely categorizes appropriations and expenditures, and the coherent presentation of its documentation as a matter of public record, to be voted on as any other piece of legislation. The prince's initiatives are "controlled" by the most popular branch of government, following close public scrutiny of these money matters. The prince will not be able to tamper with public funds without alerting his subjects to his predatory actions.

"The whole work of financial management, so vast and complicated, can be reduced to two very simple operations: *appropriations* and *expenditures.*" One of the most important innovations in state finances has been the State Budget, which brings these operations to light on a year-to-year basis. Within that document is an estimate of revenues from various taxes and their allocation toward various state goals.

In short, each minister, responsible for his own department, prepares his own budget, which he submits to the Minister of Finance. The latter's duty is to prepare a budget for the whole government based on other ministers' requests. The legislature amends and votes on the budget plan, like any other bill. The budget is a yearly submittal and in it the economic health of the nation can be gauged while government expenditures can be tracked on a department by department basis. Any requested increase will have to be justified as the budget goes through multiple readings and revisions in the legislature. Before it is voted, the plan is submitted to the public and dissected and discussed by all interested parties.

Although it is voted on like any other piece of legislation, the budget is no ordinary measure. It is as much a political as it is a financial statement. Its bulk of figures, when properly analyzed, reveals the basic commitment of the government and the broad outline of domestic and foreign policy. "This impressive document is published, printed, and reproduced in a thousand newspapers and reveals to all eyes the domestic and foreign policy of the state and its civil, judicial, and military administration."

Montesquieu continues his discussion of the budget in the Nineteenth Dialogue. All other financial reforms are an emanation and refinement of this budgetary system, which is standard in all modern, well-regulated societies. Proper budgeting requires the balancing of expenditures and revenues. In this matter, there has been recourse to "a very prudent expedient." The legislature votes the revenue and appropriations parts of the budget in turns. Having first passed the revenue part, expenses can be tailored and allocated accordingly. Desired expenditures will not then be determinative of the revenues to be raised. Rather, given revenues will be the frame for essential expenditures. This will keep individual legislators from getting carried away by any spending excesses. The two elements of the budget will then be harmonized by a comprehensive vote of the legislature.

Machiavelli would like Montesquieu to address the matter of emergency spending beyond the scope of the State Budget. "But can it be that expenditures are restricted to only what has been voted by the legislature? Is it in the power of a legislative body so to cripple the executive, to forbid a sovereign to appropriate for unforeseen expenses through emergency measures?" In fact, exactness is not always possible or expected. Changing political circumstances—a foreign attack, for example—may require unanticipated expenditures for which there is no budgetary provision. The system simply has to admit a certain amount of elasticity.

Machiavelli ties to exploit this loophole to elude the limitations set by the budget process elaborated by Montesquieu. Montesquieu closes off any such opening. The limitations to any emergency spending are necessarily very strict if legislative prerogative is not to be sacrificed. Regardless of changing circumstances, there remains only a finite amount of resources. "Political events cannot force financial realities to change from one moment to another."

Emergency appropriations must be ratified by the legislature in any case. If it is not in session, they must be ratified when it reconvenes. If it is, they must be authorized by going through the ordinary legislative process. Sufficient revenues must exist to cover any spending, otherwise a supplementary appropriation must be attached to such a bill. Moreover, Montesquieu explains, all unused appropriations must revert to the general fund. They cannot be set aside for the prince as discretionary spending in future years. If diverting funds is the design of the prince, it is made even more difficult by a system of line-item budgeting and subsidiary accounts for each department and government agency.

That is, expenditures within these budgets are further broken down into easily categorized expenditures common to all agencies. Each subsidiary account, personnel expenses, for example, receives its own appropriation. This sets a limit on that particular spending. Any unused portions of an allocation must revert to the general fund. There is to be no transfer among accounts. Otherwise, "by an ingenious subterfuge," the prince could evade the legislatively designated destination of spending and we would return to arbitrary finance. A treasurer and a board of auditors oversee the whole arrangement to guarantee the regular movement of monies and the accuracy of bookkeeping.

A Revolution in Fiscal Practices

Machiavelli facetiously confesses to be "dumbfounded" by all this and to have been taken at his most vulnerable point. As a practical matter, he applauds the application of strict accounting techniques to state fiscal affairs and the orderly approach to the movement of monies. He will adopt these reforms but not the "plethora of precautions" he calls "puerile." For his part, he speaks from a more exalted view of things. He is a "statesman" not an accountant. In fact, he will adopt "all these marvels" of accounting, all these financial reforms and have them redound to the splendor of his reign.

He is perhaps not so "dumbfounded" by Montesquieu and as vulnerable as he lets on. In a surprising statement, he claims that the question of finance is, of all political concerns, the one that lends itself most easily to the maxims of *The Prince*. The spirit of reform that Machiavelli will bring to such matters is consistent with his statements in Part One, where he attempted to lay bare the essentials of his political teaching, for which he claims "eternal relevancy."

In effect, Machiavelli asserts here, as before, that Montesquieu's science describes a system as it ought to be, not how in fact states conduct real affairs. It is foolish to be guided by what never attains in the real world. "I answer that it is necessary to will the possible and that what holds universally cannot but be done." He will look to the real practices of states that only theoretically operate under the financial system outlined by Montesquieu.

He accuses Montesquieu of elevating the standards of private morality as the standard for political action. The principles that have supposedly brought the budget process to its "perfection" are those which inform "household management." He might have pointed out that "economics" as "household management" was the original meaning of the Greek word but we are here dealing with modern societies that operate on different, more complex principles. Indeed, any move toward "perfection" for Machiavelli is premised on getting away from such antiquated and ill-conceived notions.

Since Machavelli has mentioned *The Prince*, Montesquieu confronts him with his own teaching on fiscal matters found there. "What I find surprising is that your financial theories are in patent contradiction with what you said in *The Prince*, where you strictly recommend parsimony for the prince, even avarice." Montesquieu, like Machavelli a short while ago, here points to inconsistencies between the person before him and the texts he has written. Given the resplendent reign Machiavelli envisions, he would seem to be acting contrary to his own maxims.[7]

Machiavelli retorts with an even more fundamental principle of *The Prince*. Above all, the prince must remain flexible and change with circumstances. This is an updated Machiavellian teaching apropos of the nineteenth century, as the subtitle of Joly's work indicates. He will act in accord with the requirements of the times and the unique opportunities they afford to despotism. Contrary to Montesquieu, we may not assume the niggardliness of modern peoples. These are not times of scarcity but, we shall see, of new hopes in the possibility of plenty, brought by a technological society, reformed to exploit it to the utmost.

Precisely because he, and not Montesquieu, really knows the character of modern peoples, he need not rescind popular sovereignty in the matter of state finances. Taxes will be duly voted and collected; the people's representatives will also approve expenditures. "The people who acclaim me do not merely tolerate the splendor of the throne. They positively crave it" and look to the prince for a vicarious sense of power. "They really hate only one thing—wealth in their peers."

Machiavelli begins his reform of the Montesquieuan system of financial management by loosening its restraints. He is like the "giant in the fairytale," he says, bound by pygmies when he sleeps. He awakes and shatters his fetters without even knowing he was tied.

First and foremost, he will take advantage of the power that the coup affords him. Just as the coup was used to introduce the necessary changes in the constitution, it will also justify the streamlining of financial management. In fact, a new budget, following his accession to power, will be declared extraordinarily "by decree." Legal ways will return in subsequent years, but with some changes, of course.

For Machiavelli, the board of auditors poses no real threat. It is a "bookkeeper's office" that cannot prevent funds from being voted and expended. As a source of information, it is perhaps of some use but its reports do not really go too far beyond the data in the budget. As a purely administrative body, it is under the prince's control. Having no power of remonstrance, it need not worry the prince. The other safeguards to which Montesquieu alluded will not be met with such forebearance. In true Machiavellian spirit, however, nothing will be changed directly. As he encounters certain regulations upon assuming more legal ways, he merely proposes to regulate a little in return.

He will do away with the division of the budgetary process into a revenue vote followed by an expenditure vote. Finances are better handled when expenditures are voted piecemeal, with expenditure decisions adjusted as you go along. His is a "diligent" government and he does not want to waste precious time by unnecessary formalities. The intent of such a measure is to let the expenditure side of the budget determine the overall balance. Extraordinary budgets no longer need to have retroactive legislative ratification. The gist of this reform is the same. It removes fiscal discipline from executive spending.

The "spirit" of such reforms extends to line-item budgeting. Where subsidiary accounts pinpointed allocated expense, Machiavelli prefers gross blocs of appropriations for each agency. This grants greater discretion in the use of funds.[8] He will retain the prohibition against the transfer of funds, but only between ministries, not within or among agencies.

At the end of the Nineteenth Dialogue, Machiavelli gives the impression that he has finished with the discussion of such matters. What he has already indicated is sufficient to show Montesquieu that he is not restrained by mere parchment barriers. As a man of the Middle Ages, Machiavelli is supposedly unversed in modern financial matters. His statements seem to reflect a certain prejudice against the detailed consideration of a topic for which he, speaking as a statesman from a former era, has a certain disdain.

For Montesquieu, however, the "reforms" Machiavelli lists are not sufficient. He may exercise greater discretion in the deployment of funds, but he is still limited by the overall budgetary "frame," the boundaries of which may be broken through but not without "peril." For Machiavelli, however, it is an "elastic" frame that can be "stretched as far as wanted." He will in any event remain "within it, never outside," he declares. In the Twentieth Dialogue, Montesquieu gives Machiavelli the opportunity to explain what he means.

Machiavelli now assumes the teacher's role from Montesquieu and begins to elaborate the devices at his disposal. Individually, the changes are too "subtle" to attract the attention of citizens, let alone signal any alarms. There is no reason that they should disquiet them any more than any other political measure. As Machiavelli prefaced this discourse, they are the common practices of all existing societies and it is from such practices, not abstract theories, that he seeks guidance.

However, such statements belie the revolutionary design he has in store for his economic policies. In fact, he posits a new role for government within the economic sphere that finally "dumbfounds" Montesquieu and silences him. It is an understanding of political economy that challenges the presumptions of early liberalism that define Montesquieu's view. What begins with a recitation of some common executive practices in budgetary matters ends with rather uncommon conclusions for economic theory *tout court*.[9]

Machiavelli doubts that the State Budget imposes any rigid limitation on the prince. For Machiavelli, it is "nothing but a provisional measure," a projection of principal financial trends. There are in fact other extraordinary budgets which correct, revise, or add to the main State Budget: emergency budgets, supplementary budgets, deficiency budgets. The financial situation at any given moment is never definitive. Machiavelli endeavors to show that there is considerable elasticity in the system to accommodate the prince.

Machiavelli proceeds as if the requirement that expenditures balance with revenues were just a matter of bookkeeping. Devices to ensure the proper "balance" are myriad. Certain projected revenues, for example, may be used to offset present expenditures. Present expenditures may also be deferred to future budgets. The extraordinary budgets can be deftly handled to disguise certain costs. They will be treated essentially as appendices to the main budget and not be subsumed under its revenue limitations. In fact, each year, you will have "many budgets." In this way, "at the end of ten years, the budget can be doubled or tripled" beyond allocations in the main State Budget.

To this point, Machiavelli has avoided the real thrust of Montesquieu's contentions. In saying that the budget itself will constrain the prince, Montesquieu means that certain fiscal realities must be faced. By and large, the artifices that Machiavelli employs are merely ways to sequester monies within already appropriated sums. They may garner substantial revenues for the prince but not on the order he wishes. More important, they do not produce any wherewithal for the prince beyond that appropriated in the budgets.

Will he, "like Julius Caesar," find fabulous sums in the coffers of the state? Perhaps he intends to discover the equivalent of the "Potosi mines," Montesquieu facetiously comments. To attain desired revenues Machiavelli has two real choices: raising taxes or borrowing. If it is true that peoples in modern states are niggardly and jealous, they simply will not stand for confiscatory taxes. It follows that Machiavelli will be forced to borrow.

The Role of Public Debt in their Respective Schemes

Montesquieu briefly seizes the initiative once again to elaborate on the system of debt financing in modern states.[10] In forcing Machiavelli's admission of his dependence on borrowing, Montesquieu believes he has maneuvered him into a position of weakness. "This is what I wanted you to say." In fact, the rest of the discussion of Part Three concerns borrowing and how Machiavelli will escape the last restraint by which Montesquieu secures the tyrant. Once again, we see Machiavelli give a step-by-step description of how he will undermine Montesquieu's scheme.

Montesquieu acknowledges the necessity of borrowing but only for all "but a few governments." Those which do resort to "such expedients do so with great caution." It is both "immoral" and "dangerous" to "weigh down future generations with exorbitant burdens beyond the limits of any foreseeable resources."

Modern states that want to escape an exclusive reliance on a burdensome and possibly self-defeating taxation turn to borrowing. These borrowing needs are handled by sinking fund arrangements, a scheme that "is truly admirable in its simplicity and mode of execution." According to such a scheme, sums can be gathered for a price (interest) and paid off piecemeal by putting aside each year a certain portion of the borrowed sum. The borrowed sum (principal) along with the interest will be redeemed in full after the time allotted the borrower. The public debt is thus liquidated by successive fractions paid yearly.

If constantly required to amortize, borrowing will not be taken lightly. The government's integrity is on the line and its solvency is a precondition for further borrowing. The people will authorize debts only when the obligation can be easily met. Surprisingly, Machiavelli shows himself as no neophyte when it comes to such matters. He points to the practice of England, which has been known to suspend debt payments on more than one occasion. For his part, he will keep the amortization scheme, which has "certain advantages."

It is Machiavelli who in fact has manipulated Montesquieu to the matter of borrowing, upon which rests the final burden of restraining the prince. At this point, the previously deferential Machiavelli heaps scorn on Montesquieu and his theories. For Machiavelli, deficit financing is a matter to be handled, not so much by financial officers, as by the press. The prince's skillful propagandists will reassure the people who ultimately authorize the debt. All of Montesquieu's previous discourse on this science is parodied and used as a smokescreen for Machiavelli's financial intrigues.

Montesquieu had previously stated that the science of modern finance fundamentally relies on the control and public accountability that the budget process affords. As it turns out, the new prince escapes the "control" of that process principally through borrowing, an action that takes place "off budget." Moreover, the press itself can be effectively employed to justify the ways of the prince as proceeding from more enlightened economic theories. The press, which was to shed all possible light on the activities of the prince, is really a tool that can be used to produce powerful effects on "the minds of bourgeois block-heads."

The limits to fiscally appropriate borrowing are disputed and are presented by Machiavelli as an outmoded understanding of things. "I want my Minister of Finance to be perfectly clear in his use of statistics. Moreover, his literary style must be impeccably lucid." The people will see that the government operates on principles different from those that guide private affairs. No one will dispute that economics is amenable to the advances seen in other sciences.

Prosperity and productivity, the keynotes of his rhetoric, will in fact be fueled, at least initially, by the expenditures of borrowed monies. The government's solvency, which is the precondition of borrowing, must not be put into question by any yearly deficit. If less than predicted, it will be reported as a real triumph. If more, mitigating circumstances will be found, which, when they pass, will permit a return to tighter management. As Machiavelli illustrates in considerable detail, there is no dearth of ways that budgetary statistics can be presented and manipulated if the common faith of the times in material and theoretical progress is not disturbed. The confidence of the prince in the power of his propaganda is nowhere more in evidence than here.

In the last dialogue of this part, the Twenty-First, Machiavelli doggedly attempts to dispel Montesquieu's prejudice against borrowing, which is touted for many different reasons. Through it, "whole families are made dependent on the government."[11] Moreover, "contemporary economics recognizes that far from impoverishing the state, public debt enriches it." It is interesting that for the second time in this part, an offer by Machiavelli to elaborate "new theories" is rejected.

Montesquieu is presumptuous enough to think that he knows such theories. He has been consistent in this respect throughout and has not changed from the very beginning when Machiavelli's opening statement is greeted as "nothing new." Though not explicitly spelled out, we may infer a new economic and industrial policy from the schemes Machiavelli elaborates. Montesquieu's presumptuousness notwithstanding, they point economic policy in a wholly new direction that challenges the fundamental presuppositions of liberalism by dramatically changing the organization of the productive forces of society.[12]

Rather than listening to a theoretical discourse, Montesquieu would first rather like to know the source of the prince's borrowed capital as well as the reasons for raising it. To provide a rationale for raising monies, the prince may always call a foreign war. It is interesting, however, that Machiavelli does not intend to use these monies exclusively for war-making purposes. A domestic end is also in view, as he explains. "Only one-half to two-thirds of such a sum need be spent. The rest finds its way into the treasury for domestic expenditures."

The rough sums that he envisions from war requisitions are three-quarters of what is allotted in the State Budget. This is clearly an enormous sum of money, equal to "the total wealth of certain states." It would certainly be beyond the capacity of any banks to finance such a sum. As it turns out, it is not Machiavelli's intention at all to seek funding from such sources. The whole idea is ridiculed as bespeaking a "dark age" mentality.

In modern times, the small cartel of money merchants is broken. Sufficient monies can be had cheaply if banking institutions are initially bypassed. The prince will issue government securities in denominations that can be afforded by the common artisan. Money will be taken from under mattresses and invested in government bonds.

Substantial sums can be generated immediately this way. Interests rates offered by banks fall in competitive bidding with the government. Machiavelli presents a scheme that intends to undermine the strength of the traditional bank. It is far better to satisfy borrowing needs by addressing all of the country's subjects—"the rich, the poor, artisans, manufacturers, anyone who has a penny at his disposal." In this way, such "excellent investments" break the monopolist hold of banks over finance and succeed in attaching "whole families" to the government.

Machiavelli will also resort to a very clever ploy. After issuing his securities, he will announce that demand has so far outstripped supply that he will be forced to return several millions to would-be investors who "rush from all sides" to buy shares rising at a substantial premium. Things get to "a fever pitch."[13] The prince's tactic will underscore the desirability of such investments and inspire an all-important confidence in a government that acts with such exemplary forebearance and honesty. "Judge for yourself how great an effect this will have on the public mind."

Machiavelli will have even more money than Montesquieu can imagine. The small cartel of private banks are replaced by "great banking institutions," now common to all modern societies. They are capable of lending to the state, at prime rates," sums equivalent to a quarter of the yearly State Budget. For all intents and purposes, government has subsumed the banking function. Later, it becomes clear that these government institutions of credit exist to lend money to large industrial enterprises and to coordinate the financial needs of the country's industrial structure.

Beyond banks, other government authorities, with their own revenue sources, are capable of lending additional sums to the government. Moreover, pension funds, health insurance plans, and savings schemes may tap even vaster sums that will be "deposited in the public treasury" where they will mix with general revenues. The subjects of the prince are modern men, preoccupied above all with security concerns that a materialistic government serves. We are here given some indication of the myriad "public services," controlled by the state, that prompted Machiavelli in the beginning to reject a parsimonious government. What were formerly matters of personal responsibility now are concerns of the state and a cover for the prince's revenue needs.

How Debts are "Dealt With"

Machiavelli has proved that there are indeed numerous schemes for securing necessary funds. The problem arises when such debts fall due. Montesquieu turns the discussion to how Machiavielli will pay back what he has borrowed. If he is not to act like the "common stock jobber," his debts must somehow be paid off. Machivaelli will presently show his interlocutor how his debts "will be dealt with." The choice of words is apt, he declares, because debts cannot always be paid but somehow always must be met. There are several ways.

He might resort to taxes. But, it will be recalled, he originally turned to borrowing in the first place to avoid resorting to this inherently unpopular step. Nevertheless, modern society is amenable to a diversity of tax measures, the burdens of which can be artfully disguised. If the tax route is not taken, it is more perhaps due to a lack of imagination and initiative than to any really formidable impediment. There are still other ways, once tax possibilities are exhausted.

The outstanding public debt can be consolidated under a uniform rate of interest and then, if need be, converted to a lower rate. Agreement to the new interest rate is accepted or the principal is immediately returned. The mentality of the common investor inhibits him from taking this option. Montesquieu really does not know these stockholders. Ever creatures of habit, they prefer an investment at a lower rate than to return their monies to their mattresses, especially when they have become accustomed to new-found paper wealth. In this way, substantial sums of interest can be annulled in a single stroke.

In effect, Machiavelli has succeeded in drawing the common artisan and workingman into his investment schemes. The small scale of their disposable income, as well as their inherent conservatism, makes them reliable supports for the grander designs of the prince. They are predictable investors, not the speculators whose placement of funds can leverage markets. Machiavelli has inculcated a new way of thinking in such types, previously untouched by economic concerns. Their new interests have been made complicit with those of the prince, and serve ends of a wholly different scale and order.

As to principal costs, recourse can be had to a different expedient. Debts can be "rolled over," that is to say, refinanced. As debts fall due, investors can be reissued another certificate of indebtedness and the due date postponed to a more auspicious time. This can be applied to all "floating debts." Montesquieu objects that the prince will jeopardize the solvency of his government and its credit standing. Its bonds will be spurned first in foreign markets and then at home.

Finally, just as Machiavelli would control the press by the press and conspiracies by conspiracies, he would control financial markets by financial markets themselves. Great credit institutions that serve the designs and needs of government would be able to bolster the price of the prince's securities if they were to sag too much by buying up great quantities. Opposite pressures can be relieved by having these institutions sell securities. By means of such action, the prince can virtually create or destroy the fortunes of investors. Montesquieu ends this discussion with a taunt. The prince's favorites, his ministers and mistresses, privy to the state's financial secrets, will be able to reap large fortunes. Machiavelli agrees that indeed the favored will be rewarded, whereas a "thunderbolt" awaits those who stand in his way.[14]

The Principles of the Economic Revolution Fleshed Out

Ostensibly, Part Three is an exercise in how Machiavelli manipulates the budget. Montesquieu has kept the conversation limited to such a topic and away from the views of "modern economists today" whose theories he already presumes to know. Nevertheless, in accord with those views, though unstated, Machiavelli holds out the promise of a vast expansion of productive capacity by a strategic infusion of public monies into the economy. Beyond the Machiavellian devices at his disposal in manipulating the budget, he can perhaps "deal with his debts" through unprecedented economic growth, centrally planned and directed. Implicit in his discussion are the germs of an economic theory that transcends the frame of understanding of Montesquieuan liberalism as it belies Montesquieu's claim to speak authoritatively about such matters.

Machiavelli calls for a new and dynamic role for government in economic society. Unlike oriental despotism, heavy sacrifices are placed on the nation to support extensive "public services" and a "brilliant" and "great" court at the apex of a large centralized administrative structure. Tremendous revenues are needed, not as Montesquieu presumes, to satisfy tyrannical appetites and to furnish the prince and his cohorts with luxuries. Through the active intervention of the government, in conjunction with the advance of technology and applied science, productivity might be greatly improved. This could generate enough public monies to retire public debts easily but also for programs that help minimize the threat of revolution emanating from the masses and assure the popularity he seeks for despotism.

The specifics of his economic program await a discussion of the grand public works programs in the next part of the *Dialogue*. The foundations for that policy lie, however, in the budgetary and banking revolution adumbrated in this part. The steps of the prince are directed by a new economic theory that can be fully measured against the background of Montesquieuan liberalism as it is presented in the *Dialogue*.

The Economic Premises of Montesquiean Economics

Montesquieu's thought is informed by classic notions of liberalism that Machiavelli at one point facetiously likens to a "dark age" mentality. His system implies a parsimonious government not only because it was understood to be dependent on requisitions from a grudging people but because of the limited role government was to perform. "The tendency of economics is to see the political apparatus merely as a necessary but very costly mechanism, whose workings must be simplified. It reduces the role of government to such elementary functions that its greatest drawback perhaps is to destroy government's prestige."[15]

Briefly, the first task facing men is to end the state of nature. Government must be instituted to control the predatory instincts of the species. The next task, equally important to man's well being, is to control government itself. This is the historic task that Montesquieu set himself in his political teaching. As Montesquieu explained earlier, government is mechanistically arranged to control itself. Furthermore, any invasion of rights was to be resisted by an enlightened populace, upon which rested ultimate authority. His arrangement presumes vigilance on the part of the people to keep government properly restrained.

The role of government was limited. Its primary function was as arbiter and guarantor of social peace. Within a protected private sphere, the liberty of the individual would find expression in the self-interested pursuit of material betterment and the accumulation of property. Unfettered from certain religious and governmental restraints, such motives would be given scope and force. Properly channeled by institutions and law, such self-interested pursuits would also serve the interests of society as a whole by protecting the wealth in which all share, through commerce and trade. It was therefore in government's interest to protect property and that private sphere as the precondition of society's prospering and as the guarantee of its own perpetuation. In sum, its natural tendency to aggrandizement had to be curbed and incentives established to restrain its activist tendencies.

A restricted role for government would seemingly give the greatest play to man's productive capacities. Competition among individual producers arises naturally, keeping the costs of production at prices accessible to consumers while encouraging innovation and enterprise. In such a scheme, the sovereign is discharged from the duty of regulating a society that, under enlightened conditions, is extraordinarily capable of self-regulation. This leaves the greatest amount of natural liberty to the individual while it conduces to the material security that was the motive behind forming society in the first place. To attempt to regulate modern society is thus counterproductive. It would expose the sovereign to innumerable delusions because of the insufficiency of human wisdom to properly supervise the myriad industries and employment of peoples. At the same time, it would require granting dangerous powers to direct such enterprises and coerce individuals from whom the strongest and most reliable motive to work has been removed. It is for these reasons that, according to Montesquieu at least, the maxims derived from the study of modern economies are "most contrary to the concentration of power."

Joly's Machiavelli, however, sees an end to such a restricted role for government. Like Marx, he presents himself as speaking from a view that sees liberal society as having reached an advanced stage. Society is now vast, diversified, and increasingly interdependent. The role of government, even as arbiter, would naturally grow apace. State finances, the subject of Part Three, becomes an increasingly important factor as government plays the central role in the economic and social nexus.

Joly's Machiavelli shows how the increased economic leverage of government might be used by the modern tyrant. In controlling the powers to borrow, spend, and tax, he controls the power to reward and punish, as the concluding reflections in this part suggest. Such are formidable weapons in the hands of the modern ruler. With such economic tools, he need not rely on a crude fear to bend his subjects to his will. "To rule today does not require committing atrocities, or decapitating your enemies, confiscating the goods of your subjects, or engaging in widespread torture." Such measures are passé, especially with other more fastidious weapons at his disposal. But beyond the exercise of such economic leverage, Machiavelli intends even more fundamental changes. He will bring into being a new social arrangement appropriate to developments that, presumably, have rendered liberal theories obsolete.

According to Montesquieu, the people are bound to an economic regime that is "inimical to despotism." Therefore, if Machiavelli is not supreme in this sphere, he will not be in the political one. The logic of Machiavelli's despotism thus leads him to an attack on society, understood by Montesquieu as effectively preserved from government encroachment because it would run counter to the material benefits modern peoples enjoy from the freedom allotted them. But, as Machiavelli points out, such benefits do not extend to the masses and economic niceties do not form part of their character. These represent vast reservoirs of peoples in the latter stages of capitalism that Machiavelli describes. Indeed, society is not as fluid or dynamic as Montesquieu implies and its benefits exclude the most numerous and turbulent classes "riveted" to work by poverty. The new prince has their interests and desires as his constant preoccupation. In winning them over, he finds the broadest base for his regime.

According to Machiavelli, social stratification has reasserted itself within modern societies. Ultimately, it is inherited wealth, an accident of birth, which perpetuates privilege. A misplaced respect for the principle of inheritance is a vestige of aristocratic times and gives rise to a class of idle rich as the modern counterpart to the idle nobility. In the end, they are as unproductive as the "intemperate gentleman's son," as Joly's Montesquieu so aptly puts it. Their existence is inappropriate to the society of the future as the land, workshops, and capital come under the prince's direction in an attempt to control the whole society as if one interconnected enterprise. In such a view, government becomes a tutelary power of vast proportions, like the society of India, which receives Machiavelli's praise in this respect at the end of the Fifth Dialogue.

According to this view, the revolutions that menace modern societies derive from the inadequate coordination of society and the putative failure of private markets to efficiently organize production and assure a broader distribution of goods that include the masses. Machiavelli's financial reforms intend to bring centralized control through the State Budget and the allocation of key capital investments to increase productivity that will reduce the revolutionary threat. If successful in attenuating class conflict, he will bring about a new form of despotism, at once marked by mildness but potentially quite enduring. We might be witnessing the beginnings of "a frightful calm," the statement that stands at the beginning of Joly's work as a kind of motif.

In the "sketch" of the regime given in the Seventh Dialogue, Machiavelli declared he would borrow certain features from the very industrial order that elicits the admiration of Monesquieu. He will bring into existence immense monopolies. "The fate of all private fortunes would become completely dependent on these vast reservoirs of public wealth." Landed wealth would be kept "in a condition of relative inferiority" through taxes which intend to destroy inherited privilege. "Independent fortunes" in industry will be controlled by competition from huge government monopolies. "The point must be reached where the state is composed of nothing but proletarians, a few millionaires, and soldiers"—the latter two groups being the least revolutionary elements in the state and the former exclusively cultivated by the policies of the prince.

The role of the market and individual enterprise as the primary engine of production and distribution comes to an end and is replaced by the sovereign's will and his dictates.

> As head of my government, all my edicts, all my ordinances would constantly aim at the same goal—the annihilation of independent powers, whether of groups or individuals, to develop the unlimited dominance of the state, making it the most powerful force in protecting, promoting, and remunerating society's activities.

With such a statement, we arrive at the furthest extreme from the limited government of Montesquieu's scheme. The individual exists solely in and through the prince, who personally undertakes decisions that were formerly made impersonally by the market. The prince directly assumes activities that were the preserve of the individual. He absorbs the social spheres that sheltered the citizen and afforded him opportunity to pursue his individual happiness. He thereby annihilates autonomy and responsibility, and the very possibilities of dignified existence.

As with the theory of despotism that originally framed the understanding of

Montesquieu and opened the discussion of this part, private property is effectively held at the sufferance of the sovereign. Indeed, we are told, there is not a "farthing" whose spending is not in some way connected to the wishes of the prince. However, all this occurs not in a primitive and backward society but in one of the most materially advanced societies of the world. Again, unlike what Montesquieu originally presumes, the despotism of the future will generate its revenues, initially at least, not from the conduct of a self-defeating war, but internally, from available resources. Unlike despotic regimes of old, "economics" is not a derivative of effective war making. Effective war making is a derivative of "economics." The modern prince will set out on his path of conquest, the subject of the next Part of the *Dialogue*, subsequent to his economic revolution.

The initial prospects for Machiavelli's revolution seemed promising at the time Joly wrote. The perpetuation of such a regime was a different matter. Joly leads his contemporaries to ponder its prospects.[16] In the reflective light of history, we partisans of liberal regimes can draw the appropriate lessons from its rise and fall.

The next chapter addresses the manners and mores of the Machiavellian regime, a "moral revolution" as profound and extensive as that in the economic sphere.

Notes

1. See *The Spirit of the Laws* XX-XXII, which deal explicitly with commerce and money. Sorel writes that Montesquieu anticipates Adam Smith in attempting to "give scientific form to the problem of political economy." See Sorel, *Montesquieu*, 148.

2. Montesquieu's remarks at this point indicate an understanding of despotism that is limited to oriental varieties. These are classically described in *The Spirit of the Laws*. His consternation in the face of Machiavelli's regime, which assumes a modern, industrial society, can be traced to such thinking. The principles of force and fear that define despotism are progressively minimized in the Machiavellian revolution. In this part, we begin to see how the promise of economic prosperity shifts the foundation of despotism by winning popular support for the despot.

3. Machiavelli is referring to arguments found in *The Spirit of the Laws* XIII 10.

4. This argument was made repeatedly in the century following Joly, that is, the century that knew the greatest wars. It is still frequently heard today. Who wants to make war when there is so much money to be made in the "global village"? When there are so many places to go and people to meet?

We have been told that the existence of a McDonalds inside countries borders is a kind of *gage* of peace. I never understood why. Is it all the "happy meals" they serve?

The proliferation of war in the future is at least as inevitable as the proliferation of McDonalds.

5. Machiavelli remarks upon the vehemence with which Montesquieu asserts his proposition.

6. There is a parallel between economic policy here stated and policy pursued by the prince in regard to the pope. Anti-clerical elements are radicalized to energize the orthodox. Essentially, different groups are politicized and played off against each other. This creates the necessity for the prince to reassert control, while satisfying one group or another in turns.

7. See *The Prince* XVI.

8. President Reagan was motivated by similar thinking when he advocated his reforms in the realm of "fiscal federalism"—federal grants to local programs. However, the consolidation of accounts was proposed to encourage greater administrative discretion in the *reduction* of expenditures.

9. What is described is uncanny in its anticipation of key elements of what later became known as Keynesian economics and more radical economic theories.

10. See *The Spirit of the Laws* XVII 18, "Of the Payment of Public Debts," where sinking fund arrangements are elaborated.

11. Contrary to the financial policies of Machiavelli's despot, who envisions a "bondholding" society, Margaret Thatcher spoke of turning her country into a "stockholding" society. This, of course, would make "whole families" dependent on the health of corporate Britain and loosen dependence on government (and unions) for the economic well-being of its citizens. The process is well advanced in America. In the span of a decade we changed from being a society of institutional "bondholders" to the "stockholder society" envisioned by Thatcher. The changes to the economy have been dramatic. The Chairman of the Federal Reserve has admitted to targeting the stock market in his management of the country's monetary policy. At the end of his tenure as President, the Democrat Clinton bragged about the Thatcherite change that took place in his administration. It should be kept in mind that the precipitous decline in the paper wealth of the untold millions of stockholders in the United States lies at the heart of the now current economic malaise. Is not this empowerment of "Wall Street" by Washington, direct and indirect, not without its own inherent dangers and potential abuses? What is now a "malaise" may later be a problem of a different order.

12. In *The Spirit of the Laws*, XXII 17, Montesquieu questions those theorists who insist that the state could "multiply riches" by turning to deficit financing. After listing the numerous disadvantages, he concludes baldly: "I know of no advantage."

13. As we in the United States all know now, investment schemes can take on a momentum of their own. "Irrational exuberance" has a way of setting in.

14. Among others, DeMorney, longtime friend and confident of Louis, became notorious for profiting in office from the financial schemes of the Second Empire.

15. Machiavelli implies that his financial revolution is meant to restore prestige to government.

16. As the quote from Montesquieu on the title page of Joly's work augurs: *"soon,"* perhaps, people would unite against such a power.

Chapter Six

THE MORAL REVOLUTION

Part Four consists of four dialogues, the Twenty-Second through the Twenty-Fifth. In the previous two parts of the *Dialogue*, Machiavelli shows in detail how he will surmount the obstacles to despotism in the political and financial system outlined by Montesquieu. Having heard Machiavelli, Montesquieu admits to not knowing "either *the spirit of the laws or the spirit of finance*" and facetiously thanks his interlocutor for having taught him both. They may now begin other topics in accord with the "wager" they have made. Machiavelli's prince is now absolute. "With such prodigious power, you will do great things," Montesquieu ironically quips in challenging Machiavelli to indicate how despotism will escape the odium in which it is normally held.

The discussion in Part Four reverts to the themes of Part One. There, Montesquieu contended that pure selfishness, implemented by Machiavellian means, could not be a consistent maxim of both prince and subject. At a minimum, if a regime is to endure, it must appeal to some notion of a greater good. It is not enough for Machiavelli to have gained complete power, even granting the momentousness of such an achievement. Machiavelli must justify the means he has used to gain rule by pointing to the redeeming ends that his despotism serves. In Part Four, Machiavelli endeavors to spell out the basis of a new "common good" between the ruler and the ruled that would endow his regime with the legitimacy necessary for its perpetuation. Machiavelli must prove his dictum that the end justifies the means, "It is finally the time to show that *good can come from evil.*"

As the discussion progresses, we are given a fine portrait of the despot as he crucially shapes the character of the people to his rule. Joly's sensitive eye as a social analyst is nowhere more in evidence than in the vivid description of the manners and mores of the Napoleonic regime. On the deepest level, however, his artfulness intends to bring to life the character of a totally new order, the expression of a new historic epoch that succeeds the "constitutional era" defined by Montesquieu.

In the opening Dialogue of this part, Montesquieu adjures Machiavelli's prince to adopt the manners, not of an overbearing despot, but of Alfred the

Great and "Godly Louis," who never ceased in their humble ministering to the poor. He also offers the ancient founders of austere republics as the proper models of one who would really seek the public welfare and the common good. Theirs was a legacy of liberty based on simplicity and decency and is meant to contrast most sharply with the legacy of Machiavelli's models, history's great conquerors and luxury-seeking emperors. Montesquieu understands himself as standing with his interlocutor "like the Atlas and the Taurus," as a republican polar opposite from the imperial Machiavelli. As it turns out, the whole movement of Part Four is led by Machiavelli to bridge the differences with Montesquieu over the principles of rule each admires. Like the "Godly Louis" and Alfred the Great, he declares himself to have the poor as the principal concern of his rule. Moreover, in the last Dialogue of this part, he shows how he will even claim for himself the mantle of champion of "liberty." At the conclusion of Joly's work, we are meant to contemplate the success of Machiavelli in satisfying the principles and passions of moderns. Machiavelli has founded a regime, not as a reactionary partisan of the Middle Ages, but by appealing to the same fundamental principles defended by Montesquieu but applied to a new historic order. A fuller elaboration of the Machiavellian revolution points to elements of Saint-Simonian thought that inspire Napoleon III and, beyond, to essential elements of modern totalitarianism.

The New "Spirit" of the Laws

In the shortest and arguably most beautifully written part of the *Dialogue*, the stereotypical view of Machiavelli, which Montesquieu shares, is shattered. What separates the two interlocutors is not merely an admiration of republican virtue and imperial grandeur but two historic epochs. Far from a limited defense of his own epoch, "bordering on the Middle Ages," Machiavelli comes to light as an apparent apologist for an epoch that transcends the so-called modern world defended by Montesquieu. He successfully brings about a "return" to despotism, but presented as an advance of the historic process, the demands of which his regime effectively fulfills.

Machiavelli declares he will bring peace, "the greatest of my benefactions," to a country previously wracked by factions. Montesquieu immediately attacks Machiavelli's assertion that his rule stands for "liberty, dignity, and strength." Such a claim can be maintained only by changing "the meaning of words" as they would apply in the republican regime described by Montesquieu.

Following the policy of Rome, the unity of the country, as indeed its "dignity and strength," is guaranteed through an aggressive foreign policy, a subtopic of Part Four. Domestic peace is premised on war abroad as all factions unite in extending the influence of the regime globally. Having helped restore stability at home through the establishment of authoritarian rule, the prince uses the collective resources of the state in pursuit of the most exalted glory as he emulates the great conquerors of history in the most diverse regions of the world. The new prince's deeds, Machiavelli implies, will be commensurate with the unprecedented power he has gained.

In the face of evident hyperbole which compares the new prince to "Alexander, Caesar, and Charlemagne," among others, Montesquieu grants that "no hero of antiquity or modern times" could rank with him. Even the example of Louis XIV pales beside him. But such musings are beside the point. Montesquieu fails to see what "good" accrues from a policy based on war, an "evil" where, inevitably, destruction and servitude follow. "This is not the time to equivocate," Machiavelli interrupts. "Glory is itself a great good," he says to one who has tasted earthly celebrity and secretly pines over its loss in hell. "All other assets accrue to the sovereign who has glory." In winning it, the prince will come to arbitrate the affairs of the world personally.

Machiavelli recurs to the past grandeur of great historical figures to frame his vision of the future. He intends to fire the imagination of the masses and unite them to a leader who, by words and deeds, gives expression to a new historic consciousness. Machiavelli attempts to end the disruptions that are endemic to liberal society by removing their most serious causes. He projects through propaganda a world-historic view that would replace the liberal consciousness by elevating the masses and uniting formerly disparate groups in a common historic enterprise.

Machiavelli seizes upon a casual reference to Louis XIV. Like the former French sovereign, the new prince will have his name associated with the apogee of an historic epoch, which rivaled the splendors of the Periclean and Augustian ages.[1] Political parallels may also be drawn in their common efforts to maximize centralization, co-opt independent groups, and emasculate institutions that might serve as independent centers of opposition.

As he competes with Louis in war, he also competes with him in constructing monuments. Here is introduced a subject of vast importance to this part of the *Dialogue* which simultaneously serves diverse objectives. In a technological and engineering feat of unprecedented dimensions, he will refurbish and redesign cities in magnificence while providing housing for his people. Machiavelli here once again touches on the key to his rule and sway over the people. They are to be impressed with the glory of the sovereign and participate through him in certain exalted emotions tied to the unprecedented power he holds. "I would want to show the people that a monument whose construction used to require centuries could be built by me in a few years." His architecture need not be tasteful by past standards, as long as it is large and "modern," as befitting the tone of a new industrial age. "The palaces of my predecessors would fall under the wrecker's ball in order to raise them anew in modern forms."

Admittedly, "the number of great actions" to achieve glory "is not limitless." The two "principal marks" of great reigns, whether that of Ramses II, Louis

XIV, or Peter I, have been "war and buildings."[2] Like these former sovereigns, he intends his buildings to dwarf the significance of the individual by its scale and have him seek identity with the strength of the prince. This will serve the prince's political principles "aesthetically" by giving expression to an imperial grandeur in which all collectively participate. At the same time, it appeases their love of equality, which all the ruled share, at least in comparison to a person of such exalted stature.

The prince also intends his building program to accommodate the people in their needs. Massive public works programs will give employment to the masses of men, formerly excluded from a stake in society and from the pleasures only the "few rich" could procure. They will be furnished housing. The spirit of enterprise will flourish in his regime but only in those occupations peripheral to the great economic tasks of the prince. Small-scale businesses will be subsumed into the massive government programs that aim at improving "the material conditions of workers, laborers, and those bent under the weight of social necessity." In underscoring the concern of the prince for the masses of poor, he finds moral justification for his rule, while discrediting the laissez-faire arrangements of the Montesquieuan system as "cold-blooded indifference" to the "wretchedness of the people."

In "an oratorical outburst," as Machiavelli puts it, Montesquieu forces a comparison between this sovereign and others, who brought not monuments of glory, but a legacy of laws, simplicity, and liberty. If Machiavelli were sincere about his solicitude for the people, he would dispose of his court and all its trappings as well as his policy of bread and circuses. In a tirade against pomp, Montesquieu adjures Machiavelli to follow the likes of Agesilaus, Lycurgus, and Gracchus and not the emperors he emulates.[3]

At the end of the Twenty-Second Dialogue, Montesquieu asserts that the greatest act of benefaction is the abnegation of absolute power. He asks Machiavelli to have his prince step down from power as the touchstone of his good faith intentions for the people. In any case, "the people that elected you would only have to express its will by asking you to descend from the throne in the name of the state's salvation." According to Montesquieu, the new prince can be counted among those "who last but a day."

Montesquieu's "outburst" interrupts the flow of the discussion. Machiavelli was to specify the "good" his rule would serve. It continues with how in fact he can guarantee the perpetuation of his rule. The Twenty-Third Dialogue elaborates the means that are available. Such considerations continue in the Twenty-Fourth Dialogue. Machiavelli begins to sketch in detailed particulars of the portrait of the new prince who begins to take on the aspect of not merely a glorious ruler but a new kind of god.

Machiavelli's Realism

In the Twenty-Third Dialogue, Machiavelli argues why the necessities of the moment prevent him from adopting the role of a modern Lycurgus in renouncing absolute power. Montesquieu is acquainted with Machiavelli's political, economic, and financial system. He will now learn "the final way" by which he will "sink the roots" of his dynasty "into the depths of the earth."

Machiavelli characterizes Montesquieu's "oratorical outburst" as misplaced enthusiasm for things which are no longer possible. In an equally vehement statement, he attempts to show that the times demand despotism. If he succeeds in showing that his rule is the last buffer against utter destruction, then what serves his rule is "good," at least insofar as it preserves against a greater evil. He seeks strength and security, not for self-interested motives or out of profligacy, but for urgent political reasons. In this light, the self-abnegation that Montesquieu demands would be irresponsible.

The character of modern society is presented in vivid and scathing terms. Machiavelli's prince cannot be an "Agesilaus, Lycurgus, or Gracchus" because he is not among "Spartans or Romans." He is "in the midst of voluptuous societies, where a passion for pleasure and war go hand in hand, where people are transported by power and sensuality and no longer recognize divine authority, paternal authority, or religious restrictions." It follows that he cannot lead by an appeal to virtue. "I control this society through its vices because it only presents me with vices." The events of 1848, not to mention 1789, have made evident the anarchic and destructive possibilities in mass revolution. Consequently, the masses must be appeased to forestall chaos.[4]

For their part, the privileged classes make common cause with the prince and embrace policies that stand between them and a Europe "aflame." In the final analysis, it is an appeal to security that justifies the Machiavellian coup and serves as the ultimate objective of the prince's policies. This is a compelling argument for the liberal Montesquieu whose design of political society is fundamentally motivated by the same desire for security but who is now forced to entertain the idea that it is best guaranteed by dictatorial rule.

If it is granted that the Machiavellian revolution has thwarted anarchy, then Machiavelli's view of history is seemingly vindicated as to the recurrent possibility and even necessity for despotism. Moreover, he has, in a sense, proved that "good can come from evil"—at least if forestalling a greater evil is "good." It follows that any steps that strengthen his regime can be viewed as justified. Machiavelli has maneuvered the discussion to the point where his principles, in the extreme situation that comes to prevail in modern times, would force at least conditional assent on Montesquieu's part. Upon such foundations, less justifiably, he would build his grand structure of tyranny. Working within the frame of liberal politics to meet the problems he identifies is not considered.

Machiavelli turns to measures that will ensure that his rule takes hold. Up to this point, he has emphasized the harsher aspects of his rule and, as conqueror, stands accused of being an "avenging angel." In mock protest, Machiavelli asks: "Am I really so harsh when I embrace, not violence, but self-effacement as my political end?" His rule in fact is not to be confused with the military despotism of old. With sarcasm, he promises to bring Montesquieu "more than one unexpected consolation" and points to certain softer features of his rule. But first, he asks indulgence for listing "a few more precautions" necessary for the prince's safety.

He will expand the praetorian guard, a personal force one-third the size of the regular army. As far as the army goes, there will be universal conscription to ensure an adequate force for his imperial policies. Continued service necessary to a professional armed forces will be encouraged by monetary incentives. The goal is state employment of the masses, bound to the prince through patriotic loyalty and employment.[5]

His rule will find support of other sovereigns interested in a tranquil Europe. He will have his "worker's Jacquerie" to go along with his praetorian guard and armed services. But, in the end, it is the prince's building program that represents the most efficacious way of finding permanent occupations for the masses. They are tied to the regime whose policies guarantee their livelihood. And the propertied classes, meanwhile, realize that this is the only means to defuse revolution. His building policy is the most important of many steps to organize and co-opt the workers while it lays down the foundations for a more integrated economy.

Attention is rightly redirected to such a policy for the multiple objectives it serves. "Have you noticed that almost all my political reforms simultaneously serve economic goals?" In a truly Machiavellian vein, reconstruction also pursues a strategic goal. The avenues of the capital, for example, will be widened. They will come to be rightfully admired for providing the most beautiful urban vistas in the world. But they also allow for the easy movement of troops. The workers who widen such thoroughfares will make the erection of barricades more difficult. They are depriving themselves of their favored means of mounting effective protests and insurrections. Moreover, important building projects will take the workers outside of the city, the center of agitation, where the government is most vulnerable to a revolutionary coup. The subsidized housing that the workers will construct for themselves will be interspersed in the environs of the city. This will isolate troublemakers and fractionalize the strength of any revolutionary movement.[6]

There will be an explosion in the growth of the bureaucracy as the role of government expands to handle the grand projects and social programs of the regime. With the new programs initiated by the prince, the bureaucrat comes to the fore. With such employment, he hopes to channel the aspirations and energies of the more talented and ambitious.

He will not neglect the "little things" to secure himself. Those who cannot be bought off will be won by honors. Equality of conditions breeds a love of distinction that can easily be satisfied by baubles and braid. Trophies, emblems, images, and statues will be erected everywhere to remind of the greatness of the prince who will designate everything under his authority with the epithet "royal." Titles will multiply and ceremony will return into vogue. As petty honors satisfy little souls at little expense, the ancient nobility is appeased by a scrupulous regard for traditions and honors which, until recently, had fallen into desuetude.

Above all, the general tone of the regime will be set by pleasure-seeking appropriate to a rich and luxurious Empire and far removed from the austerity associated with ancient republics or the peculiar asceticism and disciplined lifestyles of many in the money-making classes of early liberal regimes. Public spectacles will rout boredom. And austere individuals who do not succumb to all such blandishments will appear singular.[7] Efforts will be made to seduce the most pure among them. In no way will the people be made to feel self-conscious in their pursuits. Rather, the fall of the pure will confirm them in their predilections. The prince will be "harsh only in what relates to politics." All other passions will be tolerated and encouraged by the prince's example.

Montesquieu had presumed that virtue would exist in substantial numbers of citizens, who would be moved to resistance to despotic rule. But Machiavelli has succeeded in impoverishing citizen character and reducing and isolating such types.[8] At the same time, he has enlisted, through self-interest, the diverse factions and groups in liberal society to the prince's cause.

The Character of Louis Napoleon

In the Twenty-Fourth Dialogue, Machiavelli will give his government its "final countenance."

In political matters, the prince must remain inscrutable. He follows the likes of Alexander VI and the Duke of Valentinois, of whom it was said of the former that "he never did what he said" and of the latter that "he never said what he did." Machiavelli thus begins the Twenty-Fourth Dialogue with reference to two prominent personages from *The Prince*, whose lives make for most profitable study for would-be rulers. As it turns out, this Dialogue contains the most frequent references to *The Prince*. Moreover, except for one interruption, Machiavelli is free to proceed as he wishes. The dialectical character of Joly's work disappears as the interlocutors hasten to finish their conversation. The resulting prose reminds one of the character of *The Prince* in the quickened pace in which it prescribes the "proper" and oftentimes shocking conduct of princes.

In adjuring the prince to be inscrutable in word and deed, Machiavelli gives the first of a series of recommendations that intend to conjure a god-like image for the sovereign. Mystery surrounds the throne. But when the prince does act, he acts with vigor. The people see him as a singular kind of law unto himself. Montesquieu interrupts Machiavelli to object to this dissimulation, which, no matter how beneficial in keeping his subjects off balance and fearful, might provoke foreigners not held "under foot." The combined strength of his neighbors would limit his power to act and ultimately overthrow such a faithless and menacing personage.

Machiavelli is momentarily forced to leave the portrait of the prince he is sketching and address foreign affairs. His foreign policy consists in offsetting the strength of his more formidable enemies by seeking allies from countries in decline. He will then manipulate them through appeals to memories of ancient glory. This would provide him "with 300,000 more men against armed Europe" for as long as he lived. After this interlude, Machiavelli can return to the task of revealing "the royal countenance" in its finished form, in virtually uninterrupted discourse.

Competent advisors will serve the prince and debate in his presence. The correct course of action will recommend itself without the prince having to commit himself beforehand. His word in fact may betray opposite intentions. Anticipating Orwell and the descriptions of later totalitarianism, he will signal his designs to the privileged few by words opposite to his acts. "When I say: 'My reign is peace,' it means there will be war. When I make an appeal to morality, it means that I am going to use force." His motives will remain obscure except to the initiated who penetrate the inner sanctums of power. The line of authority will constantly shift to prevent the coalescence of cliques that may grow presumptuous.

His press will talk constantly of the grandeur of the reign and the love of his subjects. It will put "into the mouths of the people the opinions and ideas, and even the forms of speech by which they communicate them." His pronouncements will be grand occasions, oracular in character. When he addresses himself to the people, he is not above a more blatant demagoguery and other techniques of mass appeal.

He will follow a great historic figure as his model. He could not "put his leisure to better use than by writing, say, the history of a great man" he emulates. Precisely like Louis Napoleon, he will be a man of the times, cultivated, a poetaster. This will lend a certain charm to go with historic stature as it appeals to intellectuals whose sympathies are necessary in helping to project the "proper" image of the prince for his subjects and posterity.[9]

At times, he must appear awesome. We are reminded of *The Prince* where it is asserted that men avenge slight wrongs but not great ones.[10] They like to feel the strength of the prince. Since they are venal, they would be ready accomplices in ventures that subdue the proud and independent.

The wrath of his "justice' would affirm their commonality with others, including their superiors. All immediately around him are vulnerable to the prince and the fate he dispenses. Restraint would be viewed with gratitude, almost as an active benefaction. The smallest gesture will be studied as a sign of his disposition. Any odious excesses will be attributed to his underlings. He is to punish with unyielding vigor but reward with alacrity. In the end, the hold of moral principle will be loosened and replaced by reference to the will and pleasure of the prince.

Machiavelli next turns to the human side of the prince. Clemency and magnanimity complement his more forceful features and soften his aspect. "Man is the image of God, and the Divinity avails Himself of severe blows as well as mercy." Since customs have softened in modern times, he will not disregard the usefulness of clemency in winning the allegiance of the multitudes.

He must appear superstitious. This will endow all his actions with a certain fatefulness to play upon the credulity of the masses. He will also be a lusty prince. This will enlist the interest and attention of the more beautiful half of his subjects. He will be envied of men and desired by women. Chivalry will return in his person. In effect, the whole of his policy is to make men forget their loss of liberty. "I can assure you that if I carefully follow the rules I have just outlined there will be little concern about liberty in my kingdom." Making the people happy and providing them with diversions is what occupies him. "A thousand different objects will constantly occupy people's minds."

"I shall even go so far as to satisfy the obsession for liberty." He returns to foreign policy where he might exploit certain opportunities to gain popular influence on the pretext of fighting for the advancement of popular causes. He would assure his fellow monarchs, however, that he embraces the cause of liberty only to stifle it.

At end, students of Napoleon III and, certainly, the contemporaries of Joly could not help but be aware that "the portrait of the prince" Machiavelli has endeavored to sketch in the Twenty-Fourth Dialogue is in perfect likeness to the French Emperor. We are left little doubt as to who Joly conceived as the practitioner of the "politics of Machiavelli in the Nineteenth Century," in the Dialogue that is at once most explicitly Machiavellian in character and tone and most detailed in its description of Napoleon III.

Loosening Repression

At the beginning of the Twenty-Fifth Dialogue, Machiavelli indicates that he will rule for "ten years" in strictly absolute fashion. It is time for severe repression, whatever the prince's efforts to mask such a reality. It might be thought that the people will be unhappy and complain. They will in fact receive their fate as deserved punishment.

According to Machiavelli, there comes a moment to loosen pressure. The prince will grant liberties. The enemies of the prince fool themselves when they think that repression will redound against the prince. It had its effect in dissipating the forces of resistance. He can grant certain liberties without them threatening him. Partisan hatred will be disarmed as he grants the necessary concession to the liberal spirit of the times. "I could even grant real liberties," he declares. "You'd have to be completely bereft of political intelligence not to see that by this time my legislation has borne fruit." In fact, "the character of the nation has changed." Absolutism has penetrated the customs and reformed the mindset of the nation. He may now enter the path of toleration without fearing anything.

An anecdote drawn from the experience of Rome demonstrates how liberty affects the souls of people. Dion relates that "the Roman people were indignant toward Augustus because of certain very harsh laws that he had promulgated. But as soon as he had the actor Piladus recalled and the seditious were banished from the city, discontent ceased." Montesquieu himself recounts this anecdote in *The Spirit of the Laws*.[11] The Romans felt tyranny more deeply when a dancer was exiled than when all its laws had been taken away. We have reached a similar point in the evolution of France.

The portrait of the prince is virtually complete. A short while before, Montesquieu had asked Machiavelli to step down from the throne as the touchstone of his good will and concern for the common good. He will relinquish power on one condition, "as a martyr" to the popular cause and as a testament to his love of the people. After his death, their love for him will turn to adoration.

The Cult of Personailty

Far from an act of self-abnegation, such a martyred death represents the height of hubris that would see the beloved prince elevated to a god-like status to rival that of the Roman Caesar, also the founder of a universal dynasty. Here we glimpse the real ambitions of the modern prince in what comes to light as a Napoleonic emulation of the Caesars and one of the deepest insights into the character of Louis.[12] The modern Caesar seeks the highest glory in the founding of a new historic order. It is based on a new religion, generated by his sacrificial death, that finds this prince, as Caesar before him, the supreme object of worship.

At the dramatic end of Joly's work, this becomes explicit.

> I don't say that I shall be respected or loved, but I do say that I will be revered and adored. If I so wished I could have altars erected for me....When I pass by, the soul of the people exalts. People run deliriously in my train. I am an object of idolatry. The father points me out to his son. The mother invokes my name in her prayers. The girl looks at me, sighs, and thinks that if only I might glance at her, perchance, she could lie for a moment in my bed... I tell you, my name will be invoked as if I was a god. When there are hailstorms,

droughts, and fires, I rush up and the people throw themselves at my feet. They would bear me to heaven in their arms if god gave them wings.

There can be no recourse to liberty, at least as Montesquieu understands the term. "In the mind and soul of my people I personify virtue. Even more, I personify liberty and also revolution, progress, the modern spirit, finally all that is best at the core of contemporary civilization."

At the beginning of this part, Montesquieu had claimed that Machiavelli would have to change the meaning of words, if he were, as he said, to personify such things. A transvaluation of values, to borrow a phrase from Nietszche, is implied in his appeal to "virtue and liberty"—a change in the fundamental significance of words that rival the changed world view inaugurated by the real Machiavelli in his use of such terms.

We are along way from the mechanistic politics of Montesquieu outlined in the first part of the *Dialogue*. Machiavelli has attempted to establish a popular despotism. In the "cult" of the prince, he has also attempted to reconcile modern rational politics with the credulous disposition of the masses and former faiths. Devotions, formerly directed to other worlds, are redirected to this world and the person of this prince, who finds legitimacy in both secular and religious terms, or rather, in an ideology that tries to synthesize the deepest sources of authority in the West.

Notes

1. See Voltaire, *Siecle de Louis XIV* (Paris: Flammerion, 1931), I , 507. The opening of Voltaire's history indicates the appropriateness of Louis XIV as an object of emulation for the new prince. He reigned over one of the four great epochs of the West. The first of these belonged to Periclean Athens, the second to the Caesars, the third to Renaissance Italy, and the last to Louis XIV, an era enriched by the three previous and therefore the culmination of an "esprit" that Napoleonic France wanted to emulate.

2. Hitler's ambitions on this score parallel those of Louis. See Albert Speer, *Inside the Third Reich*, trans. Richard and Clara Winston (New York: Macmillan, 1970), 8. Speer had a theory of "ruin value" that attracted Hitler's interest. The buildings of the Third Reich, in terms of their materials and statics, were to be designed on the order of Roman models and their condition after the passing of a thousand years. (This was the Thousand Year Reich and the first Reich, Charlemagne's Holy Roman Empire, lasted this long.) As in the *Dialogue*, an economic consideration also inspired the erection of the Third Reich's monuments. The money spent on public buildings, like that spent on armaments, injected the capital necessary to revive a depressed economy. It created the artificial demand for goods that alleviated the employment problem. As in the *Dialogue*, the buildings policy was meant to speak to and represent certain ideological goals of the regime.

3. In no way does the real Montesquieu adjure moderns to follow the likes of the ancient founders. One cannot read the description of Lycurgus's "singular" institutions without strong feelings of antipathy. See *The Spirit of the Laws* IV 6 and 7. Joly's distortion of the thought of the real Montesquieu is clearly evident here.

Ironically, the real Machiavelli, in fact, touts ancient founders as appropriate models for curing the "peculiar" diseases of modern politics.

4. Machiavelli's defense of his despotism in fact parodies the wisdom of ancient founders—recommended by Montesquieu for his emulation—when he constructs constitutions tailored to the character of the people he finds.

5. The secret to Saddam Hussein's political longevity may lie in the pursuit of similar policies.

6. One thinks of Sarcelles, on the outskirts of Paris.

7. This is the Paris of Offenbach, we should always remember. More to the point, Joly indicates that he knows very well how his contemporaries view him, indeed an "austere" and strange individual against the background of the Second Empire. He later indicates that there is no dearth of individuals who can be counted on to subdue the few proud and "independent men" of the times.

8. The "impoverishment" of the character of the people is precisely how the court that tried Joly saw him as depicting the effects of Napoleon's policies.

9. French presidents who followed DeGaulle have shown themselves of one mind with Joly's Machiavelli on this score. They have felt compelled to demonstrate their affinity for literature (Mitterand) or art (Pompidou). Even the staid Giscard apparently wrote a romantic novel. The family name—d'Estaing—though a bought title, was no electoral handicap. The contrast with America is striking. The "populist" streak in American democracy inclines to suspicion in matters that the French see as *de rigeur* in their leaders. The only recent exception to "populist suspicion" in the U.S. was JFK (and perhaps FDR). Like Louis Napoleon, Kennedy burnished his reputation before running for president by writing a history of great men—a Pulitzer-prize winner, to boot. He and his wife were genuinely at ease in the world of culture. It is for this that he is known as being the most "European" of presidents. Family wealth, athletic good looks, prep schools and Harvard, an attractive, intelligent, French-speaking wife, beautiful children—were all critical elements of his charm. It rendered his life, not suspect, but *féerique,* and for a brief moment Washington (of all places) became "Camelot." He seduced a whole generation of "the best and brightest." What the Machiavelli of Joly's *Dialogue* says is pertinent here. The intellectuals he seduced would perpetuate his memory through their writing. Doesn't the "Kennedy myth" have something to do with this?

10. See *The Prince* III.

11. The reference to Dion can be found in *The Spirit of the Laws* XIX 3.

12. The nephew Augustus stood to his uncle Julius as "civilizer" to "conqueror." Louis probably saw himself in a similar light with regard to his relative. I argue that his "civilizing" mission was undertaken in the element of Saint-Simonianism, the topic of the following two chapters.

Part III

The Saint-Simonian Elements in the New Modes and Orders

Chapter Seven

THE SAINT-SIMONIAN HISTORICAL ELEMENTS

Saint-Simonianism and Louis Napoleon

The influence of Saint-Simonianism on Napoleon III was more commonly noted among contemporaries of Louis than among later historians of the Second Empire. For example, Sainte-Beuve is widely reported to have hailed the arrival of Napoleon III on the French political scene as "Saint-Simon on horseback," the historic embodiment of that thinker's thought.[1] Such a view of the Emperor gets its fullest articulation in Joly's *Dialogue*.

According to Octave Aubrey, the influence of Saint-Simon was a lot more than something Napoleon absorbed from the intellectual atmosphere of nineteenth century France. While a political prisoner for five and half years in the fortress of Ham, Louis Napoleon read deeply in the corpus of Saint-Simon and even annotated his works.[2] Like other despotic ideologues of later times, Napoleon remarked upon the formative experience of his years of study in prison—"my university," he later dubbed it. Albert Guerard repeats the more common view of the Second Empire—a "gilded age" of pleasure seeking and profiteering that witnessed "the triumph of materialism in all its forms." However, he sees "another aspect to the period," more revealing of the Emperor himself and "his deeper views." Like observers contemporary to Napoleon, he links such levels of thought in the Emperor to Saint-Simonianism.

According to Guerard, "without being formally associated with the Saint-Simonian school, he was animated by its spirit." In particular, he notes the religious character of such thought expressed in its "fundamental principle" that "the first duty of government is to promote the welfare, material and moral, of the most numerous and poorest class." Furthermore, "it is significant that a number of Saint-Simonians, Father Enfantin, and the Pereire brothers, without abjuring the messianic hopes of their youth, became prominent business leaders under the Second Empire."[3]

Twentieth century historians of the Second Empire, who are aware of Saint-Simonianism, may see it as having some bearing on diverse social and economic projects of the Emperor, but they typically do not see it as having any coherent political influence. Saint-Simon and his intellectual progeny are best studied with other curious thinkers of the day, such as Fourier in France or Owen in Great Britain, who proposed radically flawed social experiments in the face of the dislocation brought on by industrialism. Most noteworthy in this regard is the thinking of George G. Iggers. He meticulously draws out the totalitarian implications of Saint-Simonian doctrine but denies any practical influence to its teaching beyond its contribution to the climate of ideas in the early nineteenth century. For Iggers, Saint-Simonianism is nothing but "a totalitarian fantasy."[4] For Joly, it gave form to the real world in which he lived.

More recent scholarship sees the Iggers thesis as an overwrought distortion of the thrust of Saint-Simonian thinking. Emphasizing certain "softer" elements in the thought of the Saint-Simonians, the Manuels see the revolution they espoused more as a "tender failure"[5] than a "totalitarian fantasy." However, they seem to agree that the Saint-Simonians exerted no great influence on political practice and stand in a line of interpretations beginning with Marx who branded Saint-Simonianism as "utopian," engaged only in sterile speculation because it misperceived the material reality of the historic process.

It is not surprising that current readers of Joly's work largely miss the Saint-Simonian connection to the *Dialogue*. It is indeed never made explicit there, though numerous references are made to "new theories" of which Machiavelli is the spokesman. In this regard, Joly seems to prefer to follow the real Napoleon who ever remained the enigmatic "Sphinx of the Tuileries." He disguised his motives, never, as Guerard says, formally acknowledging his association with the Saint-Simonian school, which stood in a certain bad repute for its esoteric practices and cultist proclivities.[6]

In establishing the link between Machiavelli in the *Dialogue* and Saint-Simonianism, we will reestablish the link between Napoleonism and Saint-Simonianism perceived early on by the more astute contemporaries of the Second Empire. Later, we will argue that the earlier view, most richly developed by Maurice Joly, can help resolve the historic controversy surrounding the Second Empire as well as the enigma of Louis Napoleon. The element of Saint-Simonian thought is the key to a full understanding of the *Dialogue in Hell* and the Emperor.

When Joly wrote the *Dialogue in Hell*, Louis Napoleon was securely in the saddle. His despotic regime was well in place. The *Dialogue in Hell* is not merely the step-by-step recounting of the establishment of this regime, as fascinating and informative as this is. Joly was convinced that the actions of the Emperor were fundamentally motivated by a new way of thinking, an ideology that gave coherence to the revolutionary steps he took. The thinking that informed Napoleon's regime is what made it so unique and portentous. We now turn to a brief elaboration of that ideology and its pretensions to world-historic significance.

The Saint-Simonian View of History

The Saint-Simonian understanding of history attempts to synthesize both ancient and modern conceptions. To the ancient way of thinking, history is cyclical. The natural laws of growth and decay serve as the pattern for the understanding of human things. Political history "made sense" not in terms of some ultimate meaning but as belonging to certain cycles—rhythms of genesis, growth, disintegration, and death. This is the fated dispensation of all things ephemeral. It is manifested in the rise and fall of political regimes that, in turn, elicits the response of historical actors. Their conduct in these circumstances remains the most profitable study for understanding the human dilemmas and our common lot.[7]

Different assumptions inform the modern concept of history. Political history is understood, not as part of a natural scheme of things and subject to fate, but as a progression in time of events largely determined by human causes and effects. As expressed by the Montesquieu of the *Dialogue*, who can be seen as spokesman for such a view, the sequence of events is also progressive.

History came to be perceived as a process, with clear lines of development. It manifests the progress of reason whose advances are cumulative, irreversible, and potentially universal in its effect. The proper posture of man, therefore, is not one of manly equanimity and moderation in dealing with limitations that cannot be changed. Rather, it is one of hopeful endeavor in the full realization that the scope of human events and nature itself is not subject to fate alone, but responsive to rational human effort.

As in the modern view, the Saint-Simonians see history essentially as a process reflecting the universal advance of reason but whose political effects are variable, as in the ancient view, passing through progressive extremes of order and dissolution. The historic process is not then an open process of simple linear progress but a varied one, with a definitive and necessary conclusion in the coming to pass of a universal society. Unlike the ancients, this greater dispensation of things is not caused by blind fate beyond human control. It is the product of human effort in the fulfillment of a rationally determined end to which all history can be seen as tending.

In the Paris Lectures of 1828, the Saint-Simonian historical view gets its most detailed elaboration. Like natural phenomena, history is shown to be subject to certain laws. And its future "behavior" can be confidently predicted when these laws stand fully revealed.

"Organic" and "Critical" Moments

"The law of history development" shows itself in two distinct and alternating states of society.[8] In the one state, which is called "organic," all human activity proceeds from a "general theory" or doctrine. "The goal of all social action is clearly defined." It is accepted and acted upon by all orders of society, according to their different capacities and functions. It engages the individual totally in his three-fold capacity as an "intellectual, sentient, and physical being." The other state, called "critical," is marked by the cessation of all communion of thought, fellow feeling, and collective action. "Society appears as a mere agglomeration of isolated individuals fighting each other."

Each of these states has occupied two periods "in a long historical series." The first organic period occurred during the religious era of ancient Greece, marked by the ascendancy of the pagan gods. It was followed by a period, commonly called "philosophic" because of the presence of such luminaries as Plato and Aristotle, but which the Saint-Simonians would "term more exactly the critical period" because it opposes the religiously-based orthodoxy that integrated and defined life in the ancient polis. Later, a new doctrine was formulated that finally established dominance over the West. The Church administered a new organic epoch which, in turn, began to dissolve in the sixteenth century, (among other things, the moment of Machiavelli, whose critique of the former order had broadened in the centuries that followed).

Critical epochs themselves can be further subdivided "into distinct periods." The first is marked by the arousal of "the most sensitive men," whose call for the end of the old established order finds a sympathetic response in the masses, loosened from all authority. This period erupts with "accumulated rancor" and issues into a burst of collective action that serves destructive purposes only. "Soon there remains of the former institutions nothing but ruins to testify that there once has been a harmonious society."

The second period in critical epochs marks the interval that separates the destruction of the former order and the construction of the new. At this point, "anarchy has ceased to be violent" but it has grown wider and deeper with the conditions of society replicating themselves in the personality of the individual in a complete divergence of feeling, reasoning, and action. It is an age (most recently, the moment of Romanticism) marked by a sickness in the soul that longs for a return to a time that unites man to his fellows by sympathetic bonds.

As the historical process evolves, it expands to cover wider and wider segments of mankind. The first organic period is identified in a precise geographic place—Greece. It is succeeded in a second such period by a system that includes "all of the Occident." It follows in Saint-Simonian doctrine that a third organic period will be universal, succeeding in turn the dissolution that affected the

West in its recent revolutionary past. Indeed, the universal ground for the Saint-Simonian future is a factor that points to its definitive character.

The new general state of mankind, which the Saint-Simonians proclaim as our future, will form the third and final organic link "in an uninterrupted chain" of history. A simple return to the happy moments in the past presents no practicable solution for modern men. The new era will not be identical with such former "organic" states but "will share striking similarities to them with respect to order and unity" which will advance to its most complete realization "in the full association of humanity." The epoch will evince an ascendancy of a new doctrine that embraces all the modes of human activity, once again reintegrating the individual to society that has been in the process of dissolution under the influence of a destructive critical doctrine.

Organic epochs are characterized by a consensus of beliefs, which the "Doctrine of Saint-Simon" intends to serve in the future. This core set of shared principles finds full expression in society and is reflected in its institutional arrangements. A unity of purpose, effectively organized and looking toward a comprehensive view of things, marks such periods as "philosophic." Strictly speaking, there have been no more philosophic doctrines "worthy of the name" than there have been "general states of mankind," a situation having occurred only twice in the past, in antiquity and the Middle Ages, the precise character of which is crucial to understanding the lines of future developments.

"Critical" periods, in turn, may be characterized as the time of the progressive erosion of the former philosophic unity that is the basis of the integrated social order. These critical periods reach their term in egoism and social confusion, creating an objective "need" for a new order, which falls to the prophetic "genius" to articulate philosophically. The Saint-Simonians identify both critical periods with a presiding figure as they identify the genius of the future "organic" order with their spiritual mentor, Saint-Simon.

It was the appearance of Socrates that marked the beginning of the end of the older order in antiquity. The defenders of this order correctly saw in his life a threat to the city's gods and its fundamental beliefs. But in ordering his death, they unwittingly had served to make his questionable life attractive and respectable, the immediate heirs and beneficiaries of which were Socrates's pupils, Plato and Xenophon.[9] In commanding this individual's death, they liberated the critical spirit and, ironically, guaranteed the "death" of the society they had intended to defend.

The appearance of Socrates, which first marks a period of dissolution, also serves history in a progressive way by making possible the eventual emergence of a new and higher historical order. Indeed, Socratic science (Neo-Platonic and Aristotlean) conjoin with Biblical revelation in the great synthesizers of the Middle Ages (Augustine and Thomas) to form the constitutive elements of a new doctrine. This is given organizational expression by the Church in the society of the Middle Ages. Critical science, it should be well noted, passes into the philosophy of the new epoch and becomes part of the theoretical underpinning of a new faith that reaches its ascendancy under the institutionalized protection of the Church and its Pope.

Such considerations mark critical epochs as inherently ambiguous— destructive from the point of view of political unity, but constructive and progressive in preparing and as a part of a "greater human association." Thus, the progress of science and philosophy has had varied political effects and may be said to be the cause of history's cyclical turns, which the ancients more narrowly observed and construed as fate.

According to the Saint-Simonians, the appearance of Bacon marks the second critical period and inaugurates the dissolution of the Middle Ages. Since the sixteenth century, "scientists all follow the road opened by Bacon."[10] With the Enlightenment, we reach the furthest reaches of Baconian science and the beginning of the death throes of the Middle Ages, whose principles and institutions suffer from irremediable attack, preparing the way for an era of revolution and social dissolution that characterizes the present crisis.

Saint-Simonianism and the *Dialogue*

In the element of Saint-Simonian philosophy, just described, we may now profitably return to the dispute between Machiavelli and Montesquieu that serves as the dramatic focus of Joly's *Dialogue*. It is their understanding of universal history that is ultimately put to question in their "wager" and this determines the sufficiency of their respective political sciences, invoked in history's name. Montesquieu elaborates his view of history in Part One and Machiavelli in the concluding parts of the *Dialogue*, where an alternative view is progressively revealed. We thus come to the full historic implications of Machiavelli's teaching eventually. It is only at the end that we come to a full appreciation of what his "founding" portends and the sense that he has elaborated a totally "new" political science, explicitly opposed to the Montesquieuan understanding of things.

The initial lines of their dispute would have us believe that Machiavelli is arguing the ancient or medieval conception of history with the most formidable spokesman of modernity, Montesquieu. The latter confidently expounds the progressive historical view that has superseded and discredited his opponent's position. Machiavelli's cyclical view of history seems to hearken back to a view that would have political life tied to an ineluctable fate which, like the natural order of things, exhibits a time of growth and decay, order and dissolution.

Montesquieu, at least, thinks he is responding to such a view when he claims that the cumulative discoveries of reason have put politics on a progressive course. Through his own efforts, man can eliminate much of the control of fate and with it the ancient debilitating fear of the living agents, "despots" and "priests," who supposedly control it. Montesquieu points to what he thinks is certain historical evidence that vindicates his position. At the same time, he underscores his own contributions to political science in opening society to reason and establishing the stable conditions for self-rule.

The material and moral advance of man is guaranteed in a regime that effectively guards against a lapse into despotism. The new "constitutional era" which Montesquieu celebrates holds no possibility for a return to an "era of revolution," anarchy, and despotic rule. The historic swings between autocracy and anarchy are overcome in a regime of "ordered liberty." This ends the turmoil that formerly marked political life and which was most acute perhaps at the moment of Machiavelli in the sixteenth century.

Evidence from contemporary events alone would challenge Montesquieu's optimism. Cognizant of the recent anarchy that shook the West, Machiavelli launches his first serious attack on the theories of his interlocutor, who is found crucially ignorant of such events. Framed in Saint-Simonian terms, the present moment reveals the active revolutionary period as having ceased with the violence of 1848. The West has arrived at that pregnant moment when the old "critical" epoch has reached its term, as anarchy has grown wider and deeper within society. It is the interval that prepares the "birth" of a new order, the founding of which is the active goal of Napoleon III.

Such considerations give the proper perspective from which to view the real scope of Machiavelli's historical understanding of things. Broader and more complex than that of the ancients, it begins to meld more fully and obviously with the Saint-Simonian understanding of history when we consider the character of the Machiavellian or Napoleonic revolution as aiming precisely at a new and final "organic" order. This leaves the "critical" science of Montesquieu open to the charge leveled by the Saint-Simonians and repeated by the Machiavelli of the *Dialogue* that it has failed to definitively solve the political problem and has, rather, issued into an "age of revolution" and instability.

The cyclical view of history propounded by Machiavelli is not, as Montesquieu imagines, the ancient or Medieval conception. Machiavelli is not in fact so limited by the time in which he lived and the thought that dominated it. Rather, Machiavelli argues in the mode of the Saint-Simonians and would have those "cycles" of political and social life integrated into the full scope of world history as part of a long and "uninterrupted chain" and process.

Machiavelli gives voice to the Saint-Simonian contention that links the historic crisis facing the West to the diminishing hold of religion and the final passing of the medieval order. Montesquieu initially perceives Machiavelli, who was "born on the borders of such an epoch," as its defender and its last effective spokesman. He sees Machiavelli's opposition to the modern understanding of politics he espouses as stemming from ignorance of more recent historical developments and a stubborn defense of the politics of an epoch—no matter how "modern" the idiom or how clever the arguments—that history has passed by.

In such an epoch, Christian doctrine provided the organizational principles of society. Repeating the charges of the Saint-Simonians, Machiavelli claims that the thought of Montesquieu, among others even less prudent, has inevitably bred individualism and atheism, whose effects have been to loosen the bonds of society, setting it upon its anarchic drift. The progress to such a point marks a definitive period that coincides with the most recent "critical" moment in the Saint-Simonian "Law of Historical Development." Its beginning can be said to lie in the Renaissance of the sixteenth century and its tentative steps toward modernity. It ends with "the great Montesquieu" whose works, especially *The Spirit of the Laws*, represent the crowning achievement of the Enlightenment and the systematized application of modern principles of thought to the understanding of politics and history.

According to Machiavelli, the necessity for order in society requires unlimited personal rule, the legitimacy of which cannot be called into question. Montesquieu claims to have discovered in "popular sovereignty," rightly understood, a new principle of rule and an alternative to the notion of "divine right," defended by Machiavelli as providing the authoritative grounding for the Middle Ages. The modern constitutional regime, organized on a popular basis, better attains the political stability sought by Machiavelli, not by despotic repression of popular will and impulses, but in their liberation and through the guarantee of freedom of thought.

The period roughly from Machiavelli and the Renaissance to Montesquieu, which coincides with the most recent "critical" moment in the Saint-Simonian "Law of Historic Development," also accords with their essential understanding of such epochs. The era over which the thought of Montesquieu presides is founded expressly on "critical" principles, opposed to the political arrangement of the Middle Ages. The success of the Enlightenment project dissolves the former order but fails to secure an enduring basis for politics, at least according to Machiavelli and his reading of contemporary history. This creates the need for a new founding to arrest the anarchy such principles have engendered. The overriding necessity for order requires a return to a political orthodoxy that once again sanctions personal rule in religious terms. The conditions that define "organic" orders as such are reestablished but in accord with certain historical principles, advanced by Montesquieu, which do no violence to critical elements of the "modern spirit."

A Return to the "Organic" Conditions of Society

In conformity with the conditions of an "organic" order, the Saint-Simonian ideologue wants to put an end to what it sees as the alienated modern soul—the disaccord that one feels between oneself and the "mind" and "heart" of one's fellows, and to put an end to a situation where satisfaction of one's "material interests" can be had only at the expense of others. In sum, to "cure" the sickness" in the soul, the individual once again must be fully integrated with his fellows in a greater community of shared "religious" purpose. It is not by coincidence that successive parts of the *Dialogue* endeavor to fulfill precisely the Saint-Simonian perspective in this regard and that the discussion as a whole ends with a description of the new "religious consciousness."

More precisely, Part Two explains how in a literate nation the Machiavellian founder will use a "free press," the chief safeguard of the Montesquieuan system, to his own advantage. It contains in outline the essentials of a new orthodoxy and the means to ensure its propagation. The security of autocratic power in modern times is crucially premised on winning over the "minds" of the subject.

The political revolution in Part Two is complemented in Part Three by an economic revolution. The prince promises a vast industrial expansion, led by the state and its use of credit, which ultimately looks toward a more complete scientific organization of the nation's productive forces. This has as its putative goal "the amelioration of the lot of the poor." They were perceived to be systematically excluded from sharing in material benefits as a result of the organization of liberal society and its failure, under uncoordinated conditions, to make good on what was promised by the advance of technological knowledge.

The political and economic revolutions in Part Two and Part Three proceed apace and are integral to each other. On the basis of unencumbered political power, the prince may undertake the reformation of society. On the basis of economic expansion, in which the poor now share, the prince defuses the principal source of revolutionary discontent and begins to win popularity to his new despotic rule. In Part Three, the "material interests" of man are enlisted to the same regime that succeeded in Part Two to win over their "minds."

Part Four represents the keystone in the structure of the Saint-Simonian regime that Machiavelli erects. It describes a revolution in "spiritual" realms that complements the revolution in political and economic realms, previously elaborated in respective parts of the *Dialogue*. The rule of the all-powerful prince on behalf of the interests of the "poorest and most numerous classes" is endowed with the higher justifications of religion, the principles of which are advanced by a new kind of leader. The new prince claims the allegiance, not only of the mind, but speaks to deeper levels of truth associated with the "hearts" of his subjects, levels to which religion heretofore uniquely spoke.

The "spirit of the age" is exalted in art and architecture that has the new prince and what he represents as its theme. Art ceases to be "critical"— individualistic" and "heroically negative"—as it manifested itself at the moment of Romanticism. As at the time of the Middle Ages, it once again finds inspiration in serving "positive" ends, giving aesthetic embellishment to the new underlying religious consensus of society.[11] Indeed, the revival of art would be the most telling element of the return to organic moments as such.

In a revolution that touches religious consciousness and the nature of civilized life itself, Machiavelli reveals the full scope of the historic change he intends. It is as a god and in terms of a new understanding of religion that the new Machiavellian prince pursues his towering political ambitions and attempts to stamp his personality on the historic order to come. He has combined the role of Romulus and Numa in a new founding that has Rome in many of its particulars as its most relevant precedent. Put succinctly, he attempts a return to the "organic" conditions that formerly characterized politics, but in the context of modernity and looking toward universal influence.

At the end of the *Dialogue* proper, Machiavelli asserts that the respective positions of the two antagonists, spelled out in Part One, have finally begun "to come together." The elements of Saint-Simonian thought which guide the Machiavellian founding reveal for us the real basis of this "rapprochement." Key principles of "critical" science that opposed the medieval order are reflected in the organization of a new "organic" society, which is offered as the third and final link in a long historical process, succeeding Montesquieu's "constitutional era."

The new order presents itself as completing the democratic thrust of history with which Montesquieu thought he was aligned in establishing the constitutional regime. It replaces the regime of individual "rights," which supposedly remain "cruelly abstract" for the majority of peoples, with a regime of unlimited power, dedicated to the "amelioration of the lot of the poorest and most numerous classes." To the thinker who stands for "progress," the return to unlimited personal rule is associated with "barbarism." The Machiavellian prince, however, presents his rule as an historic advance that draws upon the deepest sources of authority in the West to justify itself in modern times. As Machiavelli argues, such rule gives concrete fulfillment to the material interests of its subjects as it also answers to deeper desires, ultimately of religious origin, which are satisfied in a this-worldly context.

The return to the "organic" conditions of society in the context of modern times, the step that essentially defines the Saint-Simonian project, explains the ambiguity in the character of Machiavelli as well as his regime. Machiavelli is not so limited by the horizon of the Middle Ages as Montesquieu initially presumes. He defends a return to a new kind of personal rule, not as a reactionary, but in terms of historic "progress." At the same time and in dramatic fashion, a "new" Machiavelli emerges which shatters Montesquieu's stereotypic view of his interlocutor and mocks the condescending posture he had assumed toward him.

The Saint-Simonian ideology that lies behind Machiavelli's thought remains unidentified in the *Dialogue*. This heightens the ambiguity of the character of Machiavelli and his regime while it gives Joly's work its dramatic power. It forces the reader for whom the *Dialogue* was intended, as it does Montesquieu, to further reflection on the character of Machiavelli and his politics. However, as that politics is associated with the infamous name of Machiavelli, the reader is led to contemplate his regime from the point of view of an unprecedented tyranny, potentially universal in scope. In this way, the literary mode of Joly's teaching opens to political lessons of great consequences to Joly's contemporaries, threatened by such a regime. Joly's way of proceeding in all this is motivated to serve didactic purposes in the most effective way.

In the following chapter, we will discuss in greater detail the character of the new regime from the point of view of the new religious foundations for politics. In the chapter after that, we will try to come to terms with the figure of Machiavelli as he has come to light in Joly's work.

Notes

1. Sainte-Beuve was literary critic at *Le Globe* and himself frequented Saint-Simonian circles. He was an apologist for the Second Empire and Napoleon III. His statement about Napoleon and Saint-Simon can be found in Albert Guerard, *France*, new edition revised and enlarged by Paul A. Gagnon (Ann Arbor: University of Michigan Press, 1969), 312.

2. See Octave Aubrey, *The Second Empire*, trans. Arthur Livingston (Philadelphia: J. B. Lippincott, 1940), 22.

3. Guerard, *France*, 312.

4. See Georg G. Iggers's Preface to the second edition of *The Doctrine of Saint-Simon. An Exposition* (New York: Schoken Books, 1972), 22. Iggers denies any appreciable and "direct relevance" of Saint-Simonianism to "later thought and practice." He stresses its large contribution to the intellectual climate of the nineteenth century.

5. See Frank M. and Fritzie P. Manuel, *Utopian Thought in the Western World* (Cambridge, Mass.: Belknap Press, 1979), 631 and 635.

6. The Saint-Simonians for a time lived on the Rue Monsigny. The sect eventually split between the followers of Bazard and Enfantin. The latter wished to establish a fantastic sacerdotal commune with very lax notions about the relationship between the sexes. His group moved to Menilmontant, where, distinguished by an extravagant way of dressing, they lived in communistic fashion. The sect was broken up in 1832 after the public trial of Enfantin whose bizarre antics and behavior, influenced in part by his readings of Mesmer, intentionally provoked jurists and audience. He was condemned and imprisoned for outrgaes against the social order.

7. See Karl Lowith, *Meaning in History* (Chicago: University of Chicago Press, 1949), 4. Lowith describes the ancient understanding of history thus:

> The ancients were more moderate [than Hebrew and Christian thinkers] in their speculations. They did not presume to make sense of the

world or to discover its ultimate meaning. They were impressed by the visible order and beauty of the cosmos, and the cosmic law of growth and decay was also the pattern of their understanding of history. According to the Greek view of life and the world, everything moves in recurrences, like the eternal recurrence of sunrise and sunset, of summer and winter, of generation and corruption. This view was satisfactory to them because it is a rational and natural understanding of the universe combining recognition of temporal changes with periodic regularity, constancy, and immutability. The immutable, as visible in the fixed order of the heavenly bodies, had a higher interest and value to them than any progressive and radical change.

8. This summary of the "Law of Historic Development" is drawn mainly from Iggers (ed.), *The Doctrine*, "On the Necessity of a New Social Doctrine" (First Session) and "The Law of the Development of Mankind: Verification of this Law by History" (Second Session).

9. For a discussion of the "critical era" of antiquity, see Iggers, (ed.) *The Doctrine*, 17 and especially 216.

10. Iggers (ed.), *The Doctrine*, 7.

11. Think of the epoch's (mankind's?) greatest artistic and architectural achievement—the medieval cathedral.

It should be well noted that Louis Napoleon showed himself very sensitive to the concerns we are talking about here when he commissioned Charles Gautier to construct the opulent Paris Opera and to give it such prominence in the reconstructed city. The Communists and Nazis were equally sensitive. They, too, thought their respective world-historic revolutions would occasion the regeneration of art.

The artistic legacy of Louis Napoleon is decidedly more mixed. It is, at its worst, tinged with Romanticism, an imitative pastiche, tending to ostentation and excess. What are we to say of Mitterand's Opera, la Pryramide, la Défense, and his library (dubbed the T.G.B., the très grand bibliothèque, in a play on the T.G.V.—Train de Grande Vitesse)? If contemporary debate is any indication, his legacy is much more *douteux* than that of Napoleon III.

The adjectives most frequently heard in this regard are "sterile," "grandiose," "shocking," "inaccessible," "pharonical," "playful," "inefficient," "iconoclastic," and "expensive." Defenders would counter that most of these things were said of Mr. Eiffel's tower. Is all this just another example of the old time-lag phenomenon, when mass tastes will eventually catch up with the avante-garde's inspirations? Or is it the case of the advance of a "negative aesthetic, "an assault (sometimes bold, sometimes whimsical) on the canons of taste itself?

Mitterand's motivations, I believe, were very much like those of Louis. France would lead the way in giving artist expression to a new age, *post-modern*, for lack of a better term. He clearly was competing with Eiffel in giving landmarks to the landscape of the City of Light. In any case, Joly was on to something when he gave such emphasis to "building policy" in his book.

Chapter Eight

THE SAINT-SIMONIAN RELIGIOUS ELEMENTS

Religion in Liberal Polities

The religious theme, first introduced by Montesquieu in Part One, assumes increasing importance as the description of Machiavelli's regime progresses. Like a motif, it is heard periodically, as in the treatment of propaganda and papal policy. But in the dramatic conclusion of Joly's work, which completes the portrait of the prince in putting the finishing touches on his "royal countenance," it emerges as perhaps the fundamental issue of the *Dialogue*, as it is in Saint-Simonian thought per se. Approaching the deepest level of the historic change described by Machiavellian politics, it likewise helps define for us the real nature of the prince's political ambition in his quest for god-like status.

Beyond the institutional obstacles to the consolidation of absolute power within the liberal system of government, the Montesquieu of the *Dialogue* lists religion as the key bulwark of the liberal regime. In the name of a common God and the ethical duties He enjoins, Montesquieu argues, we find legitimate appeal from worldly rulers who would order what is contrary to our paramount concerns and the clear canons of conscience. "Nations that avow Christianity will always escape despotism, for Christianity elevates man's dignity and places him beyond the reach of tyrants. It develops moral forces over which human power has no sway," he asserts. The check is not limited to Christian nations. As *The Spirit of the Laws* demonstrates with regard to oriental despotism, the scope of what the Sultan may command is effectively limited by overriding religious duties that he is bound to respect, if he is to attain any measure of security and not fall victim to public odium.[1]

In distinction to the world's other great religions, the Montesquieu of the *Dialogue* reserves for Christianity a special status. It is the fountainhead of what has nurtured the West's common culture. As it has evolved in the course of history, its profound and pervasive influence has come to serve the social and political mores of the liberal regime, whose very possibility, initially at least, seems to be limited to the Christian West. When asked where his principles find current application, Montesquieu responds: "almost all the countries over which the Roman world formerly extended," listing Christian nations exclusively.[2]

Among other things, he argues that the disposition to work and worldly betterment, as well as the attributes of character that help sustain the conditions for productive enterprise, are tied to deeper cultural attitudes, ultimately of religious and Christian origin. "Societies that live by means of work, exchange, and credit are essentially Christian, for all such powerful and varied forms of industry are basically applications of several great moral ideas derived from Christianity, the source of all strength and truth." [3]

Through Christianity, the ferocity of man is softened and his energies redirected from war to more social means of livelihood, including wider and wider segments of society as participants and beneficiaries. Modern industrial society evolves out of the great moral truths of Christianity. It arrives at a stage where personal attachments and dependencies dissolve, where the modern social order itself becomes the "engine" where "power is generated." According to Christianity, man stands as an equal before God. He will eventually stand as an equal before all earthly powers. Such is the power of the Christian moral teaching—"source of all strength and truth"—that it has come from its primitive beginnings as an obscure Eastern sect to change the entire face of the world.

Doctrinal changes introduced by Protestantism were key to transforming the Christian world of the Middle Ages. They had the practical effect of elevating the status of the city of man, which was originally clearly subordinated to the city of God in the earlier Christian teaching.[4] In the all-important matters it ministered, the Church and its Pope claimed supremacy over the Emperor.

The Church held that salvation was possible only through its sacraments and the mediation of priests. To break the hold of its corrupting influence, Protestantism preached that man stood face to face with God in a personal relationship. Salvation was a matter between man and God without the interposition of Peter's institution to guide men, or, more likely, lead them astray. In Protestant doctrine, reform of this world became incumbent upon the religious man as his holy duty. The manifest works performed by the individual in this world were the key to salvation and visible rewards its chief sign. Such convictions changed the fundamental orientation of men and redirected their energies to this world. We are now at the point where the Montesquieu of the *Dialogue* can maintain that Christianity has effectively imbued the whole of the secular realm with its spirit. Machiavelli, who sees the modern world as having faded into "atheism" and mere "materialism," does not appreciate the subtle but profound transformation that Christianity has brought to it, Montesquieu argues.

Protestantism's influence on the political realm has been formidable and pervasive. The claims of individual conscience it raised in opposition to Church and monarch—institutions that were formerly seen as divinely sanctioned—

prepares the teaching of secular individualism that underlies liberal theory and gives rise to notions of popular rule and representative government. Significantly, it is the same claim of conscience that lies at the origin of the move toward religious toleration, which is expressly guaranteed in the liberal regime. The Montesquieu of Joly's *Dialogue* points to a political arrangement "where the state has strictly segregated religious authority from worldly politics." Political power is out of bounds when it infringes upon religious prerogatives belonging to its protected sphere.

According to Montesquieu, "the peoples of the Christian era" may have "had more difficulty putting constitutions in harmony with the dynamics of political life" because of the original religious or papal dominance over the secular realm. But through religious tolerance, a politic balance has been struck. Modern men have "profited from the lessons of antiquity," where religion existed in harmony with civil laws, and "with infinitely more complex civilizations, they have arrived at more perfect results."

Religious freedom can be said to expand the sphere of individual liberty while it also subtly works toward the progressive accommodation of the religious and the secular realm that informs Montesquieu's view of history. Socially, a multiplicity of sects is the product of such tolerance, which, in turn, acts to reinforce its guarantee. Each sect, prohibited by its size alone from attempting to dominate politics directly, attaches itself to the regime that preserves the conditions of its existence and effective propagation. This helps solve the problem of allegiance to the earthly city, potentially strained for such groups in the secular commonwealth, particularly in the face of certain actions necessary to the perpetuation of earthly powers that the religious conscience, strictly speaking, would proscribe.

Prelates no longer dictate to politicians. "The words of preachers are limited to terms found in the Gospels," Montesquieu states. Nevertheless, they play an important role in molding the character of citizens in a private capacity. Their humane influence counters the principle of self-interest given scope in the liberal regime and keeps it in proper bounds. It helps restrain the appetites in ways that make civilized existence possible. The "humble and gentle" message of the Gospels proves "the stumbling bock to degenerate materialism."

As a result of such a political arrangement, religion's voice on public policy is heard indirectly or only on matters that elicit the widest possible consensus among numerous sects. This encourages the emergence of a public teaching that imparts a higher tone to the realm of public life, the distilled elements of a basic Judeo-Christian moral teaching, yet devoid of dogmatic divisiveness. This helps forge national unity in bringing to the people a shared perspective of what is ethically appropriate. Indeed, a common religious idiom becomes the mode of national self-expression. The example of America is pertinent here. Its happy experience owes much to just such arrangements.[5]

According to Joly's Montesquieu, toleration preserves politics from a doctrinaire religious spirit that threatens social harmony and which, as history attests, may lead to the most sanguinary civil wars. At the same time, it employs the Christian teaching to its most politic advantage, indirectly spreading and deepening its social influence. According to objections raised by the Machiavelli of the *Dialogue*, however, the multiplicity of sects that issue from the liberal arrangement is seen to further fractionalize social life whose unity and cohesive force, in the ancient polity, is traced to the dominance of a unique social and civil religion.

Secular Religion and the New Order

A close reading of the *Dialogue* finds in religious influence the most important current of historic change. Accordingly, the historic project of the *Dialogue*'s Machiavelli can be shown to rest fundamentally on certain religious principles, effecting a revolution that advances upon Protestant Christianity and the liberal order that issues from it. Succinctly put, it is a revolution that tries to reestablish the strict unity of political and religious life in the ancient city, but sundered by Christianity and further fractionalized by Protestantism. It looks to a new and universal civil or secular religion that puts forth as its putative goal the practical fulfillment of the Christian ethical teaching, already acknowledged by Montesquieu as exerting a pervading influence on our worldly conduct.

The character of this "religion" can be traced to the teaching of the "new Christianity," proclaimed by Saint-Simon shortly before his death.[6] His followers elaborated the doctrine and placed it in the context of a more rigorous and systematic historical account. According to the original teaching, morality has only one principle, best expressed by the Gospels in its essential form when it commands universal love. Unlike physical science, which shows a discernible progress, the moral truth does not vary with time but remains eternally valid. Only its historical applications and embodiment are relative.

Originally, the Gospel's proclamation was a radical and revolutionary principle. As the Montesquieu of the *Dialogue* states, the pure teaching of the Gospels, "so humble and so gentle," was strong enough to destroy by itself "the Roman Empire, Caesarism, and its power." By the sixteenth century, the Christian principle, now embodied in a universal Church, had been perverted and stood itself in need of regeneration. It had come to serve only the interest of the Church as an institutional, not a moral, power. As Machiavelli points out, far from its primitive beginnings, Christianity was now aligned with the "absolute power" of monarchies in the service of reactionary causes that would protect its worldly influence.

Saint-Simon arraigns the papacy before the bar of primitive Christianity toward a revolutionary end. The original teaching of Christianity, "so gentle and so humble," must again find positive application in the society of the future which is institutionally reorganized to embody the true Christian "spirit" once again. The present Christian world had to be recast to reflect the progress of history and science, which had advanced to the point where "the amelioration of the lot of the poorest and most numerous classes" could be effectively fulfilled, both materially and morally. The present Church stands as an obstacle to the future fulfillment of its own moral truths. Its pope, revealed in such a light, is properly seen as an "anti-Christ" and his followers heretical.

According to Machiavelli in the *Dialogue*, the decline of the hold of the traditional Christian religion is the root cause of the crisis of the time and propels the final descent into the anarchy sapping Europe in the most recent events hidden from Montesquieu. The reestablishment of a religious foundation for politics marks a new "organic" moment and the only basis for an enduring social order. This makes the religious question the ultimate political question for Machiavelli as for the Saint-Simonians, who themselves herald the rejuvenation of religiosity against the background of Enlightenment skepticism and the opposition of the established Church.

The New "Christianity" in the *Dialogue*

In accord with the "new" Christianity, the Machiavellian prince of the nineteenth century declares the "welfare of the masses" to be "his constant preoccupation." In the context of the *Dialogue*, such a goal can be seen as an extension of the historic progress of Christianity. It justifies the authoritarian reordering of society while it endows its institutions with new moral meaning. In taking up the cause of the "poorest and most numerous classes," the new prince simultaneously finds not only the broadest base of political support but moral legitimacy as well.

In the *Dialogue in Hell*, Machiavelli accuses Montesquieu of having a less than orthodox view of God's role in history. According to Montesquieu, God's presence is no longer marked by his active intervention in the affairs of the world, through miracles and punishments, to correct man's wayward course. Rather, divine presence is manifested in the "Eternal Wisdom" that inexorably guides man's destiny. Such wisdom is revealed in collective history to the foremost minds that participate in it through their individual reason. While there is apparently no providence of a personal Being, the design of things, manifested in the workings of reason, is beneficently disposed toward man, ordering things to a progressive course.

Inplicitly, Machiavelli's position is somewhat different and follows Saint-Simonian doctrine. It emerges in the *Dialogue* as an extension of Montesquieu's thinking, not in a reaction to it. According to the dogma of the "New Christianity," the duties to a personal Godhead recede. "Critical" thought and positive science rightly have purged religion of insubstantial anthropomorphic and meta-physical supports. As with Montesquieu, the presence of God is made known through history, understood according to the Scientific "Law of Human Devel-opment." Divine providence and the eschatological hopes of primitive Christian-ity find concrete fulfillment at the conclusion of history in a society effectively organized to fulfill the "essential truths" of Christian morality on a universal scale.

In this historicized theodicy, the Christian Godhead, who formerly occupied a transcendent realm, makes way for the Saint-Simonian ruler, who presents himself as the living embodiment of "Eternal Wisdom," given "form" and struc-ture in a final and determinative historic order. Like a medieval pope, he is the "anointed representative" of the Divine Presence but makes his claim to "infalli-bility" on scientific grounds—a new orthodoxy supported by absolute power, artfully reinforced through propaganda and ceremony, which a large portion of Part Four in the *Dialogue* is devoted to explaining.

At the end of that section, we noted a certain "imitation of Christ" as the conscious policy of the new prince. Indeed, by his "martyred" death man stands "redeemed" and a "new world" arises. Such a powerful symbol strikes a deep chord in the traditional Christian, now conditioned to shift his allegiance from transcendent to secular realms. Using the metaphor favored by Montesquieu, the prince's death will give "birth" to a new world order that brings fulfillment to the secular hopes and ambitions of the so-called party of "progress" and of "new ideas." Such a synthesis promises to bring peace to the "cultural war" between traditionalists and secularists. As Machiavelli states at the conclusion of the *Dia-logue*, the masses will want to construct "altars" to such a ruler's memory—more in the style of the mausoleum in the Red Square (or the Invalides) than the crypts of medieval Cathedrals, we can well imagine.

The new "organic" order that inspires the Machiavellian founding is the best background to view the more specific policies and goals of the prince. The papal affairs of Napoleon III, for example, which have long vexed historians of the second Empire, come into new light as tied not to mere political maneuvering but a more fundamental historic change. Joly intimates the deeper intentions un-derlying a policy that was commonly understood as undertaken only to placate the conservative voices of the prince's political constituency.[7] The relation of papal authority to secular power sounds an important motif in Machiavelli's *The Prince*, whose teaching can be used to shed considerable light on the policy of Joly's nineteenth-century Machiavellian prince. More precisely, however, it can be fully appreciated only in terms of Saint-Simonian thought and a world his-toric order premised on finding institutionalized expression for a religious revo-lution on a scale even greater than that administered by the Christian Church of the Middle Ages.

Paradoxically, the nineteenth-century prince seeks to undermine the papacy by coming to its defense. Initially, this wins the plaudits of the more conservative elements of the new regime. Actually, it intends to so compromise the political existence of the Vatican as to make it a dependent appendage of its defender who profits from the peculiar authority it lends to his new rule. As the new prince uses the institutions of liberalism to cover and disguise his political revolution, he can also be seen to use the authority of the papacy and extant Christianity to move beyond it. As with the prince's revolution in political and economic realms, his religious revolution moves in circumspect ways that hide its more radical agenda.

The Spiritual Father's position will gradually be usurped by the representative of the new historic order, succeeding that over which the Church ruled at the apex of its power during the Middle Ages. The Church, with its retrograde political policies, is no more than an anachronistic reminder of a former order whose vitality has long since passed, sapped by a revolution of thought which culminates with the Enlightenment movement. The eclipse of its prestige is underscored by contemporary events that find the Vatican under military siege by the forces of modern nationalism.[8]

Ultimately, the prince in the *Dialogue* (Napoleon III) would want to definitively terminate the role of the Church, the political influence of which was necessarily baneful, at least according to the original critique of Machiavelli in *The Prince*. Viewed as a worldly institution, its inevitable effect was to compromise the source of its own legitimacy, expressed in its moral teachings, in bowing to the inevitable exigencies of politics. Its worldly conduct mocked its otherworldly pretensions; yet, its authority, accepted by other powers on faith, guaranteed the perpetuation of its unhealthy influence.

The essential spirit of *The Prince*'s critique of the old Christianity finds expression in an amusing "bon mot" related by Joly's Machiavelli in the *Dialogue*. Machiavelli explains how he will act in such a regime. "I would be like Alexander VI and the Duke of Valentinois. There was a saying about Alexander VI at the court of Rome, 'that he never did what he said,' and about the Duke of Valentinois 'that he never said what he did'." Machiavelli's prince is to follow such political men who kept their ultimate aims "impenetrable." Yet, as a deeper reading of *The Prince* reveals, the necessity for such "dissimulation" was rooted perhaps as much in the character of the times as the character of these particular men.

The worldly pope, Alexander VI, "never did what he said." What he said ever remained the essence of Christian charity, but what he did was motivated by political necessity. On the other hand, Borgia "never said what he did." His murderous acts had to remain shrouded. His plans could not be articulated without offending the Christian temper of the times and exposing himself to rightful retribution as an enemy of God. Borgia and Alexander complement each other in furthering their imperial ambitions in Italy. The one provided the moral authority to cover the crimes that such a goal dictated.

On several occasions, the Machiavelli of the *Dialogue*, like the Machiavelli of *The Prince*, adjures the modern founder to follow the likes of Borgia. Yet, a good reader of *The Prince* knows, peculiarly enough, that Borgia failed. The real Machiavelli overstates the case when he says that a "great malignity of fortune" frustrated the Duke of Valentinois. He could have secured himself by a crime he apparently could not contemplate—removing Pope Julius—to guarantee another, like Alexander, complicit with his schemes.

The Machiavellian prince of the nineteenth century would follow through on the "implicit" steps recommended by the real Machiavelli. His actions in Italy intend to render the pope subservient to his own imperial ambitions. But such acts ultimately look to a more radical solution—the effectual destruction of the power of the papacy, whose influence is already on the decline. Such a project is more audacious than the murder of a pope. It strikes not only at the temporal seat of the pope's power but his moral authority, in the summoning of the masses to a new moral order. It is backed by political power, unprecedented in scope, that would always elude the medieval papacy despite its unholy alliances.

To escape the "great malignity of fortune" that plagued Borgia and Alexander, the division of secular and religious authority, shared by these two figures, would have to be terminated. This is precisely what the Machiavellian prince of the nineteenth century seeks to accomplish in succeeding to Caesarian power as the leader of a "civil religion." Accordingly, the Saint-Simonian prince will preside over institutions that are at once "political and religious," which, by giving unified expression to claims of both secular and moral progress, allows him to succeed to complete and uncompromised authority. The unification of spiritual and political powers effectively ends the fatal division of the world introduced by Christianity. It strikes at the source of strength of the liberal regime by ending the contradiction of authorities that the Montesquieu of the *Dialogue* labored so hard at keeping in "vital tension" and equilibrium.

According to the Saint-Simonians, the religion of the future, as in all previous "organic" moments, is called upon to take its place in the political order, or, "to be exact," the political institutions of the future, "when considered in their totality are to be religious institutions."[9] The potential for a new kind of despotism can be stated in terms of Montesquieu's argument in the *Dialogue*. Religious ethics lose their position of independence as a sanction and check upon the authority of rulers and a new political doctrine sanctifies worldly rule in higher religious terms. Such rule does not admit the legitimacy of appeals on the grounds either of natural rights or individual conscience.

It is Montesquieu who argues that, contrary to appearances, the influence of Christianity has not waned and can be seen to have infused the secular realm with its spirit. Machiavelli would give an ironic twist to such a contention when it is drawn to its most radical conclusion in the Saint-Simonian thought he expresses. Historical development does not merely evince Christian influences but the actual congruence of the secular and the religious realms. This occurs in the final historical stage that is viewed by the Saint-Simonians as bringing this-worldly fulfillment of the deepest aspirations of the universal religious consciousness first given expression by Christianity but effectively and finally organized in the new revolutionary state.

The Germs of Totalitarianism

The unprecedented authority that this lends to the future ruler may be seen in terms of the universal scope of his rule. Unlike modern autocracies, traditional despotism, or the despotism of the Roman Empire, this ruler alone will determine matters that were formerly perceived to be beyond the province of politics, indifferent to its concerns, or rightly belonging to individual conscience. Such universal and unbounded authority, sanctioned by the higher laws of history and effectively implemented through modern technology, clearly anticipates later totalitarianism. They share a recognition of the growing importance of the masses, as a result of the democratic thrust of the Enlightenment, in any calculus of future history, as well as an effort by a new kind of leader to enlist their passionate allegiance to a new world order.

The attempt to endow secular politics with the higher justifications and devotions formerly associated with the psychology of religion may be viewed as a common ideological trait of totalitarianism and has long been a staple of scholarly efforts that have tried to come to terms with such phenomena. It was Raymond Aron who developed the idea of "secular religions" in *France Libre* in 1944. He explains himself thus:

> I proposed to baptize as 'religions seculaires' those doctrines which take the place of faith in the contemporary mind, and which locate man's salvation here on earth, in a far-off future, in the form of a social order yet to be created. As religions of salvation, these doctrines lay down the supreme values, and these are embodied in an earthly goal and a missionary party. Thus the zealots of these religions can embrace an unconditioned Machiavellianism in all good faith.

Such doctrines, he goes on to say, "offer an historical perspective," interpreting "past, present, and future in their own way."[10]

In the essay in which Aron writes, he asks after so many years of Nazi scholarship, whether a "mystery" remains in coming to terms with the Nazi phenomenon. Among other things, he implies that his original description of modern despotism through the concept of "secular religion" may remain the most helpful and comprehensive. In the politics of Saint-Simon, we see not only one of the earliest examples of such ideology but the most explicit application of the notion of "political religion." The "new" Christianity provides the cultural matrix of a final world order, ministered by one who would have himself viewed as a god-like being, governing as if by a new version of divine right in the name of the higher truths of history and its all-inclusive process. In such a light, Joly's Saint-Simonian regime may be seen as the archetype of totalitarian phenomena. Machiavelli delineates its essential conditions in the same manner that Montesquieu in the *Dialogue* explicitly endeavors to delineate the essential "conditions of freedom."

One brief concluding remark remains. I hope it goes without saying that the "new Christianity" maybe "new" but it is not really very Christian at all.

Notes

1. While Montesquieu does say that religion in despotic regimes serves to compound the fear in the sovereign (see *The Spirit of the Laws* IV 14), he also indicates the constraints it puts on him. A belief in the afterlife and divine retribution, for example, mitigates the power he holds over his subjects in forcing them to transgress what religion proscribes. See *The Spirit of the Laws* XXIV 14.

2. This is, of course, Samuel P. Huntington's argument in his brilliant and provocative work *The Clash of Civilizations* (New York: Touchstone, 1997). However, Huntington argues that respect for individual rights and freedom, whose origin lies in the West, will largely remain confined to the West. There is very little grounding in hopes for liberal polities in other "civilizations" of the world, Christian Orthodox, Muslim, etc. In this, I think him closer to the real Montesquieu than the one who appears in the *Dialogue*.

3. While Christian countries "live" by "credit," the failure of Muslim countries to adapt to the exigencies of modernity can be tied to religious prohibitions against it. See *The Spirit of the Laws* XX 19.

4. Cf. Acquinas, *Summa Theologica* Ia, Q. 1, art. 8, ad. 2. Thomas also speaks of the Christian's duty to accommodate oneself to the earthly city while also endeavoring to perfect it. Of course, he does not contemplate this outside the ministering of the Church.

5. How a multiplicity of sects moderates religious zeal as it helps accommodate one sect to another is beautifully explained by Adam Smith in *An Inquiry into the Nature and Causes of the Wealth of Nations*, Edwin Cannan, ed., (New York: Modern Library, 1937), 745. It deserves full citation.

> The interested and active zeal of religious teachers can be dangerous and troublesome only where there is, either one sect tolerated in the society, or where the whole of a large society is divided into two or three great sects; the teachers of each acting by concert and under a great discipline and subordination. But that zeal must be altogether innocent where the society is divided into two or three hundred, or into as many thousand small sects, of which no one could be consid-

erable enough to disturb the public tranquillity. The teachers of each
sect seeing themselves surrounded on all sides with more adversaries
than friends, would be obliged to learn that candor and moderation
which is so seldom to be found among the teachers of those great
sects whose tenets being supported by the civil magistrates are held
in veneration by almost all the inhabitants of extensive kingdoms and
empires, and who therefore see nothing round them but followers,
disciples, and humble admirers. The teachers of each little sect, finding themselves almost alone, would be obliged to respect those of
almost every other sect, and the concessions which they would mutually find both convenient and agreeable to make to one another,
might in time probably reduce the doctrine of the greater part of them
to that pure and rational religion, free from every mixture of absurd-
ity, imposture, and fanaticism, such as wise men in all ages of the
world wished to establish.

6. The text of the "New Christianity" can be found in Saint-Simon, *Social Organization*, 81-116.

7 . Such accounts typically indicate the extremes to which Napoleon must have been
moved to placate his conservative constituency. He was forced to abandon his sympathy
for nationalistic causes, particularly as it manifested itself in Italy, where as a youth, he
fought in its behalf.

8. It goes without saying in all this that Machiavelli's despot was only the first modern tyrant to underestimate the strength of the Papacy and the peculiar "divisions" it has
at its disposition.

9. Iggers makes the same point in his Introduction to *The Doctrine of Saint-
Simon*, xlii-xliii:

In order not to misunderstand the Saint-Simonian emphasis on religion as vague mysticism, one must realize that the Saint-Simonian
conception of religion was essentially institutional, an extension and
secularization of the Roman Catholic Church. . . . The Saint-
Simonians saw in the Catholic Church a pattern of autocracy applicable to the organization of society as a whole.

10. Raymond Aron, "Is There a Nazi Mystery?" *Encounter* (1980): 32. Aron thought
that he had by and large resolved the historic problem of Nazism. This was before the
phenomenon and indeed all history had been *re-problematized* by the postmoderns. The
term "totalitarian," like "holocaust," is promiscuously used today. For example, we are
told by the postmoderns that belief in any "truth" is "totalizing" and dangerous. This apparently makes even Jefferson and his truths—human equality and government in the
service of basic human needs—totalitarian in spirit. It is patently clear, if not *self-evident*,
that something is amiss in all this.

Where I once studied, I would pass daily into an academic building that had "The Truth Shall Set You Free" chiseled in stone above its portal. It was a Jesuit school and the quote, from Acquinas, I think, was appropriate. In the Brave New World of the post-modern university, I propose we sandblast old Thomas. Or, better yet, we could hoist a banner and cover him. Something along the lines of cigarette labels could be written on it. "Warning: The 'Truth' Has Been Determined To Be Dangerous as Well as Toxic to Your Mental Health and Our General Well-Being." This banner could be easily taken down when the new movement in thought passes.

Sydney Hook, citing the American philosopher Charles Pierce, once spoke of the importance of the "ethics of words." See "How Democratic Is America" (A Response to Howard Zinn) in *Points of View*, Robert E. DiClerico and Alan S. Hammock, eds., (New York: McGraw Hill, 1995), 14. From his wall, Humpty Dumpty observed those who "employ" words outside of their proper context. He might say that words like "totalitarian," as used today, should be "paid overtime." This chapter is written to recover the proper dimensions of the phenomenon of totalitarianism and to vindicate Joly and Aron in their efforts to come to terms with it. The last chapter would like the reader to consider the "holocaust" in its proper context. Like Sydney Hook, I submit that the promiscuous use of such terms is itself very, very dangerous and distorting. Abusive acts can all too often follow abused words. There may indeed be an ethical responsibility in using certain words correctly.

Parenthetically, I used to think that Charlie Chaplin had also solved the "Nazi mystery" and got Hitler just about right. His was too conventional a view of the dictator and dictatorship, however. When his very unconventional crimes—"against humanity"—were revealed, Hitler disappeared as a subject for comedy. For those who had firsthand experience of the regime, nothing was funny about Nazism. A German philosopher once thought that even poetry, post-Hitler, was henceforth impossible.

All this does not hold true for later generations. Hollywood even made a sit-com of life in a German P.O.W. camp. What person of any sense or sensibility is not appalled by the depiction of the frat house atmosphere that reigns there. While all this zany fun supposedly takes place, real men, women, and children were being starved, gassed, shot, and otherwise exterminated in other such "camps." These things are dreadful, obtuse, vulgar, and popular.

Recent movies show that the Mussolini era in Italy can be laughed at. (Of course, Fellini did that too, but with a dose of surrealism). Perhaps Mussolini's De Orco-like fate was purgative. Anyway, Mussolini's Italy did not burden later generations with the same crimes as Hitler. Twentieth-century history (as life in general) weighs lighter on Italians than on Germans. Maybe that's why Mussolini's party could be resurrected and even share in governing there?

One wonders if the old Fascist dog still has much bite. Even Fascists, post-Thatcher, see the marketplace and its peculiar disciplines as requisite to "getting the trains to run on time." One only hopes that Marx was correct when he saw the tragic moments of History as repeating themselves only as farce.

Part IV

The Drama of the *Dialogue*

Chapter Nine

Joly and the Portrait of Machiavelli

Thinkers who have come into contact with Joly appreciate his talents and insights and unfailingly remark upon the gross abuse that the *Dialogue in Hell* has suffered at the hands of posterity. However, the real nature of this abuse and a true appreciation of Joly's text presume an adequate understanding of the more subtle intentions and teachings of the *Dialogue* which heretofore have been not sufficiently addressed. This requires greater concentration on the dramatic elements of the *Dialogue* whose careful construction has been overlooked by scholars whose interest in Joly derives from their greater concern with the *Protocols*.

In his essay on Joly, Hans Speier summarizes a view of past scholars that he shares, in part, but would also like to refine and correct.

> While critics have often pointed out that Joly's sympathies are on the side of Montesquieu, it would be more correct to stress that in the *Dialogue* he shared Montesquieu's moral preferences but regarded Machiavelli's knowledge of politics as superior to that of his adversary.[1]

Speier senses the need for more clarity in coming to grips with the enigmatic character of the author of the *Dialogue in Hell*, but his statement, despite his intentions, brings greater obfuscation.

When taken at face value, his comment on Joly's critics leads to some insupportable conclusions that do no justice to Joly, an author Speier obviously respects, or the subtlety of the text, the real significance and continuing relevance of which Speier wished to present. Indeed, the most astute commentator on the *Dialogue in Hell* would unintentionally force the issue of a more adequate treatment of Joly, whose thought and way of writing is again underestimated and escapes the scholar most capable of grasping its finer points.[2]

Montesquieu is devastated by the arguments of Machiavelli. Following Speier's line of thought, certain perplexing questions arise. If Joly's sympathies lie with Montesquieu, why would he seem so utterly to refute his position? Can we really maintain a preference for a morality that is erected upon baseless assumptions? Joly would be presenting us with a very unpalatable choice. We might have our "moral preferences" but at the sacrifice of reason.

There really is no choice in such a case. Given the limitations of Montesquieu in the portrait of him presented by the *Dialogue*, we are led to side with Machiavelli.[3] However, if we leave it at that, we would be forced to conclude that Joly's effect, if not his intention, is immoral in seeming to serve the cause of despotism. Finally, we might begin to wonder at the perversity of such a man so obviously in contradiction with himself. We shall see that the resolution of these contradictions begins with a more adequate understanding of the character and thought of the Machiavelli in the *Dialogue in Hell*.

Dissatisfaction with Speier's account of Joly requires a return to the text. Indeed, a closer investigation of details reveals a certain sympathy to elements of Montesquieuan thought, not within the *Dialogue* proper but outside it, so to speak, in A Short Introductory Statement and on the Title page. These are the only places where Joly addresses us in a direct manner and not through his interlocutors. They are the logical starting places for distilling a more adequate understanding of Joly and deserve proper emphasis.

There are two quotes from *The Spirit of the Laws* on the title page.

> Soon we should see a frightful calm during which everyone would unite against that power which had violated the laws.

> When Sulla thought of restoring Rome to her liberty, this unhappy city was incapable of receiving that blessing.

These quotes are keyed to Joly's deeper intentions.[4]

In the former, we are presented with a glimpse of the future. The statement would aptly refer to the rule of Joly's despot and his violation of the statutes and organic law of the liberal regime as well as, perhaps, the more fundamental laws of religious origin that are the basis of civil life. Inaugurated in violence, his rule moves toward a peace that could be described as "frightful," if not chilling, due to the apparent success of the despot in overcoming the resistance of his subjects and winning acceptance to their own servitude. We are, however, on the verge of a great social upheaval and may stand in only an interval of a calm before an even more dreadful storm.

In the second quote, Joly presents an ancient partisan of liberty, Sulla, who attempted to restore Rome and its Senate to republican principles. However, there were only the feeble remains of virtue. The succession of Caesars that followed failed to arouse Rome from its lethargy and steadfastly riveted the chains of servitude. When the people struck blows, it was at the tyrant, not the tyranny.[5]

A case can be made that Joly himself takes advantage of this "frightful calm" to teach his contemporaries of the crisis that is ripening and the despotism that is upon them. It is not unlike the despotism that engulfed Rome in the rule of the Caesars who followed in the wake of Sulla's failure. His addressees, who are not fully cognizant of their situation, dictate the manner in which he presents his teaching. In revealing the tyrant, Joly indicates what makes the present so perilous and tries to arouse his contemporaries from their lassitude. In this regard, his intentions are similar to those of Sulla, although the methods markedly differ, to say the least. He prompts the test of their virtue in the face of the modern Caesar and, conscious of Sulla, doubts their response.

We may see the quotes as an expression of a political crisis that Joly thought was brought to a head by recent Napoleonic policies. Political upheaval remains a distinct possibility in the face of a political order, the closest antecedent of which is Imperial Rome. The possibility for liberty rests in thwarting the aims of that order without unleashing a dangerous anarchy. In the first quote, the destruction of the regime is held forth as a distinct and perhaps imminent possibility. The undertones of mass anarchy make the present moment a truly delicate one, calling for a political teaching that is at once prudent, as well as revealing and frank. Joly's solicitude is not unfounded. He basically accepts the analysis of Joly's Machiavelli regarding the character of his contemporaries. We have only to look to the anarchy of the Commune and its murderous repression, when, indeed, the Napoleonic Empire suddenly fell in war with Germany.[6] And as citizens of the world at the beginning of the twenty-first century, we have fresh experience of the mayhem that can follow from the collapse of a powerful despotic empire.

Joly's name is not found on the Title page of his own book. Given the nature of the material in the book and his presentation of the ways of the Napoleonic regime, he presumably does this for prudential reasons of a personal kind. He has his book published in Brussels, a place that was more congenial to projects like his own.[7]

In his preface, he writes that his book will be published anonymously. Giving his name is not important, all considerations of prudence aside. The work does not represent personal views. It is the "public voice" and a "call to conscience" that is contained therein. It is meant to speak in disinterested tones. At least according to its author, we are not to doubt his "moral intentions" or his opposition to despotism.

In A Short Introductory Statement, we also see how the author views the regime described in the *Dialogue*. He does not simply identify with the teaching of Machiavelli therein. Machiavelli's regime is present reality. The day that it was "enthroned" is "all too distant." It is a regime whose continued existence rests on "corruption" and is an insult to "integrity," as a reading of the last part of the *Dialogue*, in particular, conveys. The proper interpretation of Joly begins and ends with what is his earliest and most open assessment of the regime and his implied intention to help coalesce the forces that would end it.

Joly indicates why he proceeds as he does. Certain of his contemporaries do not accept "harsh political truths." Their sensibilities would be outraged. These are sons of the Enlightenment, sophisticated and worldly. They trust in the powers of reason to ameliorate political and social life. Indeed, politics is no longer the predominant concern of the educated. Joly's addressees are literate men of goodwill, though politically naive. He intends to teach them "harsh truths about contemporary politics" through a dialogue "that is not without its lively pleasures." The *Dialogue in Hell* is the vehicle by which he delivers his stern teaching that couches an anti-Caesarian conspiracy. The ultimate resonance of the conspiracy theme, so prominent in the *Dialogue*, can be appreciated at this point.

Joly's Mode of Writing

Joly chooses the dialogue format to present his teaching even though it might initially cause his work to be mistaken as a purely literary endeavor. A fictional presentation would prove to be more appealing to his addressees and perhaps an aid to getting a distance on themselves and their times proper to a correct perspective. A political tract might be seen as coming from partisan sources, while a more theoretical work would lose the majority of his intended audience. We soon see that Joly is not at all writing fiction, nor can the cause he serves in his attack on Napoleon be seen as narrowly partisan.

In his preface, Joly expressly puts before us the question of his way of writing, a mode that has been adopted with certain diverse and specific intentions in mind. Beyond it, we may glean additional reasons in the body of the text for his proceeding the way he does. These are found in the detailed sections on propaganda and the press. In these passages, the peculiar sensitivity of the new regime to written material of a political nature is revealed, as the control of thought becomes crucial to the success of the new despot.

Joly explains through his Machiavelli that a long political tract would not engage the interests of his reading public. Moreover, such an endeavor would put the author under the immediate suspicion of the secret police, oftentimes with dire consequences, as was explained. Joly's literary mode allows him to reach his proper audience in a manner that engages their interest, while it allows him to escape the closer scrutiny of the censors and the police, who are tolerant and even encouraging, by their laxness, in areas that do not involve direct political concerns.

If the return to a guarded orthodoxy marks the politics of the Second Empire, prudence recommends a mode of writing to express opposition to proper audiences and to escape persecution from official quarters. Machiavelli and Montesquieu wrote in a former such epoch. They may in certain ways be a model or inspiration for such an endeavor on the part of Joly, whose skills are perhaps sharpened by his study of their texts. In fact, the mode of writing adopted by Joly may prove serviceable in multiple ways, as important for prudential considerations in avoiding the scrutiny of several groups as it is in enlisting the attention of several levels of more sympathetic readers.

Albert Guerard notes how censorship and the persecution of writers in this epoch forced individuals (like Joly) to a greater exercise of wit that resulted in a clear gain for both art and thought.

> The repressive laws were for the journalist a blessing in their disguise. If, until the closing years, writers could not indulge in violent personal attacks, the loss to genuine freedom was small. If they had to use wit, allusiveness, and irony in the exhilarating game with the censor, the result in thought and art was clear gain. Napoleon III was spared, but Tiberius of Rome and Soulouque (Faustin I) of Haiti were mercilessly criticized.[8]

In the short autobiographical sketch written while imprisoned in 1870, Joly recounts how he decided upon the dialogue format he chose. The *Dialogues sur le Commerce des Blés* by the Abbé Ferdinand Galiani (1770) is mentioned as the model. There, the controversial friend of d'Holbach and Mme. d'Epinay had departed souls wittily discuss tariffs, grain trade, and other important matters. The format was designed to hoodwink the censors while attacking the politics of the time. "While walking on the terrace along the river near Port Royal in bad weather," Joly came to his idea of a conversation in hell between Montesquieu who "represents the policy of justice," and Machiavelli, who describes the "abominable policies" of Napoleon III. Joly specifically indicates the necessity for a "disguise" for writers during the Second Empire.[9]

He probably anticipated a certain celebrity for the *Dialogue*.[10] If he were apprehended by the police for the opinions expressed therein, his defense would be aided by the complex elements of his thought, which would provide him a flexible scope for his response. At the very least, this would prove frustrating and embarrassing for prosecutors. As a canny lawyer himself and very familiar with the conduct of Parisian courts, Joly could use a judicial forum to his advantage in publicizing his book and pressing his attack on the Napoleonic regime.

His literary mode avoids a mass readership which, given the quotes on the Title page and the possibilities of anarchy, must be preserved from any political teaching that would for whatever reason enflame its passions. Already, this separates Joly from more doctrinaire liberals who ultimately see no threats from the dispersion of political opinion. The author of the *Dialogue in Hell* shows a more complex understanding of the relationship of thought to society than that presented by the spokesman for liberalism in his text, who, in many respects, represents a certain naive and doctrinaire view of liberalism.

But where the masses are preserved from certain teachings that would enflame passions, the proper addressees of Joly's work, those educated types who would be the victims of Napoleonic politics, are to be politicized through Joly's harsh lessons. These are the elements in a regime that set its tone and are the target of the prince's covert efforts of suppression and seduction, as explained in Part Two of the *Dialogue*.

The Portrait of the Philosopher

Finally, beyond such readers, there are other addressees, more attentive readers who are able to appreciate the multiple levels and more subtle intentions of Joly's work. In the deeper reading of the Machiavelli of the *Dialogue* lies a portrait of the philosopher, less conspicuous than that of the tyrant he has endeavored to reveal, but equally impressive in its own right. This subtler portrait may now come into better focus.

We have noted Joly's use of Montesquieu on the title page as opening the *Dialogue* to an interpretation that is antagonistic to despotism and sympathetic to a republican cause. But the hidden key in interpreting the drama of the text rests with Machiavelli, whose thought dominates the *Dialogue* as a whole. Proper understanding of the Machiavelli there presented reveals a character that is not the same as his reputation would depict him. We shall find that Joly presents a more sophisticated portrait of Machiavelli that rises above a naive connection of his name with evil and tyranny. The true Machiavelli comes to light as a philosopher benevolently motivated toward men, as illustrated, ironically enough, by his treatment of his interlocutor in the *Dialogue*.

It is obvious from the outset that Machiavelli is a master of irony. It is in fact employed in his very greeting of Montesquieu, in order to effectively "size up" this celebrated personage. Montesquieu confesses to being very inept in such arts of conversation. At the end of his encounter, he has the strong impression that the portrait of tyranny just sketched is meant as consummate irony.[11] Yet, it is at this point that Machiavelli is his most serious. Far from an ironic presentation, he reveals that his tyranny is current in the world. It is often the case that whenever Machiavelli is most facetious, Montesquieu is most earnest. His seriousness is similarly misinterpreted. In either case, Montesquieu is constantly gulled until the end, when Machiavelli dramatically reveals the most recent events that have escaped Montesquieu's purview.

The final disclosures to Montesquieu are meant to underscore the serious use of Machiavellian irony. In a seemingly playful dialogue, a "friendly wager" issues into a teaching of tremendous consequence to Montesquieu. Its impact is greatly heightened by its mode of presentation. The effect of the conversation is not unlike the intended effect of the *Dialogue* on its readers, who are suddenly brought to certain very sobering revelations in a book whose seriousness is initially disguised.

As readers, we are encouraged throughout the *Dialogue* to ponder the irony of Machiavelli and the enigmatic character of Joly's presentation. We shall find that by resolving the one, we shall resolve the other. There are two points of access to Machiavelli's intentions, which allow us "to get behind" his irony, as it were. They are presented to us at the very beginning of the *Dialogue* and at the very end.

At the end of the *Dialogue*, Machiavelli reveals to Montesquieu the actuality of the tyranny he has described.

> What I have just described—this mass of monstrous things before which the spirit recoils in fright, this work that only hell itself could accomplish—all this is done, exists, and is prospering in the light of day, at this very hour, in that place on the globe that you have recently departed.

To this point, Montesquieu has been consistently complacent in the face of Machiavelli's attack. He was first sure of the cause he defended. Later, he takes consolation from the fact that he is only involved in a theoretical discussion, an impression that might have let Machiavelli score some easy debating points which later prove so consequential. In a surface reading of the text, we also assume that Machiavelli has identified himself with the regime he has described. Here, however, he condemns it in no uncertain terms. The condemnation itself reminds us of Joly's own statements in his preface, the most forthright revelation of Joly's views and intentions.

The circumstances that surround Machiavelli's utterances at this point lead us to believe in his sincerity. Machiavelli is being spirited away by the onrush of sinister souls who have haunted the conversation throughout. In his last statement to Montesquieu—for eternity—and the denouement of the whole conversation, irony would be singularly out of place. In his frankest and most dramatic moment, Machiavelli distinguishes himself from the "Machiavellianism" he has described. His statement of the political truth, which he so intransigently pursues, does not, it seems, necessarily imply moral approbation. His last statements also constitute a critique of worldly glory and a subtle rebuke to Montesquieu.

Throughout Machiavelli's discourse, we have understood the greatest good for political men to be glory. This is without doubt the chief motive of the new prince, who wants to achieve enduring glory in the most ambitious and lasting of political foundings. Haunting their conversation are men who, according to Machiavelli, also sought celebrity in their earthly existence from various political endeavors. The enigmatic presence of such figures in fact serves an important dramatic function in the *Dialogue* beyond a periodic reminder of the context of their conversation. In pointing out the present shame of such men, with whom Montesquieu was perhaps intimate, Machiavelli reminds us of the predominance of fortune in political affairs and the evanescence of even the greatest fame. Formerly prominent, these men have been brought low by events, subsequent to their deaths, that mock their life's achievements.

The drama of the moment prompts the question as to whether or not the men of the Enlightenment had in fact laid the foundations for this Napoleonic tyranny. The real Montesquieu poignantly expresses a similar thought in *The Greatness of the Romans and Their Decline*. There he wonders if all the history of the Roman Republic, a history resplendent with the accomplishments and virtues of heroic individuals not seen since, existed only to appease and satiate the happiness of five or six monsters in the Empire.[12] The grand "spectacle of things human," when contemplated from hell, would diminish even the greatest pretensions to worldly glory and lasting achievement.

It is therefore significant that the Machiavelli of Joly's *Dialogue* reveals himself on earth and in hell as personally unmoved by the motive of political glory that he analyzes in the great actors on the world stage. However, he would have been capable, at least by knowledge, if not fortune, of attaining its heights, it seems.

At the very beginning of his encounter with Montesquieu, Machiavelli shows his imperturbability in the face of his personal plight in hell. According to the Joly portrait, his situation is not unlike his life on earth, which is interpreted in the *Dialogue* as devoted to inquiry and the search for truth. In fact, his situation is perhaps an improvement over his lot on earth which, as Montesquieu points out, saw the defeat in Florence of his republican political cause during a lifetime marked by harassment and disappointment, ending in torture and misery. Here at least, he may find the world's great minds whom he may engage in conversation. Given the present reality on earth, Machiavelli has escaped a worse hell and, in a certain sense, leads a blessed existence free from less important cares and concerns.

Machiavelli's subsequent handling of Montesquieu is marked by what seems to be a harshness that borders on cruelty. He is devastating in the manner by which he disabuses Montesquieu of his reputation and his putative standing before God. Yet, his harsh lesson to Montesquieu is not unjust, if we are to hold the truth at all important. It also conceals a certain humanity. In forcing him to confront his former illustrious cohorts, who are passing nearby, Machiavelli forces Montesquieu to realize the vacuity of glory and the present atrocities in a world which he apparently loves too much. Under the present despotism, it is not a world to be regretted. Machiavelli would seemingly want to impress Montesquieu by his example and teach him the pleasures of his lofty detachment from the vanity that infects his interlocutor.

We remember that knowledge of recent events has escaped Montesquieu, who has met only the deceased from long ago and far away in his wanderings in hell. Apparently, he earnestly seeks to be "filled in" on these events if only for present confirmation of his theories. At the end of his conversation with Machiavelli, he is shown passing before his eyes his chagrined contemporaries who could inform him of it. The point is that one or another of such men will disabuse Montesquieu of his illusions. Machiavelli, in his apparent harshness, would do so in a way that points to his liberation from his ignorance and vain concerns.

Machiavelli predicts that after their confrontation, Montesquieu will anxiously seek him out and wander eternally in his pursuit. This is the reverse of the beginning of the *Dialogue* where it was Machiavelli who sought out Montesquieu. Machiavelli has brought to Montesquieu a concern for philosophy and inquiry born of the recognition of certain harsh truths and the realization that the human, political problem has not been solved. In this search is not only liberation but a recognition of the true human situation and the highest manifestation of our human autonomy.

As hell is depicted in the *Dialogue*, it is a stopping place for the deceased before judgment day. The proper attitude would seem to be one of introspection and an examination of conscience before one makes his defense before the tribunal of God.[13] In the case of these two interlocutors, an examination of conscience would involve an examination of political history. More than perhaps all other men, they are personally responsible for the conditions of the world.

Joly characterizes his work in his preface as "a call to conscience." This is the distinct effect of Machiavelli's "harsh" teaching on the Montesquieu of the *Dialogue*, though his conversation begins "pleasantly enough." This Montesquieu does not initially recognize his human responsibility, nor is he adequately philosophic. He trusts that the political problem has been solved and exalts in his own role in providing the solution. He therefore feels himself personally secure in hell and in God's eyes. The conversation with Machiavelli is his shock of awareness on these scores.

Joly's Montesquieu is not the philosopher of *The Spirit of the Laws*, a point to which we will return shortly. The latter has been sacrificed to Joly's literary mode. The Montesquieu of the *Dialogue* is more the contemporary liberal, a man of good intentions but one who would be the dupe and casualty of Napoleon's politics. Joly's text is a call to conscience (and consciousness) to such types.

Machiavelli and Joly tell such men of the eternal possibilities of despotism and its new and future forms.[14] The politics of the future will not, as Joly sees it, be menaced by a reaction to the Enlightenment but by a regime that emanates from it. It does not appear bloodthirsty. As the great contemporary of Joly, Alexis de Tocqueville, described his own fears in this regard, it has the capacity to degrade men without tormenting them. Its real threat, obscured for these reasons, can be characterized as destroying human autonomy and responsibility to the point where Joly's call, like that of Sulla, falls on deaf ears.

The task of the future is to confront the political situation realistically. Through Machiavelli, we are made aware that the moral good is not supported by mere goodwill or by the evolution of a history which orders affairs to continual progress. Such good is the product of active human concerns that begin with the active concern for the truth. In the context of the *Dialogue*, only this would justify us in the eyes of God. On this basis, it is Machiavelli who can face God's tribunal with equanimity, despite the infamy attached to his name and his condemnation by inferior earthly judges.

We would be well reminded of a most perspicacious statement that the sixteenth-century playwright Christopher Marlowe attributes to Machiavelli, who appears in his play, *The Jew of Malta*. There, the Florentine philosopher boldly confesses that "there is no sin but ignorance."[15] There could be no more succinct and fitting epigram to describe the character of the Machiavelli that appears in Joly's work of "fiction." It is the forthright statement of the philosopher that points to what is so impressive in the Joly portrait.

Lifting Joly's and Machiavelli's Mask

A clearer appreciation of Joly's thought and intentions emerges in a deeper probing of the character of Machiavelli as he appears in the *Dialogue*. As Speier stated, Joly regarded his Machiavelli's knowledge of politics as superior. But this is not, as Speier formulates it, contrary to his more subtle moral intentions or his liberal sympathies. A case can be made that Joly's Machiavelli harbors republican intentions in his open teaching of tyranny, just as he has a humane end in view in his harsh treatment of his interlocutor. This is consistent with a certain sophisticated view of Machiavelli that Joly seems to share, at least as revealed by the teaching and drama of the *Dialogue*.

The parallels between Joly and this subtler portrait of Machiavelli, as philosopher and republican partisan, are manifold and present us with hints as to the character of the author of the *Dialogue in Hell*. Like this Machiaveli, Joly shows himself to be indifferent to reputation in hiding what is most deeply revealing of himself in his service to his disinterested call to conscience.

Like Machiavelli's *The Prince*, Joly's work is subject to misinterpretation. At one extreme, both Joly and Machiavelli are seen as openly teaching and advocating tyranny. At the other extreme, they may be seen as involved in a purely "literary" endeavor. Montesquieu, who wants to pass his time pleasantly with his interlocutor, prefers this latter interpretation which has Machiavalli, as the author of *The Prince*, merely trying to paint the characters and exploits of his time in the most vivid colors.

It is more than coincidence that Joly refers specifically to the possibility of these very same misunderstandings with regard to his own work. But he warns in his preface of the careful construction of his book. Beyond pleasant fictions, moral causes are being served in a "call to conscience" and deeper, enduring political truths revealed.

In this same preface, Joly reveals his disapprobation of the regime he will shortly describe. At the end of his conversation with Montesquieu, Machiavelli reveals his disapprobation of the regime in terms strikingly similar to those of Joly. His dramatic and disquieting revelation sheds light on the motive for his search of Montesquieu in the beginning. Machiavelli's knowledge of contemporary affairs has rendered him anxious for the future of civil life. It is not for mean or malevolent purposes that he searches out Montesquieu, but to engage him, liberalism's great spokesman, in a conversation to come to terms with its problems.

We are not to assume that the defeat of Montesquieu is tantamount to a definitive defeat of the cause of freedom. Machiavellianism triumphs precisely because of Montesquieu's ignorance about what has come to pass. The manner by which Machiavelli enlightens his "adversary" would allow for the reconstruction of the case for liberalism, without illusions, and fully cognizant of what is at stake. The Machiavellian regime is described as leaving extant the institutions of liberalism, while changing the spirit of its operations. The *Dialogue* might perhaps be seen as attempting to rekindle that spirit in the face of the despot and the possibility of a renewed outbreak of anarchy.

The Montesquieu that Machiavelli finds in hell is ignorant of contemporary events and singularly complacent. Machiavelli guides the course of their conversation accordingly. What was sought out as a conversation between two philosophers becomes a didactic enterprise on the part of Machiavelli, served by irony. But at the beginning and at the end of their conversation, the real intentions of Machiavelli are manifest. The Machiavelli of the *Dialogue*, properly understood, is Joly's spokesman and the enlightenment of Montesquieu is really the enlightenment of the reader who shares most of his fatal prejudices.

Machiavelli states that his political teaching was intended for princes and people alike. He has shown the truth to people as he has to kings. He says that Machiavellian princes are not in need of such teachings. They do not learn anything from Machiavelli that they do not know already. The real effect of the open teaching of the techniques of tyrannical politics is to enlighten the people. They stand to learn what threatens them and are made to see politics in a realistic light.

The success of the tyrant requires duplicity and cunning. The open teaching of tyranny removes this possibility by fully revealing the tyrant. Through Joly's conceit of a dialogue in hell, Machiavelli is describing the despot Napoleon III, shorn of his disguise. In what appears as a theoretical discourse between two eminent philosophers, Joly is actually presenting a brutally realistic portrayal of contemporary life. Like the Montesquieu of the *Dialogue*, the readers are blithely ignorant in the crucial sense of what has recently come to pass.

Joly's Machiavelli hints at the intended use of his teaching. He states that Montesquieu's *The Spirit of the Laws*, in its teaching on liberal government, might be a great aid to Machiavellians who seek to overthrow such regimes. Ironically, it has been Machiavelli's guide throughout the conversation with Montesquieu, and Machiavelli shows that he is capable of accurately quoting its text. The implication is too transparent to miss: the detailed teaching of tyranny in the *Dialogue in Hell* could properly serve his audience for their own defense. At the beginning of their conversation, Montesquieu wonders how Machiavelli, a staunch republican in life, could be the mentor of tyrants in his writings. The conclusion of the *Dialogue* would lead us to believe that no such disjunction exists. A republican cause is being served in the very writing that seems to bless tyranny.[16]

That the *Dialogue* intends enlightenment of his contemporaries is obvious at certain points. Periodically, Machiavelli feigns ignorance. This allows Montesquieu to discourse on liberal institutions and the intentions behind certain political, social, and economic arrangements. Through Montesquieu, we have a reteaching of the general theory of liberal politics. But through the various discussions of Machiavelli, particular attention is drawn to the sensitive points that hold together the political and social fabric of liberalism. The proper addressees of the *Dialogue*, those concerned with the fate of free government, are prompted by Joly to contemplate the threats that emanate from modern dictators as well as the means by which liberal institutions may be shored up and fortified against the new vulnerabilities that Machiavelli has identified.

Joly shows where the present danger can be found. It is not in a reactionary and rapacious tyranny but in the modern Caesar, whose genius lies in appealing to the passions of the masses and in representing their satisfaction as the legitimate exercise of their rights. Joly recurs to the "timeless wisdom" of Machiavelli to remind us of the eternal threat of Caesarism to republican government. The test of liberal government is to adapt itself in countering what was to be the future threat to its perpetuation, foreseen by Joly in the politics of Napoleon.

In his stunning portrait of modern tyranny, Joly makes his "call to conscience," which demands of his contemporaries as much a moral as an intellectual effort. Implicitly, in the absence of the Enlightenment faith in progress, it is an effort that rests on the determination to be free. Critics who fail to see the moral dimensions of Joly's *Dialogue* fail to see what is at its core.

If we are permitted to speak of Joly's own view of history, we might say that it clearly does not reflect a process of guaranteed progress. Indeed, it is in the guise of progress that Caesarism threatens to establish itself. Nor, if men are essentially free, can a universal conclusion to historical development be presumed, as the Saint-Simonians and future historicist thinkers down to our day would argue. Joly's primary intention in the *Dialogue*—to issue a "call to conscience"—

is based on the premise of man's irreducible freedom and his capacity as a moral being to respond to his call.[17]

History is open-ended. There can be no scientific certitude in such matters because the future is necessarily indeterminate, always dependent on the contingent actions of men and women. Situations are presented that elicit numerous possible responses that are a constant test of the virtues of history's actors. The shaping of events varies according to the influence of these actors, more so with regard to the Machiavellis and the Montesquieus, of course, but in some degree as well from the more modest efforts of people like Joly.

Speier describes Joly as being equally outraged by the despot as by the ease with which the people let themselves be corrupted. In concentrating on the weaknesses of the majority of men, he leaves himself open to a charge of a certain irascible moralism, a claim that is substantiated by what little is known of his personal life. But, this charge might be leveled only by those, like the subjects of the Empire, unaware of their own corruption. Moreover, he anticipates such charges in the body of the text when he shows an awareness of how singularly strange types like himself will appear among his contemporaries and future generations. His call may fail, as did that of Sulla, but not from simple moralism.

Joly appears to be appealing to the sterner virtues of ancient republics and he might have found himself more at home in such times than in his own century, for which he displays a certain loathing and contempt. Yet, it is such sterner virtues that are under attack in the soft despotism described in the *Dialogue*. Joly seeks to revive it in his call to conscience as the essential condition for the possibility of republican regimes, even in modern times. In this light, we can appreciate more fully the peculiar appropriateness of his identification with the severe Sulla as well as the more Catonic tones in which he casts his critique of modern life.[18]

At end, it might be helpful to situate Joly with regard to the two great protagonists in the *Dialogue*. For Montesquieu, man becomes master of his destiny as human reason progressively brings order to the physical universe and political world. For Machiavelli, man is subject to a fatality he cannot ultimately fathom or control. Joly might be said to incline toward the pessimism of the *Dialogue*'s Machiavelli. This is what the experience of the Second Empire forces upon him. But in his call to conscience, he acknowledges man's capacity to affect and better his future. For Joly, it seems, man is neither the lord of history nor its plaything. He would agree with Alexis de Tocqueville, when he counsels prudent human action born of the recognition of human freedom and its ineluctable limits. Our task is to act responsibly within the margins of freedom that the constraints of history leave us. Like his great contemporary, Joly is acutely aware of the decline of civic courage and honorable love of freedom in his fellow citizens. The action that is called for at the moment Joly writes requires clarity of vision and a revival of this civic courage. The *Dialogue* attempts to provide the first and spur the second.

Concluding Remarks

Before closing our discussion of Joly, it might again be helpful to elaborate somewhat further his presentation of the two great interlocutors in his work. It would be unseemly to leave the discussion of the *Dialogue* with the impression that Joly's portrait of Montesquieu and Machiavelli is definitive. The concluding remarks that are in order are not meant to detract from Joly's achievement but to be more just to the great thinkers he employs in his work. They will also let us more fairly assess Joly's contribution to our political understanding.[19] We turn first to Montesquieu.

In *The Spirit of the Laws*, Montesquieu broadens and historicizes the "logical" classification of regimes found in Aristotle's *Politics*. He famously delineates both the nature and animating principle of the fundamental political alternatives. The republican regime is motivated by virtue, the European monarchy by honor, and despotism by fear. Curiously, Montesquieu's regime of liberty lies outside this classification. It is found in modern England, of course. But, even more curiously, its name is not mentioned. We today fail to grasp its "newness"—this regime of political liberty, this commercial "republic" embedded and hidden in the "forms" of monarchic government. There, law is no longer the measure of man but his instrument.

Joly is correct in sensing that its lessons somehow lie at the core of Montesquieu's teaching. One is tempted to say that the new political "model" for man falls outside the alternatives that history has heretofore offered. It is a regime outside the "natural" alternatives, so to speak. Its happy circumstance is literally a historic (and geographic) accident of history. By offering England as a model for the future, Montesquieu shows, perhaps paradoxically, how "history" may be used to better our condition and escape our "historic fate."

In contrast to the regime of liberty, whose influence will be found in the future, the ancient city's time has forever passed. At first blush, Aristotle's classification of regimes seems exhaustive. Indeed, the ancient city can be governed, it would seem, in virtuous or vicious ways, by one, a few, or many. There is inherent logical appeal in such a classification But it actually applies "exhaustively" to only a very narrow political alternative—the ancient polis.

According to Aristotle, how a city lines up within this schema is what fundamentally determines its way of life. Montesquieu implicitly attacks Aristotle and offers a different conception of the ancient city and what may be judged as "virtue" therein. The "virtue" of the ancient city is not to be judged by its approach to human excellence. It is manifested in a "love of country," regardless of the numbers of individuals who nominally rule. A "patriotism" burns in the ancient soul that is hard for moderns to conceive. This is its animating "principle"—what gives it "life"—and what distinguishes it as an historic alternative.[20]

But, for Montesquieu, the historic moment of the polis has passed. and its passing (contrary to the Romantics) is not to be regretted. In despotism, all are equal before the despot—equally abject, that is.[21] In the ancient city, "equality" belongs to a constricted group of citizens who enjoy their privileges at the expense of a larger class of slaves. Like despotism, the ancient city is an outrage to our rightful sense of basic human dignity while life there mutilates the soul, even of the privileged, by a rigor that resembles the dryly cruel and austere life of the monastery.

Outside of Aristotle's ambit of experience lies modern England, of course, but also the medieval Christian monarchy. At the time that Montesquieu wrote, this historic alternative was at its apogee. And Montesquieu's France was, but for the most recent past, the most beautiful flower of this historic moment.

The latter half of *The Spirit of the Laws* divides about equally between a segment that describes the modern regime of commerce and a segment that describes feudal law. The former was written under the invocation of a muse. Its passages shine with new luster. The latter is dark, dense, opaque, and labyrinthine. They belong to the scholar, not the poet. But it is here that the soul of France will be found and the labyrinth will lead all the way to a band of men, loyally pledged to one another, in a German forest.

When Montesquieu wrote, he thought that the soul of France had been corrupted. The luxurious court of Louis XIV had suborned honor, the life principle of the regime. The "forms" of medieval honor remained. Indeed, they were respected in ever more exaggerated ways. But the noble merely played at "honor," hypocritically, while he actually sought favor, abjectly, from the reigning sovereign. His stout independence and noble indifference to material blandishments had eroded. In a word, France was adopting the manners of Byzantium.[22]

Montesquieu sensed a coming revolution that would, a century and a half later, undermine the medieval monarchy and render it passé. Where it did perpetuate itself, it would exist (as Walter Bagehot would put it) only in the "decorative" part of modern constitutions and far from where "efficient" power was exercised. As with the ancient city, its vital juices now only nourish poetic imaginations.

The *Persian Letters* was Montesquieu's most pessimistic (and accurate) assessment of the predicament of France. The long absence of Usbek from his Persian seraglio leads to anarchy and revolution that overturns the natural order of things, as the women blindly revolt against their absent god. The horrific lessons for France can be drawn from the homely example from the East.[23] The Enlightenment's attack on the Christian God will see His withdrawal from the political world. His absence will bring unprecedented revolutionary anarchy that will bring the political world to capitulation before the power of a new kind of god—

not the Prince of Peace, for sure, but the man that Clausewitz called "*the* god of war." The earthly city, built on the ruins of the City of God, will not bring historic liberation but a return to a despotism in a new and more virulent form. Montesquieu's prescience should be well noted and alert us to the power of a political analysis that reaches beyond centuries.

Montesquieu's preferred solution for France's predicament was certainly not "England." A turn at this time (the Regency of Louis XV) to the modern commercial republic would fly in the face of extant institutions and the most deeply etched lineaments in the French soul. Rather, Montesquieu wanted to recover the ancient vitality of his country by a return to its feudal origins. Contrary to the naive "progressive" as he appears in the Joly portrait—enamored of England as the only historic alternative for the times—the real Montesquieu may be seen as a "conservative," at least in what regards France. We might even call him a "reactionary"—a term of even greater opprobrium in the "progressive's" vocabulary.[24] But Montesquieu's preference for this solution was done knowingly and the subsequent history of his country, when cut off from its "natural" origins, bears him out.

Cut loose from its roots, France will in fact relive and suffer the whole course of history as if in microcosm. Periods will be marked by turns to the constitutional arrangements of England. These will lapse into despotism but not before a brief interlude (with Robespierre) that will try to reintroduce the regime of republican virtue. There will be Restorations of the medieval alternative as well as periods of Empire that recall Rome and its fate under the Caesars. Things will not settle until 1958, if we can count on the recent past projecting itself into what now beckons and is called the "new Europe."

Montesquieu is a modern. He did not sketch a "best regime." Such "heavenly principalities" are something "to be prayed for" (perhaps) but cannot provide effectual guidance for men today. There is, however, a palpable sense of the "worst regime" and its hovering presence—despotism. We could say that the *summum malum* is all too present and real while the *summum bonum* is all too distant and ambiguous. Accordingly, Montesquieu designs his politics to escape the "worst" and to cultivate prospects for the implantation of the "best" that is available to us. In this light, he sees England as escaping the "worst" the best. The medieval monarchy, on the other hand, despite moderating institutions and a religious grounding, would be perpetually menaced by the "worst."

But a choice of modern England over even the remnants of medieval France could be made only with great reservations. The modern regime is characterized by a vigilant sense of protecting one's own space as well as frenetic and self-forgetting enterprise. Such life threatens the greatness of soul that finds its proper soil in regimes that are historically passé. By the middle of the nineteenth century, at the time of the Second Republic, the monarchic alternative had completely exhausted itself in France. At this time, Alexis de Tocqueville, admirably, takes Montesquieu's lead in trying to infuse the modern life that is our fate with the ennobling characteristics that it naturally resists.[25]

At end, Montesquieu's assessment of despotism is much richer and complex than that found in the *Dialogue in Hell*. And any transition to "England" as a solution for modern man is a much more troubled, if still desirable, prospect. This our contemporaries, who see a world of liberal politics and marketplace economies as imminently before us, would be well advised to ponder.

Montesquieu has been called the "Hippocrates" of politics. He makes a tour of our fundamental political alternatives to help us purge them of nefarious, even mortal, tendencies. This is done, not in the spirit of facilitating the benign and ineluctable movement of history. Indeed, a reading of *The Greatness of the Romans and their Decline* is sufficient to cause anyone to question any hope of permanency to political life, especially any notion that would see man as permanently perfecting himself through history. Rather, he acts in the spirit of the good physician, with humanity and wisdom, and more often than not he recommends a medicine or a regimen of moderation that would cause those most in need of his counsel to balk.[26]

Montesquieu has also been called the preeminent political (or philosophic) sociologist. Contrary to Aristotle, the question of who rules does not provide a sufficient entry into a statesmanlike political understanding of things. Man is shaped by many "forces"—historical and social—that are equally if not more important than questions of regime, narrowly understood. The statesman must be cognizant of soil, climate, religion, history, mores and manners, and their intricate interplay in setting the course for the future. Again, contrary to ancient philosophy, consideration of what they termed "the best regime" cannot possibly furnish appropriate light for modern men. For this we need the capacious intelligence of someone like Montesquieu, who has made the tour of our fundamental historical alternatives with a view to what is concretely possible, not theoretically desirable.

Nevertheless, abiding links still tie Montesquieu and Aristotle together. For both, prudence is the foremost virtue in our practical affairs. They are preeminent among political philosophers, ancient and modern, in counseling political moderation. What crimes have been committed in the last two centuries in the name of "humanity," cut off from moderation, and bathed in the rhetoric of "progress"! How pathetic are most of our contemporaries who facilely claim for themselves this virtue! The humanity of the author of *The Spirit of the Laws* is of a wholly different order, it goes without saying.[27] Montesquieu (and Aristotle before him) reveals for us the limits of the "progress" we can hope for. They remind us (too late for twentieth-century man) that moderation is not the enemy of "progress" but its essential condition. In this light, the naive and optimistic Montesquieu of Joly's *Dialogue* seriously distorts "ce grand homme." The real Montequieu, sober but hopeful, is lost from view in the *Dialogue in Hell.*[28]

How then are we finally to assess Joly? One of the alternatives for post-Revolutionary France was Imperial expansion. It was Joly's view that Louis was successor to Napoleon I's ambitious megalomania. But the Napoleons were only in a certain sense the historic counterparts to the Caesars. Present in their politics was something Raymond Aron detected and analyzed in later regimes and which was absent from the Roman alternative. Modern despotism, unlike the ancient variant, is crucially "ideocratic."[29]

Napoleon I projected power that escaped the most formidable French kings. He reverted to the forms of the past in France to advance modern thought. This was the decisive thing that made his appearance emblematic of modernity and the revolutions and wars of the future. It was "world-historic" ideas and not merely French prestige that put his armies on the move.

He crucially reshaped the "civilizing mission" of France, which was displaced from the realm of culture and made politically aggressive. He would topple the tottering monarchs of Europe, whose legitimacy was being undermined in the thought of its "wisest" men and in the sentiments of its poorest citizens. Joly sees Napoleon III as harboring similarly grand ambitions but endeavoring to give historic form to the thought of Saint-Simon and his followers, a more radical interpretation of the Enlightenment project, as we now see, hopefully more clearly. Joly is the analyst par excellence of ideocratic despotism as it first manifested itself in the nineteenth century. Raymond Aron is the analyst par excellence of the more menacing and devastating ideocratic despotisms of the twentieth century, which found inspiration in the thought of Marx and the racist *epigones* of Nietzsche. Their lifeworks were complementary and, rightfully viewed, we owe to them a new political awareness and a new sense of our vulnerabilities and possibilities.

My endeavor has been to emphasize the Aronian elements of Joly's thought. Therein lies what is best in him and what deserves most praise. I would praise Aron as the most Montesquieuan of modern political analysts if it were becoming for someone like me to praise these latter figures.[30]

There are also problems with Joly's treatment of Machiavelli who emerges in the deepest reading of the *Dialogue* as a philosopher whose political predilections, like those of Joly, lie with republicanism. Joly is perhaps too quick in dismissing or explaining away the tyrannous pronouncements of *The Prince* and the shocking design of his teaching. His perception of Machiavelli is shared by many learned students of the Florentine who see his writings merely as the forthright statements of "realpolitik." As Joly himself maintains, it is as absurd to blame Machiavelli for describing politics as it really is as it would be to blame a geologist for his analysis of earthquakes.

For all its "learnedness," such an interpretation may in fact be a hindrance to a finer appreciation of the real Machiavellian teaching which is perhaps better approached, initially at least, through the more naive view of Machiavelli as indeed a purveyor of evil. The learned view is a product of the essential Machiavellian project. It therefore underestimates the truly radical character of its teaching, the sense of which is grasped only in a sympathetic appreciation of the philosophic world against which Machiavelli is revolting.

Machiavelli's teaching assumes souls formed by this world, the truth of which, by this late date, is no longer entertained in "learned" circles. The magnitude and audacity of Machiavelli's project escapes more recent interpreters who, importing categories of thought of a later date, might explain Machiavellian thought as the product of its time, conditioned by the moment in which he wrote. Or, worse, they might "psychologize" and trivialize an enterprise like *The Prince* as merely an effort to secure employment. Interestingly enough, both of these views are present in the *Dialogue* as Montesquieu's putative conception of the real figure of Machiavelli, whose reputation is finally acknowledged to be undeserved in either case.

The nature of Machiavelli's preference for republicanism is indeed a key to his thinking. *The Prince* praises republics for providing the most stable foundations for political orders. The Roman Republic in particular is repeatedly cited in his works as the proper ground for virtue. By recurring to Rome as an eminently respectable political model, Machiavelli recurs to pre-Christian times. A revolutionary understanding of virtue emerges from the study of ancient republics which crucially informs the project of the future as it renders Christian teachings and ancient political philosophy itself radically suspect.

In the final analysis, Joly's Machiavelli appears as the intransigent seeker of truth, despite personal consequences. His service to and sympathy for liberal republicanism, as portrayed in the *Dialogue*, would question the older conception of such a figure, while it also robs him of all moral controversy. The real Montesquieu has been sacrificed to the literary and didactic requirements of the *Dialogue*. Perhaps the real Machiavelli has also been sacrificed, though even more unwittingly, and with full conviction in the exactness of his more sophisticated portrait.

We might agree with Joly that Machiavelli was fundamentally motivated by the search for the enduring principles of political order, whose breakdown was acutely felt in his times. But this did not lead to a simple defense of former times and admiration for political conditions informed by the principle of "divine right." It is an all too obvious distortion to align Machiavelli with positions embraced by "conservative" partisans of the early nineteenth century or with Christian principles of rule that predominated in the Middle Ages. More important, the Machiavelli of the *Dialogue* is adamantly opposed to the regime he has just described as the "work of hell itself." He is not the sympathetic spokesman for the "new theories," promoted by Napoleon and the Saint-Simonians. Yet, as our analysis of the chapter on the religious founding indicates, there is perhaps an abiding affinity between the real Machiavelli and the Saint-Simonian doctrine that informs the project that Joly's Machiavelli describes.

The Saint-Simonians, like the real Machiavelli, ultimately look to security (or order) as the great desideratum of political life. Again, like the real Machiavelli in his praise of Rome, the political virtues appropriate to their historic project are nurtured in the element of a civil religion. In a call to reinfuse society with the elements of a revitalized Christianity, they may be seen as standing at polar opposites from the Florentine. In the end, however, the apparent revolt of the Saint-Simonians against Machiavellianism essentially takes place on Machiavellian grounds.

In jettisoning the transcendent elements of that faith and leaving its moral core, the Saint-Simonians intend to overcome the fatal division of the world introduced by traditional Christianity. This was classically diagnosed by the real Machiavelli as the deepest cause of political strife in holding politics to precepts it cannot follow. It is also the source of man's alienation from the earth, while it prevents him from even contemplating the steps necessary to secure its blessings. Machiavelli would be far from "recoiling in fright" from the spectacle of the harsh and despotic steps necessary to achieve a return to the conditions of political health, grandeur, and human happiness, as the Saint-Simonians see it.

Were we, unlike Joly, to take more seriously the scope of the real Machiavelli's vision, we might approach a truer appreciation of such an enigmatic figure. He is more than a mere analyst of tyranny who would warn and enlighten others about harsh truths in the real world. And he is more than a mere republican partisan. We would do well to take at face value his self-proclaimed mission as a new "Columbus." He has discovered a vast continent of thought that accommodates the likes of Bacon as well as Saint-Simon and his followers. From this perspective, the distortion of Machiavelli on Joly's part proceeds, ironically enough, from an underestimation of the thinker he so admired in the pages of the *Dialogue.* It is also a misreading of his moral intentions. These are much more ambiguous than Joly seems to realize. They should be much more questionable to one so ardently and intransigently moved by such considerations.

Notes

1. Speier, "The Truth in Hell," 23.

2. The sensitivity of Speier to an esoteric form of writing as a vehicle to reach several levels of audience in the same work is demonstrated in his essay on Grimelshausen. See Hans Speier, "Grimmelshausen's Laughter," in *Ancients and Moderns*, Joseph Cropsey, ed., (New York: Basic Books, 1964) 177-212.

3. Note the emphasis given Machiavelli on the Title page by capitalizing his name. The key to the *Dialogue* surely lies with him.

4. See Montesquieu *The Spirit of the Laws* III 3 and XIX 27.

5. Sulla's effort on behalf of the Republic is analyzed in greater detail in Montesquieu, *Greatness of the Romans* XI. Consider the comparison of Sulla and Augustus in

light of the *Dialogue* and Joly's stance vis-à-vis the modern Caesar.

> But in Sulla's whole life, even in the midst of his acts of violence, a republican spirit was revealed. All his regulations, although tyrannically executed, tended toward a certain form of republic. Sulla, a man of passion, violently led the Romans to liberty; Augustus, a scheming tyrant, conducted them gently to servitude. Under Sulla, while the republic gained its strength, everyone cried out against the tyranny, and while tyranny fortified itself under Augustus, people spoke of nothing but liberty.

Montesquieu also composed a *Dialogue between Sulla and Eucrates.* After gathering all power in Rome, Sulla abandons his station in weariness and disgust with his contemporaries. Joly's weariness and disgust is almost palpable.

6. According to a jingle at the time, the choice facing France was "Cavaignac" (order) or "le mic-mac" (chaos). Paris had not seen such anarchy since the Revolution. The army's repression of the Paris Commune insurgents was ruthless and chilling. Cavaignac was the Minister of War who designed the plan of battle against the "Reds."

7. The Belgian police had a close working relationship with the French police of the Empire. Belgian cooperation helped keep Paris informed of the refugee press. The French Ministry of Foreign Affairs occasionally persuaded Belgian authorities to suppress anti-French literature. Joly is aware of the complicity between France and smaller, easily intimidated countries on her borders. He is thus aware of the risks he ran in going to Brussels to have his work published. However, the freedom of the press that existed in Belgium made it a natural place for those like Joly to gravitate. Despite efforts of the police, the volume of clandestine literature that filtered through such channels was considerable. This included the latest works of Victor Hugo, Louis Napoleon's nemesis. See Howard C. Payne, *The Police State of Napoleon Bonaparte 1852-1860* (Seattle; University of Washington Press, 1960), 158.

8. Guerard, *France*, 309. The historian hits upon something important. Looking to the experience of the Soviet Union, some have remarked that censorship, not to mention the grossest repression, was conducive to great literary effort. Freedom—post-Empire— does not match up (as yet, anyway). Can what is observed in the Soviet Union be generalized to history as a whole? Can it be possible that artistic freedom stultifies high art? It would seem that the human spirit needs deprivation and a profound sense of lack to stimulate creativity. Nietzsche, in his portrait of the "Last Man" and many other places, has much to say about all this. Rousseau, too.

The ancients (Thomas, included), thought that creativity was something divine (as with the "divine Homer"). Its source was not deprivation and aspiration but a fullness of being.

Those conservatives who fret over the state of contemporary culture and its coarsening effect on the national character are correct. It certainly does seem that rock and roll is here to stay and, as it continues to go down in history, we are fated to dig it to the end.

I wonder if Vaclav Havel is even writing today. If Solzhenitsyn today wrote a great novel, I would feel more confidence in the ancient view of things.

9. See Bernstein, *The Truth About the Protocols*, 15-17.

10. Joly was adamant that his book was serious and meant to be taken seriously. He was at pains to distinguish it from "lampoons" and mere "pamphlets." This did not mean that his work would not appeal to his contemporaries in a manner similar to such writings. Albert Sorel beautifully captures the character of those who write and read such material. When "men of letters" (like Joly or Montesquieu) write "lampoons "or "pamphlets," the "men of the world are amused by them, courtiers condemn them, the author goes to prison, and the reader rubs his hands." Joly knew very well that he risked prison. I also think he thought his reading public would "rub their hands" before trying to grab a copy of his work. He hoped, once in hand and read, they would then be led to deeper reflection.

11. Thomas Babington Macaulay seems to think that Lord Bacon sees *The Prince* as "merely a piece of grave irony." It can best be understood as attempting to "warn nations against the arts of ambitious men." The reader is referred to the Appendix for further discussion of these matters.

12. Montesquieu, *Greatness of the Romans* XV.

13. In an interesting interlude in the *Dialogue*, a moment arises that shifts the attention of the interlocutors to questions of God's ultimate justice. A pregnant silence is Machiavelli's response. Obviously, we do not find a Christian "hell" in Joly's *Dialogue*. For example, there is no talk of hellfire, as in Christian mythology of the afterlife. There is talk of "banks" and "shores." This, in fact, reminds us more of Hades, the ancient conception of afterlife, where we find the rivers Styx and Lethe. Perhaps the judgment of a Christian God is not forthcoming. The revelation of this fact would, however, destroy the spur to knowledge and personal responsibility that Machiavelli endeavors to bring to bear on his interlocutor (and presumably the reader). Joly might be indicating to sympathetic readers that he shares the real Machiavelli's skepticism with regard to any hopes for "ultimate justice."

Socrates, of course, brought changes to the orthodox conception of Hades. He gave an account that would have philosophy as the most needful thing for humans. Those parched souls who greedily drink the waters of Lethe do not find relief. Rather, they are drugged into oblivion before their souls reenter the world from which they have departed. The whole human drama is to navigate the passage of Lethe in a manner that will not defile the soul. As it turns out, only the philosopher can do this. All other men, out of ignorance, have chosen defective "souls"—lives of pleasure or honor—as their fate in the next life. There is no rest for cities until philosophers are kings. Apparently, there is no rest for the soul until philosophy rules therein. Indeed, "only the truth will set you free," the reconstructed myth of Er seems to say. "Er" is another noble lie, is it not? Its tale would make the listener more philosophic. Is Joly's Machiavelli also perpetrating a lie to nobly benefit Montesquieu? These thoughts are prompted by Joly's account. I wouldn't put it past him that he intended to guide the reader to them. See the "myth of Er" in Plato's *Republic* 614a-621d for the Socratic transformation of Hades.

Before being accused of mistranslating the Title of Joly's work, it should be pointed out that a literal rendering would be *Dialogue in Hells*. This is curious, to say the least. Perhaps Dante's afterlife, with its circles of hell, inspires Joly.

14. Joly was, of course, right when he indicated that we stood, not before a benign end to history, but a new era of unprecedented despotisms. There are those who see that that era has definitively come to end with the fall of Soviet Communism. Daniel Mahoney thinks otherwise. It cannot be treated as a mere "episode,"—"an historic parenthesis,"—as it were. Totalitarianism is not something which "contemporary democrats need not reflect about at any length or with any sustained seriousness" as if it were of "merely historical or antiquarian interest." He puts what I want to say very well when he says that "reflexive dismissal of reflection about totalitarianism as part of a distant Cold War past ignores the permanent lessons that can and ought to be discerned from the lived experience of totalitarian despotism." See his Introduction to "Aron and Arendt and the Origins of Totalitarianism" in *In Defense of Political Reason*, 95. Aron (and Joly) would certainly agree.

15. See Machiavelli's "Prologue" in Christopher Marlowe's "The Jew of Malta" in *The Complete Plays of Christopher Marlowe*, Irving Ribner ed., (New York: Odyssey Press, 1963), 179. Machiavelli's statement—"there is no sin but ignorance"—is shocking to Christian ears and its conception of sin. Indeed, the *original* sin was to want to eat the fruit of the tree of knowledge and be the equal of God. Marlowe's Machiavelli, however, expresses sentiments not too distant from the founder of political philosophy, Socrates, (if we are indeed permitted to speak of "sin" in the context of pagan philosophy). Consider his statement that "knowledge is virtue." Ultimately it is as shocking to pagans as, perhaps, it is to Christians. Think through what Socrates was really doing by changing myth in note 12 above.

16. The author of the "Memoir of Machiavelli" (unidentified) writes that Machiavelli once responded to someone who reproved him for the teachings of *The Prince* with the following retort: "If I taught princes how to tyrannize, I also taught the people how to destroy them." That Machiavelli really once said this may be taken with a grain of salt. (See Chapter 1, note 2). Nevertheless, this author (Bohn himself?) tries to "make sense of Machiavelli" accordingly. "He probably develops in these words the secrets of his writings," he continues. "He was willing to *teach* both parties but his heart was with the republic." The "quote" from Machiavelli can be found in *The History of Florence*, xix. Joly basically agrees that such thinking best explains Machiavelli. Indeed, best reveals his "secrets."

Rousseau seems to be the most eminent thinker to share this view of *The Prince*. "In feigning to give lessons to kings, he gave great ones to peoples. *The Prince* of Machiavelli is the book for republicans," he declares. See *Social Contract* III 6. The 1782 edition of this work also had the following note attached to what was just quoted:

> Machiavelli was an honest man and a good citizen. But attached to
> the house of the Medici he was forced by the oppression of his coun-
> try to disguise his love of liberty. The choice alone of his execrable

Heroes manifests fairly clearly his secret intention and how contrary
the maxims of *The Prince* are to those of his *Discourses on Titus
Livy.* And his *History of Florence* shows how this profound political
man has up until now had only superficial and corrupt readers. The
Court of Rome censored his book severely, and rightly so. It was
what was being depicted in the clearest of lights.

17. Joly's view of history is not, it should be stressed, just a variation of "one damn
thing after another" school. Like Tocqueville, he could see inevitable trends that have
permanently changed political things. The process of democratization in the West is the
most massive and important of these trends, for sure. He would also point to certain
"constants" in the human condition that don't change—ambition and pusillanimity, for
example. His endeavor was not to rise to a philosophic view of history but to warn his
contemporaries about how the "constants" could change even what appears to be the
most auspicious of historic circumstances. Albert Sorel quotes Montesquieu as follows:
"As men have at all times had the same passions, the occasions giving rise to great
changes have been different, but their causes always the same." This is why the *Greatness of the Romans* stays fresh and instructive. I believe Joly held to similar views and
that is why he thought his little work would provide timeless lessons for those who love
liberty. For the Montesquieu quote, see Sorel, *Montesquieu*, 63.

18. According to Speier, Joly "was a lonely man devoted to moral principles and apparently never forgave anyone who did not live up to his standards. Perhaps his keen insight into politics and society was sharpened by a passionate desire to remain pure and
morally inviolate. If so, he paid with his life for such rigor." Speier, "The Truth in Hell,"
21.

19. My remarks benefited greatly from the penetrating insights of Pierre Manent on
Montesquieu as well as Daniel J. Mahoney's sensitive and illuminating remarks thereon.
See Pierre Manent, *La Cité de L'Homme* (Paris: Fayard, 1994). See also Daniel Ma-
honey's review essay on Manent's book "Modern Man and Man *Tout Court*," in
Interpretation 22, no. 3 (Spring 1990): 417-438.

The best book I have read that is exclusively on Montesquieu is Thomas L. Pangle's
Montesquieu's Philosophy of Liberalism (Chicago: University of Chicago Press, 1973).

20. See *The Spirit of the Laws* XI 9 entitled "Aristotle's manner of thinking." This
small chapter follows hard upon Montesquieu's discourse on the institutions of contemporary England. Ostensibly, it is a criticism of Aristotle for his misconceptions concerning monarchy. It is, in truth, more sweeping.

21. Who is not stunned by the shortest chapter in the whole of *The Spirit of the Laws*,
which gives an "idea" of the mentality of the despot and what despotic power really entails. Montesquieu writes:

When the savages of Louisiana are desirous of fruit, they cut the tree
to the root, and gather the fruit. This is an emblem of despotic government.

Was there not an even greater "savage" mentality in Soviet despotism that "cut down" ten million *kulaks* in the name of increasing agricultural production? This could serve as the "emblem" of Leninism. See *The Spirit of the Laws* V 13.

22. Montesquieu's words undoubtedly apply to his contemporaries:

> The character of the majority of courtiers is marked by indolent ambition, mean-spirited pride, lust for wealth without labor, antipathy to truth, flattery, treachery, perfidy, neglect of all engagements, contempt for civic duties, dread of virtue in the prince, and hope based upon his weaknesses—above all, an ingrained habit of sneering at virtue.

We should bear in mind that, in Montesquieu's thinking, once the animating principle in a regime is corrupted, there is little possibility to revive it. His hope for reform of France and the recovery of honor to avoid revolution was probably a slender one. The above quote can be found in Sorel, *Montesquieu*, 176 and is taken from *The Spirit of the Laws* III 5.

23. Exotic thinking and new ways of doing things would seduce the mind of France as they seduced the mind of Usbek. France's encounter with the secular apostles of the new order would make it impossible for it simply to return to the old ways. The Enlightenment would change the West, as Montesquieu clearly saw. (So, too, would it change Usbek's East.) He would want to bequeath what is best from the changes that were upon us all.

24. His reputation as a "conservative" is of longer date than the reputation that Joly would fix on him. It was in fact the first reaction to his thought. Helvetius, a not unfriendly contemporary of Montesquieu, criticized the author of *The Spirit of the Laws* because he was too fixated on the past and because he tried to ameliorate defective regimes and practices. "I know but two classes of government," he wrote, "the good and the bad; and the good are yet to be found." This is the mind of the ideologue who, in accepting nothing short of perfection, would jeopardize what good man can attain. Who cannot see in Helvetius the intellectual mindset of today? His remarks on Montesquieu can be found in Sorel, *Montesquieu*, 163.

25. What is absent from the modern world is the sense of a secure place for the human spirit, which gives rise to a noble use of leisure, taste, and refinement. According to Pierre Manent, this was present in France until the 1960s. It was then that the quintessentially French "aesthetic education" (to use Schiller's term) succumbed. It was, more precisely, when Daniel Cohn-Bendit, on the streets and with a smirk, drove the last and perhaps the greatest representative of old France from political office. The young wanted new heroes. It should be pointed out that in America and France, the new ones did not last too, too long. See Manent, *La Cité de l'homme*, 43. Before Aron, Montesquieu and Tocqueville were the most noble and intellectually defensible efforts to "plaidoyer pour L' Europe decadent."

26. The French nobility at the time Montesquieu wrote was not likely to appreciate his message: to wit, they were unaware of their own corruption and were leading France

to revolutionary destruction. Nor would they like to take the "medicine" of a return to ancestral ways that this political "Hippocrates" recommends.

Similarly, today's Americans would not likely relish being told that their "optimism" is hopelessly naive and breeds arrogance. Indeed, "radical surgery" would be necessary to disabuse them of this character trait, since all the horrors of the last century apparently were unable to do so. Nor should such "surgery" be undertaken, anyway. This is because much of what is best in the American "spirit" is also inextricably bound up with their optimism. At the source of our "arrogance" are standards that we apply not only to others but to ourselves. America at its best is constantly striving, internally and externally. Complacent self-absorption would be its downfall.

Ultimately, I believe, our optimism stems from a certain belief in morality that sees in the acts of a moral agent of goodwill the necessary and sufficient condition to affect change. Among other things, it discounts the fragility of the moral horizon that envelops civilized life.

All other countries identify themselves with a brief shining moment in the past. They sense that their best as a people somehow lies behind them. More prominent in their memories are the tragedies that still weigh heavily upon them. But what is the world to make of a people whose past weighs so lightly? To Americans, the past is mere grist for the future, not a huge boulder that blocks their way. They are continually building their historic home, only to abandon it before living therein, ever moving confidently forward. It is always just dawn in America. This is a people that has, as yet, not suffered a historic tragedy, at least not at the hands of others. Is this optimism the "tragic flaw" in a people that has heretofore not known tragedy?

A look to the pain of Vietnam (it would take "radical surgery" to remove it from my generation) may be instructive. The "flip side" of American optimism is a tendency to withdraw from the world when it proves recalcitrant to its "spirit"—which it inevitably will do, probably more often than not.

Vietnam began, I am convinced, in all optimism and with all good intentions. The war was conducted with our characteristic faith in technology, that is, that "calibrated bombing" would soon end it. We assumed that the "rational" incentives that would move Americans would move the Viet Cong. But Vietnam did not end quickly or well.

The "experience" has been interpreted in at least three different ways. Some Americans believe that we were, in a sense, "stabbed in the back." Our policy would have been vindicated had not certain elements—nearly "treasonable"—not blocked our efforts. Our real enemy was "within." Some Americans reacted with hostility to the world that proved so recalcitrant to them. "You're on your own now: *Débrouilléz-vous.*" Retreat from the world and a markedly lower profile followed the experience. (It is likely that Congress, much maligned, effectively represented the majority of Americans in this regard.) Equilibrium, tentative at best, followed only a decade later. And some Americans, like the first group, saw the problem as lying within but attributed it, not to dissident elements, but to something more fundamentally wrong. It is this group that the first group finds treasonable. It may indeed be the case that our deepest domestic divisions, still with us, have a foreign policy origin.

All these reactions pointed to a new "isolationism," which is really not a policy option anymore but nevertheless remains as a permanent temptation to Americans in the aftermath of their failures—the "flip side" of their optimism, I would argue. It is part of a post-Vietnam mentality that makes us turn to an "exit strategy" as the first priority in the use of our power, while the darker side of America's former involvement in Asia now forces us to tolerate no casualties to American soldiers and none to enemy civilians, not to speak of unacceptable "collateral" damage. Such presumptions drive the technology of our weapons systems. But what is astonishing is that our commanders in chief seem to accept these parameters as a basis for any military engagements. This cannot remain the basis of effective foreign policy, at least given the dangers of the world and the global responsibilities that we have assumed. Our Secretaries of State need a little talking to in the gardens of Rucellai.

Historically, Vietnam has been called a "non-event." This is arguable. In any case, there will inevitably be other Vietnams in America's future, which might indeed alter the course of human events. If Vietnam is in any way an instructive precedent, Americans will withdraw from the world, brood in their tent, Achilles-like (Holden Caulfield-like?), nursing their grievances. A plaintive "come home, America" will again be heard and, if the pain is deep enough, the bruised son will come back to the maternal call. Meanwhile, the pieces of the world will fall into place without American participation or influence. This will be unfortunate for America. It is not shallow patriotism that makes me think it will be unfortunate for the world, too.

At end, if American optimism cannot and should not be rooted out of the American character, it should, nevertheless, be made more clear-sighted, sober, and mature. In a word, it should be more "Montesquieuan." This, I think, would help forestall the appearance of other Vietnams in the future and would ultimately equip us to deal with them better when they happen.

Speaking of Montesquieu, and probably with the French uppermost in his mind, Albert Sorel stated that "when men tried to return to order, moderation, liberty, they returned to him." He also thought that Montesquieu's greatest gift to posterity was "something better than precepts." This is what I am talking about. "He left a method making it possible to develop his thought, and to apply it to cases that he never had foreseen." See Sorel, *Montesquieu*, 188 and 209.

27. The multimillionaire rock star, who has climbed the greasy pole of what passes for fame in contemporary America, even passes for "humane." This is when he or she gives a concert for AIDS victims or rain forests and doesn't take a cut in receipts. *Imagine!* Thomas Pangle even thinks there are "limits" to Montesquieu's "humanity." He writes that Montesquieu believed "that in order to benefit humanity one must never permit the sense of humanity to blur one's clarity of vision." Indeed, without this "clarity of vision" claims to "humanity" are all too often self-indulgent vanity. See Pangle, *Montesquieu's Philosophy of Liberalism*, 172.

28. Chapter 10 of this work is a historic survey of the various views of Napoleon III. It is also a polemic against the way history is done today. These remarks on Montesquieu should be kept in mind when reading this later chapter. Among other things, they show

that contemporary historicism is not the final word on the proper relation of man to history.

29. Hegel, famously and in a moment of epiphany, literally saw the Emperor in Berlin as the apotheosis of modernity. At Jena, shortly before, the Holy Roman Empire was dissolved by his force. The modern Caesar was upon Europe. Stendhal had glimpsed the phenomenon even in Italy. We could have had a key to the character of his conquests by his actions in Egypt. A host of scientists disembarked with his armies at the mouth of the Nile. There were 167 of them—civil engineers, astronomers, physicists, chemists, medical men; also musicians, writers, and artists. They would unlock the mysteries of mankind's deep past as they would infect ever after the life of the East. When former sovereigns conquered, they brought court jesters. Napoleon brought *savants*. In the age of world empire building to follow and the revolutions and wars of the last century, "ideas" would prove to be the most important arm in conquerors' arsenals. I follow Daniel Mahoney in use of the term "ideocratic" which, I think, he coined.

30. It is not appropriate for "intellectual valets" to praise such "heroes" of thought. I also realize that to confess to having heroes, intellectual or otherwise, is today something quaint, if not bemusing. But I have made my pilgrimage to La Brede, Montesquieu's ancestral home. The best Americans, by the way, in an age of heroes, forthrightly declared their admiration for Montesquieu. They called him "the celebrated Montesquieu" and at the most important moment in their history followed "the legislator of nations" as their guide. It should also be noted that Montesquieu has pride of place in Aron's magisterial study on sociology and its greatest practitioners. He is one of the few legitimate "philosopher-sociologists" in his view. See Aron's two-volume study *Main Currents in Sociological Thought* (London: Penguin Books, 1967).

Part V

The *Dialogue* and History

Chapter Ten

Solving the Enigma of Louis Napoleon

The historical controversy over Napoleon III remains strong even to this day. A good example of the more prominent views of the Emperor and his times is documented by Samuel M. Osgood in an edition of works entitled *Napoleon III*, part of a series of publications on "Problems in European Civilization." Professor Osgood presents a most useful compendium of the thought of historians and thinkers of both the nineteenth and twentieth centuries who are justly recognized for their analyses of Napoleon III and his regime. It illustrates well the nature of the ongoing controversy and the major lines of interpretation, each of which are strikingly different and claim many eminent partisans.[1]

Given this controversy, Joly's *Dialogue* has great value. As a close observer of Napoleon III and his times, he gives us useful insight as one who had actually observed and painfully experienced his rule. However, our claim for Joly is much greater than one that would treat the *Dialogue* merely as a contribution to historical studies by a contemporary of Louis Napoleon. In the breadth of his analysis, Joly can account for the many views of Napoleon III and, to a great extent, harmonize many of the most disparate interpretations. It may be that Joly's portrait of Louis Napoleon is simply the best and truest likeness to the historic character of the French Emperor.

Because of certain historicist notions he holds, Osgood would deny any claim that would present itself as constituting a more or less definitive understanding of an historical era. His position in this respect represents by now the long-standing thinking of the history profession as a whole. It also shares presumptions with the more radical post-moderns. It might be said of this latter group that they provided "metaphysical grounding" for the profession's historical intimations.[2]

Because such views increasingly reflect the prevailing orthodoxy among contemporary historical thinkers, they are perhaps accepted all too easily and unthinkingly. They will be critically examined here in some detail at the outset. After, we will turn to specific historical interpretations that would compete with Joly's understanding of the Emperor and his regime.

For Professor Osgood, the historical controversy concerning Napoleon III is to be expected, being rooted in the very nature of historical studies.

> History is no more the mere enumeration of facts than science
> is the sole gatherer of data. Any historian worthy of the name
> must approach his subject from a definite frame of reference,
> develop a thesis, and reach certain conclusions on the basis of
> available evidence. Unfortunately, Clio is the most fickle of
> muses. While she is at the historian's side to suggest the type
> of questions, she is nowhere to be found when it comes to
> formulating the answers. Left to his own devices the historian
> labors under severe handicaps. The unearthed evidence is of-
> ten fragmentary, the established facts are open to a variety of
> interpretations and, most damaging, he can never rerun the ex-
> periment to test his hypothesis.[3]

Scientific exactitude would seem to be the yardstick by which Osgood measures historical studies. At first view, history seems very much like modern natural science, properly understood. Like the scientific method, the historical method cannot be understood as a passive process and the mere collection of data. Like modern science, we might expect history to advance beyond primitive hypotheses to infinitely more refined explications of historical phenomena. Again, like modern science, historical understanding may be open-ended. It may tolerate numerous hypotheses until research confirms one or the other or points to a new and more conclusive theory—a "paradigm shift" in the historical understanding of things, if you will.[4]

However, history is necessarily more inexact than modern science, according to Osgood, because of the nature of its subject matter, which deals with human beings in a political context. The "facts" of history are past events beyond present observation. They cannot be re-tested and the "experiment" rerun. It follows that controversy is endemic to historical study. It is subject to inevitable disputes on a theoretical level among the many hypotheses that are offered to explain phenomena, and, "most damaging" of all, its "facts" can never be wholly adequate or "controlled" to yield the evidence necessary to confirm one interpretation or another.

In this light, it is perhaps more accurate to liken history to poetry rather than to science, and Osgood intimates as much when he says that it is subject to "Clio." Because its subject matter involves human beings, its proper realm belongs more to the muse than to the laboratory.

Following Osgood, a clear image of the status of history eludes us. The character of history seems to lie somewhere between that of science and poetry. While it wants to attain the rigor of science in its study of human phenomena, it is forced to draw upon the poet's peculiar powers to fathom the human soul and plumb the depths of human character in his reconstruction of the past. However, in distinction to poetry, the role of inspiration in its field seems to be constrained by its function to explain past events. The historian is not free to enter the realm of fantasy. The ambiguity of history and the powers it calls forth leaves scope to the intuition of the historian but not so broad as to do serious injustice to given facts, however controversial or fragmentary.[5]

Osgood's reference to an "historian worthy of his name," a name that he obviously prizes as one of honor, sheds some needed light on his conception of the historian's enterprise. According to Osgood, the historian develops a thesis based on available evidence from a "definite frame of reference." The key to the nature of history as irretrievably ambiguous and "fickle" perhaps lies here. The historian who is called to interpret past events does so from a certain point of view or frame of reference. This frame of reference itself would change with the movement of history, so historians continually stand, so to speak, on new grounds from which they observe the past. The differing views of past events are inevitably a part of the historical process itself. Subsequent views are not necessarily superior to less recent ones but are rather indicative of a change of perspective that cannot, given the open-ended nature of the historical process, mount to a view of the whole.

The manner in which Osgood introduces and presents the conflicting historical accounts of Napoleon III confirms this as his deepest view of the historian's enterprise. By and large, the main lines of interpretation are shown to change dramatically over time, establishing new perspectives. It is the capriciousness of the historical process itself that ultimately explains the frame of reference and the character of the "fickle" muse who presides over the historian's enterprise. In the realm of history, there are only eternal questions, we are told, with no definitive answers.

The Changing Views of Napoleon

Osgood's volume begins with the scathing portrait of Louis Napoleon by Victor Hugo, the literary giant of the nineteenth century who suffered exile under Napoleon's rule.[6] Hugo accuses his nemesis of "buffoonery" and of being "grotesque," dubbing him "Napoleon Le Petit," a man whose meager talents and lofty pretensions reveal him as totally unfit to have usurped the stage of history.

A similar thought is present in the analysis of Karl Marx, another contemporary of the Emperor.[7] Citing Hegel, Marx claims that all great events and personages reappear in one fashion or another on the great stage of history. Looking to the coup of Napoleon Bonaparte and his world-historic revolutionary achievement, Marx sees the achievement of his nephew as perhaps vindicating this thought of Hegel, but with a caveat. On the first occasion they appear in tragedy, in the second, in farce.

It was the searing prose of Hugo and the weighty authority of Marx that long colored perceptions of Napoleon III and finally, perhaps, prompted later scholars from a new "frame of reference" to struggle out from their influence. Marx, who observed the Napoleonic regime firsthand, and Hugo, who also suffered under it, were, in the minds of some, too close to the phenomenon to appreciate it properly. To Osgood, or at least some of the historians in his volume, such a "frame of reference" might rightfully yield to another that has available a greater store of historical data and is freer from the distortion born of personal experience.

The change in perspective on Napoleon III proceeded slowly. It was long understood that his election to the Presidency of the Second Republic owed much to the "magic of his name."[8] This view continued to denigrate Napoleon, as the key to his political success is found more in an accident of birth than any intrinsic merit. It was challenged by F. A. Simpson who saw in Louis Napoleon the considerable talent to seize and mold what fate had to offer.

The revision of Napoleonic historiography reaches the high-water mark in 1943 with Albert Guerard's *Napoleon III*. In the Emperor's foreign policy, Guerard sees Napoleon in the role of a "prophet" and as a forerunner of Woodrow Wilson. His desire was to convene a Congress of European powers like the Congress of Vienna, which would reorganize the continent, not on the basis of monarchic legitimacy, but as the future League of Nations, on the basis of the principle of the right to self-determination. Napoleon III may be indicted at the bar of history for being a failure, but he cannot be condemned, for he worked toward a future that is "still our hope today."[9]

Similarly, in domestic policy, Guerard credits Napoleon with espousing a democratic ideal toward which the future would inevitably move. Guerard believes that technological progress, widespread literacy, and the spread of cheap newspapers have removed the obstacles to direct democracy.[10] Indeed, "if we do not believe in direct democracy now, it is because we don't believe in democracy at all."

Guerard's critique of Marx and Hugo is implicit and is meant to speak to the Napoleonic historiography influenced by it. In opposition to Hugo, and a line of interpretation perhaps proceeding from him, Guerard claims that Napoleon's failure should not brand him as a fool or a knave any more than it would Napoleon I, Saint Louis, Lafayette, or Wilson. In opposition to Marx, he claims that Louis Napoleon's regime is "not a feeble caricature of the First Empire, but something altogether different and, in our opinion, of far more vital interest."[11]

In his *Liberalism and the Challenge of Fascism,* J. Salwyn Schapiro sees in the regime of Napoleon III the precursor of Mussolini's Italy and Hitler's Germany. Schapiro writes from a frame of reference acutely sensitized by the events of the Second World War and what it portends for the future of liberalism and a free world. According to Schapiro, the organization and policies of the Second Empire bear a striking resemblance to the fascist dictatorships of his time. He would take strong exception to Guerard and the rest of the revisionists who find "vitality" in Napoleonic policies and the "future hopes" for Europe. Schapiro sees in the plebiscitory democracies extolled by Guerard the possibilities of a frightening form of tyranny backed by popular support. It's the actual experience of Hitler's Germany that would illustrate the full range of such a regime's horrors.[12]

Given Osgood's historicist presumptions, the subtitle of his edition *Napoleon III—Buffoon, Modern Dictator, or Sphinx?* is patently disingenuous. The historical figure of Louis Napoleon is necessarily enigmatic and sphinx-like, and this editor of "The Problems in European Civilization" says as much. The historical problem of Napoleon III cannot be definitively resolved if, as Osgood implies, each view makes a claim to a certain "validity" from its own particular perspective.

The "problem" of Napoleon III is even more complicated than Osgood might have it. Not only is the historian himself historically conditioned in his view of the French Emperor, but so is the student whose access to Napoleon III is through works that are, in a certain sense, already fundamentally dated from his point of view. It is as if the real phenomenon of Napoleon III retreats with every effort to understand it. It is not merely a fickle muse who presides over the historian's enterprise but a perverse "evil genius." Apparently, we cannot avoid the subtle subjectivism of the historian or even the student who is conditioned by a historical horizon that interposes itself between the phenomenon of Napoleon III and its scholarship.

The Problems of Contemporary Historiography

At this point, certain problems with Osgood's position manifest themselves. If forced at the outset to grant that historical truth is irretrievable, we might expect the slackening of scholarly effort or the trivializing of the historian's task. Serious scholarly effort can be undertaken only in the belief that the past is open to human understanding and that it crucially affects our understanding of things important.

Within Osgood's *Napoleon III*, we have evidence of the trivializing of historic themes and a scholarship marked by frivolousness on the one hand and pedantry on the other. As students of Joly, we might be surprised to see Napoleon's efforts to control the minds of his subjects through the manipulation of public opinion as nothing too disconcerting. Rather, he is understood as employing methods which might "evoke the admiration of such moderns as George Gallup and Elmo Roper."[13] We may also wonder if the strained literary analogies of calling Napoleon a "Chekovian romantic" or the "Hamlet of history" illuminates anything beyond its pretentiousness.[14] To say the least, such scholarship contrasts with the seriousness of Joly. In 1864, the year the *Dialogue* was published, Joly thought he discerned a project that would crucially affect the fate of free men. In the depth of his analysis, he exposed some of the currents of modern political life that were, most ominously, to determine subsequent history.

Osgood would have us understand that history, as it unfolds, changes the perspective of the historian and that this crucially influences the interpretations of the past. It follows that the Schapiro view of Napoleon III, sensitized by the phenomenon of Hitlerism, differs from that of contemporaries of the Emperor, who were cut off from such a perspective and were perhaps too close to events to perceive them dispassionately. It is curious then that of all the works in the Osgood collection, it is Schapiro, writing in the aftermath of Hitler, who stands closest to Joly, a contemporary of Napoleon III. Writing from "different frames of reference," the two thinkers assess things in remarkably similar ways. According to them, Napoleon's regime is best understood as an unprecedented attempt at founding a new form of despotism.

Moreover, of all the essays in Osgood's collection, the most disparate interpretations are those of Guerard and Schapiro. We find that the former work was published in 1943 and the latter in 1949, that is to say, both from a perspective that was familiar enough with the phenomenon of Mussolini and Hitler. We may begin to wonder if indeed the historian's thought is so time-bound that it cannot rise to a detached view of the past and that scholarly effort, even beyond centuries, cannot attain similar views in independent approaches to historical reality.

Osgood implied that all historical perspectives, even the most serious, are inherently limited. Alternatively stated in a more positive way, the views of historians can make similar claims to being valid. It is at this point that the bankruptcy of Osgood's position shows itself. The theses of Guerard and Schapiro are diametrically opposed in crucial respects. If they are both to claim a share of validity, then the real phenomenon of Napoleon III may be said to disappear for all intents and purposes. We cannot claim that the policies of Napoleon III "present the hope for us today" and the prototype for Hitlerism, unless we assume that the proponents of these views are fascists, which, most certainly, they are not.

If we were to simultaneously defend the views of both Schapiro and Guerard, then the reality of Napoleon III becomes so vacuous that we might be discouraged from any effort at understanding him in the first place. Thought through, Osgood's position would lead to the trivializing of history. It turns history into a certain kind of historiography that places the emphasis not so much on understanding history as the historian. This is the undeniable bent of Osgood's Introduction and his preoccupation in the individual précis that introduces each historical piece. It is a narcissistic view of the historian that forgets his more humble task of explication. In the end, the "historian worthy of his name," in Osgood's sense, is not.

Furthermore, Osgood's conception of history and the historian's enterprise would also blunt our moral sense, the development of which, in the ancients' view—one thinks of Plutarch, in particular—was one of the chief benefits of historical study. The proper study of history was seen to lend sublimity to our lives by presenting us with situations and personalities beyond the reach of our daily occupations. In such situations, we are called to exercise our moral judgment in affairs of state that critically serves our civic education.[15] The ethical relativism that is the upshot of Osgood's position destroys the important critical functions of the study of history. We cannot simply leave the phenomenon of Napoleon III at "Buffoon," "Modern Dictator," "Hope for the Future," "Elmo Roper"—whatever. If we are to believe Joly, the view espoused by Osgood would also lead us to our peril. The germ of future history lies in the policies of Napoleon III. To Joly and more traditional historians, Osgood's approach would render inscrutable what needs greatest light, what speaks to the knowledge and well-being of future generations.

In denying that historical understanding can be definitively reached, or, alternatively, in maintaining that history is necessarily enigmatic, we are presented with an unexamined dogmatism that masquerades as openness to all historical views. For some of the reasons indicated, we cannot rest satisfied with such a position and would do well to approach our subject matter in a different, less dogmatic, and more modest manner.

The Freshness of the Old Historical Approach

From Osgood's remarks on the nature of history, we might be tempted to see historical studies as flawed because they cannot attain the exactitude of science. In the thought of Aristotle, we can find the proper corrective to the prevailing view of history and historical studies, insofar as Osgood may be deemed a representative spokesman.

In the *Nichomachean Ethics*, Aristotle writes: "Our discussion will be adequate if it achieves clarity within the limits of the subject matter. For precision cannot be expected in the treatment of all subjects alike." With evident common sense, Aristotle might accuse Osgood and others of a kind of foolishness for wanting to hold history to strictures it cannot meet. Because it fails in this regard, we are not justified in deeming it fundamentally enigmatic. Clarity can be had, but within the limits of the subject matter.

> For a well educated man is one who searches for that degree
> of precision in each kind of study which the nature of the sub-
> ject matter at hand admits. It is obviously just as foolish to ac-
> cept arguments of probability from a mathematician as to de-
> mand strict demonstrations from orators.[16]

On the one hand, we should expect conflict among historians. This is because the subject matter of history is controversial, dealing with the great political questions, sometimes, indeed, "eternal questions," whose answers determine the lives and happiness of human beings. A historian "worthy of the name" is not, as Osgood insists, a mere codifier of facts or events but must assess the thoughts and actions of men with regard to important matters. For us to come to a reasonable understanding of the past through the use of history, we are forced at some point to deal with the various deeds of historical actors and the opinions of historians themselves. On the other hand, we would be surprised if considerable light were not shed on historical problems through these same opinions. Intelligent men motivated by questions that passionately interest them, men of outstanding heart and intellect, like Hugo and Marx, are bound to understand something of what lies under investigation. Indeed, dealing with the eminent historians in Osgood's edition, "the presumption is that they are right in at least one or perhaps even in most respects," as Aristotle intimates. In consciously choosing provocatively different views of Napoleon III for his edition, Osgood has perhaps obscured vast areas of similarity. Following Aristotle, we might indeed find controversy beyond shared views, but we would be loath to endow it with too much significance, in the manner of Osgood.[17]

Osgood grants too much importance to conflicting historical opinion. The various perspectives of historians confirm a view of history that was Osgood's from the outset—that is to say, the irremediable enigma of history. Yet, this original view is not without controversy. Indeed, the questions it raises are more controversial than the views of the historians in his edition, whose more limited and modest theses do not presume to rise to a view at such philosophic heights. Rather, they endeavor to understand a concrete historical personage, Napoleon III, and can be judged independently by the ability of their interpretations to explain in a plausible and coherent manner the events and problems of his reign, brought to light in many revealing ways by the efforts of other historians.

Before we would "resolve" the controversy regarding Louis Napoleon in the manner of Osgood, it would be better and certainly less presumptuous to seek a different course. We want an interpretation that can account for the regime of Napoleon III in a way that will also allow us to comprehend some of the reasons why it has been the subject of so much historical attention and dispute. We rest dissatisfied with Osgood, who presents the absurd spectacle of wanting to deal with the Napoleon III controversy by a position that is at once dogmatically accepted and inherently more controversial.

Toward a Better Understanding of Napoleon III

Moreover, contrary to Osgood, the conflicting interpretations of Napoleon III might point the way to a more adequate understanding. Two opinions that obviously conflict, as in the case of Schapiro and Guerard, might shed light on areas of one another's interpretation that would otherwise remain poorly illuminated. The conflict would be a spur to a more adequate interpretation, either by resolving the differences in their views by a third more inclusive and superior interpretation, or when the two are totally irreconcilable, by exercising our best judgment as to the adequacy of one or the other. In effect, in leaving the controversies in his *Napoleon III* inconclusive and "enigmatic," Osgood abandons the historian's task where it might well begin in seriousness.

In fact, a line of interpretation developed from Joly may lead "within the limits of the subject matter" to the best and truest appreciation of Napoleon III. Beyond all the works in Osgood's edition, it represents the most comprehensive view of the Emperor and his regime and can account for the others' views in doing justice to their particular insights. Its analysis of the political, intellectual, and material forces of the Second Empire can serve as a basis from which to judge the adequacies of competing and less comprehensive positions. Of particular importance to the Joly analysis of Napoleonism is the role that Saint-Simonian thought plays. The reader is asked patience, for we must turn again to it to resolve the ambiguities of his rule.

A Return to Saint-Simonian Thought

The Saint-Simonians perceived the core of the contemporary crisis to be an intellectual one, manifesting itself in the apparently irreconcilable conflict between two traditions of thought. These traditions were characterized as "liberal-humanitarian" and "conservative-authoritarian."[18] The first tradition of thought finds expression in Enlightenment politics and a view of legitimate state authority as derived from individual rights. According to the secular strain of the second tradition of thought, the principles of the Enlightenment misrepresent the nature of the state and would tear apart the fabric of society.

There are no universal rights of man as man predating civil society. There are only rights of men within particular societies, guaranteed by specific institutions. These are informed by age-old historical forces and not by abstract reasoning about man in his "natural state." Far from being an artificial creation, civil society is coeval with human existence and is its condition. History demonstrates that the doctrine of natural rights leads to a revolutionary politics. The regime it would erect, by recurring to consent as the source of legitimacy, tends to disturb the salutary prejudices and habits of the citizen. These are the matrix of civil society and serve to put the necessary authority of the state beyond question. The root of legitimacy in the "conservative-authoritarian" tradition of thought is thus found not in consent but in prescription and the duties to a sovereign that are owed, not conditionally, but as part of a sacred heritage.

The Saint-Simonians saw revolutionary thought as serving a "critical" function that dissolved the ancient authority and prepared the way for the reintegration of society and a state whose authority rested on new principles. Their project was an attempt to harmonize the two traditions of thought and much of its ambiguity lies therein.

The Saint-Simonians lay emphasis on the "humanitarian" aspects of the first tradition of thought in elevating the practical teaching of Christianity to the status of a new religion. Society is to be oriented by the progressive amelioration of the material, moral, and intellectual conditions of the poor. They intend thereby to affect a synthesis of Christianity and the scientific revolution, which was originally heralded by Bacon (following Machiavelli) in a call away from an orientation by "heavenly principalities" and toward "the relief of man's estate." In jettisoning the transcendent elements of Christianity, the Saint-Simonians wanted to retain their moral code, which would then be practically implemented by a scientific society. Science, which is morally neutral, insofar as it increases human power over nature but does not determine the ends for its use, would then serve moral objectives.

Politically, the Saint-Simonian revolution calls for the supplanting of liberal institutions by an authoritarian state. Political power culminates in a leader whose legitimacy is based on an appeal to "genius" in the name of a revolutionary historical project. The liberal system of government was seen as defective in institutionalizing conflict among groups of men and by cutting off from citizens a horizon of higher shared purposes and the leaders who can give effective voice to them. In the Joly analysis, the doctrine of popular sovereignty, which emanates from consent theories of liberalism, finds its proper ground, not in individual voices, but in the all-powerful despot who practically fulfills the historic interests of the people.

Some of the radically democratic features of the first tradition of thought are retained in the policies of Napoleon III. The role of the plebiscite, for example, is to forge direct identification of the masses with the leader, in whose person they are to find the representation of their higher moral and collective selves. As Joly indicates, Napoleon leaves liberal institutions intact, but gutted, and finally replaced by an authoritarian and hierarchical politics. Positions of power were to be filled, not as in conservative regimes, by an aristocracy of birth, but by an aristocracy of "merit." The leader will fill its ranks with those distinguished by dedication and service to the new society.

What emerges in the Joly analysis is a regime that would graft the "humanitarian" aspects of the one tradition of thought to the "authoritarian" and hierarchical politics of the other tradition. Authoritarian politics replaces liberal institutions but is severed from a conservative social order and is oriented toward material progress. The Saint-Simonians accept the standards of what constitutes a healthy "organic" society from the "conservative-authoritarian" tradition of thought but want to reintegrate society on a moral basis that takes for its objective goals that derive from the "liberal-humanitarian" tradition. It is no longer the prescriptive elements of a social order that endow it with legitimacy but its orientation to the future and the fulfillment of the emergent demands of history.

The Napoleonic regime, as presented by Joly, displays a discrete but subtle combination of strains of thought that are fundamental to post-Revolutionary modernity and formerly thought irreconcilable. Rather than demonstrating the validity of historicist premises, the controversy over Napoleon III can be traced to this fact and the peculiar Saint-Simonian synthesis.

A Return to the Controversy

It is from this source that light is shed on both Guerard and Schapiro and the discrepancies in their thought. Guerard identifies with the "humanitarian" aspects of Napoleon III's regime. This distinguishes his empire from that of Napoleon I, whose revolution advanced by the sword and unthroned kings, finally to enfranchise property owners and their narrow class interests. For Guerard, it is the social goals of Napoleon III that render his regime "more vital," democratic, and humane.

In emphasizing the humanitarian aspects of Louis Napoleon's regime, Guerard reveals himself to be remarkably unperturbed in the face of the authoritarianism that is its political counterpart. The Saint-Simonian view shares with the ideologies of the twentieth century a call for the universal transformation of society as a mandate of history. Authoritarianism and violence are perhaps inherent in such a call and are required in doses proportionate to the radicalism of their visions. So strong is the hold of a "humanitarian" future on the mind of Guerard that he seems willing to exonerate the violence and authoritarianism of Louis Napoleon even in the face of failure.

Unlike other historians, Guerard does not misconceive the anti-liberal bias of the Napoleon regime. He praises the attempt to inaugurate direct democracy in a modern industrial society as the litmus test of our sincerity for democratic principles. Such a regime is taken for granted to be desirable. The spread of cheap newspapers, among other things, makes it feasible. What is astonishing is that Guerard can make such a claim in the face of Hitler, who was indeed "educated" on cheap newspapers.

Up to now, we accused Guerard of being perhaps too complacent in the face of violence and the authoritarian aspects of Napoleonic rule. He is merely perhaps too sanguine about the hold of morality, in the absence of liberal institutions and a restraining system of checks and balances, over the minds of the citizenry. Given unscrupulous rulers and their access to modern communications, it is doubtful whether the better motives of citizens can be relied upon to guarantee a moral politics. In the end, it is Guerard's moral convictions that exonerate Napoleon's crimes in the name of "humanity" and it is his faith in the power of these convictions that leads him to a culpable political naiveté.

Still other historians fail altogether to perceive the anti-liberal bias of Napoleonic government. This is the case of Theodore Zeldin, who sees Napoleon as trying to establish in France the liberal and parliamentary government of nineteenth-century England.[19] Zeldin's interpretation hinges on a proper understanding of the last years of Napoleon's reign which, according to certain historians, intended to transform the Authoritarian Empire into the Liberal Empire.

A reading of Joly makes us suspicious of any interpretation of Napoleon that would make of the Emperor a sincere partisan of liberalism. Liberal ideas of liberty—limited government and individual freedom—do not represent the expressed Napoleonic idea of the liberty that was to "crown the edifice" of his government. Deference on Napoleon's part to liberal institutions was, at first, a matter of lip-service to effect a transition to a regime of a wholly different character, where liberty is reflected in a "return to loving obedience" to a ruler and to laws that issue from an historic mandate.

The "liberalization" of the regime was a response to a series of setbacks that were "to transform the resolute conqueror of power into a wavering, fumbling Emperor."[20] Joly, writing at the height of Napoleon's power, did not face the ignominious conclusion of the Napoleonic regime. Nevertheless, a line of interpretation that accepts the Joly analysis would see the liberalization of the Empire in the manner of A. F. Thomson, as illuminating the problems of autocracy in attempting to modify itself and placate its critics, without losing control.[21]

The interpretation of J. Salwyn Schapiro would correct any view that misperceives the autocratic intentions of Napoleon and, contrary to Guerard and others, its more ominous implications. To Schapiro, Guerard's politics represents not the rightful extension of democratic principles, but some of the key elements of modern tyranny. Schapiro cites Nazi apologists themselves who claim that the regime of Napoleon is in fact the only relevant historical parallel to the rise of National Socialism.[22]

Schapiro implies that Napoleon shared the same political goals as the National Socialists, which were rooted in a common recognition of the inadequacies of liberal institutions to solve the social problems of the day and mend the cleavages that threatened society. The solution lay in authoritarian and plebiscitory leadership and in re-channeling revolutionary socialism, through certain social policies, toward a virulent form of nationalism.

According to Schapiro, the Second Empire did not differ in kind from Hitlerism but was merely a weaker version of that phenomenon. He lays particular emphasis on the fact or observation that *"the weakness of the fascist pattern of Napoleon lay in that it did not include totalitarianism."*[23] By this, Schapiro means that Napoleon never attempted to "coordinate" the political, social, and economic life of France into a uniform and unified system run by a dictatorial machine.

Moreover, Schapiro continues, such coordination would have been impossible due to certain external factors. Among these he lists the fact that France was primarily an agricultural nation with no large combination of basic industries or a large organized class of workers. In addition, there was not yet in existence the easy and rapid means of communication and transportation—radio, motion pictures, automobiles, and airplanes, which can be readily used by the dictator for propaganda and other purposes. For these reasons, totalitarian control was beyond the reach of the nineteenth-century dictator who only anticipates his twentieth-century counterpart.

It is interesting in light of the many similarities between them that this reading of Napoleon's intention clashes with that of Joly. Though unfamiliar with twentieth-century totalitarianism, of course, Joly sees an attempt at similar politics by the nineteenth-century Saint-Simonian despot. The Saint-Simonians understood both the present limitation and future opportunities for such social coordination. Such control would be progressively augmented with the advance of scientific society as the principles of material "progress" and authoritarian "order" came to be increasingly reconciled.

For all of Schapiro's contribution in drawing attention to the parallels between Napoleonism and modern tyrannies, he fails to make explicit what distinguishes the former from the latter. Napoleon intended a social revolution different in kind from the National Socialists. The light of Joly and the Saint-Simonians reveals a profound difference between the goals of Napoleonism and Hitlerism. The former can in no way be represented as the latter "in a diluted form." Napoleon may be said to accept certain "humanitarian" aspects of the "liberal-humanitarian" tradition in adopting the relief of man's estate as the social goal of his authoritarian politics. In fact, it is this element of that tradition which has risen to the status of a practical religion, having the amelioration of the lot of the poor as its central tenet.

In alluding to Napoleonism as merely the herald of Hitlerism and its weaker nineteenth-century version, Schapiro fails to appreciate the truly radical nature of National Socialism and is guilty of confusing the proper understanding of the two phenomena. National Socialism may be said to reject the whole "liberal-humanitarian" tradition of which Napoleon accepts and elevates a part. According to the Nazis, "1932" effectively "repeals 1789," that is to say, a revolutionary tradition that was advanced in certain elements of the thought of the Saint-Simonians.[24]

The National Socialists would reject what we have described as the "humanitarian" aspects of Napoleon's policy as a perversion of the natural order, which has the strong serve the weak. For the Nazis, this would represent the extreme of Western decadence by instituting a rule marked by hedonism and animated by a form of "pity" that is elevated to the status of a new religion. Certain historical interpretations, (Guerard's, among others), have insisted upon the "weak" but "well-intentioned" motives of Napoleon. Indeed, he wasn't made of the stuff of Julius Caesar, or his uncle, Napoleon I, not to mention Hitler and the Nazis.[25]

An interpretation that simply sees in Napoleon III the premonitions of Hitler fails to grasp what made the latter unique. In rejecting Western tradition, it was not a conservative reaction that was intended but something revolutionary in its own right. The Nazi revolution wanted to go beyond even nationalism and the nation state in erecting a new form of hierarchical rule, universal in scope, which contemplated the reinstitution of slavery in the service of "higher culture" and the racially pure.

In the end, Guerard's and Schapiro's interpretations grasp certain aspects of the phenomenon of Napoleon III but fail to appreciate others that would make their analyses more accurate and complete. Guerard may be criticized for failing to grasp and appreciate the implicit tyranny in the autocratic principles of the emperor because he passionately shares his social goals. Schapiro may be criticized for failing to appreciate those goals, which crucially distinguish Napoleonism from Hitlerism and make it perhaps an early prototype of modern despotism but one that is less radical and "softer." The valid parts of their theses point to their mutual deficiencies and a more comprehensive interpretation that Joly would admirably serve. The Saint-Simonian elements in the Second Empire begin to resolve the ambiguities in the person and policies of Napoleon III. Through such a line of interpretation, the sphinx's riddle begins to be solved, as the two most disparate interpretations are reconciled from its point of view.

Marxian Class Analysis

Beyond Guerard and Schapiro, Karl Marx explains Napoleon's election and consolidation of power in terms of the structure of French society at the time, with particular emphasis on his relation to the peasantry. Such is the authority and influence of Marx that Marxian class analysis has dominated much of subsequent scholarship. Though they would insist that the key to Napoleonism lay not in relation to the peasantry but to other classes, subsequent scholars are perhaps not aware of their deeper indebtedness to Marx. Their scholarship shares a view of history as materially determined and dependent on the alignment of certain social forces, however differently interpreted.

According to Marx, an understanding of the underlying social forces can resolve the sphinx-like character of the Second Empire and the apparent contradictions in the rule of Napoleon III.

> The conditions of peasant life in France are the solution to the riddle of the general elections of December 20th and the 21st which carried the second Bonaparte to the top of Mount Sinai—not to receive laws but to give them. [26]

The Eighteenth Brumaire traces the changes in the condition of peasant life between the Empires and its critical political effect. By the revolution of Napoleon I, serfdom was abolished and the peasant, formerly tied to a manor and lord, became a freeholder. The roots of this system of small landholding struck deep and "cut off the supply of nutriment upon which feudalism depended." Peasant landholding bred a staunch sense of individualistic proprietorship. This development represented a social advance over the feudal system. It served as a buffer for the bourgeoisie in guaranteeing against a reactionary coup de main of the old overlords.

By the time of the Second Empire, a system that had first enfranchised and enriched the French country folk now served their exploitation. The Revolution had put in place a system that encouraged free competition and enterprise in the rural districts where agriculture was practiced. It was productive enough to permit the initial growth of industry in the cities. However, the inevitable result, over two generations, was the pauperization of the former peasantry and their exploitation, not by feudal lords, but by the urban usurer. Real modernization in the countryside was effectively blocked by the hidebound conservatism of the peasant who resisted the application of new techniques of cultivation and husbandry. The patchwork nature of the countryside and the small scale of the farming enterprise proved resistant to market forces that would break the hold of that tradition.

The inefficiencies of petty landholding became markedly apparent in its incapacity to support the needs of the burgeoning towns. The local proprietor found it increasingly difficult to support himself and his extended family. His sons were drawn to the ranks of vagabondage or absorbed into the *lumpenproletariat* of the city. The local proprietor found himself bilked by the creditor and increasingly pressed by taxation resulting from the revenue needs of an increasingly sophisticated society.

In trying to maintain the capitalist order, the bourgeoisie became the natural ally of the priest and the prefect against the schoolmaster and the mayor. The former impresses upon the peasant the fatality of its lot and preserves it from the influence of more enlightened educators and popular representatives. The credulous masses could be made to see the cause of their ruin not in the social system but in "higher" causes, the chastening hand of God that brings to bear a fateful drought or a bad harvest.

Prior to 1848, there were fewer than 250,000 voters in France. In the 1848 elections to the Constituent Assembly, the franchise reached over 9,000,000, which included the peasant as the vast majority. Such a constituency was prepared for the appearance of a Moses who would lead them from the wilderness, which was, in actuality, the social condition of modern society that resulted in bondage to the bourgeoisie. The sudden leap to universal manhood suffrage created a political void that was filled by Louis Napoleon and "the magic of his name."

Napoleon III ended the political confusion by authoritarian leadership. His "commandments" had for their object the defense of the status quo and the values of traditional French society. The first two "idées napoleonnes" called for the defense of private property, in deference to the interests of the petty landowner, and in defense of the interests of the bourgeoisie. In occupying such ground, the second Bonaparte wanted to extend the principles of the first Bonaparte. Yet, subterranean forces of society had changed so as to render the politics of Louis into a feeble caricature of his uncle, a farcical parody that stood, not for revolutionary advance, but for the more retrograde elements of society.

In Marx's analysis, the peasantry constitutes a kind of "class" with distinct interests that distinguish it from other classes in society. Their farms are of a size to support only extended families and allow for no division of labor or scientific principles of agriculture. A score of such plots, like individual atoms, form a larger entity, the village. These combine in turn and form aggregates called departments, through which a strong central authority, inherited from the feudal past and modernized to suit the times, exerts its control. To accede to this power is the prize of all revolutions and has a compelling allure for conspirators and romantic adventurers like Louis Napoleon.

Although the peasants share certain interests, they find no organized expression. The poor quality of communications and social intercourse that marks life in the countryside requires that their interests be represented. They cannot assert those interests in their own name. Napoleon III appears as that representative but also as a "lord and master" whose authoritarian rule will protect the peasant against other classes.

Nurtured in superstition, the peasants accept the second Bonaparte as the Messiah and the savior of the old order established by the first Napoleon, whom, by this date, they have come to deify. According to Marx, the political influence of the peasantry find its "last expression" in the autocratic regime of Louis Napoleon. It is through an appeal to the peasant that Napoleon not only comes to power but rules, always dependent on satisfying such a constituency for the continued popularity that is required in his plebiscitory rule.

In the cities, the threat from revolutionary elements likewise drives the bourgeoisie to the strong government of Louis. In a view unclouded by sentiment or superstition, the bourgeoisie sees in Napoleon the savior of the same order that supports their interests and an instrument that could be wielded to serve their will. In thus coming to the defense of property in the city and countryside, Napoleon seemingly stands for a harmony of interests that coalesced behind him in the landslide election of president in December 1848.

Yet, what served for purposes of election is the cause of the contradictions of his rule. In fact, the interest of the peasants no longer coincides with the interests of capital and the bourgeoisie, as during the reign of Napoleon I. The election of Napoleon only masks the profound conflict of interest that marks the relation of the bourgeois to the peasant and which rends society at large. It is a conflict characterized by the exploitation of the city over the countryside, and, within the city, of the bourgeoisie over the proletariat.

The peasants would find their natural allies in the more progressive elements of the urban proletariat. The coalescence of such forces promises to end the contradictions that rend society by the radical overthrowing of the capitalist order that exploits them both. To forestall this, Louis wants to keep the interests of the different classes distinct and increase their separate dependency on the central power of the state. "That is why his government alternatively seeks to win and then humiliate this class or that." It is a policy that can give to one class only by robbing another. While Louis wants to be the benefactor of all classes, his policy ends up arraying them all against himself.

The contradictions inherent in such a rule reflect the contradictions inherent in society and create the pressure that leads to the enormous expansion of the state's power. The dictatorial coup d'état of 1851, which ended the Second Republic, is an event that proceeds logically from what is required to maintain the social order. The after-effects of this event are constantly felt as Louis is forced to a "miniature coup" every day against the forces that would gather strength and align themselves against him. He attempts to resolve the contradictions of society through continual conspiracy.[27]

The expansion of state power finds expression in a huge bureaucracy, "well fed and well dressed," which creates an "artificial caste" alongside the other classes of society. For them, the survival of the regime is a "bread and butter question." Their goal is to draw "Californian prizes out of the state treasury." This caste attempts to regulate the pressures of class conflict that plays itself out within the constraints of autocratic rule. The culminating point of the "idées napoleonnes" is the preponderance of the army, whose ranks will be filled with members of the proletariat. The most incendiary elements of modern society are co-opted and enlisted to the established order and framework of traditional French society. At the same time, the material interests of the working class are appeased through certain social policies.

Under the First Empire, the army was filled with "the flower of peasant youth" who defended the glory of the nation and a revolution through which they came to own their land. The narrow lives of the peasant were sublimated to a nationalism that appealed to their collective selves as it advanced their private interests. The army of the Second Empire was less sublime in seeking to expand the coercive powers of the state. Its "heroic" feats consisted of police raids to bring the peasantry to heel.

A huge bureaucracy and army, supported by a burdensome taxation, puts further internal pressure on the regime. This is relieved by an imperialistic policy that risks defeat in foreign wars and only delays the dissolution of society. In any event, the state finally exhausts itself and falls along with the social structure that supports its heavy weight. Before it collapses, the opposition of the state to the true interests of society is displayed "in all its nudity." This robs the state of all dignity and renders it loathsome and ridiculous.

Marx sees a revolution forthcoming. In fact, the regime of Napoleon III prepares the way for revolution that alone can resolve the profound contradictions in his empire. Put in place by Louis is a centralized structure of government that is indispensable to modern society. The industry and commerce that temporarily thrive under this strong government augment the ranks of the working class in whose interest the revolution will come and under whose direction it will fall.

By revolution, this class will inherit the machinery of government that will construct a new society based on common property and a rule in the common social interest—what came to be called the "dictatorship of the proletariat." It is this class alone that has a true social mission. Its consciousness is formed by common productive enterprise in the increasingly interdependent network of industrial society. Its self-interest serves the common interest in a revolution that unleashes the unlimited productive capacities of society with a view to benefits shared by all productive members according to their needs.

The intellectual vanguard of the working class is already present in France and is articulating the growing consciousness of the working class and the future demands of history. Napoleon's string of decrees can only forestall the day of the "true socialists." They have correctly perceived the material nature of history that demands the social revolution that Napoleon III attempts to thwart.

In this light, history proves itself to be quite cunning. Napoleon has served the future in spite of himself. He has augmented the ranks of the working class and helped create the government machinery that their leaders will employ after the revolution. Moreover, his parody of Napoleon Bonaparte has freed the nation from the yoke of tradition in robbing imperial rule of all sublimity. The future will rise upon the ruins of the militarist and bureaucratic government "which was created as a counterblast to feudalism," the "last expression" of which was the regime of Louis. Napoleon III displays the bankruptcy of state authority nakedly revealed to be a conspiracy against society itself. In the absence of a tenable tradition, France will be open to the future, which proceeds according to principles of scientific history, articulated by Marx himself.

While a Marxist revolution will end the contradictions of society, it may also be seen to reconcile the elements of "tragedy" and "comedy" in the human condition that Marx sees reflected in the respective politics of the two Napoleons. The "absolute moment" in the historical process that Marx occupies comprehends the necessity of both Empires in the construction of the future. The "tragic" failure of the first Napoleon is mimicked in the "comic" failure of the second. But from the most comprehensive view, the ultimate triumph of history robs the human condition of its tragic dimension, while it makes less ludicrous what serves a higher purpose.

The Marxian Historians

Prominent later historians followed the lines of class analysis so richly articulated by Marx but found the essential character of the Second Empire revealed, contrary to Marx, not in relation to the peasantry, but in relation to other classes. Alfred Cobban, for example, sees the Second Empire as basically a bourgeois regime.[28] It is significant that his analysis places due emphasis on the Saint-Simonians in whose economic programs are found the elements that inspire and give coherency to Napoleon's policies. Yet, Cobban fails to elaborate adequately on this connection and is as guilty of distorting Saint-Simonian thought as he is the Second Empire. Cobban shares with Marx a conception of history as materially determined. According to Cobban, the "only real and worthy" achievement of the second Empire was in economic affairs and this justifies his preoccupation with these matters. He is mistaken when he attributes a similar frame of reference to the Saint-Simonians.

Cobban states that Saint-Simon's "best title to fame" may be found in a little parable. Suppose France were to suddenly lose leading scientist of all kinds, artists, architects, doctors, bankers, merchants, iron-makers, industrialists in every branch, masons, carpenters, and workers in every craft. The country would obviously "sink in the scale of civilization." But, on the other hand, suppose it kept such men but lost the whole royal family, all the ministers and councilors of state, prefects, judges, archbishops, bishops and other ecclesiastics, and, in addition, ten thousand of the wealthiest landlords. A humanitarian country like France would grieve such a loss, we are told, but it would not be materially affected. "In other words," Cobban sums up, "Saint-Simon was asserting the primacy of the productive classes of society, of economic over political ends."[29]

Cobban's "summing up" gives a misleading impression of Saint-Simon and is a bland misreading of the radical implications of the parable. Saint-Simon was not merely asserting the primacy of economic over political ends. Far-reaching political implications are suggested by the parable, even as outlined by Cobban. The expendable personages represent whole classes and institutions that formed the bulwark of traditional French society. The "simple" parable perhaps hides a most revolutionary politics. This would see in the elimination of the traditional elements of French society an advance of civilization, if replaced by a regime that institutes the rule of the few based on talent and their capacity to contribute to society as a whole, morally, intellectually and, of course, economically.

Cobban has interpreted Saint-Simon as asserting the primacy of the productive classes of society that includes "artists" as a constitutive element. Of all groups in society, they are the least apt to being defended on such grounds. In such an anomaly, we are alerted to Cobban's distortion of Saint-Simon, despite what the "simple" parable intends to show.

According to Saint-Simon and his disciples, a more rational and integrated mode of production was a key to the attenuation of the class struggle in the present and to material progress in the future. However, they were not asserting the primacy of the economic or material to other modes of human activities that embrace the sentiments and intellect of man. In fact, material and scientific progress, if not subordinated to moral ends, would lead to social conflict. The artist, albeit "unproductive" in the "material" sense, was to serve the reintegration of the individual to society by giving "spiritual" expression to the religious ideas that bind society and give it moral direction. In giving preeminence to the material aspects of Saint-Simonianism, Cobban is guilty of neglecting the more important elements and objectives of that philosophy that guide economic policy.

Cobban's narrow focus aligns the Saint-Simonian movement with the class interests of the bourgeoisie which, indisputably, but not exclusively, gained by a number of Napoleon's policies. According to Cobban, bourgeois financiers did not promote the Second Empire, it was the Second Empire that promoted the bourgeois financier. As Joly indicates, in the third part of his work, the advance of commerce and industry was essentially dependent on the availability of credit and capital. During the Empire, there was founded the Compteur d'Escompte, the Credit Foncier, the Credit Agricole, the Credit Mobilier—a virtual financial revolution, whose institutions are still in existence today. This helped furnish the commercial and mortgage finance to promote, among other things, the system of railways, roads, steamships, the reconstruction of cities and towns, and the launching of various industrial and agricultural enterprises.

A wave of economic expansion followed with impressive gains in the production of steel, coal, and iron that were to help build the modern infrastructure of France. Inspired by a Saint-Simonian plan of 1832 and put into effect by Baron Haussman, an ambitious public works project sanitized, modernized, and redesigned the city of Paris. This included the renovation of the Bois de Boulogne and the widening of avenues such as the Champs Elysées. As mentioned before, its architectural achievements were crowned by Charles Gautier in the construction of the Paris Opera. Saint-Simonian universalism was later to inspire the construction of the Suez canal and an end to a world conventionally conceived as divided by an East and a West.

Joly's *Dialogue* shows a greater comprehension of the Saint-Simonian elements that, Cobban insists, stand behind Napoleon's policies. He is blind to the despotic elements in Napoleon's regime, the immense ambition of the Emperor, and the historic dimensions of his project. These cause us to question a "bourgeois" interpretation of the Second Empire as far too limited. As he has oversimplified the Saint-Simonian parable by neglecting its revolutionary implications, he has done the same with the phenomenon of the Second Empire itself. Cobban downplays certain policies that served social interests beyond those of the bourgeoisie and included the mass of workers in particular. The presence of these elements too would cause us to question an interpretation that conceived of Napoleon as exclusively serving the bourgeoisie and as the historic representative of their material interests.

For Henrick Nicolaas Boon and others, Napoleon inaugurated social legislation that rendered him as much an innovator in such fields as "Bismarck and Cavour were in politics."[30] Among other things, Boon cites the development of credit unions, the improvement of housing, the founding of retirement funds, and aid to cooperative movements as evidence of his enlightened stance. He also reads into such policies certain political motives. Napoleon was attempting to lead and channel the aspirations of "the growing multitude" in order "to satisfy their legitimate material and social demands, thus rallying them to the Empire and turning their minds away from politics."[31]

For all of Boon's fine appreciation for the innovations of Napoleon, whom he likens to a "Columbus," he is perhaps not appreciative enough of the real nature of his founding which lies in visionary policies, beyond counterrevolutionary objectives. For Boon, Napoleon was perhaps following England's example in these innovations but was "ahead of his times" in France in seeing the need for new policies and institutions which did not materialize until a later age. However, the opposition of Napoleon to the English system, both politically and socially, is made abundantly clear in Machiavelli's articulation of the policies of the Emperor in the *Dialogue in Hell*. There, Napoleonic politics is revealed as the very antithesis of Montesquieuan or English liberalism.

Full Circle?

Marx's deprecatory view of Napoleonic politics as essentially reactionary and in the service of traditional French society is perhaps not too far distant from that of Zeldin and others who credit the Emperor with no political vision at all. He was commonly perceived, from the escapades of his youth, as having a romantic temperament bent on adventurism. For Zeldin, success was his goal and this depended on knowing which way the wind was blowing. In sum, he was probably a determined believer in the merits of neither liberalism nor despotism but "an opportunist above all else."[32]

Through seemingly contradictory analyses, we might also arrive at Zeldin's rather disparaging conclusions. This would mark a return to the beginnings of Napoleonic historiography, which has none too high an opinion of Louis, but as a summary of the reflections of the most eminent commentators on the times.[33] The Emperor's actions would, by turns, have for their motives policies that are at once reactionary, economically progressive, and counterrevolutionary, as respectively revealed, for example, in the essays of Marx, Cobban, and Boon. We would perhaps distill from such policies the incoherence of the romantic adventurer with no grander vision than what inspiration and intuition prompted in changing circumstances. To say the least, this asserted lack of coherent policy would contrast most sharply with the view of Napoleonism in the *Dialogue in*

Hell, which integrates economic, political and social realms into a world-historic project.

That Napoleon III was an opportunist, as charged by Zeldin, cannot be denied. However, such an accusation is not very revealing as it legitimately can be leveled against any and all political men. That he was a mere opportunist would be denied by Joly, not as his defender, but as part of a more serious charge. He is accused of harboring Caesarian ambitions and of seeing the time ripe for launching a project to satisfy them. He is a worthy object of study, even in his ultimate failure, as reminding of the eternal possibilities of the Caesarian threat, when towering ambition is engaged in the founding of new modes and orders and given opportunity in the critical moments that history will always offer.

In this light, Louis is certainly not a determined believer in the merits of either liberalism or despotism, as commonly understood. Those like Zeldin end up accusing Napoleon of rank opportunism because the real nature of his enigmatic policies escapes them. They may in their own right be accused of the same culpable naiveté that infects the Montesquieu of the *Dialogue* when he addresses the politics described by Machiavelli from the perspective of certain doctrinaire notions of liberalism and with certain limited notions of despotism. It is precisely this limited perspective that Joly wants to educate in his description of the modern Caesar.

In the final analysis, Napoleon is an opportunist and perhaps a romantic, but these qualities are nourished in the element of Saint-Simonian philosophy. The deepest insight into his romanticism might likewise come from a Saint-Simonian source. His founding recurs to certain elements of the ancient city and the life of the Middle Ages as necessary to a new world order—the reestablishment of the "organic" conditions of politics in modern times.

The Saint-Simonian thought that Joly offers as the most fundamental and revealing phenomonon of Napoleonic politics meets the charge of mere opportunism. In it we find an appeal to the principles of progress and order and a politics that would want to resolve their disparate claims. The failure to appreciate this politics, by Zeldin and others, would have it understood as mere dalliance, indicating an on-again/off-again love affair with liberalism and despotism, when its real goal, at least in the mind of the convinced ideologue, is an historic solution to the human problem consonant with the highest of ambition, which neither liberalism nor mere despotism can serve.

The analyses of Cobban and Boon help to correct the ultimately disparaging conclusion of Zeldin. In the economic policies that supposedly served the class interest of the bourgeoisie and the social policies that benefited the working class, they respectively point to Napoleonic policies that attest to a broader vision. Such analyses would also help to correct Marx's view that Napoleon's policies are reactionary and promote the interests of the most retrograde elements of French society, especially the peasantry.

Such scholars emphasize unique aspects of Napoleon's policies and present partial aspects of his rule that may be harmonized in the Saint-Simonian perspective of Joly. Thus, we find in Joly, as in Marx, that the root strength of Napoleon's plebiscitory rule lay initially in the peasantry. The Emperor does not want to disturb the prejudices of such types, nor their gullible natures, in order to impress upon them the tenets of a new religion with himself as a secular kind of Pope, a new "Moses," as Marx called him. Interestingly enough, for Marx too, the perpetuation of the regime depends upon preserving the vitality of the religious impulse but to mask and exculpate the "sins" of an exploitative and reactionary society, not to introduce the conditions of a new "organic" and final order.

Through his banking revolution, the Emperor intended to lay down the basis of a sound infrastructure, the precondition for an enormous burst of productive activity. But this was not, as Cobban suggests, to serve the class interests of the bourgeoisie. The Emperor was not intent upon expanding the parameters of private enterprise but to begin a move toward centralizing the economy and exerting social control. Indeed, the social policies to which Boon points show that the regime was not narrowly partisan and bourgeois in Cobban's sense.

In emphasizing the different policies of the Emperor from the point of view of classes other than the peasantry, Cobban and Boon point away from Marx's interpretation. Marx legitimately stands criticized for placing too much weight on the relations of the Emperor to the peasantry to explain the whole of the regime. Moreover, they also point away from the deeper influence of Marx in an interpretation of history that is obliged to see politics in terms of material class interests. Such a class analysis shows itself incapable of grasping the elements of the Saint-Simonian revolution which the Emperor, according to Joly's analysis, tried to effect. It requires taking the "idealist" view of history seriously and shows that the historian's task to understand the past in its own terms is perhaps ill-served and distorted by Marxian reductionism, as powerful a mode of analysis as it is, particularly in the thought of Marx himself.[34]

At first view, Joly's portrait of Napoleon III is most distant from the portrait of Victor Hugo. Parenthetically, the editor of *Napoleon III—Buffoon, Dictator, or Sphinx?* is probably least sympathetic to Hugo who appears too splenetic and ready to dismiss the Emperor. However, a close look at Hugo in the light of Joly reveals striking similarities and a common intention in their respective publications.

Both perceive the despotic character of the Emperor and its novel elements. Moreover, both endeavor to galvanize republican opposition to his rule, though they take different routes. Hugo puts emphasis on the petty qualities of the despot which are set in relief by a comparison to ancient despots who showed a grandeur of soul even in the depth and extent of their criminality.

The focus of Joly's work also brings to consideration the differences between ancient and modern despotism. As we have shown, Napoleon recurs to certain ancient or medieval elements in his rule in order to advance upon the Enlightenment project and erect a new and final historic order. Put another way, the distinguishing characteristic of the despotism of the future lies in the role that ideology plays in investing modern despotism with a revolutionary project of millenarian objectives. Joly's *Dialogue*, between the two giants of modern thought, Machiavelli and Montesquieu, reintroduces us to the themes of political philosophy and, through the doctrines of the Saint-Simonians, to newer currents of thought that open the way to modern totalitarianism. It is in such terms that we are perhaps provided the best access to the study of such a phenomenon.

Notes

1. Samuel M. Osgood, ed., *Napoleon III—Buffoon, Modern Dictator, or Sphinx?* (Boston: D. C. Heath, 1966). The text includes an Introduction that presents the editor's view of the problem of Napoleonic historiography.

2. I realize that I open myself to ridicule by associating the post-moderns with the search for "metaphysical foundations" of anything. They are almost by definition opposed to all "metaphysics" and any "foundational" mode of thinking. We are forced to oxymoron to characterize them (and this would probably not bother them either since they believe that "binary oppositions," embedded Western categories of thought, are radically suspect anyway). In this light, it may be better to speak not of their search for "metaphysical foundations" but of their search for "anti-foundational foundations." If it is still impossible to speak of them in such a way, we might prefer to see their thinking, not as "foundational" at all, but as "strategies" to "destabilize" "logocentric" thinking per se. At end, one wonders why they do not apply their thinking to themselves. Why is their thought not a mere "will o' the wisp" like all other thought, i.e., radically questionable?

In any case, the post-moderns see history as radically illusive. The traditional historian in his attempt to recover the past "as it was" is therefore horribly (or comically) deluded. For Derrida, for example, "differ*ance*" and an inevitable "slippage" in language make effective "communication" between generations impossible. He speaks of the "aporia" of discourse and the disassociation of words from any "reality." For Foucault, changes in "power relations" make different eras fundamentally incomprehensible to one another. We cannot come to know what is "true" about the past or to independent judgments of what each era holds as "true." Language and ideas privilege certain hegemonic groups and are themselves instruments of power. "Knowledge" is not liberating; it is, rather, "authoritarian," or "phallocentric." They are among the now many thinkers who have forced the adjective "totalitarian" from its *political* context. It is the quintessential description of Western "logocentric" *thinking*, we are told. The upshot of all this is to disestablish all prevailing notions of "truth." One may naively ask where this leaves us, and the West? There is irony in the fact that such thinkers assume the heroic pose in purging political life of all possibility of heroism. Are they not, in spite of themselves, leading a generation by the hand to the land of the "Last Man"? See Gertude Himmelfarb,

"Postmodernist History" in *On Looking into the Abyss* (New York: Vintage Books, 1995), 131-163. To my mind, there is no greater defender and practitioner of "the traditional approach" (she would call it the "modern" approach) to historical studies than Ms. Himmelfarb. In case it is not clear, this is what I argue for in this chapter. She made even clearer to me the importance of the issue.

It is interesting that she sees Theodore Zeldin as a transitional figure from "traditional/narrative" history to post-modern historical thought. Among other things, he is regarded as one of the most authoritative historians of the Second Empire. She writes the following:

> Theodore Zeldin was one of the first historians (as distinct from philosophers of history) to launch a serious, sustained assault upon modernist history. That history, he claimed—traditional narrative history—is dependent upon such 'tyrannical' concepts as causality, chronology, and collectivity (the latter including class as well as nationality). To liberate history from these constraints, he proposed a new history on the model of *pointilliste* painting, composed entirely of unconnected dots. This would have the double advantage of emancipating the historian from the tyrannies of the discipline, and emancipating the reader from the tyranny of the historian, since the reader would be free to make what lines he thinks fit for himself. (138.)

It is perhaps no coincidence that we will come to know Zeldin as the interpreter of Napoleon III that saw no core to his personality or programs.

Osgood's case is interesting in light of all this. He comes before the post-moderns took hold and falls somewhere between the traditionalist approach and the more radical brand of historicism. His thinking, typical enough, shows how the profession could easily be seduced by the latter mode of thought.

3. See Samuel M. Osgood's Introduction to his *Napoleon III*, xi.

4. This mode of thinking originates with Thomas Kuhn. I do not know if Osgood had him in mind. Perhaps. Kuhn's idea of a "paradigm shift," originally referring to the process of scientific discovery, has been embraced by many post-moderns as indicative of the process of Western thinking *tout court*, historical thinking included. See Thomas S. Kuhn, *The Structure of Scientific Revolutions* (Chicago: University of Chicago Press, 1962).

5. Contemporary "historians" are not as loath as Osgood to enter the realm of fiction. I mention in this regard Edmund Morris and Rigoberta Menchú. In his "biography" of Ronald Reagan, the former forthrightly blended a fictional account of the President with the massive facts of his life. "Wholesale history; retail poetry," we might say. The dangers of this should be obvious. In a very real sense we *are* our past. To understand ourselves and guide our future, we must come to understand it honestly. The traditional historian endeavors to do this, fully conscious of the important role he or she plays in service to the truth and civilized life. The traditional disciplines of the craft, which favor

objectivity, are what makes his enterprise so difficult (and rewarding). Himmelfarb deserves extensive quotation here. See *On Looking into the Abyss*, 136, where she writes the following:

> Critical history puts a premium on archival research and primary sources, the authenticity of documents and reliability of witnesses, the need to obtain substantiating and countervailing evidence; and at a more mundane level, the accuracy of quotations and citations, prescribed forms of documentation in footnotes and bibliography, and all the rest of 'methodology' that goes into the 'canon of evidence.' The purpose of this methodology is twofold: to bring to the surface the infrastructure, as it were, of the historical work, thus making it accessible to the reader and exposing it to criticism; and to encourage the historian to a maximum exertion of objectivity in spite of all the temptations to the contrary.

The Morris approach leaves history open to all those with interests apart from history as traditionally conceived. These interests might be ideological or monetary, to provide grist for Hollywood's entertainment mill, for example. In the case of Rigoberta Menchú, who went into denial about her fictional distortions of what happened in Guatemala, it may be fame and notoriety. Who knows? The point is that we risk losing contact with the noble civilizing functions of the historian's true enterprise.

I was much moved by an anecdote about Richard Nixon that Henry Kissinger related. (Most university people I know can see nothing poignant to anything relating to Richard Nixon.) During the crisis that saw him leave the presidency, he forced Kissinger to get on his knees with him. The God he was praying to was really the God of History. He would correct the wrongs he thought he had suffered in life. (Does this remind us of certain parts of the *Dialogue*? Well, it's in there.) His contributions to his country would eventually be seen in a correct light. This God of historic judgment, ruthlessly honest, is the best we have until the appearance of the real God and the Last Judgment. It chastens even the most hardened of historic actors. Contemporary historians don't know what they are doing when they fool with it. See Edmund Morris, *Dutch: A Memoir of Ronald Reagan* (New York: Random House, 1999); Rigoberta Menchú, *I Rigoberta Menchú An Indian Woman in Guatemala* ed. Elizabeth Burgos-Debray; trans. Ann Wright (London: Verso, 1984). and David Stoll, *Rigoberta Menchú and the Story of All Poor Guatemalans* (Boulder, Colo.: Westview Press, 1999). Stoll was prompted by injustices to history to write his exposé.

Parenthetically, isn't what these authors do similar to what Hitler did with the *Protocols*? What the *Protocols* reveal is "historically" true even if the "Wise Men of Zion" never really historically met. In other words, it doesn't matter if what someone vouchsafes is *factually* a fraud.

Richard Crosby put things very well when he said to me that once upon a time we found the implications of the fact/value distinction disturbing. "Now not only are values the realm of fantasy, so are facts."

6. Osgood, ed., *Napoleon III*, 1-5. The Osgood excerpts are taken from Victor Hugo, "Napoleon the Little," in *The Works of Victor Hugo* (New York: Nottingham Society, *circa* 1907), VIII, 15-20; 192-195.

7. Osgood, ed., *Napoleon III*, 23-33. The Osgood excerpts are taken from Karl Marx, *The Eighteenth Brumaire of Louis Napoleon*, tr. Eden and Cedar Paul (New York: International, 1926), 23-24; 128-144.

8. See the selection from Charles Seignobos, "The Magic of a Name," in Osgood, ed., *Napoleon III*, 14-16. Osgood's translation is excerpted from Seignobos's essay in *Histoire de France Contemporaire*, ed. Ernest Lavisse (Paris: Hachette, 1921), VI, 124-127.

9. To make light of Louis's "failures" in such a way begs the facts—massive facts—of his reign. Many other scholars join Guerard and see the Emperor even in failure as basically "well meaning" (as if this were enough to exonerate him). It was Louis who wanted to end the order of Vienna that was imposed on Europe after the defeat of his uncle. This order was designed to prevent the emergence of another Napoleon. And Louis was, well, another Napoleon. His ambitions brought military defeat to France and Europe was cast loose from Richelieu's moorings. From being divided and weak, Germany became united and strong. French dominance on the continent ended.

Both he and Bismarck were playing with fire. Bismarck played better. Conflagration came only after he departed the scene. Louis played with it less well. Destruction came immediately to France. His failures were not trivial, nor can we sympathize with the most egregious of them. Joly wrote in 1864, when Louis dominated France and was extremely influential in Europe. He did not contemplate the end in his book. In the spirit of Joly, we would be tempted to say that the failure of great ambition (as with Lenin and Hitler) has great consequences. Meanwhile, with the end of "Vienna," new monsters were slouching their way into Europe. See "Two Revolutionaries: Napoleon III and Bismarck," in chapter 5 of Henry A. Kissinger's magisterial work, *Diplomacy* (New York: Touchstone, 1995), 103-136.

As ruler of the "superpower" on the continent, "Le Petit" thought he "stood taller than the rest" and that his way would lead the way for the rest of the world. The quick reversal of his fortunes might serve as a cautionary tale for us today.

10. Who is not familiar with the same arguments today regarding the internet and the "new" technologies. We are told that they herald the promised land of universal democracy to which everyone aspires.

11. See the selection from Albert Guerard, "A Forerunner of Woodrow Wilson," in Osgood, *Napoleon III*, 57-65. This is excerpted from Albert Guerard, *Napoleon III* (Cambridge, Mass.: Harvard University Press, 1943), 176-192; 221-222.

12. See J. Salwyn Schapiro, "Heralds of Fascism: Louis Napoleon Bonaparte," in Osgood, ed., *Napoleon III*, 81-87. This is excerpted from J. Salwyn Schapiro, *Liberalism and the Challenge of Fascism* (New York: McGraw Hill, 1949), 320-331.

13. See Lynn M. Case, "A Voice in the Wilderness," in Osgood, ed., *Napoleon III*, 65-70. This is excerpted from Lynn M. Case, *French Opinion on War and Diplomacy During the Second Empire* (Philadelphia: University of Pennsylvania Press, 1954), 270-

277. Some post-moderns, unlike Case, may be said to consciously engage in the "trivialization" of history. If history is ineluctably a matter of "interpretation," everything can be turned to material for the irony and wit of the "interpreter." Up until now, they seem to have stopped short at the Holocaust, although I believe it is only a matter of time until some "transgressive" hero of thought really cashes in on the Holocaust's potentialities.

14. The "Chekovian romantic" label belongs to A. F. Thompson. See his "From Restoration to Republic" in Osgood, ed., *Napoleon III*, 99-102. This is excerpted from an essay with the same title in *France: Government and Society*, J. M. Wallace-Handrill and J. McManners, ed., (London: Methuen 1957), 212-217.

15. Plutarch wrote about heroes and has us experience some of the most exalted times that humans ever knew. Tacitus, on the other hand, wrote about "dark times." In *The Annals* he wrote that history's "highest function" was "to let no worthy action be uncommemorated, and to hold out the reprobation of posterity as a terror to evil words and deeds." The commemorative task fell largely to Plutarch. Tacitus's task was emphatically the more melancholy one. See *The Annals*, tr. Alfred John Church and William Jackson Brodribb (Chicago: Great Books, 1952), XV, 60.

Anything this author knows about Tacitus is thanks to the late James Leake, to whom he gives belated thanks. The moments when the human spirit finds a hospitable field to display all its rich potentiality are rare, he once said to me. For the most part, human beings must operate in "dark times" (a phrase he used often in his thesis). They are forced to carve out a niche in the world where, unmolested, they find what dignity and fulfillment they can. The grandeur of Tacitus, according to him, was to reveal the actions of virtuous men against a somber background. What they could do was limited, but it shone, nevertheless—perhaps, all the more. Seneca is the model.

I remember the enthusiasm when Jim discovered the works of a Tacitus scholar who lived behind the Iron Curtain. In a deft use of Latin quotes and footnotes, he esoterically conveyed the moral truths about the squalid regime he lived under. What could a man do in such "dark times"? As a functionary, soften an inane or brutal directive? Or, as this man—a scholar—let the light of the truth shine wherever possible? He had put his "message in a bottle" and cast it forth. No better person in the whole world could have picked it up.

For scholars like these, the truth was something sacred, I feel compelled to say, not a toy to be "deconstructed" and played with.

16. *Nichomachean Ethics*, 1094b10-25 and 1098b25-30.

17. Aristotle's comments in his *Poetics* are very pertinent to our discussion of Osgood and contemporary historiography. They may help "educated men" to better understand that "degree of precision" which the study of history admits.

In this regard, it is interesting that, for Aristotle, Homer's muse is superior to Clio. That is, poetry is more philosophic than history. This seems counterintuitive. After all, history deals with what really happened and poetry belongs to fiction. But being true to the facts of the past forces us to acknowledge a large element of chance in human affairs. And what belongs to chance can never be fully intelligible. The best poetry excludes chance and can be more "meaningful" than history, not to mention the kinds of lives we all lead today.

These remarks have benefited from Laurence Berns's fine essay "Aristotle's *Poetics*" in *Ancients and Moderns*, Joseph Cropsey ed., (New York: Basic Books: 1964), 70-87, esp. 80ff.

18. This is Iggers's characterization in his Introduction to *The Doctrine of Saint-Simon*, xiii.

19. See Theodore Zeldin, "The Myth of Napoleon III," in Osgood, ed., *Napoleon III*, 88-94. This is excerpted from an article of the same title as it appeared in *History Today*, (February 1959), vii, 103-110.

20. See Adrien Dansette, "Louis Napooleon: A Vignette," in Osgood, ed., *Napoleon III*, 13. Osgood's translation is excerpted from Adrien Dansette, "Louis Napoleon à la conquet du pouvoir" in *Histoire du Second Empire* (Paris: Hachette, 1961), I, 384-386.

21. See A. F. Thompson "From Restoration to Republic," in Osgood, ed., *Napoleon III*, 102.

22. See Schapiro, "Heralds of Fascism," in Osgood, ed., *Napoleon III*, 86. Among others, Schapiro cites the Nazi Franz Kemper in this regard.

23. Schapiro, "Heralds of Fascism," in Osgood, ed., *Napoleon III*, 86. (Schapiro's emphasis).

24. Among other things, such statements indicate the millenarian aspects of Nazi thought. The democratic thrust of history since 1789 was not inevitable or definitive.

25. Unlike Xenophon's "humane" hero, Cyrus the Great, who manically gloated over the sight of battlefield cadavers, it is interesting that Louis Napoleon reportedly wept when he contemplated his casualties. He was not like his uncle in this regard, or like Caesar. Joly would probably interpret such tears as of the "crocodile" variety. I'm not so sure. Napoleon I was said to have said: "I have an income of two hundred thousand men a year." And "what does a man like me care about a hundred thousand lives?" See Guerard, Napoleon III, 172 and Xenophon, *Cyropaedia* I. iv. 24.

26. Marx, "Eighteenth Brumaire," in Osgood, ed., *Napoleon III*, 31.

27. François Mitterand wrote a rather splenetic book criticizing DeGaulle and the Fifth Republic called *The Permanent Coup d'État*. The title is obviously inspired by Marx's *Eighteenth Brumaire*. As President, however, he sounded more like Goldilocks. When he then spoke of the Constitution of the Fifth Republic, he said "this one is *just right*."

28. Alfred Cobban, "A Bourgeois Empire," in Osgood, ed., *Napoleon III*, 75-80. This is excerpted from Alfred Cobban, *A History of Modern France* (Middlesex, G.B.: Penguin Books, 1961), II, 160-169.

29. Cobban, "A Bourgeois Empire," in Osgood, ed., *Napoleon III*, 76.

30. Hendrik Nicholas Boon, "The Social and Economic Policies of Napoleon III," in Osgood, ed., *Napoleon III* 41-50. Osgood's translation is excerpted from Hendrik Nicholas Boon, *Rêve and realité dans l'œuvre économique et sociale de Napoleon III* (The Hague, the Netherlands: Martinus Nijhoff, 1936), 65-70; 146-156; 167-168.

31. Boon, "The Social and Economic Policies," in Osgood, ed., *Napoleon III*, 44.

32. Zeldin, "The Myth of Napoleon III," in Osgood, ed., *Napoleon III*, 90.

33. One would hesitate to say that Napoleonic historiography has returned to a disparaging and dismissive view of Louis Napoleon, given the publication of Philippe Seguin's book, *Louis Napoleon le Grand* (Paris: Grasset, 1990). In his polemic with Victor Hugo, it is curious that the head (in a double sense) of the RPR would want to burnish the memory of the Emperor. Certain "elective affinities" exist, perhaps, between them. General De Gaulle sheared France from its imperial holdings. But he designed the Fifth Republic so that France could act in the world with "imperial weight." He carried himself, at least in official duties, in a regal manner. A certain predilection for the grandeur of a powerful, if not imperial, France perhaps finds its way into the thinking of the man who carries on the General's legacy. This predilection is far from foreign to the contemporary French political class.

Moreover, the RPR today sees France as going through an "industrial revolution" as profound and consequential as that over which Louis presided. Such revolutionary change will "come from above" and remain *solidaire* with "the most numerous and poorest classes." At first view, the orientation of the RPR appears to be not too distant from that of the nineteenth-century sovereign, benignly interpreted. Such a view fails, I think, to take the more controversial elements of Napoleonism into account, or fails to understand them. To my knowledge, as Seguin has pointed out, there is still no public building, no street sign, and no metro stop named after Louis Napoleon in Paris. (I once had an undistinguished meal at a bistro near the Butte Chaumont appropriately named *Napoleon III*. It was the Emperor who had changed this former garbage dump into an urban park that could be characterized as, well, "proto-Disney," a Maxwell Parish fantasy come to life in concrete and papier mâché. His "imaginative" reconstruction of the castle ruins at Pierrefond clearly anticipates "fantasyland." Saint-Simon has a charming street named after him in the twentieth *arrondissement* studded with *pavillions* that would have housed the "poorest and most numerous classes" in the nineteenth century but would now cost a fortune. And metro stops are festooned with the names of prominent nineteenth-century Saint-Simonians.) Historical amnesia seems to surround the Emperor. I find it curious and interesting that someone like Seguin takes pains to end the anathema.

34. One of the burdens of this work is to show that "ideas," contrary to materialist historiography, do indeed have consequences, as do historic personalities and political phenomena, in addition to classes and social phenomena. Raymond Aron, among others, had a deep appreciation for the *Eighteenth Brumaire*. Of Marx's works, it strayed most from the strict materialism that guided his historical view. See Daniel Mahoney and his interesting comments thereupon in *The Liberal Science of Raymond Aron* (Lanham, Md: Rowman & Littlefield, 1992), 35. Marx once boasted that he had "stood Hegel on his head." The great sweep of history that he had understood "idealistically" had to be understood "materialistically." Recently, we have seen Hegel get back on his feet, as he now strides once again in intellectual circles around the world. For all this, Marx has not been "stood on his head," in turn. For the moment he has been pushed aside, if not toppled. See Gertrude Himmelfarb's essay "From Marx to Hegel," in *On Looking into the Abyss*,

50-73. Could it be that the long dominance of Marxian class analysis in our historical studies has received a devastating blow?

By now it should come as no surprise that I would recommend Montesquieu to fill the place in our academies that has been occupied far too long by Marx and Marxians. His capacious view of human things would release us from the straitjacket of historical determinism and economic reductionism. What is needed at the very least is a revival of the Montesquieuan spirit, a sense for the full panoply of human things, its richness, and subtle interconnections.

Chapter Eleven

The Protocols of the Elders of Zion

The Discovery of the *Dialogue*

In 1921, a British correspondent to the London *Times*, Phillip Graves, happened upon one of the original copies of the *Dialogue in Hell* while stationed in Istanbul. It is highly possible that this rare find had been transported to Turkey by a Russian émigré after the Revolution of 1917.[1] Graves was the first to make the connection between the *Dialogue* and the *Protocols of the Elders of Zion* which, by the time of the discovery, had been widely published throughout the world. His own newspaper in fact had published the *Protocols* and had editorialized on the Jewish peril, basing itself on its "revelations."

Scholars have traced the *Protocols* forgery mainly to two literary works. By far, however, the *Dialogue in Hell* was the most prominent and substantive source. The forger's plagiarism was extensive as whole passages were copied directly from the *Dialogue*. "In all, over 160 passages in the *Protocols*, totaling two-fifths of the entire text, are clearly based on Joly. In some of the chapters, the borrowings amount to more than one-half of the text, in one, (Protocol VII) to almost the entire text."[2]

The other source for the *Protocols* was found in a novel written four years after the *Dialogue* entitled *To Sedan* (1868). That work contains a chapter describing a secret congregation of world rabbis in Prague, a centennial event in that city's cemetery. The novel was written under the pseudonym Sir John Retcliffe, actually a Prussian clerk and rabid anti-Semite named Herman Godsche, who had developed a penchant for writing sensationalist literature. At the cemetery and in the presence of Satan, the rabbis, representing the twelve tribes of Israel, relate their successes since their last meeting in furthering their secret plan for world domination.

In concocting the *Protocols*, the fabricator combines the arguments of Machiavelli in Joly's *Dialogue* with some of the more lurid elements of Godsche's tale. He borrows from Joly his considerable political acumen for identifying the opportunities for modern despotism in the vulnerabilities of contemporary society but has Machiavelli's despotic cause pronounced by world Jewry who, as in *To Sedan*, are revealed to be in sinister pursuit of a long-standing goal of universal rule.

Konrad Heiden, who gives a leading role to the *Protocols* in his study of Hitler, writes of the powerful blend of elements contained therein.

> Godsche's feat was childish and none too convincing. But suppose you take these rabbis conspiring in their cemetery and give them the worldly wisdom, the contempt for humanity, the seductive power of Joly's tyrant. Don't just make them avaricious braggarts, make them subtle and crafty: make them speak the accursed satirical wisdom of Machiavelli, in deadly earnest. Finally, confound the fabulous nocturnal conspiracy with an international Jewish Congress which actually did convene to discuss such sober matters as the problem of immigration. Then, we have before us, in all its bloody romantic horror, the demons of Jewish world domination gathered in a Congress and fixed in a protocol.[3]

Despite the airing of Graves's discovery, the Jewish myth did not die off. It likewise survived the 1934-35 "Bern Trials" where it was charged by Swiss Jews that the former Fuehrer of the Swiss National Socialists had been guilty of violating the law against "improper literature" (*schundliteratur*) by circulating the *Protocols*. The Court concluded upon testimony of Graves, noted international scholars, and former Russian officials:

> I hope that one day there will come a time when no one will any longer comprehend how in the year 1935 almost a dozen fully sensible and reasonable men could for fourteen days torment their brains before a court of Bern over the authenticity of these so-called "protocols," that, for all the harm they have already caused and may yet cause, are nothing but ridiculous nonsense.[4]

This is in fact the reaction of any reasonable person in reading the fantastic account of the *Protocols*. The Court was at pains to document its fraudulence, however, given the political use to which the *Protocols* was being put.

Yet, like a virus, the myth proved to be extraordinarily resilient. It did not respond to the application of sensible men in 1935 because, for all its "nonsense," it was allied to strains much stronger than reason. Efforts were subsequently made to prove the Semitic ancestry of the obscure Joly and to trace his peculiar insights to "diabolical Jewishness."[5] But for Hitler and others, the findings of the Bern Court were not telling, even in the face of a documented forgery.

The "inner truth" of the *Protocols* was proof against those who sought to discredit the document's authenticity. This was Hitler's already stated position in *Mein Kampf* and was offered in response to Graves's original discovery. It redeemed the *Protocols* from such levels of attack, however reasonable, and aligned the document with esoteric truths that only Hitler's demonstrable genius and claimed affinity for such matters could sufficiently plumb.[6]

The Fabrication of the *Protocols*

With the *Dialogue* identified as the source of the forgery, the events behind its fabrication were pieced together over the years in a collective effort of scholars and other interested parties. By most accounts, Ilya Tsion, a Russian expatriate and an avowed enemy of Count Sergei Witte, the liberal finance minister under Nicholas II, had come into contact with Joly's work in his Swiss exile. He adapted Joly's critique of Louis Napoleon to the figure of Witte and this version fell into the hands of Peter Ratchkovsky, who was ordered by Witte to burglarize Tsion's home to obtain the manuscript.[7]

Ratchkovsky was in Witte's service as head of the French bureau of the Ochrana, the Russian secret police, and had become a master of intrigue and forgeries. Russian witnesses at the Bern Trial corroborated testimony that pointed to Ratchkovsky as the fabricator of the *Protocols*. In all probability, it was under the direction of the unscrupulous Ratchkovsky that the Joly text was again gleaned and woven with the conspiratorial elements of Godsche's tale into the first version of the *Protocols of the Elders of Zion*.

The version that comes down to us was sponsored by the Ochrana and published in 1905. It was an appendix to a tract entitled *Small Signs Betoken Great Events; The Antichrist Is Near at Hand*, written by Sergei Nilus, who was personally acquainted with Ratchkovsky. This mystic's ambition was to pierce the Tsar's entourage and replace a healer of French origin as the Tsar's favorite.

Such machinations and intrigues raise the question as to Ratchkovsky's motives in all this. With the *Protocols* as the set-piece, no less was sought than a national counterrevolution against the inroads of liberalism countenanced by Witte. The aroused passions of the people wedded to the power of the most autocratic state in Europe were to help serve the reactionary reconstruction of Russian society. It was in the atmosphere immediately following the debacle of the 1905 war with Japan that the *Protocols* were enlisted to enflame the masses and, through Nilus, to subvert the thinking of the Tsar.

Walter Laqueur, who became convinced of the crucial importance of the *Protocols* on the Nazi revolution during his research for *Russia and Germany*, noted Western scholarship's failure to appreciate the strong strains of Russian influence on the formative period of Hitler's Germany. This was not the fault of Konrad Heiden who writes in *Der Fuehrer* that, through the Ochrana conspiracy, Russia had become the "spiritual mother country of modern fascism, as it later became the world center of Communism.[8]

The Crisis Atmosphere of Postwar Europe

Heiden reconstructs the situation in the aftermath of the Revolution and the White Russian army's retreat from the East. The sense of catastrophe contributed to the strong impression the Nilus text was to have on such men as Alfred Rosenberg. According to L. Poliakov, Rosenberg was to give form to Hitler's inchoate race hatred as one of the main ideologues of Nazism and the author of the *Myth of the Twentieth Century*, a work which "leads in a straight line from the *Protocols*."[9]

Rosenberg fled Russia during its revolution and met Hitler in Munich, itself in the throes of revolutionary unrest. He was steeped in the anti-Semitism and the anti-Bolshevism of the White Russians, many of whom later fled to that troubled city. In Nazi ideology, anti-Semitism and anti-Bolshevism were enmeshed. The Kremlin was dominated by Jews and conspired for world revolution in the name of Communism. Did this not lend credence to the myth of the *Protocols*? It seems it was Rosenberg who introduced the *Protocols* to Hitler, who immediately came to share the enthusiasm for its "esoteric truths." Though the *Protocols* myth struck deepest roots in Germany, it was widely disseminated throughout the world. Copies circulated in Boston and New York after the war. In 1920, Henry Ford's newspaper, *The Dearborn Independent*, printed the document in full. Since then, it has been translated in all major languages. It may astonish us to hear that Herman Cohn conjectures that the *Protocols*, after the Bible, was the century's most widely-read text.[10]

The universal appeal of the *Protocols* testifies to the prevalence of a now perhaps forgotten mood of pessimism, despair, and confusion that belonged to the subterranean level of thought in the nineteenth century only to emerge full-blown after the collective experience of the horrors of the First World War. In the traumatic aftermath of that war, moderate political regimes came under increasing strain. The fate of liberalism was sorely tested, particularly in Germany, bearing the onus of having been imposed on that country as a consequence of a defeat that was portrayed by its domestic enemies as a betrayal. A regime that struggled for the support of citizens whose allegiance was toward other forms of government was ill-equipped to handle the punitive aspects of the Versailles Treaty and to face the difficulties of the Depression. To revolutionaries of both the right and the left, the global impact of the deepening economic crisis signaled the general bankruptcy of the old order and the prelude to world revolution, the course of which found Germany in a truly pivotal position in Europe, geographically and otherwise.

The *Protocols* Myth as the Explanation of Crisis

The myth of the *Protocols* provided an explanation for the impasse of liberalism while elevating the Jew to the central role in the denouement of the world's drama. According to the Nazis, liberalism's relation to the Jew was the most revealing phenomenon of that regime. The extension of rights to the Jew was the acid test of its universalistic principles. However, the extension of such rights, according to them, actually served the Jew's ultimate plans by allowing them to work within society and under its protection to effect its undermining.

The Nazis maintained that in the person of the Jew liberal society had accepted into its fold a most intransigent enemy. Liberal tolerance is inwardly spurned and exploited by the Jew to further his secret goal of racial domination, which the crisis of liberalism and the Great Depression prepare. The rights accorded to the individual prove serviceable to the Jew, who shows that the real forces of history ultimately lie not in abstract and universal principles, but along racial lines and according to a conscious project.

The imminent collapse of the liberal order brings world domination, always the secret motive of the Jew, closer to realization. The "truth" of the *Protocols* offers spectacular evidence of the existence of an age-old plot. In further linking the Jew to Communism, which makes conspiracy and violence legitimate means to their political end, that plot becomes at once more real, explicit, and immediate. This enabled the Nazis to enter the contest for world domination with the Jew on distinct ideological and racial lines.

For the Communist, the class contradictions of capitalism are inherent and tied to the material conditions of society that define the workings of history. For Hitler, however, there is another reality behind the movements and conflicts of history. The existence of a Jewish masterplan, revealed in the *Protocols*, demonstrates the essentially conspiratorial causes of the movements of history in the light of which the momentous events of the day can be comprehended—indeed, "small signs betoken great events."

As the active agent of history, the Jew assumes the central role of history that Communism understood to be played by cold and impersonal forces. The complexities and contingencies of history are reduced and explained by the person of the Jew who gives "meaning" to such distraught times. The "inner truth" of the *Protocols* opens the way to hatred and fear where we find the most potent source of energy for Hitler's historic movement.

According to Hitler, the class struggle between capitalist and Communist, which now occupied the center stage of history, was actually manipulated by the Jews. From time to time, as in the *Protocols* revelation, the curtain that hid them parted and gave glimpses of what Hitler in fact said existed. Wasn't the Russian Revolution in large part brought to success by Jewish Bolsheviks? And wasn't the Rothschild fortune the pillar of moneyed capitalism? Hitler's privileged perspective allowed him to illuminate for others the hidden truths that put an end to the great deception.

According to Hitler, the class struggle was orchestrated by the Jews for their own profit and eventual domination. The Red Menace strengthened the hands of capitalism led by Jewish financiers who consorted with the sovereigns of the nation states of Europe as equals. Their indifference to the plight of the working classes played into the hands of the Bolsheviks, also led by the Jews, who violently conspired against these same nation states. Society, so riddled and exhausted, would ultimately fall to Jewish direction in any case.[11]

The continued success of the Nazi movement confirmed the faith in Hitler as having apprehended the esoteric truths of history, while any reverses would also show the "reality" of the Jewish threat. Thus, the "truth" of the *Protocols*, if not the document itself, became an irrefutable article of faith and the linchpin of Nazi ideology.

The *Protocols* held a deep fascination for Hitler and his cohorts. The historic success of the Jews to survive and prosper in alien and hostile surroundings was impressive. For them, the perseverance of a recognizable "Jewish" identity throughout the history of their dispersion attested to the fundamental importance of race and "blood" inheritance. In the absence of the Nazis, Hitler thought that the future lay with the Jews as depicted in the *Protocols*. They represented the first historically conscious group whose plans for world domination involved the maintenance of racial purity.

Beyond their use in mobilizing a mass movement, the *Protocols* reflect even more fundamental levels of Nazism which touch the core of its supposed "inner truths." Hitler shares with the Jews of the *Protocols* a racial view of history as well as their plans for world domination. For this reason, the *Protocols* have been noted not only as a rationale for the Nazi movement but as a perverse source of inspiration. The delusion of universal Jewish domination became the basis of the illusion of the future dominion of the Nazis. Himmler is reported to have said that "we owe the art of government to the Jews, namely to the *Protocols* which the Fuehrer has learned by heart."[12]

The Deeper Connection between the *Protocols* and Nazism

Despite their "crackpot manner," framed in terms of mysticism and superstition, Hannah Arendt saw the *Protocols* as noteworthy for "touching upon every important political issue of the day."[13] The *Protocols* are anti-national in principle. "The wise men of Zion" share Hitler's belief that the nation state is fundamentally unsound and that world empire will replace the present forms of political arrangements. Not content with a revolutionary seizure of power in one country, they see world conquest as possible through organization alone, regardless of the superiority of numbers, territory, and state power they face.

According to Nazism, history is not a rationally determined process. Reasonable and "moral" motives are not what move those individuals who act in history and determine the course of whole epochs. History bears the stamp of the "genius" of these individuals who share strong affinities with the "artist-creator" in their profound and mysterious inspirations and their capacity to move others. Hitler saw himself in such a romantic mold even as the painter of postcards in pre-war Vienna. If history is not predetermined in any way, it can be made. For the Nazis, the future is a project and struggle. It can be fashioned in the full consciousness of the power that man holds over it and thus offers possibilities, beyond the present debilitating moralities of the moment, that animate the strong to reassert their superiority and reclaim their right to the earth, usurped by Jewish deceit.

The struggle for the future takes shape in the light of the "inner truth" of the *Protocols*. Present in the world is a materially determined instinct. This is racially embodied in the Jew in its most thoroughgoing form, as a product of the exigencies of survival caused by their dispersion and unique history as a people. The Nazis see themselves as redeeming the world from a Jewish fate that is gaining through their hidden efforts, coordinated in the various key centers of the world where events have scattered them.

They want to awake the slumbering Hun and set him rampaging in a Europe once again grown soft. In the person of the Jew and what he represents, they are brought to the hatred and cruelty proper to their historic task of reanimating a "decadent" West, counter to the reigning dogmas and ethics, and toward the Nazi ideal. For Hitler in *Mein Kampf,* the most extreme contrast to the Aryan is the Jew.

Jewish "deceit" is more than a casual association but is rather a racial characteristic, historically conditioned. It is reflected in the *Protocols* in their centuries-old conspiracy that is brought to imminent success in the context of present political degeneration and international revolution. Borrowing from thought that can be traced to Nietzsche, such deceit is seen as present at the source of the common heritage of the West, the Judeo-Christian faith which, in its origins, is no more than a pious fraud, inspired by the Jews.

Through the remarkable transformation of values, implicit in the decadent Christian world view, the Jew has perpetrated the greatest of revolutions and his ultimate vengeance on the world by elevating a slave morality in the place of the master ethic, the element of his oppression. The National Socialists will bring a counterrevolution against Semitic culture that has wrongfully gained the West and subjected the strong, not by force of arms, but by false doctrine. The world will once again be restored to health and vigor as the master is called again to rule in good conscience and to inherit the earth that is rightfully his.

The Christian core of Western culture reflects those Semitic influences identified as alien, Eastern, and slavish. Herein lies the key to the history of the West that then saw in the triumphs of Communism the secular advance of Semitic cul-

ture, culminating in a universal, materialistic, and democratic ethos. This represents, not the proclaimed liberation of humanity through history, but disguised
Jewish dominance and the end of higher culture, always the preserve of a spiritual elite and the exclusive legacy of the Aryan race.

The future will see the mystic bond to the Aryan and Nordic past reestablished in a counterrevolution against Jewish heritage that has dominated modern
history. In the words of Rosenberg, the struggle is to "revitalize the cells of Nordic conditioned peoples; it contains the reinstatement to ruling authority of those
ideas and values for which everything that signifies culture for us stems." On the
deepest level, the present struggle is a kulturkampf which restores the Aryan to
the proper source of his strength and identity.[14]

A "new-yet-old" type of German is called who proclaims and embodies
"new-yet-old" values, the warrior ethic of the blond beast and "Nordic honor,"
essentially the inverse of Judeo-Christian values, identified disparagingly as
humility, submissiveness, and watery compassion. The truly radical character of
the Nazis is revealed in opposition to such values while engaging convictions
that call for loyalty to the living ruler and the earth, redeemed for the strong.

Through world conquest, the future is to be prepared for the introduction of
pure Aryan culture. While such "forward-looking" men of culture, aided by eu-
genicists, are already busy forming the new man, others are busy eradicating the
Jew, his nemesis, from the world. The ovens at Auschwitz are the necessary upshot of their racial policies. They also mark the distance from the hold of Judeo-
Christian doctrine and are the clearest manifestation of the ultimate principles of
where Nazi doctrine leads.

It is in the thought of Rosenberg that we see reflected the deeper levels of the
"truth" of the *Protocols*. Through his learnedness, the view of the *Protocols*
takes on dimensions beyond those of a common racist tract. The Manichean, obsessive world of Hitler's anti-Semitism is redeemed in the element of kultur and
the systematic exposition of racism that could contemplate the "final solution."
This anchors the document in a greater reality whose mystic appeals are untouched by the revelations of Graves or evidence from a court of law that reflects perhaps liberal (and ultimately Jewish) justice but not history's "greater
truths."

The *Protocols* Continued Legacy

Hitler was not the last to be influenced by the *Protocols*, or to use its teaching politically. It suffices to mention one of the spiritual fathers of contemporary
pan-Arabism, Abdel Nasser, who came out publicly in support of the *Protocols*,
claiming in a 1958 interview that it contained all that is needed to know about
the Jews. Stalin used the conspiracy myth, with Jews as the agents of imperialism, to secure the execution of Jewish members of the Czech Central Commit-

tee. The myth was to serve as the pretext for a renewed terror in the so-called doctor's plot, preempted only by Stalin's death.

The myth has thus shown itself adaptable to the most diverse politics and ideologies. It has found most ready application against the state of Israel, where it emerged from the context of the Palestinian problem to take on growing influence throughout the world. In the 1967 war, translations of the *Protocols* were found in the backpacks of captured Egyptian soldiers. Kadhafi has sponsored its translation and distribution to the developing world. The Saudi government has handed out copies to visitors and at its embassies. Pro-Khomeni Iranians distributed it on college campuses in the United States during the summer of Israel's invasion into Lebanon.

Daniel Pipes again draws our attention to the *Protocols*, claiming that Arab politics have given it a new lease on life.[15] Pipes lists some of the advantages of the myth for the Arab struggle. Among other things, it makes Israel's very existence sinister. It explains away the defeats of Arabs at the hands of Israel by linking them to a movement of international force and significance. In putting Zionism in the vanguard of international imperialism, the Arab cause takes on world historic importance. This serves to keep destructive passions stimulated while it reaches beyond the region to win broader sympathies in the former colonies of the developing world.[16]

In the years following the war, relatively little notice was taken of Muslim anti-Semitism, though it appears blatantly in the charter document of the PLO. In a classic example of Orwellian inversion, Zionism is there declared to be a political movement "organically associated with international imperialism that is racist and fanatic in nature and fascist in its methods." Western attitudes changed in the 1970s with OPEC and the astounding leverage it lent to the Arab world in projecting their cause against Israel beyond the region. The world has been witness since to a progressively wider assimilation of this PLO view that gained a certain "respectability" in light of the forums where it was pronounced and applauded. In 1975, a resolution equating Zionism with racism was approved in the U.N. Assembly. In 1979, the Havana Conference of the Non-Aligned linked Zionism to hegemonism and condemned it as not only racist but as a "crime against humanity."

The Israeli people, many of whom are the real and tragic victims of racist politics, are now seen as its perpetrators. In such a remarkable perversion of thought and history, the enormity associated with Hitlerism is associated with Jewish Israel. Its conspiratorial agenda in league with the imperialist powers stifles the developing world and is matter enough to exonerate Hitler's crimes. Such thinking gives color to the PLO effort as the vanguard of an anti-fascist movement and engaged in a liberation struggle that allows them to pursue violent methods without moral taint. It is for these reasons that the revocation of the offensive clauses in the PLO charter, mandated by the Oslo Agreement, were so protracted and controversial.

These are not beliefs to be trifled with. Nor can such thinking be turned on and off, like a light switch. The tragedy is that the justice of the cause for Palestinian statehood does not need such support. Such thinking is perhaps the greatest impediment to rational dealings with Israel and the outside world upon which a secure peace hinges.[17] It infects the man in the street as well as elite opinion, as any reader of *Al Ahram* can attest. It forces the most enlightened leaders of the Arab world to capitulate to it and deprives these people of a future worthy of themselves, their magnificent past, and hopes for the future.

A danger in all this is to so blur and misconstrue the Hitler phenomenon as to deprive it of its horrible reality for a generation of young people who have no firsthand experience of anti-Semitism and its murderous possibilities. This has helped pave the way to a renewed and wider application of anti-Semitism promoted by both the extreme left and right as fitting in with the goals of their respective revolutionary agendas. Pipes underscores his real concern about Muslim anti-Semitism as it affects Jews in the Middle East but also as it affects Jews outside the region. The Arab obsession with Israel has been fed by a fund of anti-Semitic ideas imported from Europe and is being given back to its Christian homelands, where political conditions again favor its spread.[18]

The End of the Taboo

The 1970s proved that Hitlerism and the world of the *Protocols* were not exorcised with Hitler's death. It was the mindset of a group vying for control in Argentina that came eerily close to gaining power. A tortured victim and chief witness to what took place there ended his days in Israel, whose relevance as a sanctuary for victimized Jews is reconfirmed by his experience as it was in the '80s and '90s to millions of Jews from the ex-USSR.[19]

France in the '80s was rocked by the rise of anti-Semitism. Public discourse, not to mention outright criminal attacks, prompted Bernard-Henri Lévy to declare that "again the [anti-Semitic] taboo has been lifted.[20] Leftists sympathetic to Third World causes worked at legitimizing anti-Semitism by linking the cause of Israel with American hegemony and imperialism. These years also saw the rise of "revisionism"—which diminished the significance of the Holocaust or denied it altogether." "Genocide" has become the common coin of political discourse in the post-Communist world. It is heard to characterize a breathtaking variety of humanity's current and past crimes while the case of the Jews, incredibly enough, is coming to be made light of. Concurrent with all this, France saw the rise of a far-right party that winked at such things and transformed the political equation in that country for a generation.

Its success has been duplicated most recently in Switzerland and Austria, where a "Le Pen with a human face" and shorn of his clownishness became leader of the party of opposition. The party ignited political controversy throughout the EU by entering the Austrian government. This is in a country that is prosperous and secure and where historic memories alone would seem enough to inoculate against such politics. Inroads have been made elsewhere by like-minded parties in Belgium and Norway. Italy has had an established Fascist party since the beginning of the last decade. Anti-Semitism is rife in all countries of the ex-USSR and breeds in the atmosphere of dislocation and confusion that grips these unfortunate peoples. Nowhere is the mix of post-Soviet politics and anti-Semitism more potentially lethal than in Russia itself. And nowhere, outside the Middle East, does the phantasmagoria of the world of the *Protocols* have more palpable hold. It seems that the "new" Europe is spawning the old virulence, long thought dead, but apparently only latent.

Nor is North America immune to such currents. Violent far-right groups have proliferated there in the recent past. Some of the more unsavory aspects of the Buchanan phenomenon flirt with an anti-Semitism that appeals to such groups. The taboo has indeed been lifted in the West. Its politics will remain destabilized by such forces for a long time to come, it is safe to say.

Our situation is made even more precarious by the breakdown of the "peace process" in the Middle East.[21] No one knows the long-term geopolitical consequences of events there and how they will play out in the politics of Israel and the Arab world. A different reaction to these events can be discerned in America and Europe. Simmering violence could cause erstwhile allies to choose different sides in the conflict. Access to oil complicates matters and could prove persuasive in settling dispositions. A wider war in the Middle East is no longer inconceivable and it could occasion a truly destructive rift between the countries of the Atlantic Alliance. Given weapons of mass destruction in the hands of the sworn enemies of Israel, is even another Holocaust inconceivable? There are those who say that Israel's "obsessive" concern with security is at the core of problems which threaten it and destabilize the world. Given the history of this century and the alignment of political forces in the world today, it is difficult to withhold sympathy for this concern.

Notes

1. Graves explained that he met a certain Mr. X (for some reason he wanted to remain anonymous), who said he was a Russian landowner with English connections. He described himself as a Constitutional Monarchist and Orthodox, who emigrated from Southern Russia after the Red takeover. He said he had bought some old books from a former officer in the Ochrana (secret police), among which was the Joly book. See Exhibit B in Bernstein *The Truth About the Protocols*, 259. The Ochrana had sharpened its skills in the revolutionary breakdown of Russian society that occurred after 1905 and the war in the East. It was therein that Ratchkovsky, the likely fabricator of the *Protocols*, operated. The Bolsheviks inherited its machinery and put it to good use for their pur-

poses. Contemporary Russia, in turn, has inherited the machinery of the Communist secret police and is, like its predecessors, putting it to "good use." It should not be forgotten
that the current President of Russia was schooled in practices now of long date.

2. Cohn, *Warrant for Genocide*, 74-75.

3. Heiden, *Der Fuehrer*, 9.

4. See John S. Curtiss, *An Appraisal of the Protocols of Zion* (New York: Columbia
University Press, 1942), 93. A good account of the Bern trial can be found in Exhibit B in
Bernstein, *The Truth About the Protocols*. Excerpts from the *Times* articles of June 16-18,
1921, exposing the *Protocols* forgery, can also be found there.

The Bern judge's sentiments are apropos of Holocaust denial. It is regrettable that
sensible men are forced to address themselves to this issue. Denying the deniers gives the
perverse and the malevolent a status they do not deserve.

5. Some said his real name was Moïse Joël.

6. See Adolph Hitler, *Mein Kampf*, trans. Ralph Manheim (Boston: Houghton Mifflin, 1946), 307-308. There Hitler writes:

> To what extent the whole existence of this people is based on a con-
> tinuous lie is shown incomparably by the *Protocols of the Elders of
> Zion*, so infinitely hated by the Jews. They are based on a forgery, the
> *Frankfurt Zeitung* moans and screams every week: the best proof that
> they are authentic. What many Jews do unconsciously is here con-
> sciously exposed. And that is what matters. It is completely indiffer-
> ent from what Jewish brain these disclosures originate. The important
> thing is with positively terrifying certainty, they reveal the nature and
> activity of the Jewish people, and expose their inner contexts as well
> as their ultimate final aims. Anyone who examines the historical de-
> velopment of the last hundred years from the standpoint of this book
> will at once understand the screaming of the Jewish press. For once
> this book becomes the common property of a people, the Jewish
> menace may be considered as broken.

Before his research on *Russia and Germany*, Walter Laqueur confessed that he was
more skeptical about the significance of the *Protocols*, evidence for which he subsequently found "overwhelming." According to Laqueur, much of what Hitler says in his
"magnum opus" is based on the *Protocols*. See *Russia and Germany*, 12 and 103.

7. This has led some to surmise that the *Protocols of Zion* are really the *Protocols* of
Tsion, an insider's joke which Ratchkovsky, apparently, would have reveled in.

8. Heiden, *Der Fuehrur*, 10.

9. Poliakov's remark is quoted in Cohn, *Warrant for Genocide*, 180. Rosenberg
wrote numerous articles touting the deep truths of the *Protocols*. Heiden singles
Rosenberg out as the key figure in transmitting the *Protocols* from Russia to Germany
and for introducing them to Hitler. See *Der Fuehrer*, 16-21. In *Russia and Germany*, 24,
Laqueur speaks of a "strange twist" of history which saw German anti-Semitism exported

to Russia in the eighteenth century and then reimported into Germany after the First World War.

10. See chapter VII of Cohn's *Warrant for Genocide,* "The Protocols Circle the World" for another description of exactly how the work came to be so widely read and disseminated.

It is interesting to note that Hitler had a portrait of Henrich Ford hanging in his office and liked to point it out to visitors. He also shared with Ford a vision of a *volk's* wagon. This could be achieved by first reducing automobiles to simple, basic components and then taking advantage of economies of scale in Taylor-like production facilities to produce a vehicle that common "folk"—the workers themselves—could afford. The idea has had a breathtaking impact on the world. In late modernity, the auto is blamed for polluting our air, heating our climate, congesting our cities, and laying waste to our countrysides. In the twentieth century, Ford's idea was also at the source of what made democracies take such deep root. This helped them to withstand the onslaught from regimes such as Hitler's. It is rare, especially in politics, to enjoy an unalloyed good.

Hitler and Ford also had a similar view of "history." Each, in his own way, thought it was all just "bunk."

11. See in particular a Hitler speech quoted at length in Heiden, *Der Fuehrer,* 118-123.The speech can also be found in *The Speeches of Adolph Hitler,* tr. and ed. Norman H. Baynes (New York: Howard Fertig, 1958), I, 21-41.

12. Hannah Arendt, *The Origins of Totalitarianism* (New York: Meridian Books, 1958), 360. Arendt earlier states (308) that the *Protocols* were "a model for the future organization of the German masses for 'world empire'." She refers to Alexander Stein, *Adolph Hitler, Schuler der Weisen Die Zion* (Karlsbad: 1936), as the first scholarly effort to analyze by philological comparison the ideological identity of the teaching of the Nazis with that of the "Elders of Zion."

13. See Arendt, *Totalitarianism,* 358. Konrad Heiden also speaks of "their deeper, genuine content" in this regard. See *Der Fuehrer,* 13. According to Norman Cohn, the prominent part played by Joly's text in the *Protocols* forgery is the reason why it often seems to forecast twentieth century authoritarianism. See *Warrant for Genocide,* 74.

14. Alfred Rosenberg, *Race and Race History and Other Essays,* trans. and ed. Robert Pois (New York: Harper & Row, 1974), 86.

15. Daniel Pipes, "The Politics of Muslim Anti-Semitism," *Commentary* (Aug. 1981): 42. His more recent book, *The Hidden Hand,* (New York: Saint Martin's Griffin, 1996) provides fuller elaboration and documentation of themes discussed in the essay. The subtitle of his work is "Middle East Fears of Conspiracy." Pipes is not very popular in circles I have recently had contact with. I think of him as the Kenneth Starr of Middle East scholars. In the face of intolerable conduct and denial from those in responsibility, he lays out in considerable detail the twisted and loopy thinking they engage in. Partisans of those he targets therefore do not like him. America, of course, is not free from the grips of "conspiracy thinking." Deep trauma for a people is the breeding ground. The assassination of John Kennedy was an episode in American history, yet it continues to spawn a staggering amount of "theories," not to mention movies that could genuinely be

called "loopy." The trauma in the Arab world has been long-standing, not episodic, and there are very real reasons that explain such feelings. I would like to draw attention to Chapter 3 of *The Hidden Hand*, "Greater Israel," as particularly pertinent to what is said here. Among other things, it would have alerted us to the tenuousness of the Arab/Israeli "peace process," given the thinking that is prevalent in the area, among "front line" peoples and the region's "core states" alike.

16. Taguieff, drawing upon the scholarship of Benard Lewis, among eminent others, makes the same points in Chapter VII of the first volume of his work *Les Protocoles*. See that chapter—"Avatars du Myth Dans le Monde Arabe: La Nouvelle Carriere des Protocoles"—and a chapter in the second volume by Yehoshafat Harkabi, "Les Protocoles Dans L'Antisemitisme Arabe," for detailed discussions of the spread of anti-Semitism in the Muslim world.

17. Hear the Ayotollah Sayid Ali Khamanei:

> There is evidence which shows that Zionists had close relations with German Nazis and exaggerated statistics on Jewish killing. . . [Zionists did this] as a means to attract the sympathy of public opinion. . . paving the way for the occupation of Palestine and justification for Zionist crimes.

Sadly, such thinking is not confined to the leader of Iran. The Khamanei quote was reported by *Reuters* 25 April 2001.

18. Pipes, "The Politics of Muslim Anti-Semitism," 42.

19. The interview with Levy was conducted and reported by Steven McBride, *Christian Science Monitor*, 12 January 1983, B3.

20. See Jacobo Timmerman, *Prisoner Without a Name/Cell Without a Number*, tr. Toby Talbot (New York: Alfred A. Knopf, 1981), 74ff.

21. Oslo was supposed to bring peace within the time frame of a decade. It is ominous now that Jewish leaders and intellectuals speak of the necessity to return to the mindset of 1948 and also speak of the possibility of a repeated destruction of the Temple in Jerusalem. When Arab leaders and intellectuals now speak of the political task before them, they reach back to the crusades and a centuries-long struggle as the most appropriate analogy for their situation.

Appendix

Macaulay's Machiavelli

What Thomas Babington Macaulay has said about Machiavelli has been very influential. Indeed, echoes of it can still be heard today. It is found in an essay that was written in 1828. This was when publication of Machiavelli's complete works appeared in Paris. It was, we presume, a notable event, given the anathema, then about 300 years old, attached to such a personage.

What is valuable in the "Memoir on Machiavelli" in the Bohn edition of the Florentine's works, already mentioned, comes from Macaulay. I also have the suspicion that Joly could at least read English and find it likely that he read Macaulay's essay. At the very least, Joly would place Macaulay "among those who have read and understood Machiavelli" and not among the "vulgar" interpreters. In any case, Joly's view of the "real" Machiavelli stands very close to that of Macaulay. It is for this reason that I beg the reader's indulgence for a brief excursus on Macaulay's Machiavelli.

Macaulay's antiquarian researches unearthed an amusing reference to Machiavelli in a "poem" called *Hudibras*. This following jingle appears there in Part III Canto I:

> Nick Machiavelli had ne'er a trick
> Though he gave his name to our old Nick.

The "poet" is heir to a now even longer tradition that associates the surname of Machiavelli with "knavery" and makes his Christian name synonymous with the "devil."

For reasons we will explore, Macaulay does not find it strange that "ordinary readers" of his day regard the author of *The Prince* as "the most depraved and shameless of human beings." Still, it seems "inconceivable" that the "martyr of freedom should have designedly acted as the apostle of tyranny." (Joly's Montesquieu expresses the same thought in almost identical terms.) Macaulay writes a bit further on:

> The whole man seems to be an enigma, a grotesque assemblage of in-
> congruous qualities, selfishness and generosity, cruelty and benevo-
> lence, craft and simplicity, abject villany and romantic heroism.

This encapsulates the mystery of Machiavelli that Macaulay proposes to resolve
in his essay. The publication of Machiavelli's complete works would then be
launched in a proper way, a way that would allow Macaulay's generation to come
to a true appreciation of the Florentine and, after all these centuries, to once again
find delight and profit from him.

After briefly treating and dismissing other "learned interpretations" (including
Francis Bacon's), Macaulay will demonstrate that Machiavelli can only be understood by reference to "his times." (Again, this is what the Montesquieu of the
Dialogue also says.) The "real" Machiavelli emerges only against the background
of a sensitive interpretation of the Renaissance and a sympathetic understanding
of the political predicament of Florence and Italy in the sixteenth century.

Briefly, Machiavelli stands at the first dawn of modernity. He is a product of
urban life in a city recognized as preeminent for its wealth and civilization, even
among other similarly privileged cities in Italy at the time. There, the mind found
itself nourished in one of the richest intellectual soils ever known to mankind, either before or after. It could flower untrammeled, in a place where authentic talent was honored, almost worshipped. It was in Renaissance Italy that free and full
expression was given the whole range of human phenomena—the low and the
high. And Machiavelli equally delighted in the depiction of both extremes.

The contrast with life beyond the Alps is sharp. There, the monarch's court
dominated and cities, such as existed, were pitiable sights. Life was lived according to certain "forms," practices inherited from the past and rooted in force and
superstition. Life outside the court was stupifyingly ignorant and poor.

If, again we may speak in such a way, the "tragic flaw" infecting Italy
stemmed from what made life there so exceptional. The civilized pursuits of urban life left no time for the brute-like martial virtues, exclusively cultivated in the
North. In many particulars, the city-states of Renaissance Italy find their closest
parallel in the ancient Greek city-states. However, the latter maintained their martial spirit by necessity, that is to say, because of the presence of the war-like
Sparta and a large body of restive slaves in their midst.

Italy, like Greece at the time of her decline, eventually became dependent on
mercenary soldiers for her defense. She fell victim to invasion and, by turns, was
forced to submit to the "brutality" of Switzerland, the "insolence" of France, and
the "fierce rapacity" of Arragon. They fought the overwhelming force with the
best arms they had, cunning and duplicity. The cultivated and refined Italian
stood in relation to his conquerors as the cultivated and refined Greek stood to the
Roman. Each disdained the other, but for exactly opposite reasons.

This is the experience that Machiavelli lived and it explains both his person
and his writings. He sought to expel the barbarians in order to secure civilization

for Italy and his people, as he knew it. The "true" Machiavelli is "the patriot."
And his patriotism is elevated by its links to higher human concerns. He lived exclusively for his country and to protect a way of life mortally threatened by out-
siders. To achieve his ultimate end, he suffered and compromised much of what
he held dear. His personal tragedy was to live at the end of a grand epoch and to
die with the consciousness that his life's enterprise was a failure.

According to Macauley, Machiavelli had his faults, but certainly not those
which the "vulgar" think. More precisely, he had "a single defect" but a "most
mischievous one."

> The great principle, that societies and laws exist only for the purpose
> of increasing the sum of private happiness, is not recognized with suf-
> ficient clearness. The good of the body, distinct from the good of the
> members, and sometimes hardly compatible with the good of the
> members, seems to be the object which he proposes to himself. Of all
> political fallacies, this has perhaps had the widest and most mischie-
> vous operation.

In sum, it seems Machiavelli's "defect" was that he was too patriotic in seeing
the interests of his country as taking precedence over the happiness of its members—including himself, we might add. If the virtues of men in the ancient city
were derived from "love of country," as Montesquieu claimed, he might be characterized as virtuous in this sense. But, Macauley seems to imply, like Montesquieu, that the ancient city has passed and such virtues are no longer appropriate
for truly modern men. Machiavelli's mode of thinking is now "fallacious," if indeed it could ever have been fully defended.

The Renaissance did not last, of course. The Counter-Reformation set in and
fixed the reputation of Machiavelli ever after. He became the convenient scape-
goat for an era that the Church now repudiated and condemned. But Renaissance
Italy saw Machiavelli differently, not as a monster, but as one of its most beautiful products. The moral horizons of the two historic epochs that separate Machiavelli and Macaulay are dramatically different and Macaulay's whole essay can be
seen as trying to revive and defend the earlier perspective that formed Machiavelli. He says some startling things and in the most beautiful prose. For brevity's
sake we will mention only one, but it is particularly illustrative.

Macaulay claims, astonishingly, that if we saw things like Machiavelli's contemporaries, that is, with all the clarity of these clear-sighted men, we would to a
remarkable degree switch our sympathies from Othello to Iago. Iago's "virtues"—wit, judgment, psychological acuity—would be more obvious. Othello
would inspire "nothing but detestation and contempt." In a similar vein, he tells
us, if we lived in fifteenth century Italy, we would better appreciate the qualities
of Francesco Sforza, an upstart "hero,"—clanless, lawless, and heartless—and
depreciate those of Henry V, a mere hero of the (much disdained) "North."

Can Macaulay be serious in heaping admiring praise on Iago and so disparaging Othello? The play is about jealousy, not just Othelllo's but Iago's. It is hard to avoid the terms of modern psychotherapy to capture the bent of such a small man with such monstrous, "green-eyed" obsessions. Furthermore, is it possible to put Sforza in the same league with the great-souled Hal? He speaks of Iago's "virtues" without speaking of the perverted use to which they were put. What about Henry's "wit," "judgment," and "psychological acuity?" In Falstaff's protégé, they are no less formidable than the same traits found in Iago. But they are put to noble use in founding a truly greater Britain.[1] At end, if all this is an indication of the moral sensibility it takes to redeem Machiavelli from his anathema, clearly something is wrong.

Essentially, Macaulay deals with the shocking things found in Machiavelli by telling us, reassuringly, that they are not really shocking after all. In effect, "this is how people thought back then. Open minds sensitized by history would see things so." This is a lamentably weak, if not "vulgar," argument.[2] Are we really to believe that everyone back then was a Machiavellian? Can anyone read Machiavelli's works and come to the conclusion that he is dealing with a common mind? That, I maintain, is inconceivable, regardless of when he was read, back then, in the nineteenth century, or even now.

I do not want to be snide in dealing with such a worthy and eminent historian. But I think we can discern in the mild "criticism" that he does make of Machiavelli, a hidden praise of the liberalism of nineteenth-century England. Following Macaulay and accepting momentarily his view that moral perspectives change radically with the times, we might be tempted to say that it is the experience of nineteenth century England that crucially shapes the historian. Machiavelli's "mischievous defect" was that he did not clearly enough see what any nineteenth-century liberal clearly saw, that government was meant to serve the "interests" of society—the happiness of the individual, however defined. "Hear! Hear! Score one for the political institutions of England!" And score two for its religious arrangements—the Anglican Church that shelters its people from ultramontane obfuscation, which, among other things, clouds our mind concerning the question of poor, misunderstood Machiavelli.

I have great reservations about Macaulay's thesis, and that of Joly, which stands so close to it. As was said with regard to Joly, to want to turn Machiavelli into a liberal robs his thought of all its moral ambiguity as well as its majestic heights. For sure, he is concerned about the people's interests. A great teacher I knew once remarked that the *whole* of democratic politics begins with several lines in Chapter IX of *The Prince*. But the teaching of Machiavelli is decidedly more oriented (if not exclusively so) by concern with the "few," the natural princes of our race (Moses, for example) and "rare" moments, such as political foundings. They are really worthy of attention for they form the horizon in which we all live. He speaks to the rare men—those not satisfied with an ample meal, a warm bed, and the envious notice of a neighbor—and he speaks to them about glory. It too has its exigencies, though "happy" men don't feel them. And a politics that neglects these exigencies is incomplete, impoverished, truncated, and vulnerable.[3]

We cannot simply ignore the shocking things Machiavelli says and recommends. Nor can we dismiss the concerns they raise as a product of vulgar minds not yet free from Romanish obscurantism. With Machiavelli, we are in the presence of one of those rare individuals. Macaulay would have us think of him, but for a common defect, as a "jolly good fellow." (It is even a "defect" that, paradoxically, does him honor). But I don't think a nation, like Britain, of such decency and propriety, would, then or now, accept what Machiavelli says as quite "cricket."[4] Nor would the country of Shakespeare easily come to such unseemly interpretations of his thought.

I sense that Machiavelli would smile at his scolding for his "mischievous defect." The Church's ban deals with far weightier matters. Its gravamen speaks of the soul and this helps put things in proper perspective.

Macaulay remains a truly grand historian and a sublime writer. However, I see the essay on Machiavelli as perhaps the exception that proves the rule of his worthiness. Machiavelli has disturbed his normally sure judgment. He always has this effect on his readers. It's part of his timelessness.

At end, we should not be so hard on old Macaulay if the historical net he fashioned failed to catch Machiavelli. He's a slippery kind of guy. I suspect that those who have engaged in the chase and really got hold of him are not the same persons that started the hunt. I also suspect that these very few individuals would be loath to tell all about the prize they caught.[5]

Notes

1. During the war, Winston Churchill was said to have attended a performance of *Henry V* in London. His box hovered close to the stage. The actor playing Hal (Sir Laurence Olivier, I believe) complained that every time he was about to deliver Henry's stirring lines, he could hear Churchill's deep and gravelly voice mumbling the words just before him. If the voice belonged to another person, one could imagine the actor stopping in mid-sentence, glaring up, and asking for silence. The point is that at Britain's "darkest hour," indeed *our* darkest hour, we would be surprised, to say the least, to find the great man sustaining himself with the words of Francesco Sforza. Churchill saved the regime Henry helped found and immortalized the glory of that "blessèd plot" that harbors a "happy breed of men."

2. I used to hear this argument in the classroom almost daily. It is also the argument of the "cultural relativists." I often found the "openness" that is this latter group's boast leading them to a defense of the most questionable, not to say heinous, practices of our species. At end, they are not really "relativists." "Openness" is their absolute—openness to the point of vacuity.

3 Abraham Lincoln speaks eloquently about the moral ambiguity of men who have glory as their ruling passion. He explicitly draws attention to Napoleon, who, like Caesar, was willing to destroy a republic and enslave free men to satisfy his ambition. Joly sees his nephew as a pretender to the same "tribe."

When Lincoln wrote the following words, the founding moment in America had passed. That "field of glory" had been "harvested." The question that the country faced was whether or not that founding would last. Lincoln deserves extensive quotation.

> But new reapers will arise, and they will seek a field. It is to deny, what the history of the world tells us is true, to suppose that men of ambition and talents will not continue to spring up among us. And when they do, they will naturally seek the gratification of their ruling passion, as others have done so before them. The question is, can the gratification be found in supporting and maintaining an edifice that has been erected by others? Most certainly it cannot. Many great and good men sufficiently qualified for any task they should undertake, may ever be found, whose ambition would aspire to nothing beyond a seat in Congress, a gubernatorial or presidential chair; *but such belong not to the family of the lion, or the tribe of the eagle*[.] What! Think you these places would satisfy an Alexander, a Caesar, or a Napoleon? Never! Towering genius disdains a beaten path. It seeks regions hitherto unexplored. It sees *no distinction* in adding story to story, upon the monuments of fame, erected to the memories of others. It *denies* that it is glory enough to serve under any chief. It *scorns* to tread in the footsteps of *any* predecessor, however illustrious. It thirsts and burns for distinction; and, if possible, it will have it, whether at the expense of emancipating slaves or enslaving freemen. Is it unreasonable then to expect, that some man possessed of the loftiest genius, coupled with ambition sufficient to push it to its utmost stretch, will at some time, spring up among us? And when such a one does, it will require the people to be united with each other, attached to the government and laws, and generally intelligent, to successfully frustrate his designs.
>
> Distinction will be his paramount object; and although he would as willingly, perhaps more so, acquire it by doing good as harm, yet, that opportunity being past, and nothing left to be done in the way of building up, he would set boldly to the task of pulling down.

Lincoln's words are impressive, not to say prophetic and poetic. As usual with him, lofty thoughts find the simplest and homeliest of expression. He gives a homily for democratic ears. Yet, it is absolutely devoid of the slightest tinge of preachiness or flattery. He says only a "general intelligence" can save our republic. All over America "experts" are redesigning our educational systems to better conform to the "Internet age." They should listen to Abe. (No doubt Lincoln felt the ambition he so eloquently speaks of).

For many reasons, this writer has peculiar satisfaction in ending his book about despotism with references to Churchill and Lincoln. For those who periodically feel the need, there's no better tonic than contemplating their words and lives to restore faith in humanity.

Lincoln's words are found in a speech he gave when he was a relatively unknown Illinois politician: "Address before the Springfield Young Men's Lyceum" in 1838 entitled "The Perpetuation of our Political Institutions." It can be found in *The Political Thought of Abraham Lincoln*, Richard N. Current ed., (New York: Bobbs-Merrill, 1967), 11-21.

4. Though if we are to believe the scandals now said to infect this peculiar and incomprehensible sport (throwing matches, fixing scores, bribing umpires, etc.), it might be just that.

5. Macaulay's essay on Machiavelli can be found in *Macaulay*, ed. G. M. Young (Cambridge, Mass.: Harvard University Press: 1967) 235-269. For those who get it into their head to track down Machiavelli, there is no better guide than Leo Strauss. See in particular his *Thoughts on Machiavelli* (Seattle: University of Washington Press, 1969).

Selected Bibliography

Aron, Raymond. "The Essence of Totalitarianism According to Hannah Arendt." In *In Defence of Political Reason*, edited by Daniel J. Mahoney. Lanham, Md.: Rowman & Littlefield, 1993.

———. "Is There a Nazi Mystery?" Encounter. (summer) 1980.

———. Main Currents in Sociological Thought. 2 vols. London: Penguin Books, 1967

Aristotle. Nichomachean Ethics. Loeb Classical Library XIX. Cambridge: Harvard University Press. 1926

———. Poetics. Loeb Classical Library XXIII. Cambridge,Mass.: Harvard University Press, 1932.

Arendt, Hannah. The Origins of Totalitarianism. New York: Meridian Books, 1958.

Aubrey, Octave. The Second Empire. Translated by Arthur Livingston. Philadelphia: J. B. Lippincott, 1940.

Bazard, Saint-Amand, and Barthélemay Prosper Enfantin. The Doctrine of Saint-Simon. An Exposition. Edited and translated by Georg G. Iggers. New York: Schoken Books, 1972.

Baynes, Norman, editor and translator. The Speeches of Adolph Hitler New York: Howard Fertig, 1958.

Berns, Laurence. "Aristotle's Poetics." In Ancients and Moderns, edited by Joseph Cropsey. New York: Basic Books, 1964.

Bernstein, Herman. The Truth about The Protocols of Zion. A Complete Exposure. New York: Covici Friede, 1935.

Boon, Hendrik Nicholas. Rêve et realité dans l'oeuvre économique et sociale de Napoleon III. The Hague, the Netherlands: Martinus Nijhoff, 1936

Case, Lynn M. French Opinion on War and Diplomacy During the Second Empire. Philadelphia: University of Pennsylvania Press. 1954.

Cobban, Alfred. A History of Modern France. Middlesex, G.B.: Penguin Books, 1961.

Cohn, Norman. Warrant for Genocide. The Myth of the Jewish World Conspiracy and the Protocols of the Elders of Zion. London: Eyre & Spottiswoode, 1967.

Curtiss, John S. An Appraisal of the Protocols of Zion. New York: Columbia University Press, 1942.

Dansette, Adrien. Louis Napoleon à la conquête du pouvoir.(Histore du Second Empire Vol. I.) Paris: Hachette, 1961.

Guerard, Albert. France. Edited by Paul A. Gagnon. Ann Arbor: University of Michigan Press, 1969.

———. Napoleon III. Cambridge: Harvard University Press, 1943.

Heiden, Konrad. Der Fuehrer. Translated by Ralph Manheim. Boston: Houghton Mifflin, 1944.

Himmelfarb, Gertrude. *On Looking into the Abyss.* New York: Vintage Books, 1995. Zinn). In *Points of View,* edited by Robert E. DiClerico and Alan S. Hammock

Hitler, Adolph. *Mein Kampf.* Translated by Ralph Manheim. Boston: Houghton Mifflin. 1946.

Hook, Sydney. "How Democratic Is America?" (A Response to Howard. New York: McGraw Hill, 1995.

Hugo, Victor. *Napoleon the Little.* In *The Works of Victor Hugo.* New York: Nottingham Society, *Circa* 1907.

Huntington, Samuel P. *The Clash of Civilizations.* New York: Touchstone, 1997.

Iggers, Georg G. Introduction. Pp. ix-xlvii. in *The Doctrine of Saint-Simon. An Exposition.* New York: Schoken Books, 1972.

Joly, Maurice. *Dialogue aux Enfers entre Machiavel et Montesquieu.* Collection "Liberté de l'esprit" dirigée par Raymond Aron. Paris: Calmann-Levy. 1968.

Kissinger, Henry A. *Diplomacy.* New York: Touchstone, 1995.

Kuhn, Thomas S. *The Structure of Scientific Revolutions.* Chicago: University of Chicago Press, 1962.

Laqueur, Walter. *Russia and Germany: A Century of Conflict.* Boston: Little, Brown, 1965.

Levy, Bernard Henri. Interview. *Christian Science Monitor.* 12 January 1983.

Lincoln, Abraham. "On the Perpetuation of Our Political Institutions." In *The Political Thought of Abraham Lincoln,* edited by Richard N. Current. New York: Bobbs-Merrill, 1967.

Lowenthal, David. Introduction. Pp. 1-20 in *Consideration of the Causes of the Greatness of the Romans and their Decline.* Ithaca, N.Y.: Cornell University Press, 1965.

Löwith, Karl. *Meaning in History.* Chicago: University of Chicago Press, 1949.

Macaulay, Thomas Babington. *Macaulay. Prose and Poetry.* Edited by G. M. Young. Cambridge: Harvard University Press, 1967.

Machiavelli, Niccolò. *The History of Florence together with* The Prince *and Various Other Historical Tracts.* Edited by H. B. Bohn. London: George Bell & Sons, 1906.

——. *The Prince.* Translated by Harvey C. Mansfield Jr. Chicago: University of Chicago Press, 1985.

——. *The Prince and The Discourses.* Translated by Luigi Ricci (*The Prince*) and Christian E. Detmold (*The Discourses*). New York: Modern Library, 1949.

Mahoney, Daniel J. *The Liberal Science of Raymond Aron.* Lanham, Md.: Rowman & Littlefield, 1992.

——. "Modern Man and Man *Tout Court:* The Flight from Nature and the Modern Difference." *Interpretation* 22, no. 3 (spring), 1995.

Manent, Pierre. *La Cité de l'homme.* Paris: Flammarion, 1994.

Manuel, Frank M., and Manuel, Fritzie P. *Utopian Thought in the Western World.* Cambridge, Mass: Belknap, 1979.

Marlowe, Christopher. *The Jew of Malta.* In *The Complete Plays of Christopher Marlowe,* edited by Irving Ribner: New York: Odyssey Press, 1963.

Marx, Karl. *The Eighteenth Brumaire of Louis Napoleon.* Translated by Eden and Cedar Paul. New York: International, 1926.

Menchú, Rigoberta. *I Rigoberta Menchú, an Indian Woman in Guatemala.* Edited by Elizabeth Burgos-Debray; translated by Ann Wright. London: Verso, 1984.

Montesquieu, Baron de. *Oeuvres complètes,* 2 vols. Edited by Roger Caillois. Bibliothèque de la Pléiade, Paris: Gallimard, 1949.

Morris, Edmund. *Dutch: A Memoir of Ronald Reagan.* New York: Random House, 1999.

Osgood, Samuel M. Introduction. Pp. vii-xii in *Napoleon III—Buffoon, Modern Dictator, or Sphinx?* Edited by Samuel M. Osgood. Boston: D. C. Heath, 1966.

Pangle, Thomas L. *Montesquieu's Philosophy of Liberalism.* Chicago: University of Chicago Press, 1973.

Payne, Howard C. *The Police State of Napoleon Bonaparte 1852-1860.* Seattle: University of Washington Press, 1960.

Pipes, Daniel. *The Hidden Hand. Middle East Fears of Conspiracy.* New York: Saint Martin's Griffin, 1996.

——. "The Politics of Muslim Anti-Semitism." *Commentary.* August 1981.

Plato. *The Republic.* Translated by Allan Bloom. New York: Basic Books, 1968.

Plutarch. *The Lives of Noble Grecians and Romans.* Translated by John Dryden. New York: Modern Library, 1864.

Revel, Jean-François. Préface to *Dialogue aux Enfers entre Machiavel et Montesquieu.* Paris: Calmann-Levy, 1968.

Rosenberg, Alfred, *Race and Race History and Other Essays.* Edited and translated by Robert Pois. New York: Harper & Row, 1974.

Saint-Simon, Henri de. *Social Organization, the Science of Man, and Other Writings.* Edited and translated by Felix Markham. New York: Harper Torchbooks, 1952.

Schapiro, J. Salwyn. *Liberalism and the Challenge of Fascism* New York: McGraw-Hill, 1949.

Séguin, Philippe. *Louis Napoleon le Grand.* Paris: Grasset, 1990.

Seignobos, Charles. *Histoire de France Contemporaire.* Edited by Ernest Lavisse. Paris: Hachette, 1921

Smith, Adam. *An Inquiry into the Nature and Causes of the Wealth of Nations.* Edited by Edwin Cannan. New York: Modern Library, 1937.

Sorel, Albert. *Montesquieu.* Traanslated by Melville B. Anderson and Edward Flayfair Anderson. Port Washington, N.Y.: Kennikat Press, 1969.

Speer, Albert. *Inside the Third Reich* Translated by Richard and Clara Winston.

New York: Macmillan, 1970.

Speier, Hans. "Grimmelshausen's Laughter." In *Ancients and Moderns,* edited by Joseph Cropsey. New York: Basic Books, 1964.

———. "The Truth in Hell: Maurice Joly on Modern Despotism." *Polity* 10 1977.

Stoll, David. *Rigoberta Menchú and the story of all poor Guatemalans.* Boulder, Colo.: Westview Press, 1999.

Stein, Alexander. *Adolph Hitler, Schuler der Weisen Die Zion.* Karlsbad, Verlaganstalt "Graphia" [printed in Checkoslovakia], 1936.

Strauss, Leo. *Thoughts on Machiavelli.* Seattle: University of Washington Press, 1969.

Tacitus. *The Annals.* Translated by Alfred John Church and William Jackson Brodribb. Chicago: Great Books, 1952.

Taguieff, Pierre-Andre. 1992. *Les Protocols des Sages de Sion.* 2 vols. Paris: Berg International, 1952.

Thomas Acquinas. *Summa Theologica.* Fathers of the English Dominican Province translation. 3 vols. New York: Benziger Brothers, 1947.

Thompson, A. F. "From Restoration to Republic." In *France: Government and Society,* edited by J. M. Wallace-Handrill and J. McManners. London: Methuen, 1957.

Timmerman, Jacobo. *Prisoner Without a Name/Cell Without a* Number. New York: Alfred A. Knopf, 1981.

Voltaire. *Siècle de Louis XIV,* 2 vols. Paris: Flammarion, 1931.

Xenophon. *The Education of Cyrus.* Translated by Wayne Ambler. Ithaca, N.Y.: Cornell University Press, 2001.

Zeldin, Theodore. "The Myth of Napoleon III." *History Today* (February 1959).

Index

Dialogue In Hell

Index

Commentary

About the Author

John S. Waggoner completed his undergraduate work at Cornell University and received his Ph.D. at Boston College. He worked as a Legislative Aide in the Massachusetts State Senate. He taught political science at Nichols College in Dudley, Massachusetts. He has also taught at the American University of Paris, the Sorbonne, and the American University in Cairo. He now resides in Washington D.C.